Guide to
Network Support and Troubleshooting

Greg Tomsho

COURSE
TECHNOLOGY
TM
THOMSON LEARNING

Australia • Canada • Mexico • Singapore • Spain • United Kingdom • United States

Guide to Network Support and Troubleshooting

by Greg Tomsho

Product Manager:
Laura Hildebrand

Quality Assurance Manager:
John Bosco

Marketing Manager:
Toby Shelton

Production Editor:
Danielle Power

MQA Technical Lead:
Nicole Ashton

Text Designer:
GEX Publishing Services

Development Editor:
Jill Batistick

Associate Product Manager:
Tim Gleeson

Compositor:
GEX Publishing Services

Editorial Assistant:
Nick Lombardi

Cover Design:
Julie Malone

BRIEF
Contents

TABLE OF
Contents

Preface

So, you want to be a network administrator. Perhaps by now you have learned how to manage a Windows NT, Windows 2000, or NetWare server. And, you may have dabbled in router and switch configurations. That's great, but how much do you know about the problems that can occur in your cabling, your NICs and their drivers, your network protocols, clients, and servers? Better yet, how much do you know about how to solve those problems? And how much can you tell me about network documentation, network security, and the tools you need to manage and monitor your network? If any or all of these subject areas have you scratching your head in puzzlement, read on!

This book is designed to give you the knowledge you need to tackle those perplexing and puzzling network support issues from the Physical layer right on up to the Application layer. Plus, you will learn about problem-solving methods and how to deal with network security issues. And to help stop problems before they even start, you will learn how to properly document your network and test and monitor your network. You will work with protocol analyzers, cable test equipment, and network monitoring and performance analysis tools. Review questions test your grasp of the concepts and terms presented in each chapter. Plus, hands-on projects at the end of each chapter walk you step by step through procedures you will use in a real-world networking environment to solve problems and provide technical support. Case projects are designed to challenge students to perform critical thinking and to research advanced concepts. Once you have completed this book, you should be able to confidently take on even the most daunting network troubleshooting and support tasks.

Chapter 1, "Networking Concepts Review," refreshes your memory on many of the terms and concepts you have probably already learned about networks. You will review the OSI model and the terms and devices associated with each layer. And you will be refreshed on the basic networking models such as client/server and peer to peer.

Chapter 2, "Supporting Networks," discusses the various approaches to network problem solving and some of the tools that can be used in supporting and troubleshooting a network.

Chapter 3, "Supporting the Physical Layer," describes the components of the Physical layer and discusses the issues involved with supporting each of these components. You will learn about the installation, testing, and support of cabling and Physical layer devices such as hubs and transceivers. Plus, you will learn about the rules you must abide by in constructing a network such as the 5-4-3 rule and its application in various LAN environments.

Chapter 4, "Supporting the Data Link Layer," reveals the details of Ethernet frames and the multitude of errors that can occur at this layer and how to resolve them. Data Link layer components such as NICs and switches are discussed in detail and you will learn how a protocol analyzer may be used to support this layer.

Chapter 5, "Supporting the Network and Transport Layers," walks you through the inner-workings of TCP/IP and IPX/SPX. You will learn how to capture packets and understand what each field in the Network and Transport layer headers mean. You will also learn about the role of routers in your network, which will help you understand some of the issues involved in supporting these devices.

Chapter 6, "Supporting the Upper Layers," takes a detailed look at the Session, Presentation, and Application layers of the OSI model. You will learn how protocols such as DNS and NetBIOS work and how to support these functions. Plus, you will examine some of the common TCP/IP applications like FTP and Telnet.

Chapter 7, "Supporting Network Operating Systems," covers some of the support issues you are likely to encounter with the various Windows operating systems and in a NetWare environment. You will discover some issues that are particular to peer-to-peer networks and issues you will likely see in client/server environments.

Chapter 8, "Network Security," describes how you can devise a network security policy and what that policy should cover. You will also learn the importance of physically securing your network. Some security risks are examined and you learn about auditing and securing your network in a variety of networking environments. Finally, firewalls and how they play a role in the security of your network are discussed.

Chapter 9, "Network Documentation," details the sometimes tedious, but extremely important subject of documenting your network. You will learn what should be documented and how to document it; plus, you will learn how documenting your network can make your support and troubleshooting job much easier. Some of the tools to make your documentation task easier are also discussed.

Chapter 10, "Tools for Network Troubleshooting and Support," covers a variety of tools you can use for testing, troubleshooting, and monitoring your network. Cable testers are discussed in detail, including what all of the testing parameters mean and how they are important. You will learn about how to monitor and baseline your network and which tools are available to help with that task.

The Intended Audience

This book has been designed for individuals who wish to excel in the information technology field as a network technician, network administrator, or help-desk professional. Students should be familiar with basic networking terms and concepts as might be found in an introduction to networking course. More advanced study, such as that provided in intermediate routing and switching courses is recommended. Familiarity with Windows desktop and server operating systems and the NetWare operating system are highly recommended. Specifically, this book is intended for coursework that might be completed in the second year of an information systems or networking degree or certificate program.

Features

To ensure a successful learning experience, this book includes the following pedagogical features:

- **Chapter Objectives**—Each chapter in this book begins with a detailed list of the concepts to be mastered within that chapter. This list provides you with a quick reference to the contents of that chapter, as well as a useful study aid.

- **Diagrams, Screenshots, and Illustrations**—Numerous diagrams, screenshots, and illustrations aid you in understanding how to troubleshoot network problems.

- **Chapter Summaries**—Each chapter's text is followed by a summary of the concepts it has introduced. These summaries provide a helpful way to recap and revisit the ideas covered in each chapter.

- **Key Terms List**—A list of all new terms and their definitions.

- **Review Questions**—To test knowledge of the chapter, the review questions cover the most important concepts of the chapter.

- **Hands-on Projects**—Hands-on projects help you to apply the knowledge gained in the chapter.

- **Case Study Projects**—Case study projects take you through real-world scenarios.

- **On the CD-ROM**—On the CD-ROM you will find a demo version of EtherPeek protocol analyzer software and InetTools from WildPackets, Inc. to be used with Hands-on projects in Chapters 4, 5, 6, 8 and 10. Also included is WildPackets' NetSense, an Expert Analysis program that further interprets the conversations captured by EtherPeek.

Text and Graphic Conventions

Wherever appropriate, additional information and exercises have been added to this book to help you better understand what is being discussed in the chapter. Icons throughout the text alert you to additional materials. The icons used in this textbook are as follows:

Tips are included from the author's experience that provide extra information related to network support and troubleshooting.

The Note icon is used to present additional helpful material related to the subject being described.

Each Hands-on Project in this book is preceded by the Hands-on icon and a description of the exercise that follows.

 Case project icons mark the case project. These are more involved, scenario-based assignments. In this extensive case example, you are asked to implement independently what you have learned.

Instructor's Materials

The following supplemental materials are available when this book is used in a classroom setting. All of the supplements available with this book are provided to the instructor on a single CD-ROM.

Electronic Instructor's Manual. The Instructor's Manual that accompanies this textbook includes:

- Additional instructional material to assist in class preparation, including suggestions for lecture topics, suggested lab activities, tips on setting up a lab for the hands-on assignments, and alternative lab setup ideas in situations where lab resources are limited.

- Solutions to all end-of-chapter materials, including the Review Questions, Hands-on Projects, and Case Projects.

ExamView Pro 3.0. This textbook is accompanied by ExamView®, a powerful testing software package that allows instructors to create and administer printed, computer (LAN-based), and Internet exams. ExamView includes hundreds of questions that correspond to the topics covered in this text, enabling students to generate detailed study guides that include page references for further review. The computer-based and Internet testing components allow students to take exams at their computers, and also save the instructor time by grading each exam automatically.

PowerPoint presentations. This book comes with Microsoft PowerPoint slides for each chapter. These are included as a teaching aid for classroom presentation, to be made available to students on the network for chapter review, or to be printed for classroom distribution. Instructors, please feel at liberty to add your own slides for additional topics you introduce to the class.

Read This Before You Begin

To the Student

This book is intended to be read in chapter sequence as much of the material discussed in later chapters relies on your mastery of earlier chapters. The completion of hands-on and case projects is highly recommended in order to reap the most benefits from this book. Throughout the book, many Web sites are referenced that provide additional or more in-depth information on the subjects being covered. The student is encouraged to bookmark these Web sites for future reference.

To the Instructor

This book covers network support and troubleshooting issues for a variety of operating systems. A versatile and flexible lab environment is essential to getting the most out of the hands-on projects and case projects. The lab requirements for this book are listed below:

Student Computers:

- Internet access
- 200 MHz Pentium or compatible PC
- 64MB RAM
- 2GB Hard Disk
- 10/100 Ethernet NIC configurable for promiscuous mode
- Dual-boot computers with Windows 98 and Windows 2000 Professional
- Access to Network Control Panel and the ability to change IP addresses

Additional Lab Requirements:

- One or more Windows 2000 Server (preferred) or Windows NT Server
- One NetWare Server
- Flexible cabling arrangement so that students may plug their computers into selected hubs or switches for various hands-on projects
- One or more Ethernet hub
- One or more Cisco Catalyst 1900 switch (or similar model)
- 100 MHz cable analyzer
- Cat-5/Cat-5E cable and termination tools
- Patch panel and jacks

Contact the Author

I would like to hear from you. Please e-mail me with any problems, questions, suggestions, or corrections. I even accept compliments! There will no doubt be another edition of this book, updated with the latest and greatest technologies and operating systems, so tell me what I did right, what I did wrong, and anything you would like to see added or deleted in a future edition. I can be contacted at *NetSupport@tomsho.com*.

Visit Our World Wide Web Site

Additional materials designed especially for you might be available for your course on the World Wide Web. Go to *www.course.com*. Search for this book title periodically on the Course Technology Web site for more details.

Acknowledgments

I would like to thank all of the individuals who provided support and guidance to this project: Jill Batistick, my developmental editor, who so often provided encouraging words when there appeared to be no light at the end of the tunnel and who fine-tuned my work to become the polished book before you; Tom Lancaster, my technical reviewer, who kept me straight when I sometimes wandered from technical accuracy; Laura Hildebrand, my product manager, who maintained patience and self-control even when deadlines were sometimes missed; all of the copy editors and quality assurance folks at Course Technology who helped make my writing look literate and error-free; and a special thanks to two students, Rebecca Rhyne and George Evans, who assisted with review questions and projects and provided their "student's point of view" on selected chapters. Finally, I would like to thank my wife, Julie, and my daughter, Camille, who showed enormous patience with me as I neglected them during the late nights and weekends I was holed away in my office.

Dedication

To my wife Julie and daughter Camille

1

NETWORKING CONCEPTS REVIEW

After reading this chapter and completing the exercises, you will be able to:

♦ Recall the OSI model and identify the hardware and software components found at each layer

♦ Understand the role of internetworking devices in a network support context

♦ Describe common networking models such as peer-to-peer and client/server models

The daunting task of supporting a complex **internetwork**—that is, two or more networks that communicate using hubs, bridges, routers, or gateways—can be both challenging and rewarding. The successful network administrator will need to draw upon a variety of skills, technologies, and techniques to meet the ever-increasing demands of today's LANs and internetworks. The variety of technologies being employed in networks today demands support personnel who are willing to continue their learning process long after their formal education ends. Having an excellent grasp of the fundamentals of network hardware and software will allow you, as a network administrator, to easily adapt to the continually changing computing environment.

This chapter reviews the networking fundamentals and terminology that will be used in later chapters. First, we examine the OSI model and relate the seven layers to networking support issues. Then, we look at various internetworking devices and discuss their role in the support of a network. Finally, we consider typical networking models and the operating systems used in these models. Later chapters will focus in more detail on each of these aspects of networking.

THE OSI MODEL

No discussion about networks is complete without reviewing the OSI model. Recall that the **OSI model** describes the travel and transformation of data as it is sent from its source to its destination on an internetwork. The OSI model consists of seven layers, each of which describes a particular job to be done by a software component, a hardware component, or both.

Each layer depends on the layer below it to complete the mission of successful data communications. This relationship is important to keep in mind when troubleshooting a system. Application layer functions, which are at the top of the OSI model, will not operate properly unless all layers below it are functioning correctly. In addition, if the Physical, Data Link, and Network layers are working in a TCP/IP network, you may be able to use **Ping** to contact another workstation, but the proper functioning of these layers does not guarantee that upper-layer functions such as FTP, Telnet, or client software will work properly.

Although today's most common network systems follow the OSI model in function, the implementation details and actual number of layers used may differ from computer system to computer system. Thus there are variations on the theme. For an example, inspect Figure 1-1. It compares the OSI model to the **TCP/IP networking model**, which is a four-layer design that combines the upper three OSI model layers into the Application layer and the lower two layers into one Network Interface layer.

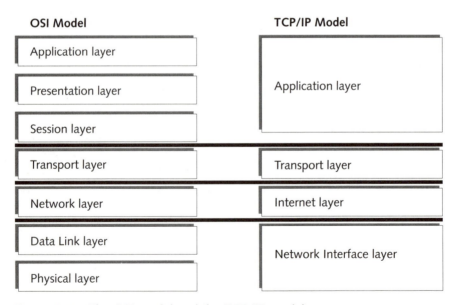

Figure 1-1   The OSI model and the TCP/IP model

Regardless of the model used, understanding what functions occur at each step of your data's journey, and what real-world hardware and software components are involved in each step, is critical to the analysis, troubleshooting, and resolution of network problems. We next look at the layers and discuss some of the support issues that may be involved with each.

Layer 1: The Physical Layer

The **Physical layer** is probably the easiest of the OSI model layers to understand. It consists primarily of things you can get your hands on: cables, connectors, **network interface cards (NICs)**, hubs, and the like. You may remember that NICs are the interface cards between a workstation and the network media. The Physical layer also describes the physical signals that make up network data, such as electrical or light pulses. In the following sections, we discuss NICs, networking media, patch panels, and hubs/repeaters. These items are all integral to understanding the Physical layer.

Network Interface Cards

The NIC is the hardware interface from a computing device to the **local area network (LAN)** media. Recall that a LAN is a local grouping of computers and devices configured to communicate through network media. The LAN might be a stand-alone network or part of a larger internetwork.

The NIC installed in your computer must have the appropriate connector to match up with the cabling you are using. Connector types include RJ-45, BNC, and AUI connectors for copper cabling. **Fiber optic** is a networking media, typically made of glass, that uses light signals to transmit data rather than electrical signals. Fiber-optic NICs are often used and a variety of connector types are available for them, including **straight tip (ST)** and **straight connector (SC)**.

Networking Media

Networking media serve as the pathway by which networking signals travel, much as roads represent the pathways by which automobiles travel. The majority of LANs today use some type of copper media to transmit signals from source to destination. Increasing in popularity are fiber-optic and even wireless media. The knowledgeable network administrator will understand the advantages of each type of medium and be able to make informed decisions regarding the one that is best for the network. Each medium brings unique issues regarding support and installation. In future chapters, we will look at some of the most common support challenges for various media types.

Patch Panels and Jacks

Patch panels and **jacks** are often-overlooked components when troubleshooting Physical-layer problems. A patch panel is a centralized connecting point, usually located in a wiring closet, for terminating media coming from the work area. A jack is the point in the work area where media are terminated to allow connection to a workstation. As with any networking component, the appropriate parts must be selected for your network media and architecture. Many mistakes can be made in the installation of these parts and, like anything else, these parts can fail. We will examine some of the problems that can crop up with these comparatively simple, yet extremely important, networking components.

Repeaters and Hubs

Rounding out the Physical layer list of components are **repeaters** and **hubs**. Traditionally, a repeater has two ports and is used to connect cable segments together to increase the length of the network. There are two types of hubs: passive hubs and active hubs. Passive hubs are much like a patch panel in that they provide a connecting point for media, but contain no active components. Active hubs do exactly what repeaters do, except that there are more ports, typically from 4 to 24. For this reason, a hub is often called a multiport repeater.

 Unless stated otherwise, the term "hub" will refer to a "multiport repeater" throughout this text.

Hubs are the simplest of the networking equipment components to install and troubleshoot. Their only job is to receive, condition, amplify, and repeat the bit signals that travel on the media. Not every hub is created equal, however. We will look in detail at some of the options available on today's hubs and the ways that they can help you manage and support your network. We will also consider what types of problems hubs can bring to your network and how to avoid and resolve them.

Layer 2: The Data Link Layer

Moving up in the OSI model, we come to the **Data Link layer**. This layer is where network packets are formatted into **frames** to be sent to their destination addresses along the physical medium. A frame defines the format in which information is arranged before it is sent to the Physical layer to be transmitted.

At this point in the OSI model, we start to talk about software components such as NIC drivers. This layer is also where **network architecture** and physical addressing are defined. A network architecture describes technologies, such as Ethernet and Token Ring, that occupy a space on both the Physical layer and the Data Link layer. The Data Link layer also provides a forum for discussion of the intricacies of switches and bridges.

NIC Drivers

The NIC is the interface between a computer and the network media. For a NIC to operate properly, the appropriate **device drivers** must be installed. It is the device drivers that format the package of data into an appropriate frame format, depending on the network architecture for which the NIC was designed. The drivers also act as the computer operating system's interface to the NIC. Before a networked computer can communicate, the NIC must be physically installed in the computer and the correct software driver for that NIC must be installed in the operating system.

Network Architecture

When designing a network, you must select an appropriate architecture for your environment. Network architectures include Ethernet, Token Ring, Fiber Distributed Data Interface (FDDI), and Attached Resource Computer Network (ARCnet), to name a few. Each of these architectures has its own rules about how data communication is accomplished, and each has rules about how computing devices access the network media and, once accessed, how data is formatted before it is sent onto the media. Due to these differences, each of these networking technologies has its own tools and techniques for troubleshooting and support.

Switches and Bridges

The internetwork devices operating at the Data Link layer include **switches** and **bridges**. Switches and bridges segment a network, but still allow communication. Both perform essentially the same tasks; a bridge is to a switch as a repeater is to a hub. The only significant difference is that switches have more ports.

Switches process frames and make filtering or forwarding decisions based on the destination's physical address. Unlike hubs, which are concerned only with the individual bit signals that travel on the media, Data Link layer devices process the actual data that the signals represent. A variety of technologies exist to accomplish this task. Because switches and bridges are more complex than hubs, the configuration and troubleshooting of these devices is a more complex task. In later chapters, we will look in more detail at some of the options available to network administrators regarding switches and hubs.

Layers 3 and 4: The Network and Transport Layers

It is at layers 3 and 4 of networking where much of a network support technician's time is spent assigning workstation addresses, installing servers, and configuring routers. The **Network layer** defines logical addressing and is responsible for the best-path selection in a routed internetwork. The **Transport layer** is responsible for reliable transmission of data, disassembly and reassembly of large data transmissions, and the ability to maintain multiple data streams between multiple applications. In this section of the chapter, we review the major protocol suites used today and discuss their role in a typical network environment. We also discuss routers, which are integral members of the Network and Transport layers.

When a networking protocol is discussed, we usually think of terms such as Transport Control Protocol/Internet Protocol (TCP/IP) and Internetwork Packet Exchange/Sequenced Packet Exchange (IPX/SPX). These protocol suites are defined primarily and collectively at the Network and Transport layers of the OSI model, so these layers will be discussed together.

IPX/SPX

Novell developed the IPX/SPX protocol to be a fast, simple-to-configure protocol for the NetWare operating system. There is little to configure, and the protocol works well, particularly in small to medium-size LAN environments. It is not completely foolproof, however, and we will see some of the problems you could encounter with this protocol.

TCP/IP

TCP/IP is the standard protocol used in networks and network operating systems today. The primary reason for the establishment of this standard has been the tremendous growth and popularity of the Internet; TCP/IP is the protocol of the Internet. Because of the huge installed base of TCP/IP devices and the comparatively complex configuration requirements, this text will primarily focus on this protocol.

TCP/IP has become dominant because of its flexibility in diverse networking environments, its ability to scale very well, its superiority in a **wide area network (WAN)** environment, and the myriad tools and applications that have been developed as a result of the Internet's popularity. Along with this flexibility and scalability comes complexity. Many a networking professional has built a career on TCP/IP expertise. Later chapters will be devoted to TCP/IP and its rigors, so for now, we can simply review some of the basic concepts of TCP/IP addressing.

Recall that a TCP/IP address is a 32-bit number divided into four **octets**. An octet is a collection of eight bits that is viewed as a single unit—in this case, a decimal value from 0 to 255. An address is expressed in **dotted decimal notation**—for example, 192.168.1.1. Dotted decimal notation, as the name implies, uses decimal numbers, separated by periods, to express a value. A TCP/IP address is divided into two parts: the network number and the host number. The use of a **subnet mask** specifies the number of bits that make up the network portion of the address.

A subnet mask is specified along with a TCP/IP address when assigning an address to a host. The subnet mask is written in dotted decimal format and is 32 bits in length, such as in the following:

> IP address: 192.168.1.1
> Subnet mask: 255.255.255.0

The network part of the IP address is 192.168.1 and the host part of the address is 1. Supporting TCP/IP networks and proper configuration of addresses, along with subnetting, are discussed in detail later in this book.

1

NetBEUI

The **NetBIOS Enhanced User Interface (NetBEUI)** protocol is a very simple, efficient protocol designed for Windows LAN environments. There is no configuration necessary and virtually no support is required. Because it is very broadcast-oriented, however, the protocol does not scale well. In addition, because there is no Network layer information included in the protocol, it cannot be routed. Very little time will be spent discussing this protocol except to mention its advantages in small, simple, Windows-based LANs.

Routers

A discussion of the Network layer is incomplete without mentioning **routers**. The routing of packets through an internetwork is the responsibility of the Network layer, and it is at this layer where routers do their work. A router examines the logical addresses of packets sent to it. It then makes a path selection decision based on the information it has about the destination network specified in each packet. This decision is based on the information stored in the routing table. In large internetworks with dozens, hundreds, or even thousands of networks, the decision-making process can become quite complex, and correct configuration of the router becomes critical in assuring working communication.

Layers 5, 6, and 7: The Upper Layers

The upper three layers of the OSI model—**Session**, **Presentation**, and **Application**—are the most difficult to relate to a particular piece of hardware or software. The purposes of these three layers are to coordinate conversations between networked applications, to translate data types if necessary, and to provide networking services to user applications, respectively.

Most network operating systems combine the functions of the upper three layers into one installable function. Examples of the software that performs these functions include **server services** (which provides access to shared resources to network **clients**, which are computers that have the capability to access shared resources on a network), name resolutions programs, and TCP/IP applications such as FTP and Telnet.

Let's now take a brief look at some of these upper-layer software participants. Later in the book, we will review them in detail when we discuss specific operating system support issues.

Client and Server Software

In a LAN environment in which computer resources, such as disk drives and printers, are being shared, two important upper-layer components must be installed on the computers: server software and client software. The **server software** allows other computers to access local resources. The **client software** is the component that allows a workstation to access remote resources.

Redirectors

On a Microsoft client workstation, the client software is referred to as a **redirector**. Windows provides a redirector for Microsoft server operating systems called Client for Microsoft Networks and one for Novell NetWare called Microsoft Client for NetWare Networks. Redirectors for other operating systems can be obtained separately.

A redirector enables a client station to perform network file operations such as open, read, write, delete, and print requests. When an application, such as a word processor, wants to open a file located on a network server, the application sends the request to the appropriate redirector. You can look at a redirector or network client as being the interface to the network for user applications. Other client software components include FTP and Telnet in the TCP/IP protocol suite. These client components must have a corresponding server component to access to be useful.

Servers

A client is useless without the complementary component of a server somewhere on the network. Examples of server software are File and Print Sharing for Microsoft Networks in a Windows environment and NetWare Core Protocol on a NetWare server. These server services comprise the functions of the upper three layers of the OSI model. It is these server components that listen and communicate with the client components on a remote system and that allow clients to access file and printer resources on the computer on which they are installed. In a TCP/IP networking environment, servers such as FTP server and Telnet server provide access to their corresponding clients.

To see how the communication process between a client and server works in relation to the OSI model, examine Figure 1-2. The left side of the diagram depicts a client application's request for network file services. Notice how each block on the left side of the diagram (the request side) has a corresponding block on the right side of the diagram. For example, the block labeled Client/Redirector has a corresponding block labeled Server Service (File and Print Sharing) at the same level in the OSI model.

TCP/IP Applications

TCP/IP is broken into four layers, as compared to the OSI model's seven layers. The TCP/IP Application layer maps to layers 5 through 7 of the OSI model. Some of the functions we find at the TCP/IP Application layer include File Transfer Protocol (FTP) and Simple Mail Transfer Protocol (SMTP). In a TCP/IP environment, each of these functions has both a client and a server component. When you are troubleshooting one of these services, you must keep in mind that the configuration on the client side must be compatible with the server-side component. Application layer support issues for TCP/IP are discussed later in this book.

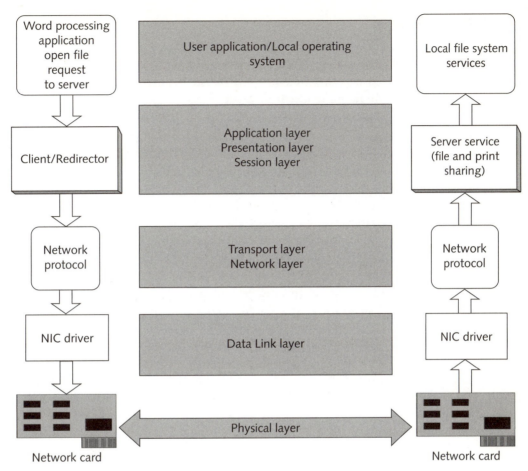

Figure 1-2   Client-to-server request

INTERNETWORKING DEVICES

Much of the challenge of designing, installing, and maintaining a network is the proper choice and configuration of **internetworking devices**. An internetworking device is a piece of equipment such as a hub, switch, or router that allows your network to grow beyond the confines of its media specifications.

You should know under which circumstances you should choose a particular device, and you must know how each device affects the operations of your network. Although we will get into the details of configuring and supporting various networking devices in later chapters, we will review the function of the most common devices here. Our focus will be on Ethernet devices, because Ethernet is the dominant network architecture in use today. We start our discussion with some Ethernet basics.

Ethernet Basics

Ethernet is a 10-Mbps, broadcast-based network architecture that dominates the LAN arena. The Ethernet network architecture is considered a best-effort delivery system. That is, when an Ethernet frame is sent onto the media, there is no verification mechanism to ensure that the frame makes it to its destination.

Ethernet is also a broadcast networking technology. When a computer wants to send a frame to a destination, the physical address, called the **MAC address**, is placed in the frame header and the frame then is sent onto the media. All stations located on that cable segment hear the message and process the frame header to determine whether the frame is addressed to them. Only the machine with the matching address will process the entire frame. Due to this broadcast method, only one computer at a time per cable segment can transmit data successfully. If more than one computer attempts to send data at the same time, the signals interfere with each other and a collision occurs.

A method must exist to determine which computer can transmit data at any given time and to detect and correct for collisions. For this purpose, Ethernet uses **Carrier Sense Multiple Access with Collision Detection (CSMA/CD)**. Within CSMA/CD, before a computer transmits data, it listens on the cable (Carrier Sense). If there is no signal, the computer can send. It is possible to have a situation in which two (or more) machines are listening at the same time, detecting no signal, and then sending (Multiple Access). When a computer sends data, it listens for signs that another station transmitted at the same time. If there is a collision with another computer's transmission, the computer will detect it (Collision Detection), wait for a period of time, and then retry the transmission. The wait period is called a **backoff**. During the backoff, a timer is set and must expire before a retransmission attempt can be made. A total of 16 transmission attempts are made before Ethernet gives up and informs the upper layers that an error has occurred.

Ethernet employs another error-checking mechanism called **Frame Check Sequence (FCS)**. The FCS is a 32-bit field added to the end of the frame header that contains the results of the **Cyclical Redundancy Check (CRC)**. The CRC is derived from a math calculation done on all data bytes in the frame to be sent. When the frame arrives at the destination, the receiving machine performs the same calculation. If the results do not match the CRC included in the frame, that frame is discarded because the data has somehow been changed, perhaps by **electromagnetic interference (EMI)** or **crosstalk**. EMI is signal interference generated from outside sources. Crosstalk is signal interference generated from wires within the same cable. The sending machine is not informed of data corruption, if it occurs. Retransmission is left to the upper-layer protocols to worry about.

We will now look at several internetworking devices and discuss their role in the network support process.

Hubs/Repeaters

Hubs work at the Physical layer of the OSI model. When a hub receives a signal on one port, it cleans up the signal, strengthens it, and repeats it out all of its other ports. It provides a single connecting point for a group of workstations and allows the network to overcome the size limitations imposed by the media in use. For example, in a typical Ethernet network using 10BaseT cabling, the limit on any one run of cable is 100 meters. Figure 1-3 shows that if a cable is connected to a hub, the workstation on the other end can communicate with another workstation at the end of another 100-meter run, thus expanding the total distance to 200 meters.

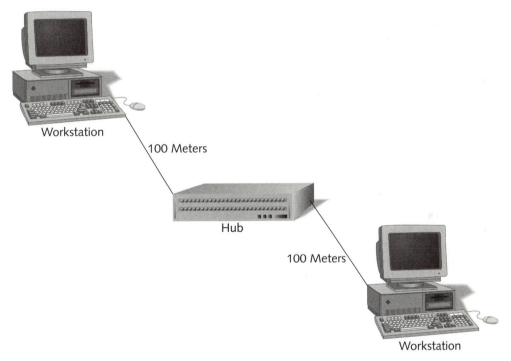

Figure 1-3 Hub expands network distance

Because a hub does not consider the destination address when repeating the incoming signals, all workstations connected to the hub must process every frame that is transmitted on the network. Furthermore, if several hubs are tied together, each hub repeats the signals to the other hubs, creating what amounts to one large **cable segment**. A cable segment is a section of cable bounded by a switch, bridge, or router port. It is also referred to as a collision domain.

Using hubs to network computers is simple and relatively inexpensive. Because of their simplicity, however, they do not scale well. The more workstations you add to a hub-based network, the higher the rate of collisions and the lower the total useful data throughput. Figure 1-4 shows how a cable segment can be expanded by using hubs. The arrow labeled Signal In represents a workstation transmission. The other arrows represent the repeated signal propagating throughout the network. Later in this book, we will discuss many of the issues related to supporting hubs and the features commonly available on hubs.

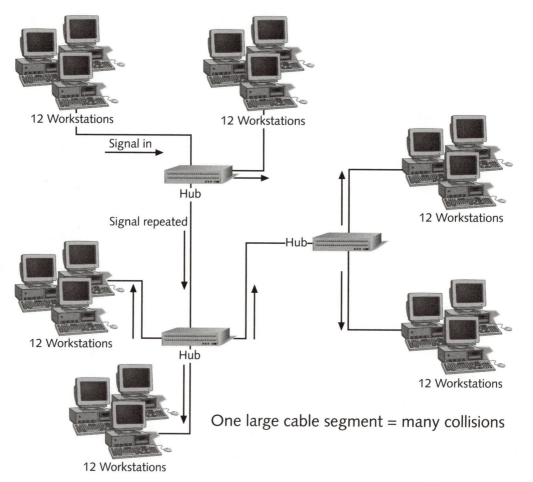

Figure 1-4   Multiple hubs form one cable segment

Bridges/Switches

Bridges and switches work at layer 2 of the OSI model. Because a switch is essentially a fast, multiport bridge, the term "switch" will be used in the remainder of this book to denote the common device of reference.

Switches perform many of the same functions as hubs do, but without some of hubs' disadvantages. Whereas hubs extend the number of workstations on a cable segment, each switch port makes a new cable segment. Each switch port constitutes a different **collision domain**. A collision domain defines the cable segments of the network over which collisions are propagated. Therefore, a network with switches has fewer collisions.

As another feature, a switch reads and processes the incoming frames and makes filtering or forwarding decisions based on the destination MAC address. A switch forwards all frames with a destination address of **broadcast** to all switch ports. A MAC address in which all 48 bits of the address are set to 1 indicates a broadcast. A MAC address is specified in hexadecimal digits. Thus a broadcast frame has a destination address of *0x*ffffffffffff, where *0x* indicates hexadecimal. In this situation, switches act much like hubs.

Figure 1-5 shows a workstation with MAC address AA sending a frame to the workstation with MAC address DD. A switch, unlike a hub, forwards the frame only out of the port where workstation DD can be found.

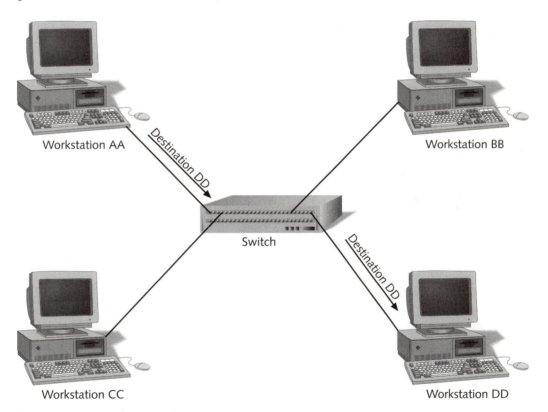

Figure 1-5 Switch operation

Routers

The router is the most complex of the internetworking devices discussed so far. Routers work at the Network layer, so they filter or forward packets based on logical addresses rather than on physical addresses. A router's primary concern is to get a packet of data from one network to another network. Whereas hubs and switches might have workstations attached to each of their ports, a router interface will have an entire network attached.

A router is used to connect networks or, in some cases, to break up a network that has become too large. Unlike switches, routers do not by default forward broadcast packets. Consequently, routers can be used to break up a network so that broadcast packets affect a smaller number of workstations. Figure 1-6 shows a simple representation of two networks connected by a router. The two networks have different network numbers. One of the networks uses a switch to interconnect hosts, and the other uses a hub. It is the router, however, that actually creates two physical networks and that allows communication between them.

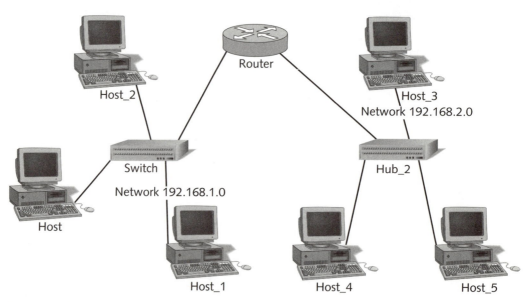

Figure 1-6   Two networks connected by a router

A router determines where to send an incoming packet based on information stored in its **routing table**. The routing table is essentially a map of all the networks known to the router, and it contains the directions on how to get to each network. Routing tables are created by the exchange of information between routers. Routers use several protocols to communicate with each other to create and maintain these routing tables. Examples include Routing Information Protocol (RIP), Opens Shortest Path First (OSPF), Interior Gateway Routing Protocol (IGRP), and Border Gateway Protocol

(BGP). The selection and configuration of the appropriate protocol for each internetwork is paramount in maintaining a healthy, efficient network.

Routers also play a significant role in network security. Failure to properly configure your routers for network security can lead to broken communications in your network or, even worse, lost or stolen data as a result of outside intrusion. Later chapters will look at many of the support issues faced by a network administrator who is charged with ensuring the proper configuration and maintenance of a routed network environment.

NETWORKING MODELS

It is not enough to know how data flows on a network, which is the focus of the OSI model. The various ways in which people and computers share data also must be understood to properly troubleshoot problems. The manner in which data and devices are shared constitutes the **networking model**.

Networking models can be classified into two categories: client/server and peer-to-peer. Very often a combination of the two will be used on a network. These models describe how resources are shared and managed on a network. Whereas the **client/server model** has centralized administration and designated server and client machines, the **peer-to-peer model** distributes the administration among all the computers, and all computers can be both clients and servers.

Both models have advantages and disadvantages and require different levels of support. In general, the client/server model is used in medium to large networks as well as small networks that would benefit from centralized administration. Client/server networks are more scalable and have a full-featured set of administration tools, as compared to the relatively simple management tools found in peer-to-peer networks. Peer-to-peer networks are usually limited to fewer than 10 computers. Therefore, client/server systems usually require network administrators who are more skilled than average in the management of a network.

We next discuss support issues for both types of network models, as unique concerns arise with each model.

Client/Server Networks

As mentioned earlier, the client/server model dictates that some computers on the network will be designated as servers and that most will be designated as clients. A server computer will run network operating system software that allows sharing of files, printers, and other resources with client computers. Some characteristics of a server computer are as follows:

- A network operating system, such as Novell NetWare, Windows NT Server/Windows 2000 Server, or OS/2 Warp
- Large amounts of RAM (128 MB and higher is typical)

- High-speed disk controllers, such as SCSI
- Large disk drives
- High-speed NICs
- Fault-tolerant features
- Tape backup
- Central user database
- Centralized management tools
- Features that allow different client operating systems to connect

To gain access to resources in the network, a user on a client computer must log into one or more network servers. Usually a password is assigned to each user for security. After logging in, a client computer then can access the resources to which the user name has been given permission. Figure 1-7 shows a typical client/server network.

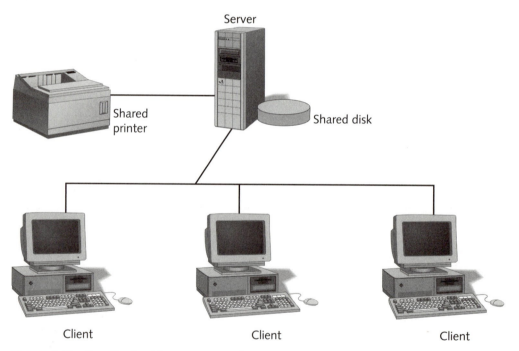

Figure 1-7 Simple client/server network

Often, a user is given a directory, called a home directory, on the server on which to store files. This directory setup allows user data files to be backed up when the server is backed up, relieving individual users from the task of doing their own backups. This is one reason that server computers must be more reliable and frequently have much larger hard disks than client computers.

A client computer runs an operating system that is optimized for single-user use and for running applications. These computers usually do not need some of the fault-tolerant and high-speed disk components that servers require. The primary goal of a client computer is to provide a comfortable interface for users to run local applications and access shared network resources.

Characteristics of a client computer include the following:

- A client operating system, such as DOS, Windows 3.*x*, 9.*x*, Windows NT Workstation, Windows XP, Windows 2000 Professional, Mac OS, or OS/2

- Network client software

- High-quality video components

- Disk controllers designed for workstation use, such as Integrated Device Electronics (IDE)

- Multimedia components

Many organizations have a variety of client computers—DOS, various versions of Windows, and Macintosh, to name a few. The servers in these organizations must be able to support connections from all these clients. When troubleshooting client/server problems, IT personnel must understand the issues involved with many types of clients and must be able to configure both the server and client operating systems correctly. Later chapters of this book will cover many of the issues you will face in a diverse client/server environment.

Peer-to-Peer Networks

A peer-to-peer network is generally less expensive to build and easier to install and maintain than a client-server network. This networking model is ideal for a network of 10 or fewer computers for which no dedicated network administrator is available and in which centralized management and security are not a requirement. In fact, peer-to-peer networks have become so popular that most computers sold today come with an operating system that has built-in, peer-to-peer networking features. These operating systems include all versions of Windows (since Windows for Workgroups 3.11), OS/2, and Mac OS. DOS and Windows 3.1 do not have peer-to-peer networking capabilities built in, although you could purchase the necessary software, if desired.

In a peer-to-peer network, each workstation can be set up to share its resources with the network and to access other shared resources. In other words, each workstation can be both a client and a server. This concept is sometimes referred to as workgroup computing. Each user has control over the access to the resources on his or her own computer. Each computer maintains its own security information. Thus, rather than use a single login to access network resources, a user may have to know several different logins—one for each computer in the network. This arrangement can become very confusing as the number of computers grows, which is one reason that peer-to-peer networks should be kept small.

Although these networks are usually fairly simple to manage, they are not foolproof. In addition, because the majority of businesses are small businesses, there are a lot of peer-to-peer networks in operation. We will look at some of the unique problems you might find in this type of environment later in this book. Figure 1-8 shows a typical peer-to-peer network.

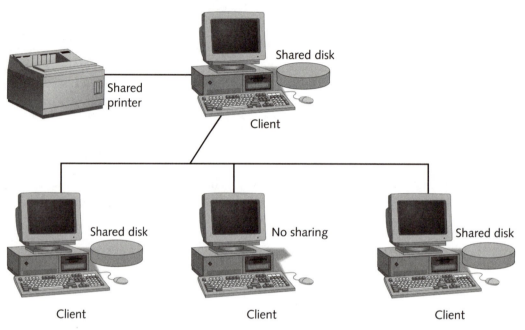

Figure 1-8   Peer-to-peer networks may have some or all computers sharing resources

CHAPTER SUMMARY

❑ The seven-layer OSI model can be described in terms of the hardware and software components we use to install and configure networks. Layer 1 relates to the cabling, connectors, signals, and hubs. Layer 2 relates to network architectures such as Ethernet and Token Ring and describes physical addressing and frame formats. Switches and bridges are common layer 2 devices. Layers 3 and 4 describe the networking protocols, such as TCP/IP and IPX/SPX, that we install on our computers, along with logical addressing and internetwork path selection. Routers are the devices that work at layer 3. The upper layers (layers 5–7) usually are discussed together. They provide the networking interface to user applications, control computer-to-computer communication sessions, and translate data as necessary. Client and server software services are found in the upper layers, as are name resolution and TCP/IP applications.

1

❑ Internetworking devices such as hubs, switches, and routers all perform different jobs, and selection of the appropriate device is critical to maintaining an efficient network. Routers are the most complex of these devices and have the most configuration options. They provide connectivity between networks, perform best-path selection, and can add security to your internetwork. Routers are concerned with logical addresses and work at layer 3 of the OSI model.

❑ Switches are used to segment growing LANs to reduce collisions. They make filtering or forwarding decisions based on physical addresses, which are found at layer 2 of the OSI model. Hubs, the simplest of the internetworking devices, are concerned only with incoming bit signals. Hubs repeat all incoming signals to all other ports after cleaning and amplifying the signals. Their primary purpose is to extend the distance limitations of the media and provide a central connecting point.

❑ The method by which computers share and access resources as well as the administration of security is described by two types of networking models: client/server and peer-to-peer. Client/server networking is used in larger networks and networks that require centralized security and control of resources. Peer-to-peer networking is best used in smaller networks where distributed control of security and resources is appropriate. Many networks use a combination of these networking models.

KEY TERMS

Application layer — Layer 7 of the OSI model, which provides networking services to user applications.

backoff — A delay period that occurs after an Ethernet collision, during which a station does not transmit data.

bridge — A Data Link-layer device that is used to segment a network into multiple collision domains. It filters and forwards data based on MAC addresses.

broadcast — A frame sent and intended to be processed by all stations; in Ethernet, it is a physical address of all binary 1s or hexadecimal Fs.

cable segment — A section of cable bounded by a switch, bridge, or router port; also referred to as a collision domain.

Carrier Sense Multiple Access with Collision Detection (CSMA/CD) — The method used by Ethernet to control access to media.

client — In general, a computer that has the capability to access shared resources on a network. It also is the software required to make a stand-alone workstation operate in a network environment.

client software — The software installed on a workstation that allows the workstation to access shared resources on another computer.

client/server model — A network of designated server and client computers with centralized administration.

collision domain — Defines the cable segments of the network over which collisions are propagated.

crosstalk — Interference of data from a neighboring wire, usually in the same cable.

Cyclical Redundancy Check (CRC) — A 32-bit value derived from a math calculation done on all data bytes in a frame. It is used to verify the integrity of the data.

Data Link layer — The layer at which network packets are formatted into frames to be sent to their destination address along the physical medium.

device driver — The software interface between an operating system and computer hardware.

dotted decimal notation — The uses of decimal numbers, separated by periods, to express a value.

electromagnetic interference (EMI) — Interference of data traveling on copper wires caused by such things as motors, electrical cables, and fluorescent lights.

Ethernet — A 10-Mbps, broadcast-based network architecture that dominates in the LAN arena.

fiber optic — A networking medium, usually made of glass, that uses light signals to transmit data.

frame — The unit of information found at the Data Link layer of the OSI model. A frame contains elements such as the physical address and the CRC. A packet is "framed" with the physical address header and the CRC trailer before being sent to the Physical layer.

Frame Check Sequence (FCS) — A 32-bit field added to the end of the frame header that contains the results of the CRC.

hub — A multiport repeater.

internetwork — Two or more networks that communicate with each other using hubs, bridges, routers, or gateways.

Internetwork Packet Exchange/Sequenced Packet Exchange (IPX/SPX) — A protocol suite used primarily at the Network and Transport layers of the OSI model.

internetworking device — A piece of equipment such as a hub, switch, or router that allows your network to grow beyond the confines of its media specifications.

jack — The point in the work area where media are terminated to allow connection to a workstation.

Local Area Network (LAN) — A local grouping of computers and devices configured to communicate through network media. It may be a stand-alone network or part of a larger internetwork.

MAC address — The physical address of an Ethernet station consisting of 48 bits and expressed in hexadecimal digits.

NetBIOS Enhanced User Interface (NetBEUI) — A simple, efficient protocol designed for Windows LAN environments.

network architecture — Networking technologies such as Ethernet and Token Ring that describe logical and physical topology as well as the media access method.

1

network interface card (NIC) — The interface card between a workstation and the network media.

Network layer — Layer 3 of the OSI model, which defines logical addressing and is responsible for best-path selection in a routed internetwork.

networking media — The pathway by which networking signals travel, much as roads represent the pathways by which automobiles travel.

networking model — The manner in which data and devices are shared.

octet — A collection of eight bits, representing one part of a four-part IP address.

OSI model — A framework for describing the travel and transformation of data as it is sent from its source to its destination on an internetwork. The OSI model consists of seven layers.

patch panel — A centralized connecting point, usually located in a wiring closet, for terminating media coming from the work area.

peer-to-peer model — A network of computers that has both clients and servers and where administration is distributed.

Physical layer — Layer 1 of the OSI model, which consists primarily of things you can get your hands on and which describes the physical signals that make up network data, such as electrical or light pulses.

Ping (Packet InterNet Groper) — A troubleshooting utility used to determine if a device with a particular IP address is available on the network.

Presentation layer — Layer 6 of the OSI model, which translates data types when necessary between communicating machines.

redirector — Software installed on a workstation that allows the workstation to access resources on a particular network operating system. Also called a requestor, network shell, or client.

repeater — An internetworking device used to extend the length of a cable segment by conditioning and amplifying incoming signals and repeating them out all other ports.

router — The device that routes packets through an internetwork.

routing table — A map of all networks known to the router. Routing tables are created by the exchange of information between routers.

server services — A device or software component that provides access to shared resources to network clients.

server software — Software installed on a computer that allows other computers to access resources on that computer.

Session layer — Layer 5 of the OSI model, which coordinates conversations between networked applications.

straight connector (SC) — A connector type used with fiber-optic media.

straight tip (ST) — A connector type used with fiber-optic media.

subnet mask — Used in combination with an IP address to specify the number of bits that make up the network part of the address.

switch — A multiport bridge.

TCP/IP networking model — A four-layer design that combines the upper three layers of the OSI model into the Application layer and the lower two layers of the OSI model into the Network Interface layer.

Transport Control Protocol/Internet Protocol (TCP/IP) — A protocol suite used primarily at the Network and Transport layers of the OSI model.

Transport layer — Layer 4 of the OSI model, which is responsible for reliable transmission of data, disassembly and reassembly of large data transmissions, and the maintenance of multiple data streams between multiple applications.

REVIEW QUESTIONS

1. One principle of troubleshooting that applies to the OSI model is that each layer _____.
   a. is independent of the other layers
   b. has built-in redundancy to eliminate errors from other layers
   c. depends on the layers below it to have successful data communications
   d. depends on the layers above it to have successful data communications

2. Ethernet and Token Ring can be described as _____.
   a. network theories
   b. network architectures
   c. network media types
   d. broadband networks

3. The Transport layer is responsible for _____.
   a. beaming information into the Data Link layer
   b. accessing the driver that moves the head of the hard drive
   c. pinging the server regularly to maintain connections
   d. maintaining multiple data streams between multiple applications

4. Which layer of the OSI model is responsible for best-path selection?
   a. 1
   b. 3
   c. 5
   d. 7

5. If you can ping to an IP address but not telnet to that same IP address, what is a possible problem?
   a. wrong IP address
   b. faulty NIC card
   c. upper-layer functions not working
   d. faulty subnet assignment

6. Which protocol works in a Windows-based LAN, requires no configuration, and does not scale well?

    a. TCP/IP

    b. NetBEUI

    c. Banyan VINES

    d. IPX/SPX

7. Which device operates at the Data Link layer?

    a. router

    b. switch

    c. repeater

    d. hub

8. Which layer of the OSI model describes the physical signals that make up the network data?

    a. 7

    b. 4

    c. 1

    d. 3

9. The Data Link layer is responsible for _____.

    a. formatting frames to be sent to their destination addresses along the physical medium

    b. processing and filtering frames based on logical addresses

    c. receiving, amplifying, and repeating bit signals

    d. describing the physical signals that make up network data

10. _____ can result from failing to properly configure a router. (Choose all that apply.)

    a. Good internetwork communication between routers

    b. Lost or stolen data from outside sources

    c. Strong security preventing loss of data

    d. Broken communication between subnets

11. Which device does a client require to operate?

    a. hub

    b. AUI cable

    c. server

    d. router

12. What happens when several computers attempt to transmit at the same time on the same cable segment?

    a. Nothing; each frame is received in perfect condition.

    b. A collision occurs.

    c. The data is scrambled but fixed by the CRC.

    d. The data is sent back to the source for retransmission.

13. Which method does Ethernet use to determine when and how a workstation may access the media?

    a. CRC

    b. token passing

    c. CSMA/CA

    d. CSMA/CD

14. Which layers of the OSI model does the TCP/IP Application layer represent?

    a. Session, Presentation, and Application

    b. Physical, Data Link, and Network

    c. Data Link, Presentation, and Application

    d. Transport, Session, and Presentation

15. What are the four layers of the TCP/IP model?

    a. Physical, Data Link, Network, and Transport

    b. Network Interface, Internet, Transport, and Application

    c. Transport, Session, Presentation, and Application

    d. Network Interface, Transport, Session, and Application

16. What are the server components responsible for in a client/server environment? (Choose all that apply.)

    a. allowing clients to access shared resources

    b. listening to and communicating with the client components on a remote system

    c. deciding whether a request for a resource is local or remote and sending the request to the appropriate redirector

    d. authenticating users to the network

17. What is the maximum length of any one cable run on a 10BaseT Ethernet network?

    a. 100 meters

    b. 200 meters

    c. 185 meters

    d. 110 meters

18. Which device is responsible for receiving a signal on one port, and then cleaning, strengthening, and repeating the signal on all its other ports?

    a. router

    b. bridge

    c. repeater

    d. switch

19. Which of the following is an error-checking mechanism that is derived from a mathematical calculation that is done on all data bytes in a frame used on an Ethernet network?

    a. CSMA/CD

    b. checksum

    c. CRC

    d. CPU

20. Which networking model is ideal for a network with 10 or fewer computers in which security is not a major concern?

    a. client/server

    b. Ethernet

    c. Token Ring

    d. peer-to-peer

21. To have access to network resources in a client/server environment, what is a required step that each user must take?

    a. Each user must log into one or more network servers.

    b. There is no required step that a user must take.

    c. Each user must log into his or her workstation.

    d. Each user must initiate a Telnet connection with the network server.

22. Which internetworking device works at the Network layer of the OSI model and filters packets based on their logical addresses rather than on their physical addresses?

    a. hub

    b. bridge

    c. router

    d. switch

23. Which device is the interface between a computer and the network media?

    a. router

    b. NIC

    c. cable

    d. hub

24. Which client component enables stations to perform network file operations such as open, read, write, delete, and print?

    a. NIC

    b. server

    c. protocol

    d. redirector

25. If you have a distance of 250 meters between a workstation and a server on an Ethernet network using 10BaseT, where do repeaters need to be placed?

    a. every 100 meters

    b. every 200 meters

    c. every 50 meters

    d. No repeaters are needed.

HANDS-ON PROJECTS

Project 1-1 Researching Terminology

In this project, you will research network terms so that you can become familiar with obtaining information that you need as a network administrator.

1. Open your Web browser.

2. In the Location or Address dialog box, type **http://www.webopedia.com/ networks/**, and then press **Enter**.

3. In the text on the left, type **multicast**.

4. Click the **Go!** button.

5. Write a summary of what the word "multicast" means and explain how it can be used in networks.

6. Click the **Back** button on your Web browser.

7. In the text box on the left, type **contention**.

8. Click the **Go!** button.

9. Write a brief summary of what the word "contention" means and explain how Ethernet deals with it.

10. Close your Web browser.

Project 1-2 Researching Protocols

In this project, you will research protocols so that you can become familiar with obtaining the information that you need as a network administrator.

1. Open your Web browser.

2. In the Location or Address dialog box, type **http://www.protocols.com**, and then press **Enter**.

3. Click the **Protocol Directory** button. Your instructor will assign you a protocol suite from the following list:

   ❏ Appletalk

   ❏ Banyan

   ❏ DECnet

   ❏ IBM

   ❏ ISO

   ❏ Novell

   ❏ Sun

   ❏ XNS

4. Write a short paper on the protocol you have been assigned, noting in which environments it is primarily used. Discuss whether the protocol is best suited for LANs, WANs, or both. List the subprotocols that are included in the protocol suite. Describe the protocol's relationship to the OSI model. Present this information to your classmates and instructor.

5. Close your Web browser.

Project 1-3 IEEE Web Site

In this project, you will become familiar with the IEEE Web site. This site belongs to a prestigious and influential association within the computer industry; learning more about this association is vital to your success as a network administrator.

1. Open your Web browser.

2. In the Location or Address text box, type **http://standards.ieee.org/**, and then press **Enter**.

3. Using the links you see on the IEEE Standards Organization page, find information on the following:

   ❏ What the IEEE Standards Organization is and how it is organized

   ❏ How to request documents from the IEEE

   ❏ Three IEEE standards that are commonly used in networking

4. Close your Web browser.

Project 1-4 Novell Support Site

Novell is a leader in the computer networking industry. Becoming familiar with its site and offerings will allow you to use the site as resource when necessary.

1. Open your Web browser.

2. In the Location or Address dialog box, type **http://support.novell.com**, and then press **Enter**.

3. Click the **Patches and Files** link.

4. Click the **Minimum Patch List** link.

5. Scroll down until you find the current support pack for the latest version of NetWare. Write down the name of the support pack file.

6. Click the support pack file name.

7. Write a summary of the contents of the support pack.

8. Close your Web browser.

Project 1-5 Request For Comments

Requests for Comments (RFCs) are used within the industry to solicit and organize input on a variety of computer-related topics. As a network administrator, you will find yourself referring to these RFCs again and again.

1. Open your Web browser.

2. In the Location or Address dialog box, type **http://www.rfc-editor.org**, and then press **Enter**.

3. Click the **Overview** link.

4. Read the Overview page and write a summary of the definition of an RFC and the process used to publish RFCs.

5. Click the **Back** button.

6. Click the **RFC Search and Retrieval** link.

7. Click the **Official Internet Protocol Standards** link.

8. Click **Edit** on the menu bar of your Web browser, and then click **Find** (**on this page**).

9. Type **Assigned Numbers** in the Find what: text box.

10. Click the **1700** link in the RFC# column.

11. Read the first several paragraphs of RFC 1700 and write a brief explanation of the purpose of RFC 1700.

12. Close your Web browser.

CASE PROJECTS

Case 1-1 Compare Client and Server Operating Systems

Identify and research two server operating systems and two client operating systems. Compare and contrast various operating systems. Prepare a report listing the details of the operating systems that you learned about in your research. Include in your report any special features or characteristics that you may have found.

Case 1-2 Tour of Your Network

Your instructor will provide a tour of your campus or classroom network. During your tour, list and describe any internetworking devices that you notice. In your description, be as precise as possible, including where you saw the component, what model of the device was being used, how it was being used, and at what layer of the OSI model the device functions.

Case 1-3 Network Architectures

Research the network architectures commonly used in LAN environments. List as many different architectures as you can. Excluding Ethernet, which was covered in this chapter, provide information on how each of the architectures accomplishes physical addressing, media access, and error handling.

Case 1-4 Sails & Snails on the Internet

You have just been hired as a consultant for a small business, Sails & Snails Industries, which has 25 desktop computers. Each user has been using individual modem dial-up as the method of access to the Internet. In addition, the company is using Windows 98 as its operating system. Another consultant has advised Sails & Snails Industries that it can reduce its total cost of operations by networking all its computers.

Based on the information provided, would you agree with the other consultant's advice? Explain your answer. If you disagree, what would your recommendations be and why would you make them?

Case 1-5 Sails & Snails Network Proposal

Sails & Snails Industries has decided to set up a network infrastructure with all 25 computers on the network and all employees having Internet access. The company has asked you to review its current environment and submit a proposal based on your findings. Recommend a network architecture and a networking model for this project. List the additional hardware and software that would be required to implement the design you select. Explain your proposal.

2

SUPPORTING NETWORKS

After reading this chapter and completing the exercises, you will be able to:

♦ Describe and utilize several approaches to problem solving

♦ Describe and use the problem-solving process flowchart

♦ Use and discuss a variety of problem-solving tools

If you are a typical administrator, you work with four operating systems, three protocols, two LAN architectures, and three WAN technologies! What is a network administrator to do? One of the most difficult things network support people face is the constantly changing technologies and the number of different technologies that must be supported. Knowing the approaches to problem solving, the problem-solving process, and the problem-solving tools at your disposal is just as important as the technical knowledge that you apply.

In this chapter, we discuss approaches to problem solving that you will utilize in upcoming chapters. You will learn about methods such as trial and error and resolve by example. You will see the problem-solving process flowchart that takes you through the troubleshooting process. Finally, you will learn about the tools available to you. These "tools" include colleagues, the World Wide Web, documentation, software and hardware troubleshooters, and test equipment.

APPROACHES TO PROBLEM SOLVING

Tackling different problems requires different approaches. Sometimes it makes sense to just try a solution and see if it works. At other times, you may have a similar system that works and you can use it as a working model to follow. At still other times, you have to buckle down and research the problem thoroughly. In this section of the chapter, you will learn about different methods and circumstances in which some methods work and others do not. This knowledge will allow you to try appropriate approaches for your environment.

Trial and Error

The trial-and-error approach to network problem solving is not very scientific and is often frowned upon by technical purists. Nevertheless, it does have its place in everyday practice and is a method that few network specialists can deny having used. There is a time and place for it, however, and this method should not be used exclusively as you can do more harm than good in some situations.

As the name suggests, the trial-and-error method of problem solving requires an assessment of the problem, an educated guess as to the solution, an implementation of the solution, and a test of the results. You repeat the process until the problem is solved. The following is a list of conditions under which this approach may be appropriate:

- The system is being newly configured, so no data can be lost.

- The system is not attached to a live network, so no other users are affected by changes made.

- You can easily undo changes.

- Other approaches would take considerably more time than a few quick trial-and-error attempts.

- There are few possible causes of the problem, which makes your educated guess at the solution a good bet.

- There is no documentation and no other resources to draw upon to arrive at a solution more scientifically.

It is not always wise to just try something and see if it works. Changes made to one system on a network can affect other nodes or make an existing problem worse. The following is a list of conditions under which the trial-and-error method is not advisable:

- A server or internetworking device is live on the network.

- The problem is being discussed over the phone and you are instructing an untrained user.

- You are unsure of the consequences of the solutions you propose.

2

- You have no sure way to undo the changes once made.

- Other approaches will take about the same amount of time as the trial-and-error approach.

Do you think that trial and error is the right approach for your problem? If so, you should follow some guidelines when you decide to take it as a route:

- Make only one change at a time before testing the results. That way, if the problem is solved, you will know which change is the solution. You can add this information to your network support manual for future use.

- Avoid making changes that might affect the operation of a live network. For example, if you suspect an incorrect TCP/IP address, do not change the address without first verifying that the new address is available to be used. Doing so could cause another device to stop working.

- Document the original settings of the hardware and software before making changes so that you can put the system back to its original settings.

- Avoid making a change that can destroy user data unless a known good backup exists.

- Avoid making a change that you cannot undo, if possible.

Figure 2-1 presents a flowchart that is designed to help you decide whether the trial-and-error approach makes sense for a given situation. Refer to this flowchart when deciding for yourself whether to use trial and error. Let us look at some scenarios and decide whether this approach is reasonable. This exercise will give you a feel for the application of this approach.

In our first theoretical scenario, you have been called to troubleshoot a new PC running Windows 98 on a client's network. The network is small, has only seven PCs, has no access to the Internet, and is set up in a workgroup environment. An unskilled employee in the company has already done some of the work, such as assigning a computer and workgroup name, but the new PC still cannot see the other PCs on the network. The protocol installed is IPX/SPX. You suspect that because the network is so small and because there is no in-house expertise, NetBEUI is the protocol being used by the rest of the computers. Unfortunately, this PC is all the way on the other end of the plant, so there is no way to check quickly. You decide to install the NetBEUI protocol and see if it works.

Looking at the flowchart, is this a reasonable situation in which to try a trial-and-error approach? Sure. Installing NetBEUI would not cause problems for the existing network, it can be uninstalled easily if necessary, and you can do the test more quickly than any other approach.

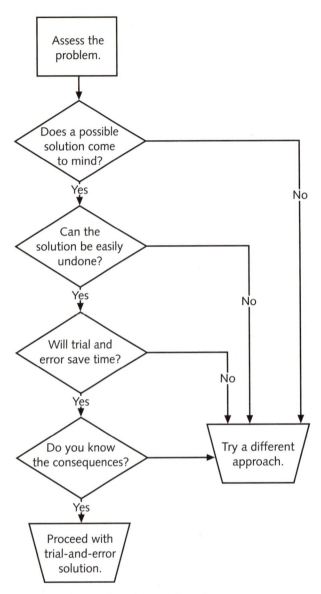

Figure 2-1   Trial-and-error flowchart

Now let's consider a second scenario. You are called to solve a problem on a network that uses a client/server approach to networking and has about 100 computers. You have done work at this firm before and you know its employees are accessing the Internet and use Novell NetWare 4.1. The problem is that a workstation running Windows 98 cannot access the Internet. You sit down at the workstation and open the Network Control Panel to check the settings. You find that TCP/IP is installed, so you check the address settings. TCP/IP is configured to use **Dynamic Host Configuration Protocol (DHCP)**.

Recall that DHCP is a method used to automatically configure TCP/IP settings on PCs and network devices. You happen to know that DHCP is not used on this network, so it must be the problem. You recall from an earlier visit that the network address is 206.17.44.0. You configure the computer with address 206.17.44.200 with a subnet mask of 255.255.255.0.

Should you use trial and error to solve this problem? Absolutely not. Although you may have happened upon the correct reason for the problem, simply choosing an address without knowing whether it is already in use can cause a conflict with another machine. The correct course of action is to consult the network documentation that lists all the IP addresses in use. This document should also have other settings such as DNS server addresses and the default gateway address. You must carefully consider the effect that changes you make have on the rest of the network. If you are unsure, play it safe and consult the documentation.

Consider a third scenario. You receive a call from a client who is having intermittent problems with a subnet. The client tells you that when workers try to access one of the firm's servers that is on a different subnet, sometimes it works and sometimes the connection times out. The network includes a total of four subnets, all connected through one router. None of the other subnets is having problems. You have seen something similar at other networks and resetting the router seemed to solve the problem. You tell the client to power down the router, wait 10 seconds, and power it back up.

Is this a reasonable way to go about solving this problem? By powering down the router, you will affect all four subnets. This action could cause loss of data, time, and possibly, even money. Additionally, you don't know if the router configuration has been saved, so powering down the router could cause even worse problems after the router reboots. Finally, you should never instruct a user to perform a procedure for which you have no way to ensure that the person is performing it correctly.

Sometimes it is quicker and easier to use trial and error to resolve problems. In fact, this option may be your only way of solving certain problems in a timely manner. However, you must be careful not to make matters worse if your proposed solution can affect other systems or cause data loss.

Resolve by Example

Resolving by example occurs when you use something that works, compare it to something that does not work, and then make the one that does not work look like the one that does. Resolving by example is one of the easiest and fastest ways to solve a problem because it requires no special knowledge or problem-solving skills on your part. When most organizations purchase computers, they purchase similar models and set them up the same way. You simply take advantage of this fact when confronted with a problem on a particular machine.

Some problems can be very difficult to troubleshoot, particularly when they have to do with an operating system configuration. In addition, hunting down the problem and fixing it may take a considerable amount of time. If you have a working example of a device that is nearly identical, however, you can copy the configuration—or pieces of the configuration—from a working machine. This effort may involve checking Control Panels for installed components, copying system files such as device drivers, copying configuration files, or even making a copy of an entire disk.

Let's look at an example. Bill is a networking consultant who is called into a client's office because two of the firm's twenty computers lock up periodically when accessing one of the company's network database programs. The database resides on a Novell NetWare 4.11 server. Bill checks the Network Control Panel on the two computers and everything seems to be in order. Bill sees the IPX/SPX protocol and the Microsoft Client for NetWare Networks loaded. The two computers can access the network, but when the database program is run, the machines invariably lock up within a half hour of use. Bill asks whether other computers run the same software and is told "yes." He takes a look at one of the computers that is not locking up. This computer also has the IPX/SPX protocol loaded, but the client is Novell NetWare Client32. Bill checks a few other computers and finds that they are all using Novell Client32. He decides to install this client on the two machines that are locking up. After several hours of testing, no lockups occur and Bill calls it a day.

What is your analysis of the situation? Bill certainly could have pulled out his network analyzer and captured network packets to try to determine what the problem was, or he could have played trial and error with different network settings to see whether he could resolve the lockups. However, with several working examples nearby, and one obvious difference between the working machines and the faulty ones, Bill did the smart thing by taking what works and applying it to what did not work.

 Sometimes it is necessary to use a protocol analyzer or network monitor to solve problems.

As with the trial-and-error method of troubleshooting, there are some caveats to using the resolve-by-example method. Here are some general rules to follow:

- Use resolve by example only when the working sample has a similar environment as the problem machine. For example, do not compare a machine having problems accessing Windows NT with one accessing NetWare.

- Do not make configuration changes that will cause conflicts. For example, do not change the TCP/IP address of your nonworking machine to the same address as your working machine.

- Do not make any changes that can destroy data that cannot be restored.

Let's look at another example. Terry is fairly new to networking, but has been tasked with the job of connecting some new computers to a stack of hubs. A similar stack of hubs already exists, and she is supposed to make these connections in a similar fashion. Armed with a boxful of patch cables, Terry starts plugging the computers into the hubs. When she gets to the last hub port, she realizes that she must save that port to connect to the second hub. She connects the two hubs together with a patch cable, but does not see a link light indicating that the connection is good. She tries another patch cable with the same result.

Not sure what to try next, Terry examines the similar stack of hubs and recognizes a switch next to one of the ports. It is a two-position switch in which one position is marked MDI and the other MDI-X. The switch is set to the MDI position. Because the hubs she is setting up are the same, Terry compares her hubs with the working hubs. The switch is set to MDI-X on her hubs, so she changes it to the MDI position in each instance. The link indicator comes on, and Terry finishes her job.

Your analysis? Because Terry had an example in a similar environment as her problem, she was able to make these changes with confidence. The hubs were not yet being used on the live network, so her changes would not cause any problems.

The Replacement Method

The replacement method of problem solving is a favorite among PC technicians. It requires the technician to narrow down the possible sources of the problem and to have known working replacement parts on hand so that they can be swapped out.

Sounds simple. In fact, it is simple—at least after the source of the problem has been identified. That is where the difficulty and the skill come in. The replacement method is effective only if the source of the problem can be determined and the source of the problem is a defective part. A lot of time and money can be wasted in replacing parts that are not really defective, so you will need to employ your troubleshooting skills before you show off your installation skills.

Follow these rules (in the order presented) when employing the replacement method:

1. Narrow the list of potentially defective parts down to one or two possibilities.

2. Make sure you have the exact part replacement on hand.

3. Replace only one part at a time.

4. If your first replacement does not fix the problem, reinstall the original part before replacing another part.

Step-by-Step Using the OSI Model

The step-by-step method of troubleshooting involves the use of the OSI model. In this approach, you test a problem starting at the Application layer and keep testing at each layer until you have a successful test or you reach the Physical layer. This method of problem solving is what most people think of as network support. It is where you need to understand how networks really work and where you must be able to use troubleshooting tools.

Networks are complex, multilayered systems. When confronted by a problem for which there is no obvious fix, it is helpful to remember the layered approach that developers have taken to make network systems work. If you reconceptualize the problem to the seven layers of the OSI model, you then can take a step-by-step approach to resolving the problem. This idea is best illustrated with an example. Let's begin by examining a simple network diagram, as depicted by Figure 2-2.

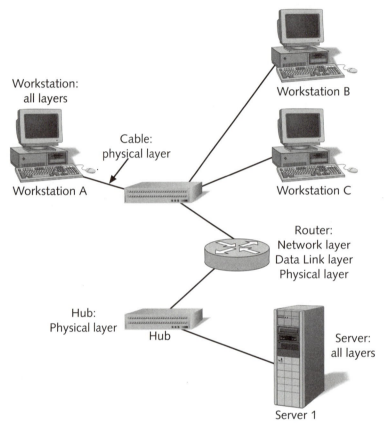

Figure 2-2   A simple network diagram

Suppose Workstation A is trying to communicate with Server 1. The user on Workstation A complains that an error occurs when she tries to access files on the server. Users at Workstations B and C are not having similar problems. No more information is available. When you arrive on the scene, you see that Workstation A is running Windows 98. The first thing you do is open Network Neighborhood to view network resources. As expected, no resources are available. Opening Network Neighborhood and checking for available network resources involves the upper layers of the OSI model. Now that you have determined that these functions are not working properly, you can start looking at the lower layers. Your goal is to find the lowest layer at which there is functionality.

2

You check the network documentation and see that TCP/IP is the protocol being used. You then verify that TCP/IP is installed correctly on this computer, so you know that you have functionality in layers 3 and 4. Time to keep moving down the OSI model. Consider the tools available to you with TCP/IP for troubleshooting. One of the most common tools is Ping. Referring to the network documentation, you try to ping Server 1. No success. Look at the diagram again. If you can communicate with the router but not the server, you can narrow your search. Try pinging the router. Again, no success.

Which layers remain to be tested? The Data Link layer and the Physical layer remain. Problems with the Data Link layer most often involve the NIC drivers or a misconfigured server. Data Link layer problems most often affect the entire network or the problem lies with a single computer's NIC drivers. Unless you have reason to believe there may be a problem with the drivers, it is best to leave them for later. Most network technicians would move on to the Physical layer because this layer is where problems restricted to one station are most likely to occur. After a brief investigation, you find that the patch cable from the jack to the workstation has gone bad, and you replace the cable. Problem solved.

Many network technicians would approach a problem by starting with the Physical layer and then working their way up. The approach you take will depend on your experience and information you may have learned from interviewing the user. What is important is that you understand all that is required for the network connection to work, which allows you to test and check all components involved using the tools available to you.

THE PROBLEM-SOLVING PROCESS

One of the most difficult aspects of network problem solving is deciding where to begin. What is described next is a general framework for approaching problems that you can apply in almost any situation. The specific actions you take will depend on the situation. The process described here can be applied to a variety of problems, both in your networking environment and in everyday life.

Let's start by listing the steps involved:

1. Determine the problem definition and scope.
2. Gather information.
3. Consider possible causes.
4. Devise a solution.
5. Implement the solution.
6. Test the solution.
7. Document the solution.
8. Devise preventive measures.

Several of the steps in this process will require multiple iterations. For example, if Step 6 does not lead to a resolution of the problem, you will probably need to go back through Steps 2 through 6 until you do have a positive resolution. Each step may require several substeps before you can move on to the next step. (We discuss the substeps in the following sections.) For example, Step 4 may require setting up a test environment to duplicate the problem and test possible solutions before implementing a solution on a live network. A flowchart of the basic process is presented in Figure 2-3.

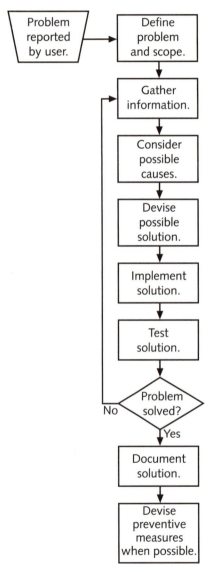

Figure 2-3   The problem-solving process

Step 1: Determine the Problem Definition and Scope

Before a problem can be solved, it must be defined. "Mary's computer doesn't work" does not define the problem well enough to create a plan of action. "Mary cannot run WordPerfect because an illegal operation occurs every time she tries to run it" is much better. A problem definition should also describe what does work in addition to what does not work. If Mary cannot run WordPerfect, it should also be stated whether she can run her e-mail program or other applications.

You need to know who and what are affected by the problem. You will take a vastly different approach if an entire floor is affected by a network problem instead of a single-user. Is the problem related to a single application—for example, e-mail—or are all functions affected? If you are working with routers, is only one router exhibiting problems or are several routers having difficulties?

Determining the scope of a problem is important not only for deciding where to start your troubleshooting process, but also for deciding what priority to assign to the problem. The malfunction of an entire network switch or server demands a higher priority than does an individual-user problem. Determining the scope quickly and accurately, therefore, is not only the first step but also an extremely important step of the troubleshooting process.

Most network problems come to the attention of the network administrator by way of a user phonecall or e-mail. This communication is your first opportunity to learn more about the problem. Although this part of the troubleshooting process is more art than technical skill, there are some questions you can ask to start you on your way:

- Is anyone else near you having the same problem?
- What about other areas of the building?
- Is the problem occurring with all applications or just one?
- If you move to a different computer, does the problem occur there as well?

 You might need to talk to more than one user to get the complete picture.

The goal of your questions is to determine a problem definition and scope. If a solution comes about as a result of this interview, all the better, but that is not the goal in this step of the process. Nor is it a goal to determine the cause of the problem. Rather, the goal of this step is to define the problem in detail and accurately determine the scope of the problem.

Examples of a problem definition and scope include the following:

- Jim cannot access the e-mail server. Other servers are available to Jim, and no one else reports the problem.

- Third-floor users cannot log into the network, but all other floors can.

- Sherry cannot print to the new LaserJet on the fourth floor. She has tried several applications. No other users have tried to print to this printer.

- Bill reports that the network is slow while accessing his home directory. Access to the Internet and other resources seem to work correctly.

After you define the problem and understand its scope, a priority can be assigned to the problem. Assigning priorities takes a little experience and a little political savvy. It is wise to have a clear understanding of what areas the organization deems most critical to its business functions. After this hierarchy is understood, a document should be created to show management in which order problems will be solved when there is a backlog.

Most IT departments are understaffed, so backlogs usually are the norm. Besides prioritizing according to business functions, there is typically some prioritizing according to who reports the problem or whom it affects. If the president of the company can't check e-mail, it is a double-edged sword if you place that problem as a number one priority. On the one hand, if you solve the problem right away, you curry favor with the boss. On the other hand, if you solve the problem right away, you must not have much else to do—so why are you always complaining that you are understaffed? In any event, after you have prioritized the problem, it can be assigned to the appropriate support person who is best equipped to solve the problem.

After the problem is ready to be tackled, you can move to the next step. It is time to dig in and get information that will help you resolve the problem.

Step 2: Gather Information

This step of the process is where your user interview skills can really shine. Most of the initial information you get about a problem will come from one or more users. Knowing what questions to ask and how to ask them can be the difference between a quick fix and an all-nighter.

Did It Ever Work?

Strangely enough, this question is often overlooked. There is a big difference between something that worked once and then stopped working, and something that never worked at all. Users often will not volunteer this information, so it pays to ask. If something once worked and now does not, you can assume something has broken the process. If it never worked at all, there's a good chance it was not set up correctly in the first place. In the former situation, you go into troubleshooting mode and continue with the interview. In the latter situation, you go into installation mode and look at it as just another thing to put on the to-do list.

To illustrate this principle, consider the following scenario. Karen receives a call from user Jim. Jim tells Karen that he cannot print to the printer down the hall. After determining that Jim is the only one having the problem as far as he knows, Karen goes into the information-gathering step. She asks Jim if he could ever print to that printer, and he replies that he could not. Karen can go into installation mode at this point. This problem has just become a simple printer installation that is not really a problem at all. Had Karen never asked that question, she might have gone into troubleshooting mode, continuing to ask questions, checking printer queues, determining printer permissions, and investing time in a host of other wasteful activities.

When Did It Stop Working?

Assuming that the problem being reported was a function that was once working and that has now stopped or changed in some way, you need to find out when the change in behavior occurred. The purpose of this question is not only to get a sense of the problem's time and date of occurrence, but also to determine what else may be going on at that time to cause the problem. For example, is another application running when the problem occurs, or does the air conditioner kick on about the time the problem occurs? This line of questioning can also give you a sense of urgency. If the user has lived with the problem for two weeks and is just now reporting it, and you have bigger and hotter fires to put out, you may be able to put this one on the back burner. The ability to listen to customers and understand their sense of urgency or frustration is a skill that a good support technician must acquire.

You also might want to ask the following:

- Does the problem occur all the time or only intermittently?
- Are there particular times of the day when the problem occurs?
- Are other applications running when the problem occurs?

Has Anything Changed?

You have to be careful with this question when you are talking to a user about a workstation problem. If a user thinks you are implying that he or she may have caused the problem, the user is likely to clam up. His or her answer is an essential piece of information. New applications on workstations, new hardware devices, and updates to existing applications or drivers all can cause problems. While you are asking the user this question, you need to consider it for yourself as well. Were any changes made to the network that could cause the problem? Were any upgrades made to the servers or were new router configurations implemented?

Never Ignore the Obvious

It's easy sometimes to get caught up in a problem, pull out the network analyzer, and start some serious troubleshooting. One of the most common problems, which thankfully has one of the easiest solutions, is the unplugged cable. Don't assume that your users will have checked this possibility. My experience suggests that a good 10 percent of network problems involve an unplugged cable. Maybe the culprit was the cleaning crew, or maybe one of your technicians did it while installing a new sound card or working on a server or router. Students in my class often complain about an inability to get to a server or router console, only to find that the device wasn't turned on.

Sometimes, you can discover the obvious when you realize that each person has his or her unique perception of a problem. For instance, descriptions such as "slow network response" are very subjective; what may be normal to one person might seem like a problem to another. Suppose an employee has been on the night shift for the last year and has recently taken a shift during the day. This employee reports that server response is very slow, but you have had no complaints from other users. It is quite possible that because the night shift works half-staffed, this employee has enjoyed the benefits of a server with a lighter load during the night, which leads to quick response times. His idea of slow response may simply be a normal response time for the day shift.

Defining How It Is Supposed to Work

It is difficult to gather solid facts about a problem if you do not have a good definition of how things are supposed to work. This point is where having good documentation of your network and a proper baseline of the network pays off. A **baseline** is a document describing the normal operation of your network. A baseline is measured after your network is configured and running smoothly. It is then repeated periodically. Periodic baselines are compared with previous baselines to determine whether trends can be seen that indicate problems ahead. For example, if average network utilization increases two or three percent per month for several months, you can prepare for a performance upgrade that will no doubt be required before too long.

A baseline of your network should include network utilization statistics, utilization statistics on server CPUs, memory, hard drives, other resources, and normal traffic patterns. This information can be compared with statistics that you gather during the troubleshooting process. It can help you determine whether reports of slow response time are valid and point you in the direction of the source of the problem if they indeed are valid. It also can help you know when it is time to upgrade the network infrastructure or servers.

 Tools available for monitoring and gathering information about your network will be discussed later in this chapter.

Step 3: Consider Possible Causes

When you have sufficient information, you can start considering causes of the problem. In this step, you consider, based on the symptoms and other information that you have gathered, what could possibly be wrong. Experience is invaluable here, as the more problems you have seen, the more likely you are to recognize the signs of a particular problem based on the symptoms. As you proceed through this step, you will probably gather additional information along the way.

2

Your goal in this step is to create a checklist of possible things that could have gone wrong to cause the problem. To get yourself warmed up to the topic, consider a situation in which an entire area of a building has lost connection with the network, but no other areas are affected. Without knowing anything else, you could construct the following list of possible causes of the problem:

- The connection in the main wiring closet to the rest of the network has failed.

- The hub or switch to which all of the workstations are connected has lost power or has completely failed in some way.

- All the workstations have acquired a virus through the network, and the virus affects their network connection.

- A major upgrade has recently been performed to all the workstations in that area and an incorrect network protocol was installed.

You could create quite a list if you put your mind to it. Of course, during the previous step in the problem-solving process, you would probably have eliminated all but a few of the possible causes. If you find yourself with a list of possible causes that goes on and on, you likely need to go back to Step 2 and gather more information.

Once you have created a list of possible causes of the problem, you can investigate and rule out or confirm each possible cause. Referring to the previous example, you would probably check the wiring closet to see the status of the devices there, or if you had a network management program, you could verify the health of the wiring closet devices remotely.

Step 4: Devise a Solution

The solution to a problem, once a likely cause has been determined, may be devised easily and quickly. In the example discussed in Step 3, assuming the cause of the problem is a failed hub, it's easy to devise the solution: Replace the hub. Suppose, however, that the reported problem is periodic loss of connection to certain resources reported by a large number of users. After you have gathered information and considered possible causes, you find that periodically several of your routers become overutilized and start dropping packets. This problem is not so simple. You do not want to rush in and replace the problem routers with bigger, stronger, faster routers, because that solution may affect other routers or other network components. Is the problem with the routers, or are the dropped packets simply another symptom of the problem? You really don't know.

Before devising a solution, it is important to consider the following:

- Is the identified cause of the problem truly the cause, or is it just another symptom of the true cause of the problem?

- Is there a way to adequately test the proposed solution?

- What results should the proposed solution produce?

- What are the ramifications of the proposed solution for the rest of the network?

- Do you need additional help to answer some of these questions?

The last bulleted item is a sore point for many network professionals. However, it is impossible to be an expert in everything, and some network problems can be too complex or the equipment necessary to adequately answer the questions too expensive for many IT departments. A broken network that results in lost productivity, and therefore lost money, can be many times more expensive than occasionally calling in experts.

Now you've got the solution in hand; time to tear into it, right? Wrong. I once implemented a major network backbone upgrade that commenced at 10 P.M. and was finally finished at 4 A.M. Planning the upgrade was a lot of work, but what took almost as much time was planning the upgrade such that if it did not work and could not be accomplished before the next morning, I could swiftly return the network to its original slow, but working condition. Such a rollback plan should be an integral part of every proposed solution. No matter which experts you call, and no matter how thoroughly you have researched the problem and planned your proposed solution, a live, working network has a funny way of throwing you curve balls.

Before you implement the solution, you must be prepared for the possibility that it will actually make things worse than the existing problem. Whether your problem and proposed solution affect an entire network or just several users, you need to know how to put things back the way they were before you implemented the solution. Things you may need to do, depending on the scope of the problem and solution, include the following:

- Save all network device configuration files.

- Document and back up workstation configurations.

- Document wiring closet configurations, including device locations and patch cable connections.

- Conduct a final baseline to compare new and old results as well as results to use as a basis for comparison in the event a rollback becomes necessary.

Step 5: Implement the Solution

If you have done a good job with the first four steps, the implementation phase of the problem-solving process should go relatively smoothly. During this step, you will create opportunities for intermediate testing and you will inform your users of your intentions. Then, you will put the plan into action.

Create Intermediate Testing Opportunities

You need to design the implementation so that you can stop and test it at critical points, rather than test the completed solution only to find that something does not work. It is far simpler to test small individual steps in which a limited number of things could go wrong than it is to test a completed complex solution in which there could be dozens or hundreds of problem areas.

Suppose you are dealing with a problem for which the solution is to add a new network segment to your internetwork to alleviate broadcast problems. You have purchased a new router and a switch to accommodate the workstations that will form the new segment. One way to go about this solution would be to hook up all the equipment, configure the router and switch, assign new addresses to the workstations, plug in all the cables, and then hope for the best. Of course, when that methodology doesn't work, where do you start looking? Is the problem the router configuration or the switches? Is your addressing scheme incorrect? You really don't know.

A better way to tackle this implementation is to have a step-by-step plan that allows for intermediate testing. For example, consider the following steps that you could use to test the new router and switch. Notice that it alternates between implementing and testing.

1. Configure the router.
2. Verify its stand-alone operation by pinging each interface.
3. Attach the router to the rest of the network.
4. Verify that all parts of the network are reachable by pinging.
5. Use the Trace utility to verify the path selection.
6. Install and configure the switch.
7. Configure workstation addresses for the new network.
8. Cable workstations to the new switch.
9. Verify connectivity within the network.
10. Connect the router to the switch.
11. Verify the ability to ping the router interface from the workstations.
12. Verify the ability to reach other networks from the workstations.
13. Create a baseline of the new network segment.

A carefully planned implementation of your solution with testing along the way allows you to catch unforeseen results at a stage in which they are easy to see and easy to fix. Once your implementation is planned in detail, you are almost ready to take action.

Inform Your Users

In situations in which your action plan necessarily affects other parts of the network and therefore other users, you need to inform your users of the possible disruption to some network services while work is progressing. Give your users plenty of time to schedule downtime of the network. Nothing can take the wind out of your sails more quickly than getting a frantic call from a boss who needs the network for a big presentation just as you are halfway through a day-long network upgrade.

One of the unfortunate duties of the network administrator is to perform major network and server upgrades and changes in the late evening hours and weekends so that as few users as possible are affected. Be prepared for this new lifestyle.

Put the Plan into Action

Once you have your checklist of actions and intermediate testing ready and you have informed your users, it is time to take action. Provided you have done everything correctly up to now, this step is the easy part. You have your list of actions; now is the time to implement them.

 Remember, it is extremely important to make only one testable change at a time.

Take notes about every change you make to the network or servers. For example, the upgrade of a driver or the change to an IP address should be documented. This way, you will know the current state of your network when your changes are complete. A well-documented network will be easier to troubleshoot and upgrade in the future.

Step 6: Test the Solution

It's 3 A.M. and you are finished with the upgrade. Time to go home, right? Wrong. It is time to test your implementation as a whole. If the issue is a simple workstation connectivity problem, you simply verify that the station can access the resources assigned to it. If it is a major network or server overhaul, the testing will be much more involved. In either case, if you have done intermediate testing during the implementation phase, this step should be relatively straightforward.

Your testing should attempt to emulate a real-world situation as closely as possible. If you are testing a workstation problem, verification that the workstation can ping a server is not sufficient. If possible, you should attempt to log into the network as a user with similar privileges as the main user of that workstation. Next, attempt to access applications that would likely be run from the workstation. Take notes about what you learned and saw.

If you are testing a major network upgrade, you probably will have already tested end-to-end connectivity during implementation. Now you need to put some stress on the network. Fire up some workstations that are on the upgraded part of the network, if possible, with the help of some assistants. Run some of the organization's network-intensive applications. Access the Internet if Internet access is included in your network. All the while, you should be gathering information about how the network behaves while you are working it. Compare your results to the results you saw before the changes were put in place. Again, take notes about the results of your testing. When you have tested everything possible, go home and get some sleep; tomorrow will be the real test, as your users pound away at your solution.

2

Step 7: Document the Solution

If you have made it this far, congratulations, you have solved a problem! It is time to take all your handwritten notes made during the implementation and testing steps and turn them into a cohesive document. This step is as important as any of the previous steps. If you successfully solved a problem, no matter how big or small, it is likely that a similar problem will arise in the future. If you took notes about the problem and the solution, you will have this documentation available as a valuable resource for solving the next problem of its kind.

Your documentation should include everything pertinent to the problem, such as the problem definition, the solution, the implementation, the testing, and the brand of coffee beans that provided much-needed inspiration as dawn approached. If necessary, you should be able to reproduce both the problem and the solution from your documentation.

Step 8: Devise Preventive Measures

Once you have solved a problem and documented it, it is desirable to do everything you can to prevent the reoccurrence of the same or a similar problem. For example, if your problem was the result of a virus that spread throughout your network and that caused considerable damage before it was found, you can implement virus protection programs on your network and tighten policies regarding software and e-mail downloads. The preventive measure is obvious and reasonably simple to implement.

Suppose, however, that your problem is one of a degenerative nature, in which your network gradually becomes slower and less responsive. Preventing this problem is not as simple as installing some software and sending a policy memo. There are some things that you can do, however. For instance, you can devise certain rules for the operation of your network. For example, you can specify that no more than 50 workstations be installed on a network segment; alternately, you can stipulate that your Windows NT servers can have no more than 200 simultaneous logins before adding a new server or CPU to the server. These types of rules will help prevent performance problems in the future. In addition, if those who hold the purse strings approve of such rules, you have instant justification for an upgrade when the time comes.

Devising preventive measures is proactive network management rather than reactive network management. If you let the problem come to you, it will always be far more serious than it would have been if you had nipped it in the bud before your network became a serious productivity liability. It is far too easy to pat yourself on the back and rest on your laurels after solving a difficult problem. The difficult part is sometimes coming up with methods to prevent the problems in the first place.

PROBLEM-SOLVING TOOLS

In this section, we discuss various tools available to you to troubleshoot, monitor, and document your network. Each tool has its place; experience will tell you what is appropriate for a given situation.

Experience

Your most effective weapon in the process of supporting your network and diagnosing and resolving problems is your own experience. Unfortunately, too many people do not get as much out of it as they could. Whether you have been limited to working on computers in the classroom and at home or have been lucky enough to be involved in a large **multiplatform network**, there are plenty of opportunities to expand your experience and enhance the value of your experience.

Make the Most of Your Experience

Few of us have photographic memories. We see something, we say we are going to remember it for future use, and we promptly forget what we saw. Sometimes, we remember some of it but many details are forgotten. In the world of computer networks, that is easy to do because so much is changing all the time.

Take notes about what you see and learn. This advice applies even if you have been in the computing world for years, but it is particularly pertinent when you are first starting out and your experiences are limited. Keep a journal of your experiences. Even if you never read it again, the act of writing the information down will help preserve it in your memory for future use. Let's say you are upgrading a system with a CD-writer. After several jumper changes, cable swaps, and driver installations, you finally get it to work. If you write down the type of system, the type of CD-writer, what worked, and what did not work, you will have a reference for the next time you have to perform a similar upgrade.

 An electronic journal is great because you can file your entries alphabetically and search for them when needed. Of course, a printout is also nice for those times when your network crashes and all electronic documentation is unavailable.

If It Happened Once, It Will Happen Again

One mistake technicians make is thinking that the particular problem they are seeing is so obscure that it is not worth the time and effort to make a note of it. This idea is a faulty assumption. Hardware and software are standardized today, and millions of people use the same or similar components in their computers and networks. Thus, if you are seeing a problem now, you will likely see it again. Make a note of it, and the next time the problem occurs to you or one of your colleagues, you can be the hero by already having the solution in hand.

Colleagues

One of the most overlooked resources for resolving problems is your colleagues and class-mates. Use the people you know as a resource. They will appreciate your coming to them for possible answers and, in turn, they will come to you in the future. Some people build up a network of colleagues and put them on an e-mail distribution list. Then, when faced with a difficult question or problem, they can easily send an e-mail to several or even dozens of knowledgeable people. There is a good chance one of them has faced a similar problem in the past and can steer the problem-solving process in the right direction.

Manufacturer's Phone Technical Support

Sometimes there is nothing left to do but call for help. Every time you install a new piece of hardware or a new application, one of the first things you should do (besides reading the installation manual) is enter the manufacturer's technical support number in your database of important phone numbers.

Information You Should Have Before Calling Support

The best time to call technical support is when you have a specific error number or message that you can report to the manufacturer. Be prepared to have a lot of other information at the ready as well. The more prepared you are, the more responsive the support engineer is likely to be. Information you are likely to need includes the version number of the soft-ware or the serial number of the hardware, the operating system and version, if it is an application problem, and the firmware revision number, if it is a router or switch problem.

You need to be as detailed as possible in giving the circumstances of the problem or error so that the manufacturer can reproduce it if necessary. Gather all the pertinent information before you call technical support; if you don't have the necessary information, you'll have to call back a second time.

Make Sure You Have Ruled Out the Obvious

Use some of the troubleshooting methods discussed earlier to rule out obvious problems, such as a defective part. If you have another part handy, use the replacement method so that you can tell the support engineer that you have already tried swapping parts. You also can try the suspect part or application on a different system so that you can report that information to the engineer. Again, the more prepared you are, the better the results you will get from technical support. In addition, if you have tried all the obvious troubleshooting techniques and can report this fact to the support engineer, you are likely to have your problem transferred to a more knowledgeable engineer or to have tech support send a replacement part.

The World Wide Web

If you can describe the problem with a few words or an error message or error number, this information is the first place to look for an answer. Most manufacturers have put considerable time and effort into building databases of problems and solutions so that their customers can research the problem themselves without ever calling the technical support line.

The World Wide Web (WWW) is one of the greatest gifts given to computer and networking professionals. What used to take days or weeks to accomplish via phone calls and driver updates on floppy disks sent by mail now can be accomplished in minutes. New network card won't install on the new version of Windows you just installed? Get on the Web and download the latest driver. Every time you try to send an e-mail you get error number 3744? Get on the Web and go to the manufacturer's Web site; enter the error number into a search and you may get a response explaining how to solve the problem.

Most manufacturers store their technical support problems and solutions in a database called a **knowledgebase** or a **Frequently Asked Questions (FAQ)** document. A knowledgebase is a searchable database that contains descriptions of problems and errors, along with known solutions, if any. It can also contain installation notes and compatibility information. An FAQ is more like a text document that contains two parts to each entry. The first part is a question that the manufacturer has either anticipated or actually received from customers; the second part is an answer to that question. An FAQ is more helpful for general installation and configuration help, although it may contain information about error messages, solutions, and compatibility issues.

Using a Knowledgebase

There is a skill to using a knowledgebase well. The old adage of "garbage in, garbage out" applies perfectly to the use of a knowledgebase. You have to provide the database search program with the right words, phrases, or error numbers to find the information you want. Even then, it can take several attempts to find what you are looking for, and you may have to sift through several entries before you come upon the information that will help in your particular case.

Figure 2-4 is a search dialog box found on Novell's Web site. It has four sections. The first section allows you to narrow your search by specifying a particular product. The second section allows you to specify the types of documents you wish to search. It is a nice feature, as you can choose only the technical documents and skip searching user manuals if you desire.

The third step allows you to specify the keywords to include in the search. The fourth step allows you to execute the search, refine the search, or clear the form for another search. The third step is where a little patience and experience pay off. When you are researching a problem, you typically want to be as specific as possible. If you have error numbers or messages, enter them. With error messages, you will get the best results if you enclose the message in quotes. For example, if the error message says "Too many open files," you can enter that exact phrase enclosed by quotation marks to get the best and fewest search results. Enter as many keywords or phrases as possible to limit the number of results returned, as you will often receive hundreds or thousands of results if the keywords you enter are too general. If your first search returns no results, cut back on the specificity of the search and try again. After a while, you will get a feel for the type and amount of information to enter.

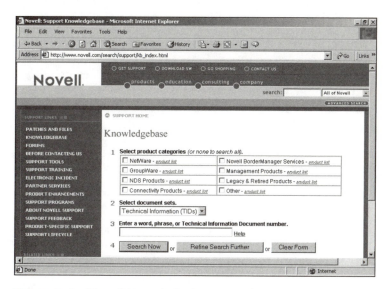

Figure 2-4   Novell Knowledgebase search screen

Many manufacturers' Web sites have different rules and syntax for specifying the search criteria, so read the help screen provided by most sites to guide your search.

Finding Drivers and Updates

One of the first things you need to do when installing a new piece of hardware, a new operating system, or a new networking device is to check whether bug fixes, driver updates, or new firmware revisions are available. Before you contact a manufacturer's technical support personnel by phone, make sure you have the latest versions or the engineer will likely tell you to call back if the problem persists after you have installed the new version.

Refer again to Figure 2-4, and you will see a link on Novell's Web site for *PATCHES AND FILES*. Most manufacturers will have a section of their Web sites devoted to the latest fixes and drivers that you can download. A word of caution—read the installation guide or readme.txt file before installing operating system updates, because there may be special preinstallation items of which you must be aware before you start the update. The WWW and phone technical support can frequently lead you to the solution to a problem you are having, but sometimes the solution can be found only within information that is specific to your network.

Network Documentation

It is one of the most disliked jobs that any network administrator has, but when it comes to knowing what is happening with a network and what needs to be done to fix a problem, there is no better resource than good network documentation. Good documentation of your network can be the difference between a five-minute fix and hours, or even days, of troubleshooting.

Everything that is important to the installation, maintenance, and troubleshooting of the network should be documented. Your documentation should read like a user's manual for network administrators. You know it is complete when you feel as though you could leave your network in the hands of a stranger for a month and when you come back, everything will still be working fine. In a strong documentation packet, you should find information in two categories:

- Network topology
- Internetworking devices

This classification is a general guideline—your network may have many more categories and subcategories. We will now discuss each category in turn so that you will know what should be included in it. If you find that the documentation you are referencing is weak in any area, you should set aside time to bring it back up to standard.

Network Topology

A picture is worth a thousand words, and that statement is certainly true for a network. Your documentation should include a network diagram showing the logical topology of your network and a physical diagram of your network showing the physical aspects of your network such as buildings and floors. Complete documentation will show a level of detail down to the floor plan and location of jacks. Figure 2-5 shows a logical topology, and Figure 2-6 shows a physical topology at the lowest level of detail.

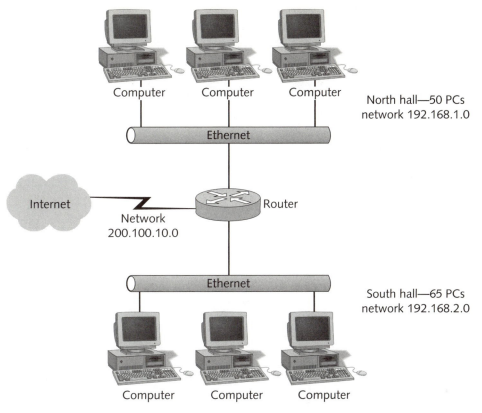

Figure 2-5   Logical topology

Internetworking Devices

Your internetworking devices will require different levels of documentation depending on the type of equipment. Simple hubs require the least information, whereas routers normally require the most amount of documentation. Besides depicting the internetworking devices in your network diagrams, you should have a listing of them in tabular form. An example of a listing of hubs is shown in Table 2-1.

A similar table should be created for all types of devices so that they can be easily located and identified when necessary. This information also helps you with your expansion plans, as you will have available the number of free ports in which to add new workstations and other devices.

Experience, colleagues, the Web, phone support, and documentation are all fine resources for network support and troubleshooting. Sometimes, however, the only place you can get the information you need is from your very own network.

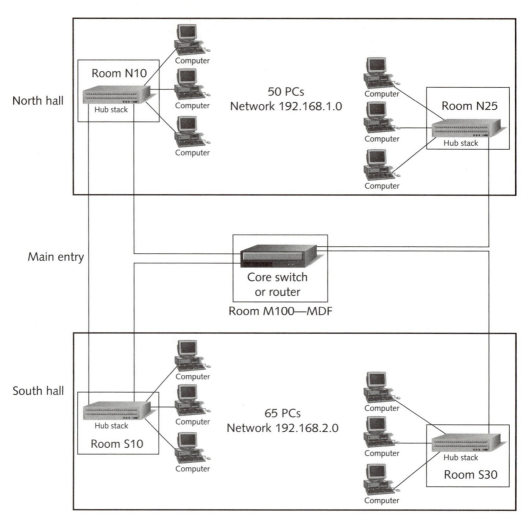

Figure 2-6   Physical topology

Table 2-1   Network equipment list

Hub Model/Serial #	Location	IP Address	MAC Address	# Ports/# Free
Cisco 424M 324234657	Room N10	192.168.1.240	00000cab3546	24/0
Cisco 424 324234658	Room N10	N/A	00000cab3305	24/0
Cisco 412 32434659	Room N10	N/A	00000cab3254	12/10

Network Testing and Monitoring Tools

The tools available to you to test, monitor, troubleshoot, and document your network range in complexity and price from simple and free to rocket-science and enormously expensive. This section will discuss primarily the low-end to medium-end products, in terms of both price and complexity.

Workstation Network Configuration

The tools necessary to determine how a Windows workstation or server is configured for the network are built into the Windows operating system. To determine which networking components are installed on a workstation and to view the properties of those components, use the Network Control Panel, as pictured in Figure 2-7.

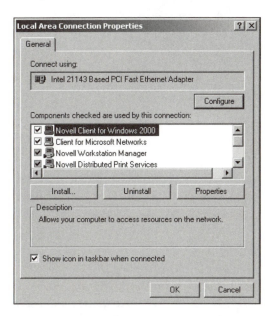

Figure 2-7   Windows 2000 network properties

To get information about TCP/IP address settings and the MAC address on a workstation, use the Ipconfig utility or Winipcfg utility. Ipconfig is a command-line utility used in Windows 98, Windows NT, and Windows 2000. Winipcfg provides the same information but through a graphical user interface rather than a command-line interface. Winipcfg is not available in Windows NT or Windows 2000 but is available in Windows 95 through Windows ME.

Figure 2-8 shows the output from Ipconfig. Both Ipconfig and Winipcfg provide you with all the IP configuration documentation that you need, including the IP address and subnet mask as well as the default gateway and DNS servers. If the workstation were set up to use DHCP, the DHCP server that provided the IP information would also be listed. One other key piece of information that the utility provides is the MAC address for the NIC. Here's a nice tip: If you are well versed in login scripts, you can create a script that runs the Ipconfig utility and redirects its output to a file located on a server. This script will give you the IP configuration and MAC address for every workstation in your system.

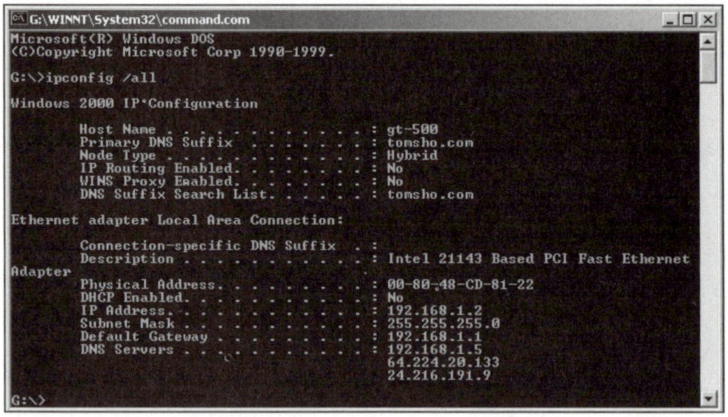

Figure 2-8   Ipconfig utility in Windows 2000

End-to-End Network Connectivity

For workstation connectivity issues, there are some useful tools built into most operating systems and network devices that support the TCP/IP protocol. The **Ping utility** can help determine whether a workstation has end-to-end connectivity with a particular destination. It also helps determine the amount of time it takes the destination to respond. Figure 2-9 provides some sample ping output.

The output of the ping command provides useful information about how long it took for the destination to respond. A long response time might indicate a heavily loaded server or network congestion between the source and the destination device. By default, the Ping utility in Windows sends four packets. If not all packets were received, that fact will be noted in the output through the percentage loss value.

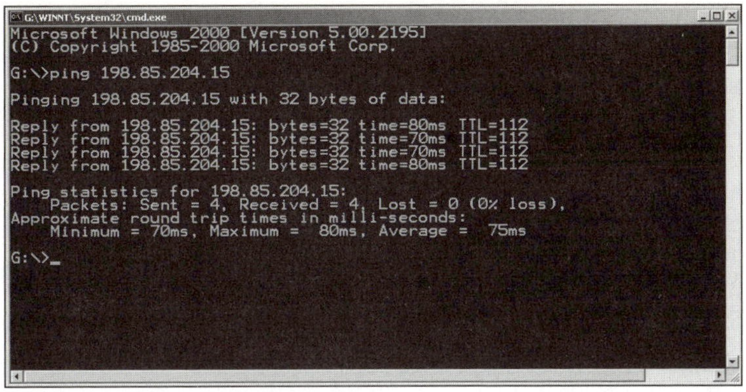

2

Figure 2-9 Ping output

Ping can be used to determine whether an IP address is currently in use on the network so that you can avoid conflicts before making an address assignment. Ping the address in question; if you receive a response, that address is currently in use on the network. If a device or workstation is powered down, however, it will not respond to the ping. In this situation, it is best to consult the network documentation, which should have a list of all IP addresses that have been assigned, before making a new assignment.

The **Trace Route utility** (the tracert command in Windows systems) can help determine the path that data takes to a destination. It is useful for determining how far in the internetwork the data travels to its destination, what delays occur at each router, and whether the data is taking the optimal path. Figure 2-10 provides some sample tracert output.

Figure 2-10 Tracert output

The Trace Route utility, like the Ping utility, provides response time information. If a particular router is slow in responding, you will see that by examining the number of milliseconds it took the router to respond. The Trace Route utility also attempts to resolve the name of the router that responds. This information can be useful in determining the geographical location or name of the company that manages the router.

 The Ping and Trace Route utilities are built into most routers and switches to aid with configuration testing and troubleshooting.

Software Network Monitoring Tools

Network monitoring tools are used get a picture of how your network is performing. You can monitor such variables as percent utilization, errors, protocol types, number of broadcasts, and origins and destinations of the majority of your network traffic.

Windows NT Server and Windows 2000 Server both come with a limited network monitoring tool that allows you to monitor network packets and utilization. These network monitors can monitor only network traffic coming to and from the server on which the monitor software is being run. While this information may be useful for determining the amount of data being directed at the server, these monitoring tools cannot give you a good picture of the overall network traffic.

For the "good picture," use Network Monitor. Figure 2-11 shows Network Monitor on Windows 2000 Server. Network Monitor is chock full of information. The upper-left corner shows network utilization and frames per second to give you an idea of current network usage. The bottom part of the screen shows which stations are sending and receiving frames and what type of frames are being sent. Microsoft makes a more advanced version of this program, which allows monitoring traffic from any source to any destination. The advanced version is available in the Microsoft Systems Management Server product.

2

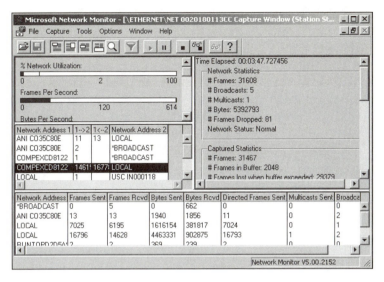

Figure 2-11 Windows 2000 Network Monitor

A program that has both network monitoring and protocol analysis features is EtherPeek from WildPackets. The network monitoring features of EtherPeek concentrate on showing graphical or tabular representations of the amount and type of data being transmitted on the network as well as the source and destination addresses of the stations sending and receiving the most traffic. Figure 2-12 gives you a peek at EtherPeek.

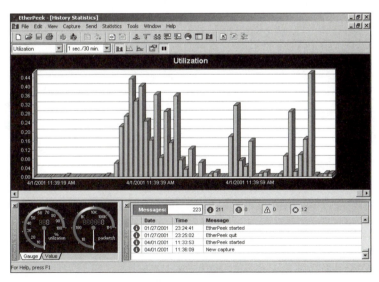

Figure 2-12 EtherPeek from WildPackets

Both EtherPeek and Microsoft's Network Monitor provide network monitoring by listening to all traffic on the cabling segment, or **collision domain**, on which the software is installed. This method of monitoring the network, while simple and effective for shared media LANs, is of limited use in larger networks that use switches and routers. In a shared media network, such as an Ethernet network using hubs for connectivity, all stations on the LAN hear all data transmissions but normally process only those packets that have a matching destination address. Network monitoring software can configure the NIC on the workstation to run in **promiscuous mode**, which allows the NIC to read and process all data packets on the segment regardless of the destination address.

Another software-based network monitoring program is Network Inspector from Fluke Networks. This program can discover devices in your network, provide trending data on your network traffic, and create a variety of reports. Reports include information such as device IP address and MAC address configurations, error reports, and available server services. Figure 2-13 shows Fluke's Network Inspector.

A popular program that has some of the same features as Network Inspector but includes additional features such as built-in automatic network mapping and event notification when a device or service becomes unavailable is What's Up Gold from IPSwitch.

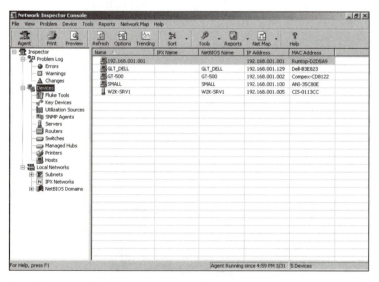

Figure 2-13   Fluke's Network Inspector

Both Network Inspector and What's Up Gold rely on an industry standard network management protocol called the **Simple Network Management Protocol (SNMP)** to communicate with devices and gather network statistics. SNMP works by distributing software **agents** on devices throughout the network. These agents are small programs that gather statistics about the network device or network segment on which they are installed. The agents then forward the data to the station that has the network monitoring software installed. This station usually is called the network management console. Because of the distributed nature of these network monitoring programs, they can gather statistics across collision domains, making them very useful in a switched networking environment.

Many manufacturers of internetworking equipment produce their own network monitoring and management software. For example, Cisco Systems produces CiscoWorks and Nortel Networks produces Optivity. Both products use SNMP and can monitor and manage enterprise-scale LANs and WANs.

Hardware Network Monitoring Tools

The advantage of a hardware network monitoring tool is that you can take it wherever you need it and plug it into the network you need to monitor. These tools are usually compact, hand-held devices that run on rechargeable batteries. They range in cost from $1000 to $10,000 or more.

Fluke Networks manufactures a line of these products ranging from the compact low-end Network Assistant to the high-end Optiview. Other manufacturers of hardware network monitoring products include Sniffer Technologies with its Sniffer line of products and DigitTech with its PC-based and hand-held lines of network monitoring and protocol analyzer products.

Software tools are your primary source for testing and monitoring problems related to the Data Link and higher layers of the OSI model, and hardware tools are your primary source for testing Physical-layer aspects of your network. Note, however, that there are no clear-cut boundaries here. You can find out plenty of information about the Physical layer with software tools, and the high-end hardware tools can be unequaled in tracking down problems related to layers 2 through 7 of the OSI model.

Protocol Analyzers

Network monitoring tools are designed to provide you with statistical information about your network, which is very helpful in documenting and baselining your network and finding trouble spots. If you want to dig deeper and examine the actual data packets being transmitted, however, you need a protocol analyzer.

A **protocol analyzer** captures data packets and then **decodes** the packets. The decoding process breaks the packet down into the network protocol headers and data and then displays this information so that a user can easily view the individual fields of each data packet. This effort can help you debug difficult-to-find problems in your network. Figure 2-14 shows an EtherPeek packet capture of a ping operation, and Figure 2-15 shows a packet decode of the ping packet.

The main part of the screen in Figure 2-14 shows summary information of the packet's capture: the source and destination addresses, the protocol, and the size of the packet. The bottom part of the screen provides a dashboard-style view of network utilization. Figure 2-15 provides a detailed look at a single packet. Each protocol header is clearly defined, and the fields within the headers are decoded.

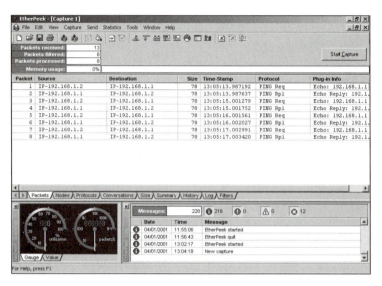

Figure 2-14   Ping packets captured by EtherPeek

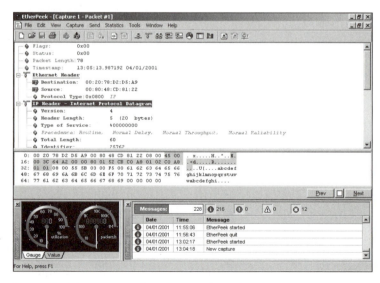

Figure 2-15   Ping packet decoded in EtherPeek

No matter how capable your workstation configuration and network monitoring tools are, these tools are useful only after you have a working Physical layer. It is at this layer that cable testers become your friend.

Cable Testers

Cable testers are perhaps your most valuable piece of network troubleshooting equipment. Cable testers are hardware products that are available with a wide range of capabilities. The simplest tester involves a simple box with LEDs into which you plug both ends of your patch cable to test basic connectivity. The more advanced testers come with two units so that you can test long runs of cabling without having access to both ends of the cable in the same place; they allow you to test a wide range of characteristics of the cable. No cable installer should be without this type of tester.

 You can purchase cable testers for all cabling types including coax, twisted-pair, and fiber optic, and you should have cable testing equipment available for each type of cabling that your network employs.

CHAPTER SUMMARY

❑ The support of a network requires the network technician to be skilled in a variety of areas. The ability to solve problems and knowing the tools available to help solve those problems are as important as technical knowledge.

❑ Approaches to network problem solving include trial and error, resolve by example, replacement, and step-by-step using the OSI model. All these approaches are part of the larger problem-solving process, which takes you from problem definition to solution documentation and preventive measures.

❑ The problem-solving process includes eight steps: determine the problem definition and scope, gather information, consider possible causes, devise a solution, implement the solution, test the solution, document the solution, and devise preventive measures.

❑ Many resources are available to help an administrator with the job of network support. They include the technician's own experience, colleagues, manufacturer's technical support, the World Wide Web, network documentation, and software-and hardware-based monitoring and troubleshooting tools.

❑ Most companies maintain knowledgebases on their Web sites containing technical support information and a driver library to assist in upgrades and system patches. Hardware and software troubleshooting tools can help determine and document workstation and server configurations, paint a picture of network traffic patterns, and show error rates and network configuration problems.

KEY TERMS

agent — A program that runs on a computer or networking device and that gathers information on behalf of a program running on a console or management station.

baseline — A periodic measurement of a variety of network statistics intended to provide an administrator with a reference for judging current network performance.

collision domain — The area in which an Ethernet collision is propagated; it is bounded by a switch or router interface.

decode — A process used by protocol analyzers that allows the display of network packets in a user-friendly format.

Dynamic Host Configuration Protocol (DHCP) — A TCP/IP standard that allows a workstation to request from a DHCP server its TCP/IP configuration settings rather than having a network administrator configure the settings manually.

Frequently Asked Questions (FAQ) — A document that contains common questions and the responses to those questions regarding the support or installation of a manufacturer's product.

knowledgebase — A database maintained by an organization that contains technical support information.

multiplatform network — A network environment that includes more than one operating system, computer type, or network architecture.

Ping utility — A utility that helps determine whether a workstation has end-to-end connectivity with a particular destination and that identifies the amount of time it took the destination to respond.

promiscuous mode — A mode of operation supported by many NICs that allows a network monitor program or protocol analyzer to view and process all network traffic on the cable segment.

protocol analyzer — A program or device that captures data packets and displays each packet in a user-friendly format for analysis by the user.

Simple Network Management Protocol (SNMP) — A TCP/IP standard that allows agents on network devices to collect network statistics and send the information to a network management station.

Trace Route utility — A TCP/IP utility found in most operating systems that shows the path that a packet takes from source to destination. The Trace Route utility uses the same technology as the Ping utility. In Windows systems, the program name is TRACERT.EXE.

REVIEW QUESTIONS

2

1. Which of the following is an approach to problem solving? (Choose all that apply.)

   a. trial and error

   b. guess and hope

   c. resolve by example

   d. step-by-step using ISA

2. If you suspect a network configuration error on a workstation and an identical workstation nearby is working correctly, what approach to solving the problem might you attempt first?

   a. Use a network analyzer to capture and examine packets.

   b. Use the trial-and-error approach to resolve the problem.

   c. Use the Ping utility.

   d. Use the resolve-by-example approach.

3. Which of the following is not a step in the problem-solving process?

   a. Describe the OSI model.

   b. Test the solution.

   c. Gather information.

   d. Define the problem.

4. Which of the following is not a goal of the "determine the problem definition and scope" step in the problem-solving process?

   a. Find out what is not working.

   b. Find out what is working.

   c. Find out how to solve the problem.

   d. Find out who is affected.

5. Which of the following is a good statement of a problem and scope?

   a. Jim is getting an error on his computer.

   b. Terry cannot access Server 2 but can access all other servers; no other users report problems accessing Server 2.

   c. Bill can't print to the LaserJet in Room 215, so it must be offline.

   d. Network access is slow for the third floor, so we need to upgrade the router memory.

6. Which situation best describes when you should use the resolve-by-example approach to problem solving?

   a. You have a good hypothesis of what the problem is and your solution is easy to undo.

   b. The problem will require several days of analysis and testing.

   c. You have a working model with a similar environment as the problem.

   d. Only a few users will be affected by the proposed solution.

7. When can you use the step-by-step layered approach to problem solving?

   a. when you can reduce the problem into layers that relate to the OSI model

   b. when you must do extensive research before defining a problem

   c. when you are using trial and error

   d. when you are gathering information from the user

8. Why is "defining the problem and scope" an important step in the problem-solving process?

   a. to see if the user caused the problem

   b. to help prioritize the problem

   c. to determine the solution to the problem

   d. to see if a network upgrade is needed

9. The main purpose in finding the number of users affected by a problem is to _____.

   a. determine whether the problem involves a user error or a network error

   b. determine the scope of the problem

   c. see which wiring closet to investigate

   d. determine how many technicians to assign

10. A solid understanding of the OSI model is necessary in which approach to problem solving?

    a. resolve by example

    b. step-by-step

    c. trial and error

    d. replacement method

11. Periodic measurements of network performance are also known as _____.

    a. network monitoring

    b. protocol analysis

    c. baselining

    d. streamlining

12. To see the path that a packet takes from its source to a destination, as well as network bottlenecks along the way, use the _____ utility.

    a. Ping

    b. Ipconfig

    c. Trace Route

    d. Display Route

13. A method used to display network packets in a user-friendly format is called _____.

    a. encoding

    b. decoding

    c. analyzing

    d. tracert

14. Some network monitors, such as EtherPeek, can monitor traffic only when it is on the same _____.

    a. hub

    b. router

    c. collision domain

    d. switch

15. A TCP/IP protocol used to gather network information and send the information to a management console is _____.

    a. SMTP

    b. UDP

    c. ICMP

    d. SNMP

16. The most important OSI layer for building a solid network foundation is layer _____.

    a. 1

    b. 2

    c. 3

    d. 4

17. Cable testers are used to test the _____ layer of the OSI model.

    a. Application

    b. Session

    c. Network

    d. Physical

18. A patch cable tester is the most complex of cable testing devices. True or False?

19. Cable testers are usually software programs you can install on your PC. True or False?

20. If you want to view the TCP/IP configuration for a Windows NT computer, you should use _____.

   a. the Control Panel

   b. Winipcfg

   c. Ipconfig

   d. Ping

HANDS-ON PROJECTS

Project 2-1 Using the Ping Utility

This exercise demonstrates the use of the Ping utility and its available options.

1. Click **Start** on your desktop, click **Run**, type **command**, and then press **Enter**.

2. At the DOS prompt, type **Ping –?**. You will see a help screen listing the various options available with the ping command.

3. To ping a workstation in your classroom, type **Ping** *address*, where *address* is the TCP/IP address of one of your classmates' workstations. List three pieces of information that the output of the ping command provides.

4. To see the name of the computer you are pinging, use the –a option by typing **Ping –a** *address*, where *address* is the TCP/IP address of one of your classmates' workstations. How did the output of the ping command differ from that obtained in Step 3?

5. The Ping command normally sends four messages. To increase this number, use the –n option by typing **Ping –n** *10 address*, where *10* is the number of messages to send to the address and where *address* is the TCP/IP address of one of your classmates' workstations.

6. The ping command sends 32 bytes of data in each message. Use the –l option to send 150 bytes of data by typing **Ping –l** *150 address*, where *address* is the TCP/IP address of one of your classmates' workstations.

7. Try to ping an address that is not known to your network. With what response does the ping reply?

8. Close the DOS window by typing **Exit**.

Project 2-2 Using the Trace Route Utility

This exercise demonstrates the use of the Trace Route utility and its available options.

1. Click **Start** on your desktop, click **Run**, type **command**, and then press **Enter**.

2. At the DOS command prompt, type **Tracert –?**. You will see a help screen listing the various options available with the tracert command.

3. If you have a connection to the Internet, type the following command: **tracert course.com**. With what does the tracert command respond? If you do not have a connection to the Internet, your instructor will provide an address that you can use. How can this command help you in the support and troubleshooting of a network?

4. This time, type the **–d** option as part of the tracert command. How does the output differ?

5. Close the DOS window by typing **Exit**.

Project 2-3 Using the Winipcfg Utility

This exercise demonstrates the use of the winipcfg command. Windows 95, Windows 98, and Windows ME can use the winipcfg command, but Windows NT, Windows 2000, and Windows XP cannot.

1. Click **Start** on your desktop, click **Run**, type **winipcfg**, and then press **Enter**.

2. Click the **More Info** button to see advanced configuration information.

3. Close the Winipcfg program.

Project 2-4 Using the Ipconfig Utility

This exercise demonstrates the use of the ipconfig command. The information that this utility provides is similar to that which is provided by the winipcfg command, but winipcfg cannot be used on Windows NT and Windows 2000 stations. You can use the ipconfig command with the Windows 98 through Windows XP operating systems.

1. Click **Start** on your desktop, click **Run**, type **command**, and then press **Enter**.

2. At the DOS prompt, type **ipconfig**.

3. Make a note of the information displayed.

4. Type **ipconfig /all**. What additional information did the /all option display?

Project 2-5 Using Network Monitor

This exercise demonstrates the capabilities of the Network Monitor program, which is built into Windows NT and Windows 2000 Server. If students do not have access to their own copies of Windows NT or Windows 2000 Server, the instructor can perform this exercise for the class.

1. Click **Start**, point to **Programs**, point to **Administrative Tools**, and then click **Network Monitor**.

2. Click the **Start Capture** button. What type of information is displayed? What are the limitations of this network monitor program?

Project 2-6 Simulate a Help Desk Call to Determine Problem Definition and Scope

This project should be done in front of the class, with the class and the instructor critiquing the performance of each student. Student should be critiqued on their ability to find out the required information and their projection of sensitivity and politeness to the caller.

1. You are working at a help desk and a customer calls with a problem. (The instructor will play the part of the caller.)

2. Using what you have learned about problem definition and scope, ask the caller appropriate questions to determine this information.

3. After you have finished determining the problem and the scope of the problem, write a clear description of both.

4. Write down what your next course of action should be to correct the caller's problem.

CASE PROJECTS

Case 2-1 The Nonworking Computer

George is confronted with a computer that will not connect to the network. He inspects the Network Control Panel; everything there seems to be in order. This computer was working yesterday, but today, when Network Neighborhood was opened, the message "Unable to browse network" appeared. This machine is the third computer of this type in the past year that has demonstrated the same symptoms. The two computers that previously experienced this problem required new NIC cards. Without further testing, George replaces the NIC card to see whether it resolves the problem.

Using the flowchart in Figure 2-1, write the answer to each question presented there and determine whether trial and error was a reasonable approach to this problem. If the solution that George proposes does not solve the problem, what should his next steps be?

Case 2-2 The Case of the Missing Drive

You are setting up a new server running Windows NT 4.0. Two hard drives are installed. After the installation is complete, you find that only one drive is found in the Disk Administrator. You power down the server, remove the case, and push on the ribbon cables going to all of the drives. You power up the server to see whether both drives are discovered.

What method of problem solving was used in this example? Was this method a reasonable choice in this situation? Explain your answer.

Case 2-3 The Problem Workstation

Diane is called in to solve a problem in which a workstation cannot access network resources. The network uses Novell NetWare and the client/server model. Upon arrival, Diane reboots the computer and recognizes that the NetWare login does not appear and that the computer goes directly to the Windows login screen.

Diane checks the Network Control Panel, and all the settings appear to be correct. The network also has access to the Internet, so Diane uses the ping command to try to communicate with one of the company's Web servers. She gets timeout errors from her ping attempts. Diane then checks the indicators on the hub into which the workstation is plugged. The link LED is not illuminated. Her next step is to test the cable from jack to patch panel; she finds that everything is acceptable. Finally, Diane tests the patch cable and sees that pin 1 on the cable is not making a connection. She replaces the patch cable, retests the ping command successfully, reboots the computer, and is able to log into the NetWare server.

What method of network troubleshooting did Diane employ? Describe the tests that she performed and relate those tests to the OSI model.

Case 2-4 Exploring Resources

Microsoft and Novell both have excellent support Web sites. Use your Web browser to go to these Web sites and research the options available for doing a search in each company's knowledgebase. Use the help screens that are available to see advanced search options and tips. Write a one-page how-to guide for conducting searches for each Web site. Compare and contrast the search knowledgebase features of each Web site. The location for Novell's knowledgebase is *www.novell.com/search/support/kb_index.html*, and the location for Microsoft's knowledgebase is *http://search.support.microsoft.com*.

Case 2-5 Creating Diagrams

Create diagrams of your classroom network. Make a logical diagram of the network that shows the logical topology as well as a physical diagram of the network that includes the approximate locations and numbers of devices and cable runs.

Case 2-6 Creating Documentation

Document the workstations and servers in your classroom network in tabular form. Design the form, including information such as model number, serial number, NIC card type, MAC address, logical address, location, patch-panel port connection, and hub/switch port connection. What other information may be important?

Case 2-7 Researching Tools

Given the list of testing and analysis tools and programs below, research their capabilities by using information presented in this book or the manufacturer's Web site. Describe what the tool does and at what layers of the OSI model it performs.

❐ Ping command

❐ Tracert command

❐ Fluke's Network Inspector

❐ Wildpacket's EtherPeek

❐ Fluke's 620 LAN CableMeter

❐ Microtest's PentaScanner

❐ Winipcfg command

3

SUPPORTING THE PHYSICAL LAYER

After reading this chapter and completing the exercises, you will be able to:

♦ Identify and describe the network components that work at the Physical layer of the OSI model

♦ Describe characteristics, installation requirements, termination, and common problems with coaxial, twisted-pair, and fiber-optic network media

♦ Describe and understand problems and characteristics associated with Physical layer devices

♦ Understand the devices and the options available to you when selecting or supporting Physical layer devices such as NICs, transceivers, media converters, and hubs and repeaters

♦ Recognize the rules imposed on media and Physical layer connectivity equipment, such as the 5-4-3 10 Mbps Ethernet rule and Class I and II 100 Mbps repeater rules

---

The proper selection of components, and the configuration and installation of a network's Physical layer, provide a solid foundation on which a reliable network can be built. All other layers of the OSI model depend upon the proper functioning of this layer, so proper planning and careful attention to the selection and installation of the Physical layer components will go a long way toward preventing troubleshooting headaches later.

In this chapter we will discuss many of the Physical layer components in a network, the characteristics of those components, and the installation and maintenance of Physical layer media and devices. We will also discuss several troubleshooting techniques you can use when problems arise.

PHYSICAL LAYER COMPONENTS

Physical layer components are usually easy to identify because they are the parts of the network that you can see and touch, as compared to the components of other layers of the OSI model, which comprise intangible software or firmware. Although it is true that the Physical layer includes signals—electric, optical, or radio frequency—that represent the bits that make up network data, the only involvement that a network technician has with these signals is providing reliable pathways in the form of tangible media installation.

The physical components of a network include the following:

- Network media
  - Cabling
  - Connectors, jacks, and patch panels
- Devices
  - Network interface cards
  - Repeaters
  - Transceivers
  - Media converters

Other network devices, such as routers and switches, have Physical layer components in the form of interface connectors and have the ability to receive bit signals, but their primary work is defined at the higher layers of the OSI model. For this reason, they are not discussed in this chapter. We will, however, discuss these devices in detail in later chapters.

NETWORK MEDIA

There is a variety of network media from which to choose when building your network. A thorough understanding of the features, characteristics, installation considerations, testing requirements, and troubleshooting methods is critical in making the best choices for your network. The media types we discuss are those based on copper wire and those based on fiber optics.

Criteria for Choosing Network Media

When choosing or supporting a media type, it is important to understand the characteristics of that particular media type. We will discuss media characteristics in a variety of categories for each media type, and you will want to keep these properties in mind so that you can use them as criteria for choosing the Physical layer components of your network. Understanding your media will also aid in troubleshooting or upgrading your network.

- Ease of installation. The relative difficulty of installation has a bearing on your choice of media. Sometimes you have to make a tradeoff between the highest quality of media available and the costs and time factors involved in the proper installation of that media. Some of the factors that must be considered are a medium's **minimum bend radius**, which limits the angle at which a cable may be bent to run around corners; the cost and time factors involved in the **termination** of the media, which involves installing connectors and attaching media to patch panels and jacks; and the physical environment (cinderblock walls, concrete floors, and high ceilings can make installation of cabling cost-prohibitive, for example).

- Testing. How difficult and expensive is it to test your media? There is no point in attempting to install a media type for which you do not have proper test equipment. Test equipment cost ranges from a few dollars for simple patch-cable wire-map testers to thousands of dollars for full-blown Category 5 and fiber-optic testers.

- Maximum length. Every media type has limitations on the maximum length for a run of cable. This constraint relates to the weakening of the signals, referred to as **attenuation**, as the signals travel the length of the cable. If the cable length is too long, the signals will be too weak to be read properly by the receiving device at the end of the cable. Cable segments can be extended by the use of repeaters, which amplify the signal, thereby counteracting the effects of attenuation.

- Maximum stations. There is a limit to the number of stations that can be installed on a cable segment for each media type. This limitation must be factored into your LAN design and remembered when you are supporting an existing LAN. For some media types, the limitation is rather restrictive and may influence your design decisions. Other media types have a fairly liberal restriction, in which case this limitation may not be a factor.

- Bandwidth capability. When choosing a media type or deciding whether to upgrade a media type, you must consider the **bandwidth** rating of the media. The bandwidth rating, measured in bits per second, determines how fast your data can be sent over the media. You must consider not only the network's current needs, but also the future needs—you do not want to have to recable your network every couple years.

- Maximum cable segments. The number of cable segments that can be tied together through repeaters to form a single logical cable segment is limited for all media types due in part to the delays that occur as the signal travels from segment to segment. In addition to media type, the number of cable segments is affected by transmission speed.

- Resistance to interference. How well a media type resists signal interference from outside sources is dependent on the construction of the media and the type of signals that the media is designed to carry. Interference to electrical signals on copper media comes in the form of **Electromagnetic Interference (EMI)** and **radio frequency interference (RFI)**. EMI is caused by electrical equipment such as electrical cables, motors, fluorescent lighting, and other sources of strong **electromagnetic fields** that are in the vicinity of your copper wiring. RFI is caused by strong broadcast signals emanating from radio and television equipment. Wireless media can be influenced by environmental conditions such as RFI and by physical obstructions such as walls and buildings. Fiber-optic media is the one media type that is essentially impervious to outside interference. Careful consideration of your environment is necessary for selecting a media type that will not be greatly affected by interference.

Let's take a look now at the various media types and see how these characteristics play a part in the support and troubleshooting of the Physical layer of your network.

Copper Media

Copper has been the standard in networking media since networking began. Over the years, there have been tremendous advances in the capabilities of copper cabling, so it is still the primary media type used in most networks. However, not every copper cable is created equal, and your understanding of the various forms of copper media is important in making correct media decisions.

Coaxial Cable

Coaxial cable is fast becoming extinct on the network wiring plan. Coax, as it is referred to in short, was the predominant media type used in Local Area Networks (LANs) in the 1980s through the early 1990s. Because of some of its limitations, it has been largely replaced by twisted-pair and fiber-optic cable as the LAN media of choice in new installations. However, a significant number of existing LANs continue to use coax. While you may not be using it in new installations, you may have occasion to support an older network that uses coax.

Two primary types of coaxial cable are used in Ethernet LANs: **thinwire Ethernet** and **thickwire Ethernet**. Thinwire Ethernet (also referred to as **Thinnet**), whose official Institute for Electronic and Electrical Engineering (IEEE) designation is 10Base2, uses coaxial cable much like the coaxial cable used to carry cable TV signals. Thickwire Ethernet is, as its name implies, a thicker, heavier cable whose official IEEE designation is 10Base5. Because 10Base5 cabling is rarely seen in networks today, little discussion here is directed toward this media type.

Both cabling types have characteristics in common with all coaxial cabling types. Both are constructed as four layers of material. There is an outer plastic cover, usually made from polyvinyl chloride (PVC), followed by a metal braid that provides shielding. The inner two layers consist of a PVC or Teflon coating, which surrounds the conducting core, usually made of copper.

Characteristics of Thinwire Ethernet

In the following sections, we discuss the characteristics of Thinnet. After reading about these and the subsequent characteristics of Thicknet, it will become apparent why thinwire Ethernet became the popular choice for network cabling in the earlier days of networking.

Ease of Installation

Thinwire Ethernet, or 10Base2, is relatively flexible, and fairly easy to install. Its minimum bend radius to bend around a 90° corner is typically about 1.25 inches, although different manufacturers may have different specifications depending on the material used.

The connectors used are common and easy to find, as are the tools required to install the connectors. The connectors required for Thinnet installation consist of a BNC cable connector, a BNC T-connector, and a BNC terminator. A BNC cable connector is fitted to each end of the cable. A BNC T-connector is used to form an intersection at the NIC for two lengths of cable, and a BNC terminator is placed at both ends of a series of cable segments. This arrangement forms the bus topology that coaxial cable is typically used to create. Figure 3-1 shows the BNC connectors.

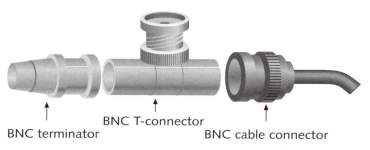

BNC T-connector

BNC terminator   BNC cable connector

Figure 3-1   BNC connectors

In a small LAN, confined to one room or a couple of rooms, Thinnet is exceedingly easy to install. You simply **daisy-chain** lengths of cable from one device to the next, with terminators placed at both ends of the LAN. A daisy-chain is formed when two or more devices are connected with what amounts to a continuous line of cable without connecting to a central device. Adding a device is just a matter of purchasing a new length of cable, attaching BNC connectors, and plugging them into the existing network. Unfortunately, this simplicity comes with a price. Adding a station to a live LAN disrupts communications on the LAN, because you will lose the necessary termination on both ends of the network during the time it takes to install the new cable.

Because coaxial cable has only one conductor, little can go wrong with the installation of connectors. Provided you have the necessary crimp tools and follow the instructions, it is a fairly error-free procedure. Because you daisy-chain the cables from one station to another, the amount of cable required is reduced compared to media that require central hubs. This fact often allows you to purchase cables of varying lengths with connectors already installed, further simplifying the process.

Testing

Testing individual thinwire Ethernet, or Thinnet, cables is simple and relatively inexpensive. Because Thinnet uses only one wire to transfer data, there is no worrying about crossed or split pairs as there is with twisted-pair cabling. Because Thinnet transfers data at a maximum 10 Mbps, the equipment needed to test at that speed is less expensive than for higher-bandwidth media. The only real concern with testing thinwire Ethernet is determining that the connectors are properly installed (no opens or shorts) and that high levels of interference do not affect the signals. One additional testing consideration with networks of this type is testing the total length of the cable segment—that is, from terminator to terminator. With other media types, you can test the length when you test each piece of cable, because each cable length attaches to a hub. Due to the daisy-chain nature of Thinnet, all lengths of cables that are chained together must be added together to find a total segment length.

Maximum Length

The maximum length of an unrepeated segment of thinwire, 10Base2 cable is 185 meters. Whether you have 5 computers in your network or 30, the total cable length from terminator to terminator can be no longer than 185 meters. Fortunately, this length can be extended with the use of repeaters. Each repeater in the network gives you another 185 meters to extend the cabling segment. Note, however, that there is a limitation on the number of repeaters that can be present as well.

You should be aware of the generous length characteristic of Thinnet. This one characteristic makes this media type a reasonable solution to connect remote stations whose distance from the main LAN exceeds the distance requirements of the media being used. As an example, consider twisted-pair media, whose maximum length is 100 meters. Suppose the network you are managing is a manufacturing company whose LAN consists of 15 computers in a small office area. You are currently using twisted-pair media. The organization needs to add a remote workstation to an area on the manufacturing floor, a distance that is 150 meters away. Using Thinnet, you can connect the remote workstation to the company LAN. See Figure 3-2. The main part of the network depicted in Figure 3-2 uses twisted-pair cabling, which limits cabling distances to 100 meters. As the hub also has a connection for Thinnet, a remote station can be added when the distances exceed 100 meters.

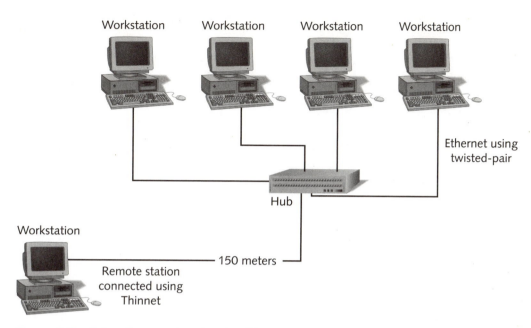

Figure 3-2   Extending a network using Thinnet

Maximum Stations

The maximum number of stations allowed in an unrepeated Thinnet cable segment is 30. This restriction is fairly rigid and may cause a growing company to upgrade to a newer media type on this basis alone. The maximum number of stations in a network that includes repeaters is 90, including the repeaters.

Bandwidth Capacity

The maximum bandwidth rating for Thinnet is 10 Mbps. This limitation is one of the factors that has made this media nearly obsolete. The media in common use today support transfer rates of 100 Mbps or more, which is a good thing given that today's LANs are pushing the bandwidth requirements ever higher. Nevertheless, 10 Mbps is quite satisfactory for a moderate-use network in which the network is used for basic file and print sharing. You might find a moderate-use network in a small office or a classroom setting in which servers are not used heavily for file sharing.

Resistance to Interference

Resistance to interference is one area in which Thinnet, as well as other coaxial cable types, shines. Due to the layer of insulating material surrounded by the metal braid, coaxial cables have a high resistance to interference from outside signals. The metal braid is the key, because it acts as a shield or reflector of Electromagnetic Interference and radio frequency interference. This characteristic does not mean that you do not have to be concerned about interference sources when using coaxial cable, but your concern should be less than with other copper cable types.

In summary, thinwire Ethernet is an aging medium that is easy to install and whose strengths are cable segment length and resistance to interference. On the downside, this coaxial media type has fallen behind in bandwidth rating and is slowly becoming obsolete in modern network infrastructures.

Installation Considerations

The following is a list of considerations you should keep in mind when installing and supporting a thinwire Ethernet network:

- Maintain a maximum cable segment length of 185 meters.
- Allow no more than 30 stations per cable segment or 90 stations overall when using repeaters.
- Use the correct cable type for LANs: RG58/U or RG58 A/U.
- Make sure that both ends of the cable segment are terminated with a 50-ohm BNC terminator.
- Have the minimum bend radius.
- Test for shorts or open connections.
- Use at most one grounding point in the cable segment.
- Make sure that all stations are connected directly to the main trunk of the cable segment.

Termination Considerations

The proper termination of a thinwire Ethernet cable is essential for proper LAN operation. Due to the bus configuration, a single loose BNC connector can disrupt your entire LAN operation. Recall that thinwire Ethernet requires a termination resistor at each end of the bus to prevent **signal reflection**. Signal reflection, or signal bounce, occurs when an electrical signal travels down the length of a wire and, when it gets to the end, bounces or reflects back up the wire. This reflection causes the signals to be scrambled.

A terminating resistor absorbs the energy of the signal when it reaches the end of the wire, thus preventing a reflection. If there is a loose connector somewhere in the middle of the bus, you have what amounts to two disconnected buses with a terminator on only one end of each bus. This problem causes complete failure of the network. Figure 3-3 depicts a small thinwire network in which one of the connectors on the second computer from the left is bad. This fault causes not only that one computer to lose communication, but also the entire network to be unusable. The Xs in the figure indicate that all computers are offline due to this problem, because you now have two physical networks with a terminator at only one end of each.

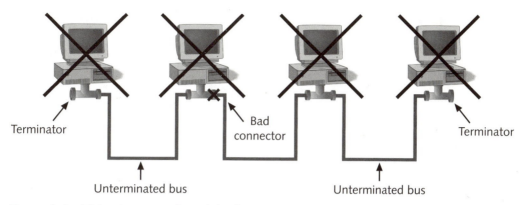

Figure 3-3   Thinwire network with bad connector

Another consideration for 10Base2 installation is grounding. Although the installation of a 50-ohm resistor at each end of the cable segment is not optional, grounding one of the terminators is optional. Some terminators come with a screw-wire or chain to attach to the grounded PC chassis to accomplish grounding. Although grounding is not imperative, it provides a level of electrical safety, preventing an electrical short circuit from causing a shock hazard through the coaxial cable.

If you do ground the coaxial cable at one end (the ground can actually be anywhere on the bus, but using one end of the bus makes it easy to find and recognize), you must make certain there is no other ground in the cabling. A second ground will disrupt the data signals. Inadvertent grounding can occur, for example, if a BNC T-connector comes into contact with the shielding of another cable or if any part of a connector or shielding comes into contact with a PC chassis. To prevent this problem, be sure that no stray wires stick out from the protective metal braid and that all cables are securely tied down to prevent shifting or twisting.

Thinwire Ethernet Common Support Issues

The most common problems with a thinwire network are related to the proper termination of the cabling and adherence to the standards for 10Base2 networks. If a 10Base2 network does not work because of the bus structure, the problem often involves multiple stations or, more likely, the entire cable segment. Isolation of the problem can be difficult and time-consuming. Here are some of the common problems to consider when troubleshooting either no connectivity or slow transmission rates.

User Has Disconnected a Cable

Users can foul up your network in a variety of ways and, unfortunately, many of the things they can easily do will disrupt the entire LAN. When users want to install a memory upgrade in their machine, what is one of the first things they do? They unplug everything from the PC before removing the PC cover. After all, this procedure is what they have been taught. This action is fine, as long as they remove the entire T-connector from the NIC rather than unplug the cables from the T-connector. If a user unplugs the cables from the T-connector, you now have two physical cable segments, neither of which has termination on both ends of the cable. The result is complete failure of the entire cable segment. Figure 3-4 shows the improper way to disconnect a PC from the network, and Figure 3-5 shows the proper method.

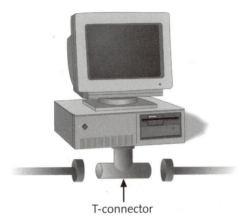

T-connector

Figure 3-4   Improper way to disconnect a PC from a 10Base2 network

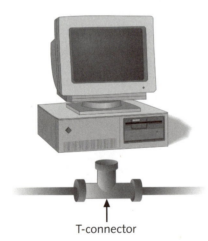

T-connector

Figure 3-5   Proper way to disconnect a PC from a 10Base2 network

3

Cable Does Not Meet Minimum Bend Radius

You may have taken painstaking care to ensure that the cabling you installed met all applicable standards, but time has a funny way of undoing your careful work. Users move their workstations, work needs to be done in the ceiling, furniture is moved, and a variety of other everyday activities occur that can turn what was once a standards-compliant installation into a puzzling problem.

If a coaxial cable is bent too sharply around a 90° angle, it can fracture or break the solid copper wire, causing attenuation problems or complete loss of connectivity. Therefore, a length of cable that has been doubled over due to something falling on it or a cable that has been stretched around a corner because furniture or workstations have been moved can cause serious problems in the network. The proper way to install a coax cable to make a 90° angle is shown in Figure 3-6.

Figure 3-6   Proper 90° bend of coax cable

Wrong Terminators Are Used

Different cable types require different terminators. Unfortunately, most coaxial terminators look more or less the same. The standard for RG58 cable used in thinwire Ethernet is a 50-ohm terminating resistor. Some terminators will simply have a color-coded band around the connector indicating the resistance value; others will be clearly marked with a resistance value. The 50-ohm terminators typically have a green band if they are not otherwise marked. The important thing is to match the correct terminator with the coaxial cable type. Otherwise, data transmission will be compromised, resulting in data errors or complete lack of transmission.

A Stub Cable Segment Is Added to the Network

A stub cable segment is one in which a T-connector is used to join two pieces of cable to extend the bus and a third connector on the T is used to add a workstation that is somewhat out of the way, as shown in Figure 3-7. This configuration should be avoided.

Figure 3-7   Improper addition of a remote workstation results in a stub segment

This type of configuration gives the electrical signals multiple paths by which to travel. It causes reflections and corrupted data. Instead of creating a stub, you should make sure that all stations are connected directly to the trunk of the network, as shown in Figure 3-8.

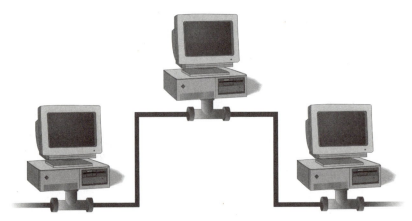

Figure 3-8   Correct addition of a remote workstation

Cable with Incorrect Impedance Rating Is Used

If you need a 50-foot length of cable in a hurry, you may run down to the nearest Radio Shack® or electronics store to buy some premade cable (cables that already have the connectors installed). Be careful`that you get the correct cable type for thinwire Ethernet. Thinwire Ethernet requires RG58 cable, which is rated at 50 ohms **impedance**. Impedance is the resistance to the flow of electric signals and is measured in ohms. Using cable types with mismatched impedance will cause all types of strange problems in your network, with the end result being loss of data or loss of connectivity. Although they look the same, you cannot use the RG59 cable that is used in cable TV because it is rated at 75 ohms. You can verify the type of cable by inspecting the outer jacket. The cable type will be printed on the jacket every few feet.

You Have Exceeded the Maximum Number of Stations

When a network is growing and you are doing all you can to support and maintain it, it is easy to forget standards or lose track of how many computers you have in a given area. If you are in a growth mode and are using thin Ethernet, keeping track of the number of workstations is vital. You cannot exceed 30 stations per unrepeated cable segment. Each workstation that you add to a network increases signal loss and contributes to overall attenuation of the signal. Exceeding the maximum number of stations could cause signals to be too weak to be properly read by the receiving stations.

You Have Exceeded the Maximum Cable Length

Just as you may easily exceed the maximum stations per segment, you may exceed the 185-meter constraint on maximum cable segment length without realizing it. If you have exceeded the maximum number of stations, that problem is easy to determine—you just count the stations. Determining cable length is not as simple. Getting out your tape measure to accomplish this task is no fun either—especially if your cabling goes into walls and ceilings, as it often does.

There is a device available to handle the problem of exceeding the maximum cable length. This device is known as a **TDR (Time Domain Reflectometer)**. You can attach this device to one end of the cable segment, which then sends a signal to the other end. By using the phenomenon called reflection or signal bounce, the TDR can measure how long it takes for the signal to travel to the end of the wire and back. Because electrical signals travel at a known speed (about one foot per nanosecond), it is a simple matter for the tester to measure how long it took for the signal to be reflected back to the TDR and then divide that number by 2 to get the length of the cable. It is not cheap, but it is very handy if you are doing a lot of cable installations. A TDR is usually part of a testing device that measures other factors such as attenuation and noise.

Keep one thing in mind when testing your cable for length: Because the TDR depends on signal bounce to get a reading, the ends of the cable must not have the terminating resistor installed. This restriction also means that you cannot test the network while it is in use!

The Cable Is Shorted or Has a Break

Poor BNC installation, failure to meet minimum bend radius, excessive tension, and wire cutters can cause breaks or shorts in your cable segment. When cables are located in ceilings and in walls, finding the source of the problem can be, well, a problem. Thankfully, the device mentioned earlier can help you track down the culprit. A TDR relies on signal bounce, which will occur at the end of a cable or at a break in the cable. Signal bounce will also occur when a short is present, such as when the copper conductor inside the cable contacts the metal braid or the shell of the BNC.

Using the TDR, you can take a length measurement. If you suspect a break or short, the length that the TDR measures will be somewhere between the TDR and the end of the cable segment. One way to determine if there is a break or a short is to measure the length with a TDR, with the terminating resistor in place at the other end. If the TDR returns a valid length, it means that the signal did bounce back and there is a problem in the cable. Now you can start from where you are and physically measure to the point at which the TDR "thinks" the end of the cable is (now you must get out the tape measure or, if you are lucky, the cable manufacturer will have put notations on the cable every few feet to indicate the length).

A general rule for troubleshooting a thinwire Ethernet LAN, if you simply do not know where to start looking for a Physical layer problem, is to break the bus into smaller segments. Break the network in half (being sure to terminate the two new ends of the segment), and test each half. The half that is still working can be ignored, and you can concentrate on the half that is not working. Repeat the procedure until you have a small enough segment that you can confidently pinpoint the problem station or section of cable.

Characteristics of Thickwire Ethernet

Thickwire Ethernet, also known as 10Base5, bears mention only for historical reasons. Although there are no doubt LANs that still have some thickwire in place, you won't find this media type being used in new installations. Thickwire, as its name implies, is much thicker than 10Base2 cabling, roughly a half-inch in diameter, making it quite rigid and difficult to install.

Thickwire's two main strengths are its maximum distance of 500 meters and its very high resistance to interference. These strengths are overshadowed by its shortcomings, however. Because other long-distance media like fiber-optic cable have come down significantly in cost over the last several years, any application that requires long cable runs and resistance to interference will likely use fiber as the medium of choice. Therefore, this discussion is all the space this text will devote to thickwire Ethernet.

Twisted-Pair Cabling

Twisted-pair cabling is the standard for the majority of new LAN installations today. Twisted-pair is a general category of copper wiring, within which there are several grades. The grades of twisted-pair cabling are classified into categories ranging from Category 1 through Category 5, with a Category 6 standard that may become available during 2001. Before we go into the characteristics of the various categories of twisted-pair cabling, let's look at what all twisted-pair cables have in common.

The name "twisted-pair" is appropriate for this type of cable, as each cable consists of either two or four pairs of color-coded insulated wires that are twisted together inside a plastic jacket. See Figure 3-9. The jacket can be either shielded or unshielded, with unshielded being the more common type used in LANs.

The twisting of the wires is a critical characteristic of the various grades of cabling, with the higher grades normally having more twists per foot than the lower grades. As electrical signals travel through wiring, a magnetic field is formed around the wire. This magnetic field can interfere with signals traveling on nearby wires, a phenomenon known as **crosstalk**. If you have ever been on the telephone and faintly heard somebody else's conversation, then you have experienced the effects of crosstalk. Crosstalk on a telephone can be annoying to people, but computers that are expecting data to be precise and in a certain format are much less tolerant.

So how do twists in the wire help? To answer that question, it is helpful to understand how the pairs of wires are used in a cable to carry data. In a typical Ethernet application, two pairs of wires are used: one pair to transmit data and one pair to receive data. When data is transmitted, a **differential signal** is used. That is, one wire uses a positive voltage and the other wire uses a negative voltage. The receiving side derives the actual data by taking the difference between the two signals. When the wires are twisted together, the magnetic field created from one wire cancels the magnetic field from the other wire. Not surprisingly, this effect is called **cancellation**. It prevents one pair of wires from leaking data onto other pairs of wires. This eliminates crosstalk.

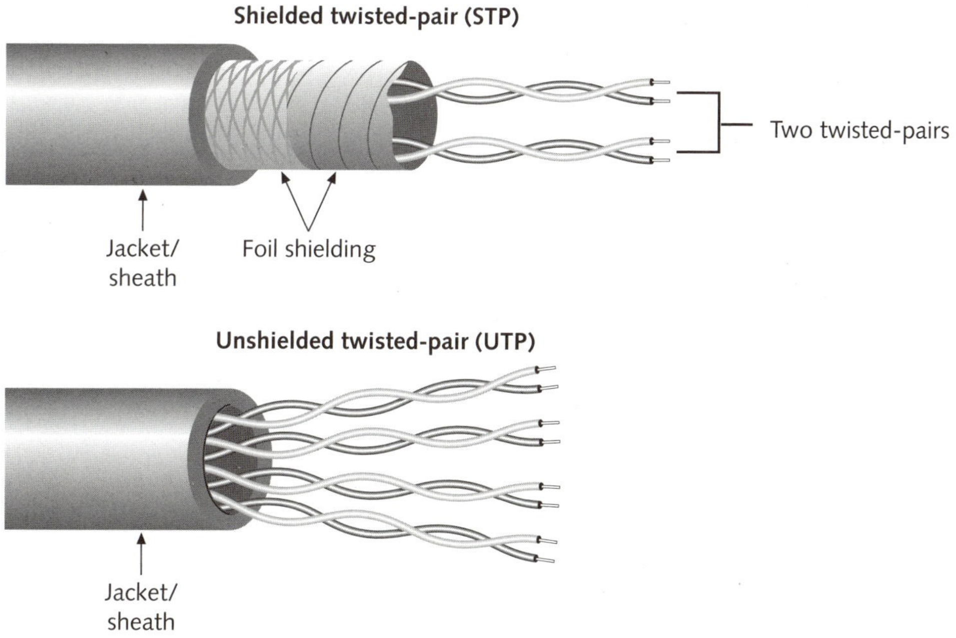

Figure 3-9   Twisted-pair cabling

Another benefit of twisted wires, along with a differential signal, is protection from outside interference. If there is noise on the line from EMI or crosstalk, the noise will be factored out when the receiving side calculates the difference between the positive and negative signal.

Let's walk through an example. Let's say that a station is transmitting a signal that represents a 1 bit. For simplicity's sake, we will say that a voltage of +5 represents a 1 bit. Using differential signaling, the positive wire transmits +2.5 V and the negative wire transmits −2.5 V. The receiving side calculates the difference between the two, so we do a subtraction:

$$+2.5 - (-2.5) = +5$$

There we have our 1 bit. Now, let's say that Electromagnetic Interference, or noise, from a nearby power source leaks onto our pair of wires and the interference is measured as +1 V. Provided that the interference is equal on both wires, the positive wire now is showing +3.5 V and the negative wire is showing −1.5 V (−2.5 + 1). The receiving side now sees the following:

$$+3.5 - (-1.5) = +5$$

The exact same result is seen because the noise is subtracted out! The data arrives safely and accurately, despite the EMI.

Notice in the previous example the phrase "Provided that the interference is equal on both wires…". This reason also explains why the twisting is important. The tighter the twists are in a pair of wires, the closer the wires will be to one another. Therefore, any noise from EMI or RFI that affects one wire is likely to affect the other wire equally. If the wires are not adequately twisted together, the noise may affect one wire but not the other, causing the data to be received incorrectly.

As discussed, several categories of twisted-pair cabling exist. These categories and their general suitability for various uses are as follows:

- Category 1
  - Standard telephone wire
  - Voice and low-speed data transmission rates, up to 56 Kbps
  - Little or no twist
  - Very high susceptibility to crosstalk
- Category 2
  - Low-speed LAN data communications, up to 1 Mbps, such as AppleTalk
  - Moderate twist
  - High susceptibility to crosstalk
- Category 3
  - Suitable for half-duplex LAN communications up to 10 Mbps
  - Moderate twist
  - Moderate susceptibility to crosstalk

3

- Category 4
    - Suitable for half-duplex LAN communications up to 16 Mbps
    - Moderate twist
    - Moderate to low susceptibility to crosstalk
- Category 5/5E
    - Suitable for full-duplex LAN communications up to 100 Mbps
    - High twist
    - Very low susceptibility to crosstalk

 Categories 5 and 5E are similar. They differ primarily in the tests they must undergo to be certified. Category 5 cabling may support up to 1000 Mbps (1 gigabit), and Category 5E should support 1000 Mbps depending on the environment and quality of termination. The latest TIA/EIA cabling standard, as of November 1999, is Category 5E. A Category 6 cabling standard is under development and should have been published by mid-to-late 2001. Category 6 cabling will support 1000 Mbps transfer rates and will likely replace Category 5E cabling in applications that require this high bandwidth. To complicate matters, a Category 7 standard is in the works but is a long way from completion. Because the proposed cabling differs significantly from Category 5 cabling and components, it may never be completed.

As you can see, the only categories of twisted-pair cabling that support current LAN environments are Category 3 and higher. Current standards specify that new installations use Category 5 or 5E, so for the purposes of this text, we will focus on these categories of twisted-pair cabling. Because these two cabling types are so similar, we will refer to them simply as Category 5. When necessary, any differences will be noted.

Characteristics of Twisted-Pair Ethernet

We have already discussed some of the general characteristics of all twisted-pair cables. Because Category 5 cabling (hereafter referred to as Cat-5) is the de facto standard for copper cabling in LANs, further discussions regarding twisted-pair cabling characteristics and support issues will be directed at Cat-5 cabling. In addition, the focus of these discussions will center on Ethernet networks.

The IEEE designation for 10 Mbps Ethernet running over twisted-pair cabling is 10BaseT. There are two options for running 100 Mbps Ethernet (also referred to as Fast Ethernet) over twisted-pair cabling. One option uses two pairs of wires, referred to as 100BaseTX. The other uses four pairs of wires, referred to as 100BaseT4. Our focus will be on the predominant 100BaseTX standard.

Ease of Installation

The installation of Cat-5 cabling is somewhat more complex than that of thinwire Ethernet, primarily due to the fact that there are four pairs of wires, making a total of eight wires, compared to a single wire with the coaxial cable used in thinwire Ethernet. The quality standards are also tighter because of the requirement that Cat-5 cabling support bandwidths up to 100 Mbps. Because there is no shielding, special attention must be given to prevent EMI and RFI. On the other hand, because Cat-5 cabling is so pervasive, there is a wealth of information available in books and on the Internet to assist you with any questions or problems you might have.

The minimum bend radius for Cat-5 cable is 1 inch, or four times the diameter of the cable. Many installers and manufacturers recommend no less than 2 inches. This choice will often depend on the quality and flexibility of the outer jacket of the cable. The connectors are inexpensive and, with some practice, easy to install; here again, attention to detail is important to maintain specifications. The cable ends require a Cat-5 **RJ45** plug. An RJ45 plug looks much like a standard telephone plug but has eight pins instead of four. Other connecting items you will find in a Cat-5 installation include RJ45 jacks and Cat-5 patch panels. These require special tools to properly terminate the four pairs of wires. While these procedures are not difficult, there is more to consider when compared to installing ends on a coaxial cable.

Cat-5 Ethernet installations require a cable segment for each workstation, connected to a central hub or switch. This arrangement of cabling is referred to as a star topology. Frequently, three separate cables are involved for each workstation. The longest section of cable runs from a patch panel to an RJ45 jack. At the patch-panel end, a patch cable connects the patch panel to a hub. At the jack end, a patch panel connects the jack to the NIC on the workstation. This topology can be seen in Figure 3-10.

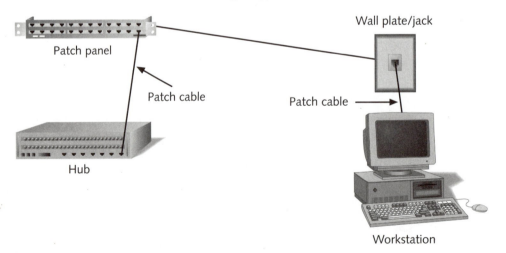

Figure 3-10   Typical workstation connection in a Cat-5 environment

Because only one station is connected to each segment of cable, adding and moving stations can be done safely without disrupting the rest of the LAN. This structure also means that more cable must be used than with the bus topology network you find with Thinnet. Thus, the installation of cabling for workstations may take considerably longer and be more costly.

Testing

The testing requirements for Category 5 cabling installations are extensive. Such installations must meet requirements for length, attenuation, crosstalk, and proper arrangement of the individual wires. Simply hooking up the cable and seeing if it works is not sufficient with Cat-5 cabling. What works in your 10BaseT network today may not work in your upgraded 100BaseTX network next month unless the installation has been properly tested and certified to Category 5 standards.

The test equipment for Cat-5 cabling installations ranges from basic testers that check for opens, shorts, and correct wiremap to digital cable analyzers that also test the length and performance characteristics of your cable installation. Only the latter testers can certify your installation for Cat-5 compliance. As expected, the prices for these testing devices range from less than a hundred dollars for the simple testers to several thousand dollars for the cable analyzers.

If your testing goal is to perform professional, certified cable installations, you will have to spring for the full-blown cable analyzer. The good news is that these analyzers are exceedingly simple to use. Plug the cable in, press a button, and within seconds you have your results. You can view results as a pass/fail option or in detail.

Maximum Length

The maximum length specification for twisted-pair cabling is less generous than that for coaxial cables. The maximum length specified for all twisted-pair cabling used for Ethernet applications is 100 meters from hub to workstation. This restriction means that the maximum distance that two workstations may be from one another, using a single repeater, is 200 meters.

While this maximum distance is considerably shorter than the maximum distances specified for coaxial cabling, it is sufficient for most LAN designs. As with coaxial cable, the total distance of your LAN can be extended by using additional repeaters. There are limitations on the use of repeaters, however, and the limitations will vary depending on the speed of your LAN.

Maximum Stations

In one specification, twisted-pair cabling is very generous compared to coaxial cabling. The maximum number of stations on an Ethernet cabling segment using twisted-pair cabling is 1024, not including repeaters. This number is high enough that it is unlikely to be a consideration in a well-designed network. A single cabling segment, or collision domain, containing anywhere near 1024 stations would have more serious problems than violating the maximum-stations specification. The number of collisions would most likely be so high that little actual data would be transferred successfully.

Bandwidth Capacity

Category 5 cabling is rated for 100 Mbps bandwidth. With additional testing, it can be used for 1000 Mbps, or 1 Gbs, transmission speeds. The enhanced Category 5, Cat-5E, is rated to carry 1000 Mbps, as will the developing standard, Category 6. If you intend to use Cat-5 or Cat-5E cabling for 1 Gbs transmissions, you must be sure that you have a cable tester designed to test for that speed.

Resistance to Interference

Unshielded twisted-pair cabling in general has low resistance to interference. Without some type of shield between outside interference sources and the data-carrying wires, **unshielded twisted-pair (UTP)** cabling is an easy target for EMI and RFI. Shielded twisted-pair (STP) cabling is an option for extremely noisy environments. Because STP cabling is more costly and requires different tools and connectors to terminate, it is best to stick with UTP Cat-5 cabling whenever possible. If Cat-5 UTP is properly installed, and all recommended installation guidelines are followed to prevent EMI, the self-shielding effect that the Cat-5 twisting provides should serve your network well in most cases.

In summary, twisted-pair cabling is the medium of choice in new LAN installations for desktop connectivity. Category 5 and Category 5E are the current recommended cabling grades for LANs operating up to 1 Gbs. While there is much to consider to achieve the goal of a trouble-free, reliable, Physical layer using Cat-5 cabling, the care that you take during installation and testing of this cabling will go a long way toward achieving that goal.

Twisted-Pair Ethernet Installation Considerations

The following is a list of considerations that you should keep in mind when installing and supporting a twisted-pair Ethernet network:

- Maintain a maximum cable length from hub to workstation of 100 meters.
- Use at least Category 5 cable.
- Make sure that all cable ends have been terminated according to applicable standards.
- Use, whenever possible, factory-made patch cables.
- Maintain the minimum bend radius.
- Make sure that you have not exceeded the maximum pull force of 25 foot-pounds.

3

- Avoid EMI sources such as fluorescent lights, electrical cables, and motors.

- Make sure that you have tested the cable with a cable performance analyzer capable of certifying Cat-5 compliance.

- Make sure that the installation is well labeled and clearly documented.

The **Telecommunications Industry Association/Electronics Industries Association (TIA/EIA)** publishes the standards that govern the use and installation of Category-5 cabling. This text will focus on some of the areas that are most likely to cause problems in an installation and explain how to recognize and solve those problems. For a more detailed look at the particular standards, refer to the following documents:

- TIA/EIA 568A—Commercial Building Telecommunications Cabling Standard

- TIA/EIA 569—Commercial Building Standard for Telecommunications Pathways and Spaces

 These documents can be purchased online at *www.tiaonline.org*.

Twisted-Pair Ethernet Termination Considerations

Proper termination and installation of twisted-pair cabling is probably the most important aspect of your Physical layer. If the cabling is terminated poorly or the use of connecting equipment is nonstandard or inconsistent, network problems will likely be numerous and difficult to track down. Strict rules apply to Category 5 cable terminations:

- Cables can be untwisted a maximum of 0.5 inch at the point of termination.

- Color-coded wires must be arranged according to the 568-A or 568-B wiring specification.

- All components used must be Category-5 rated.

As much effort as has been put into explaining the purpose of the twist in twisted-pair, the reason for the first point should be obvious. The termination of a Cat-5 cable at the jack or patch panel is where you are most likely to run into problems, especially if you use factory-made patch cables. It takes a little practice, but you should strive to make the amount of wire that is outside the jacket as short as possible and maintain the twist even outside the jacket if that is feasible. See Figure 3-11.

Figure 3-11   Correct patch-panel termination

There are two predominant wiring standards for Cat-5 cabling: 568-A and 568-B. You can use either throughout your network, but you should use only one. A common problem occurs when patch panels are wired using one standard and jacks are wired using the other. The difference between the two standards is the wiring of the transmit and receive pairs. On 568-A wired equipment, the two transmit pins from the workstation's perspective are the green pair and the receive pins are the orange pair. On 568-B wired equipment, exactly the opposite is true.

If you look at Figure 3-12 carefully, you will see that the actual wiring is identical; it is the color-coding that differs. Some manufacturers take advantage of this fact and color-code the punch-down terminals on their jacks and patch panels with both standards indicated. This way, you do not have two order numbers for the equipment depending on whether you are using the 568-A or 568-B standard.

When you install cabling, you must ensure that all of the connection components match the category of cabling you are using. Patch panels, jacks, and RJ45 plugs must all meet Category 5 standards. Also, you cannot mix cabling or connector types of differing impedances in the same circuit. Cat-5 UTP has an impedance of 100 ohms, whereas shielded twisted-pair has an impedance of 150 ohms; as a result, they cannot be mixed on the same cabling segment. Remember that a Cat-5 cabling segment consists of up to three lengths of cable: a patch cable from the workstation to the jack, a cable from the jack to the patch panel, and a patch cable from the patch panel to the hub.

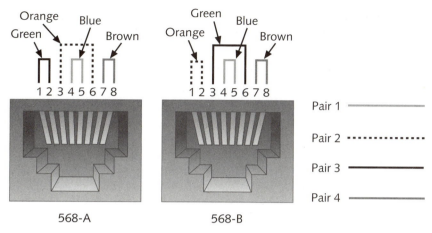

Figure 3-12   568-A and 568-B wiring standards

Twisted-Pair Ethernet Common Support Issues

The most common problems with a 10BaseT or 100BaseTX network are related to the proper termination of the cabling and adherence to the appropriate standards for devices and installation. Luckily, because only one workstation is connected on each physical cable segment, problems with a single connector or cable tend to affect only one station. This statement is not always true, but, to account for the star topology of twisted-pair Ethernet, in which each station is connected to a central hub, hub manufacturers have built features into the hubs to help isolate problems. This section will concentrate on issues that primarily occur on individual cable segments.

User Has Disconnected a Cable

Unlike the 10Base2 bus topology network, cable disconnection affects only the user who did the deed. This problem is easy to fix and almost as easy to find. If the cable end is lying on the floor, you know what to do. On the other hand, if the cable appears to be plugged into the NIC, you may dismiss a disconnected cable as the cause. Don't! Users who disconnect the cables from their computers often display one of two tendencies when replacing the cables: being too delicate or being too forceful. An RJ45 plug sometimes takes a little effort to make a good connection; you need to push only until you hear the key click into place. Sometimes users won't take this step, so check it out before assuming that the connection is good.

Another thing that can happen is that a user may plug the modem cable into the NIC, and vice versa. It doesn't seem possible, because the RJ45 is bigger than the RJ11 used for modems, but if there is a will, there is a way. Here is a tip: If the hub to which the user's workstation is connected is close to you, check the indicator light on the hub before paying the user a visit (assuming that you know the port into which the user's station is plugged; here is one place where good documentation pays off). Every Ethernet hub has one or more LEDs associated with each port. One of the LEDs will be labeled "Link". If the user's cable is functional and connected, the link light will be on; otherwise, it will be off. If it is off, check the cable connection.

When a user replaces the PC cables, he or she often uses either too much force or too little force. The first person's efforts are borne of the "If it doesn't fit, I'll make it fit" philosophy and can result in broken pins or jammed-in connectors. The timid user will barely push the cables onto the connectors, afraid that one wrong move will "break it," resulting in cables that fall out of the connectors or that do not make full contact with the pins.

Cable Does Not Meet Minimum Bend Radius

Failure to meet the minimum bend radius can occur if you do not use some type of cable channel to route your cables through ceilings and walls. Twisted-pair cabling is relatively flexible and can get bent around a corner or an obstruction in the ceiling without your being aware of it. Remember, for Cat-5 cable to go around a 90° corner, a loop of at least 1 inch of cable must be used to circumvent the corner. Because it is so flexible, you need have little concern about breaking the wires.

One of the main concerns with too sharp a bend in Cat-5 cabling is that the pairs of wires will become flattened, affecting the geometry of the twists. This issue can make the cable susceptible to noise and crosstalk. The problem will usually show up as slow performance or a high number of transmission errors, usually CRC errors. Manufacturers of cable raceway and cable channels frequently provide corner pieces that guarantee the specified minimum bend radius. If you use cable raceway—and it is highly recommended that you do—be sure that it meets the bend radius specifications for the type of cabling you are using. More bend radius than required is acceptable; too little is not.

Wrong Category of Cable Is Used

Some older cabling installations may have Category 3 cabling installed or, worse yet, Category 1 cable, also known as silver satin. Silver satin cable is the flat, silver-colored cable that you find used to connect telephones or modems. Unfortunately, some NIC manufacturers once shipped these cables along with the network card, and some unsuspecting network or PC technicians would use them. These cables might even work in a 10 Mbps Ethernet network if they were used only as patch cables, but they wouldn't pass any performance tests and could introduce a high rate of errors into your network. Category 3 cable is perfectly fine for 10BaseT networks but what happens when you want to upgrade to Fast Ethernet? Category 3 cannot be used for Fast Ethernet and is less reliable than Cat-5 for 10BaseT. As of this writing, the accepted cabling type for any new installation is Category 5E. Existing Cat-5 is acceptable but will require additional tests if 1000BaseTX will be used.

You Have Exceeded the Maximum Cable Length

One hundred meters (328 feet) seems like a long way until you have to run a cable from one end of the manufacturing warehouse to the other. Of course, you would know better, but you are not always the person running the cable. Many companies that contract out their computer work have an in-house maintenance crew, and it is the maintenance crew that frequently runs the cable.

If your job is to terminate, test the cable, plug it into the hub, and configure the workstation, what do you say when the cable tester shows the length at 115 meters? To stay strictly within standards, you need to give the bad news to the maintenance crew. In a 10BaseT network that has a couple of repeaters at most, you can probably live with 115 meters. But don't think about upgrading to 100BaseTX. Many of the specifications for Cat-5 cabling are based on worst-case scenarios assuming 100 Mbps Ethernet. With 10 Mbps Ethernet, you have a little headroom to bend the standards. Next year, however, you may not be the network consultant who is called to upgrade the company to 100 Mbps Ethernet, and the folks who are called won't have a lot of nice things to say about your competence if you let the 115 meters go. If you exceed the maximum cable length and your 10 Mbps Ethernet connection is working, document your findings along with an explanation and recommend a run of fiber or, if the design allows, a repeater.

Sometimes, even the knowledgeable network technician can accidentally end up with a cable length greater than 100 meters. Cat-5 cable has foot markings every 2 feet, so you can easily determine how many feet are in a run of cable. If you are close to the limit, you may forget about your patch cables. For this reason, the 568-A standard specifies 90 meters for the cable run between the jack and the patch panel. This choice leaves up to 10 meters for the combined length of the two patch cables. When figuring your cable run, think 90 meters (about 295 feet)—not 100 meters.

The Cable Was Pulled with Too Much Force

The end result of exceeding the maximum pull force for a Cat-5 cable (25 foot-pounds) is similar to making a sharp bend with the cable. The cable twist is compromised. The result will be excessive crosstalk or noise resulting in high error rates or lack of connectivity. If you work up a sweat pulling the cables, or if you have to wrap the cable around your hand to get a better grip, you are pulling too hard and need to find a better pathway. Twenty-five foot-pounds is not a lot of force. After the cable is run, it should not be under any tension.

Two Standards Were Used to Terminate the Cable—Transposed Pair

The use of different cable termination standards will result in no connection from the workstation to the hub. If the jack is terminated using the 568-A wiring standard and the patch panel is terminated using 568-B, you end up with the transmit wires on the workstation connected to the transmit wires on the hub and the receive wires connected to the receive wires. This problem is known as a **transposed pair**. It is equivalent to speaking into a telephone earpiece while listening on the other end.

If you do make a mistake and purchase 568-A patch panels and 568-B jacks, for example, you can correct the problem by putting the green wires where the color code indicates orange, and vice versa, on either the patch panel or jack, but not on both. This choice will undoubtedly confuse the next technician who inspects your work years after you have left the company, so the better option is to return the products and trade them in for the correct standard. There is actually a valid use for a transposed pair on a patch cable—known as a **crossover cable**.

No Standard Was Used to Terminate the Cable—Split Pair

A cable can be terminated without following either the 568-A or 568-B wiring standard and it may still work to carry 10 Mbps Ethernet. An aspiring cable installer may have heard that an Ethernet cable is wired straight-through. That is, the wire on pin 1 of one connector goes to pin 1 on the connector on the other side of the cable, and so on for all eight pins. In fact, this setup applies to a standard twisted-pair Ethernet connection. It therefore seems reasonable to just line up all four pairs of wires—green, blue, orange, and brown—and add the connectors. You get something like Figure 3-13.

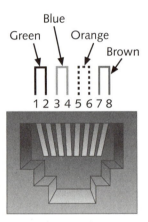

Figure 3-13   Incorrect straight-through wiring results in a split pair

This approach may even work for 10BaseT Ethernet, but this cable will not pass performance tests. Remember the reason for the twists in the wires. The effectiveness of the twists depends on the differential signals in the same circuit to cancel out each other's electromagnetic field. For this to happen, the wires have to be twisted around each other. In twisted-pair Ethernet, the transmit signals are on pins 1 and 2. In Figure 3-13, this is done: The green pair is on pins 1 and 2. The receive signals are on pins 3 and 6. In the figure, that would be one blue wire and one orange wire. The receive signals are split between the blue pair and the orange pair. Cable testers indicate this as a **split pair**. A simple wiremap tester will not detect a split pair. A split pair usually results in excessive crosstalk because you no longer have the benefit of the cancellation effect.

In practice, this wiring arrangement may work for 10BaseT because the lower signal frequency makes the cabling less susceptible to crosstalk. When you upgrade to 100BaseT, however, your problems will range from high rates of errors to no connectivity at all.

Crossed Pair

A crossed pair is fairly easy to spot and will be detected by the simplest of cable testers. It occurs when the wires in a pair cross, making a connection to the opposite pin on the other side of the cable. For example, one wire in your green pair is connected to pin 1 on one side and pin 2 on the other end of the cable. The result will be a failed wiremap test and no connectivity.

Wires Are Untwisted More Than 0.5 Inches at the Termination Point

It is difficult to work with short lengths of wire. The tendency of some technicians is to strip off several inches of the cable jacket, untwist the wires, and terminate the cable. While this approach may make for a faster, easier job of cable termination, it may result in poor connections and high error rates. This type of termination leads to crosstalk and increased susceptibility to EMI and RFI. Once again, maintaining the twist at the ends of the cable is paramount. The termination shown in Figure 3-14 is unacceptable and must be redone.

Figure 3-14   Unacceptable termination of Cat-5 cable

Cable Jacket on Patch Cable Is Not Under Strain Relief

When an RJ45 plug is installed on a Cat-5 patch cable, the jacket of the cable must rest under the strain-relief bar before crimping. Failure to do so will cause the wires to shift inside the plug, causing intermittent connections or no connection at all. After crimping the RJ45 plug, be sure to tug on the connector to ensure that the jacket is firmly secured by the strain-relief bar. See Figure 3-15 for an example of a good RJ45 plug installation.

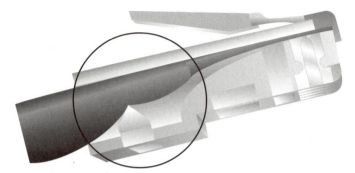

Figure 3-15   Correct RJ45 plug installation

RJ45 Contact Blades Are Not Making Contact

The copper contact blades in an RJ45 plug are pushed by the crimp tool and slice through the thin insulation on each wire, thereby making an electrical contact with the wires. There are several reasons why this procedure may fail:

- Not enough force used on the crimp tool: Some inexpensive crimp tools require considerable force to make an adequate crimp, and weak hands may not be up to the task.

- Wires not pushed far enough into the RJ45 plug: Before crimping the connector, verify that all eight wires are pushed all the way to the front of the plug.

- Faulty RJ45 plug: Occasionally, an RJ45 plug will be defective and the contact blade will not work no matter how hard you squeeze the tool. In this case, throw the plug away.

For these reasons and many more, it is advisable to use factory-made patch cables whenever possible. They may cost a little more, but the added reliability is well worth the cost, and you can spend your time designing and installing the network rather than making and troubleshooting patch cables.

Cables Are Too Close to an EMI Source

TIA/EIA 569 states that communications cables must maintain a minimum distance of 5 inches from fluorescent lighting fixtures or power lines over 2 kVA. A minimum distance of 24 inches must be maintained from power lines over 5 kVA. Do not run data cables over the top of fluorescent lights, and do maintain a separate conduit for data and power cables—with these precautions, you should be safe. Furthermore, avoid running cables near any large power sources such as heaters, motors, and generators or radio frequency sources such as microwave, radar, or X-ray equipment. If you find that network disturbances occur periodically, such as once or twice per hour, look for cabling near

3

heaters and air conditioners, as the interference may be coming from these sources when they kick on.

Cables Were Not Tested for Cat-5 Performance

Many of the problems already mentioned would be cause for Category 5 performance test failure. The initial operation of your cable installation can be certified to be free of most of these defects if you test the cabling with a performance analyzer immediately after installation. The tests that the analyzer must be able to perform for Category 5 compliance as specified in EIA/TIA TSB-67 (Transmission Performance Specifications for Field Testing of Unshielded Twisted-Pair Cabling Systems) are as follows:

- Wiremap
- Length
- Attenuation
- Near-end crosstalk (NEXT)

Additional tests are specified in the latest revision of EIA/TIA 568-A for Cat-5E cabling and are detailed in TSB-95:

- Insertion loss
- Return loss
- Equal-level far-end crosstalk (ELFEXT)

As of this writing, EIA/TIA 568-A states that all new installations must pass the more stringent Cat-5E tests. Existing Cat-5 installations may be recertified as Cat-5E by performing these additional tests on all cables.

A certified cable run today does not necessarily mean a certified cable run tomorrow. Environmental conditions change, cables get pulled or shifted, office furniture is moved, and new heating and air conditioning systems are put in, all of which can affect your cabling installation. Network cabling is the foundation of any network. It is your job to ensure that you are informed of any changes that occur in the workplace that could affect the cable plant. You will easily be able to determine if workplace changes affect your cabling if you have maintained accurate and complete documentation.

Fiber-Optic Media

Fiber-optic cabling is the media of choice for campus backbones and long-distance communications. Because fiber optics uses light signals traveling through glass rather than electrical signals traveling through copper, many of the reliability problems associated with copper media are not an issue with fiber. Thanks to its many advantages, fiber is even being accepted as a replacement for copper media for workstation connectivity. However, its higher price and more fragile termination procedure keep fiber from overtaking copper as the desktop media leader.

Characteristics of Fiber-Optic Cable

Fiber-optic cabling includes a very-small-diameter cylinder of glass at its core, surrounded by another, thicker layer of glass called the cladding, which in turn is protected by a thin plastic coating. The core of the fiber carries the optical signals that form the data. Depending on the application, there may be one or several of these fibers wrapped in a strength member made of Kevlar or a fiberglass rod. This entire structure is enclosed in a jacket of plastic, usually PVC. See Figure 3-16.

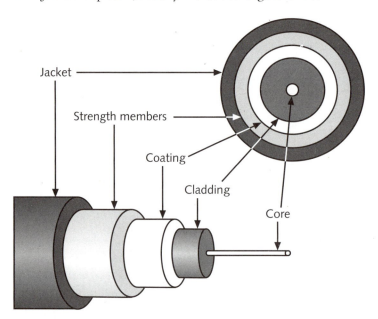

Figure 3-16   Fiber-optic cable

There are two categories of fiber-optic cable: single-mode and multimode. While there are distinct differences between these two fiber types, most of the characteristics of fiber are common to both types. The primary differences relate to the diameter of the signal-carrying core and the light source it is designed to carry. The most common multimode fiber has a core diameter of either 50 or 62.5 microns, and single-mode fiber typically has a core diameter between 7 and 9 microns. The glass cladding, which surrounds the core and reflects light back into the core, is 125 microns thick for both types.

You will typically see the specifications written as something like 62.5 μm/125 μm or 8 μm/125 μm, where μm stands for micrometer or one-millionth of a meter. Multimode fiber uses **light-emitting diodes (LED)** as the light source. Multimode fiber gets its name because the core is actually composed of several strands of glass along which multiple streams, or modes, of light travel. Single-mode fiber uses a single stream of light generated by a laser. As you might expect, single-mode fiber can carry signals for a considerably greater distance than can multimode fiber due to the stronger light source of the laser. Single-mode fiber and single-mode fiber equipment are also more expensive than their multimode fiber counterparts.

Fiber-optic signals are given as wavelengths, expressed in nanometers (nm). It is important to know what optical wavelength your network equipment uses when transmitting signals so that you can test the fiber using that wavelength. Multimode fiber applications typically use one of two wavelengths, 850 nm or 1300 nm, whereas single-mode fiber applications usually use a wavelength of 1550 nm.

We will focus on Ethernet LAN applications when discussing fiber-optic cabling, as discussions on WAN cabling are beyond the scope of this book.

Ease of Installation

Ethernet over fiber-optic cabling is referred to as 10BaseF, and Fast Ethernet over fiber is known as 100BaseFX. The 10BaseF category is broken into three subcategories: 10BaseFL, 10BaseFB, and 10BaseFP. 10BaseFL (where the "L" stands for "link") is asynchronous with a maximum segment length of 200 meters using a star wiring topology. 10BaseFB (where the "B" stands for "backbone") is synchronous fiber with a maximum segment length of 2000 meters using a star topology. The synchronous nature of 10BaseFB allows more repeaters to be used in series. 10BaseFP (where the "P" stands for "passive") has a maximum segment length of 1000 meters and uses a passive star topology. The most common types used are 10BaseFB and 10BaseFL.

Fiber-optic cabling comes in a variety of packaging formats depending on whether it is being used indoors or outdoors and how many fibers are in a single outer shell. There can be a single fiber strand inside a jacket of PVC or dozens or even hundreds of fibers wrapped inside a heavy plastic outer shell. Like the other media types, fiber-optic cable has a minimum bend radius specification that must be observed.

Due to the different packaging of fiber, it is best to check with the manufacturer for the details on bend radius. A variety of methods are used to terminate the fiber ends and secure the connectors. These methods range from using glue that is heat-cured or cured by ultraviolet light to fairly simple crimp-on connectors.

One thing that all types of fiber have in common is that you must have a precision stripping tool to remove the thin plastic coating around the cladding and a glass-cutting tool, called a **cleaver**, that will cut the glass without fracturing it. The prices of these tools range from a few hundred dollars to well into the thousands of dollars. The particulars of fiber termination are beyond the scope of this book, but suffice it to say that the installation of fiber-optic connectors is much more expensive and requires somewhat more skill than copper cabling terminations.

Fiber-optic cables are frequently terminated with one of three connector types: ST, SC, or a newer, high-density connector, MT-RJ. See Figure 3-17.

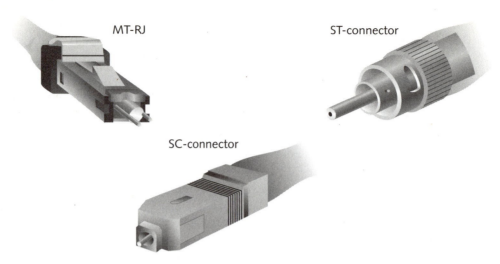

Figure 3-17   Fiber-optic connectors

Fiber-optic cable can carry a light source in only one direction. For LAN applications, then, each connection requires two strands of fiber: one for transmit and one for receive. Of the three connectors mentioned, only one—the MT-RJ—terminates two strands of fiber in a single connector. Therefore, two connectors are required for each device connection.

Other fiber-optic connector types include FC-and MIC-connectors. FC-connectors are often used in fiber-to-the-desk applications. MIC-connectors, which use a single connector for two fiber strands, are found most often in FDDI networks.

Testing

Fiber-optic cabling is unique in that you can actually see whether the cable run is capable of carrying data. Because the signals take the form of light pulses, you can take a flashlight with a narrow beam, shine it in one end of the cable, and, if there are no breaks or other obstructions in the cable, see the light come out the other end. This process will work over hundreds of meters.

Strangely enough, this flashlight method is used by some of the IT personnel at a major fiber-optic cable manufacturing plant (because they make and terminate fiber for a living, they have a high level of confidence in their work!). This method is inexpensive and simple to perform, but it doesn't certify your installation for operation. The problem with not having a more scientific test is that if something goes wrong in the network, many manufacturers of fiber-optic networking devices will not guarantee their products unless testing has been documented on the cables. While most of us simply toss the warranty card out of the way when unwrapping our new network toys, it may be a good idea to read the warranty information once in a while so that you are aware of your responsibilities. The good news is fewer things can go wrong with fiber-optic signals because there is no such thing as crosstalk, EMI, or RFI.

The main concern when testing fiber is the amount of optical signal loss from source to destination—that is, the attenuation rate. The primary equipment used consists of two pieces: a transmitter, or light source, and a receiver, or power meter. Signal strength in fiber-optic cables is measured in dBm, which are decibels referenced to one milliwatt. Signal loss is measured in dB, or decibels, which is a relative reading—that is, one power reading compared to another. In other words, signal loss can be measured only after the power meter has been calibrated to the light source so that a comparison can be made of the signal strength before the test and then again after the test.

The amount of loss that is permitted depends on the equipment you are using at the transmitter and receiver ends. Manufacturers will publish power specifications for the transmitter and specify the minimum signal strength required for the receiver to accurately read the data. Using this information, you can determine whether the amount of signal loss in your cabling is within the required limits. Test equipment that measures optical signal loss does not come cheap; it costs $1200 and higher.

Some other parameters you may need to test include cable length and propagation delay. These tests are usually available only with high-end testing equipment (which can cost thousands of dollars). These measurements are typically necessary only when you are transmitting data at very high rates (1 Gbs), as the length and delay specifications for such high-speed communications are much more strict than those for 10 Mbps or 100 Mbps Ethernet.

Maximum Length

Fiber-optic cable used to connect workstations in a star configuration to a central hub is referred to as 10BaseF or 100BaseFX, depending on the bandwidth being used. The type of cabling is specified as multimode fiber. The maximum distance allowed from the hub to a workstation for 10BaseF is 2000 meters. For 100BaseFX, the maximum distance in a shared-bandwidth network using repeaters depends on several factors, including the number and length of copper segments in the network. The maximum distances are considerably shorter than those accepted with 10BaseF, and you should consult your equipment manufacturer for any lengths over 100 meters. 100BaseFX connections to switch ports can extend as far as 2000 meters over multimode fiber and for much greater distances using single-mode fiber.

Bandwidth Capability

As previously mentioned, fiber-optic cable has enormous bandwidth carrying capability. Both single-mode and multimode fiber have been used to carry data at gigabit speeds and beyond. Tests have been done successfully at 50 Gbps over multimode fiber and at higher rates using single-mode fiber. The bandwidth then depends on the devices and NICs installed in your network.

Resistance to Interference

Fiber-optic cabling has no equal in terms of its resistance to interference. Fiber-optic cabling is completely resistant to a wide variety of interference sources, including EMI, RFI, X-rays, and microwaves. About the only thing that will interfere with a fiber-optic transmission is a backhoe. This problem, much to the chagrin of the cable and telephone companies, is not uncommon with buried fiber-optic cables. Because fiber-optic transmissions rely on pulses of light to generate signals, the only thing that can interfere with the transmission—short of breaking the glass—is another light source. As long as you have not stripped the cable down to the glass cladding, you should be fine.

Fiber-Optic Cable Installation Considerations

The following is a list of considerations that you should keep in mind when installing and supporting a fiber-optic Ethernet network:

- Use the correct mode of fiber to match the network equipment.
- Use connectors that are appropriate for the mode of fiber.
- Maintain the minimum bend radius.
- When pulling fiber, make sure that you pull on the strength member, not the jacket.
- Test the fiber using the appropriate wavelength to measure loss accurately.

Fiber-Optic Cable Termination Considerations

Provided that you have not broken the fiber while installing it, and that you have not wrapped it too tightly around any corners, the only thing that can really go wrong is improper termination of the fiber-optic cable. Because the termination of the fiber ends is so critical and the equipment is somewhat costly, some of the major fiber manufacturers sell preterminated cables in a variety of lengths. Whether it is 2 fibers or 100 fibers that you require, you can purchase them preterminated to your specifications.

If you decide to go it alone, it is highly recommended that you attend an approved fiber termination class so that you can practice on somebody else's equipment. Fiber-optic connectors are expensive, as much as $25 for single-mode connectors in single quantities. Be sure you know the proper procedures before proceeding because the connectors cannot be used more than once.

One of the easiest mistakes to make—and one of the most costly—is to take a connector made for multimode cable and install it on single-mode cable, or vice versa. This mistake can be made easily if you have large trunks of cable that include both types of fibers. Single-mode fiber and multimode fiber look the same, so the only way you can tell them apart is by the color-coding of the jacket, which the manufacturer will provide.

3

It is also recommended that you choose a connector type that is well supported by the networking equipment manufacturer. In addition, after you choose the connector type, stick with it because all of the patch panels and patch cords you buy will have to match it.

SUPPORTING PHYSICAL LAYER DEVICES

Media represent only half of the Physical layer equation. The internetworking devices to which the media connect must also be supported. Devices operating at the Physical layer of the network are primarily concerned with two things: How are bit signals encoded, and what should be done with the bit signals once they are received? Bit signal **encoding** is the method used to represent a 0 or 1 bit on the physical media. Depending on the function of the physical device, different actions may be taken by the device once bit signals are received. This section looks at four of the more common Physical layer devices:

- Network interface cards—Receive the bits and send them to the Data Link layer for further processing.

- Repeaters and hubs—Receive bits, and regenerate and retime the bits before repeating them out all active ports, thereby extending the network beyond the normal range of the media.

- Transceivers—Attach to a **media-independent interface**, such as an attachment unit interface, providing the correct physical connection for the media type in use.

- Media converters—Convert one media type to another, such as twisted-pair to fiber-optic.

NETWORK INTERFACE CARDS

NICs provide computers and other devices with an interface to the network media. They also handle the details of receiving and sending bits and accessing the media. The importance of selecting appropriate NICs for your workstations is often overlooked. Several options are available for NICs, and the choices you make can affect your network performance and manageability. NICs also function at the Data Link layer and are discussed again in Chapter 4, so we will cover only the Physical layer aspect of NICs here. This section covers NIC bus types, supported media types, operating speed, and several advanced features that you may want to consider when choosing a NIC.

NIC Bus Types

The bus type that you select for a NIC can affect the performance of your workstations and servers. The bus types listed below represent the most common choices available today for PC workstations and servers.

- ISA—An old but still available choice on today's PCs.

- EISA—An improvement over ISA but an obsolete bus type superseded by PCI.

- PCI—Clearly the dominant bus type for network interface cards and soon to be the only option for new PCs. The PCI bus offers many advantages over the other PC bus types.

Of the three bus types listed, PCI is preferred for its faster data transfer rates. The PCI bus comes in two speeds and two bus sizes. The original and most common PCI bus runs at 33 MHz and is 32 bits wide. Newer implementations support 66 MHz and 64 bit-wide data paths. At 33 MHz and 32 bits, the PCI bus can theoretically support data transfers up to 133 Mbps. The more realistic maximum throughput for a NIC is 80 Mbps to 90 Mbps, which should be more than sufficient for most applications. The 66 MHz, 64-bit PCI bus can theoretically support up to 532 Mbps data transfers but your RAM, CPU, and operating system would all have to support the wider data path to achieve this goal. The 33 MHz, 32-bit PCI bus is sufficient for NICs running up to 100 Mbps. Unless you need a 1-Gbps NIC, there is no compelling reason to find a system that supports the faster PCI bus.

NIC Media Types Supported

An important consideration when selecting a NIC is the media types supported by the card. NICs can be purchased that support the major media types, such as twisted-pair, 10Base2, and fiber-optic. You can also purchase a NIC that supports two or even three different media types. The least expensive option usually supports a single media type—for the majority of installations, that is probably twisted-pair. For example, one company used 10Base2 cabling but wanted to upgrade to Category 5 twisted-pair. Thankfully, the NICs that were installed in the existing PCs had both 10Base2 and twisted-pair connectors, so the transition involved only a couple of hubs and the cable installation.

Some organizations purchase NICs with an **attachment unit interface (AUI)** rather than with a particular media connector. An AUI is a 15-pin interface that allows you to connect a **transceiver** that supports the media type of your choice. The transceiver contains the transmit and receive circuitry and the appropriate connector for the media used. For example, one company uses NICs with AUIs and then connects fiber-optic transceivers to the AUI, with fiber-optic cable going to the desktops. This scheme is actually a less expensive solution than purchasing fiber-optic NICs.

NIC Features

NICs support a variety of features, and not all NICs are created equal in this respect. Check carefully for the features supported before you choose a NIC, because the least expensive cards may not support the features that are important to you. Some of the features discussed here include front-panel indicators, wake-on-LAN, remote boot, and bus mastering. When choosing a NIC, be sure to keep in mind the cost and time required to support your network. Many of the least expensive NICs that do not have all of the

3

extra features may operate adequately in your network but not make the grade when it comes to troubleshooting or supporting newer technologies in the future.

Front-Panel Indicators

The indicator lights on a NIC are used only when there is a problem. When you need them, however, their usefulness cannot be overstated. The indicator lights typically come in the form of green LEDs, but sometimes you will see red or amber LEDs that may be used to indicate different functions. The most basic indicators on a NIC, and the minimum that you should consider, are the link indicator and the activity indicator. The link indicator is usually green and will be on when the NIC is properly connected to the cabling system and a connection has been established to another device, usually a hub or a switch. When a network device is first attached to the cable, this light is the first thing to check. If the link LED is not on, make sure that the cable is attached to the hub or switch and that the wiring is correct.

The activity indicator flashes when data is detected on the cable. It does not necessarily indicate that the NIC detects data that is addressed to that station, but only that data is on the network cable.

Other indicator lights may include collision indicators, indicators of the link speed, and duplex-mode indicators. The collision indicator is usually amber in color and flashes when a collision is detected on the network. If you happen to work at a good vantage point to a NIC with a collision indicator, you can get a rough idea of the number of collisions that your network is experiencing by monitoring how often the LED flashes. If the LED stays on for an extended period, it may be time to break out the network monitor to see what is generating all of those collisions.

If your NIC can operate at more than one speed—10 Mbps and 100 Mbps, for example—there may be two separate link indicators: one for 10 Mbps and one for 100 Mbps. This setup is useful for determining whether your NIC is connecting to that expensive new 100 Mbps switch at full speed. Chapter 4 discusses some reasons and remedies if the NIC is not able to connect at the speed you expect.

The duplex-mode indicators, if present, indicate whether the NIC is operating in full or half-duplex. **Half-duplex** means that a device can send or receive data at any given time, but cannot do both simultaneously. **Full-duplex** means that a device can send and receive data simultaneously. If the NIC supports full-duplex operation and is connected to a switch that supports full duplex, the full-duplex indicator will be on. A NIC can run in full-duplex mode only if the network device to which it is attached is a switch, because a hub can operate only in half-duplex mode.

Wake-on-LAN

The **wake-on-LAN** feature available with some NICs allows an administrator to remotely turn on the computer by sending a signal to the NIC. This feature requires a computer that supports the remote power-on function. In the PC arena, an ATX motherboard is required, because these motherboards allow certain components such as NICs, modems, and keyboards to be continually powered, even if the main unit is turned off. The wake-on-LAN feature allows an administrator to turn on a computer in the network, upgrade software, and perform other maintenance tasks without physically going to the computer to turn it on. Additional software that supports remote management functions is also necessary for this feature to be useful.

Remote Boot

Remote boot is a feature in which the NIC has a set of ROM chips installed that query the network for an operating system that the workstation can load across the network. This feature allows diskless workstations to boot an operating system that otherwise would have been installed on a hard drive. This feature was popular in the later 1980s and early 1990s when hard drives were comparatively expensive. Inexpensive IDE drives made this feature largely unnecessary, however. The concept of Windows terminals has again made remote boot capabilities a feature that you may want to consider if you will employ Windows Terminal Server, which now comes standard with Windows 2000, or the Citrix WinFrame product.

Desktop Management Interface

Desktop Management Interface (DMI) is a standard framework for managing and tracking components in a PC or server. This feature provides administrators with the ability to remotely manage and inventory computers on their networks. A console program is installed on a workstation or server and communicates with the DMI-compliant computers throughout the network. For more information on this and related standards, see *www.dmtf.org/standards/index.php*.

RMON Data Collection

Remote Monitoring (RMON) is a standard software interface that allows network administrators to gather network statistics remotely. When RMON is supported by a NIC, the NIC can send network statistics to a remote network management station for analysis and display.

Bus Mastering

Bus mastering allows a peripheral card, such as a NIC, to access the computer's system bus without the intervention of the CPU. This feature allows the NIC to transfer data in and out of memory without the constant attention of the system CPU, thereby enabling the CPU to perform other tasks.

Encryption

Many operating systems today build encryption techniques into their network protocols. Windows 2000, for example, offers IPSec encryption with its IP stack. Some NICs

3

can offload the operating system from some of the encryption duties by building the functionality into firmware on the NIC. This tactic allows the computer CPU to handle other tasks while the NIC performs the encryption algorithm.

NIC Configuration and Support Issues

Plug and Play operating systems generally provide for a painless installation of NICs. Most often the operating system detects the NIC after it has been installed or during the installation of the operating system, and then it installs the correct driver. But what about operating systems that are not Plug and Play? If you are lucky, the operating system already has a driver available for the NIC installed and, through a series of tests, can detect the correct NIC and install the driver. Occasionally, this procedure may fail and you need to do some troubleshooting.

Windows NT is a good example of an operating system that does not support Plug and Play and that can fail to recognize the installed NIC. In such a case, you must have the driver disk ready and know the model number of your NIC. In some cases, Windows NT will fail to select the correct IRQ and port number. If the NIC is Plug and Play compliant, you may need to run the diagnostic program that comes with the NIC and disable the Plug and Play feature. This approach allows you to set the NIC to a particular IRQ and port number; you then can set those values in the Windows NT Network Control Panel. The same is true of NetWare servers—NetWare is not a Plug and Play operating system. If it fails to recognize your NIC and set up the drivers correctly, you may need to tell NetWare the IRQ and port settings for the NIC. These issues are usually important only with ISA bus cards, as PCI bus cards choose the IRQ and port based on information from the system BIOS.

The features on the NICs installed on your network can have significant performance implications for your network, workstations, and servers. Generally, desirable features, particularly on a high-bandwidth network such as fast Ethernet, include bus mastering, built-in encryption capabilities if your network uses encryption, and a PCI bus running at the fastest and widest bus width supported by your system. Wake-on-LAN, RMON, DMI, and other management features are desirable in large networks where remote administration of workstations is advisable.

Now it is time to turn our attention to the Physical layer devices into which you will be plugging your NICs.

REPEATERS

The simple repeater is one of the more basic layer 1 devices. The basic repeater has two ports and is used solely to extend the reach of the network. In the past, repeaters were seen most often in 10Base2 or 10Base5 bus networks to allow the total network size to extend beyond the restrictions imposed by the media. You can still purchase simple two-port repeaters for 10BaseT and 100BaseT networks. More commonly, multiport repeaters (or "hubs") are used in twisted-pair networks. Simple two-port repeaters follow all of the same rules as do multiport repeaters, which are discussed in the next section of this book. The only differences are the number of ports and the availability of advanced features, which are more likely to appear on multiport repeaters/hubs than on simple two-port repeaters.

One category of repeaters bears special mention. Long-haul repeaters claim to extend your network distance well beyond the specifications for the media, by as much as 600 or more yards. While these products may work in some situations, they are not compliant with current standards and their use should be carefully considered before implementation. It is probably better to depend on long-distance media, such fiber-optic cabling, and sound network design to accommodate situations that call for connections over a wide area.

HUBS/MULTIPORT REPEATERS

Once twisted-pair media became the mainstay in new LAN installations, hubs emerged as the primary internetworking devices used to connect computers. The tide has been shifting toward layer 2 switches in recent years and will probably continue to do so, but hubs are still an effective and inexpensive way to connect your computers together in a LAN.

In its simplest form, a hub has four or more ports and some indicator lights. It has the relatively simple job of receiving a signal on one port and repeating the signal out all the other ports that have a device connected—hence the term "multiport repeater." The signal is cleaned up, and some retiming and amplification of the signal occurs, so that the signal can travel another 100 meters or whatever distance the media type specifies. Hubs can have many more features than just these basic required functions, however, and it is important to know what is available when choosing or supporting a hub. This section covers the basic features found on most hubs, and then we look at some of the more advanced features that usually cost more but that can be indispensable in supporting your network.

Hubs—Basic Features

When you are shopping for a hub, there are some basic features that you should expect to receive with any device. Of course, the first thing you want to consider is the number of ports on the hub, which can vary from 4 to a maximum of 24 ports on a typical stand-alone hub. There are also chassis-based hubs, sometimes called concentrators, which have slots into which you can plug hub cards. These concentrators have a backplane through which the hub cards communicate. A concentrator is ideal when you have many ports to support or when you need to mix and match features, because slots on the concentrators can accept cards that support different devices or media types. Figure 3-18 shows an example of a stand-alone hub and a chassis-based concentrator. Notice that the concentrator has many free slots for other card types. The hubs pictured, as well as most available hubs in all price ranges, support all of the basic features common to hubs: indicator lights, an AUI or 10Base2 connection, and an uplink port.

16-port stand-alone hub

3

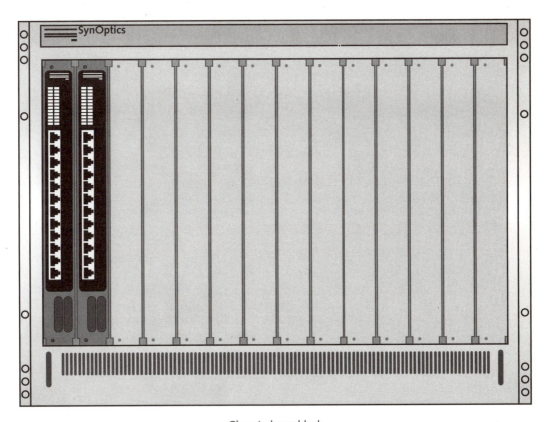

Chassis-based hub

Figure 3-18   Stand-alone and chassis-based hubs

Indicator Lights

Just as NICs have indicator lights to indicate link status and possibly other conditions, hubs usually have indicators for link status, collisions, and activity. If the hub supports two speeds, such as 10 Mbps and 100 Mbps Ethernet, there may be an LED for each port indicating the speed of the connection. There is a link status LED for each port on the hub, which is one of the first places to look if a user reports an inability to connect to the network. In this situation, the user's NIC card can also be checked as previously mentioned. Nevertheless, the hub is often easier to see and reach than the user's PC, which is frequently stuffed underneath desks, making the back of the PC difficult to see. On rare occasions, you may see one side of the cable, either at the NIC or at the hub, showing a good link status, and the other side showing no link. This problem is almost always due to a faulty RJ45 crimp on a patch cable.

Hubs may have only one collision LED or one collision LED for each port. The difference is not too significant—in a shared media environment such as hubs provide, all stations hear all collisions, so one LED is sufficient. Just as with NICs, the collision indicator can give you a general idea about the frequency of collisions in your network.

There may also be one activity LED on each port or a single one for the entire hub. If there is an LED on each port, it may flash whenever the station on that port sends data, so you can get a general idea of which stations are doing the most sending. Hubs that have a single LED to indicate activity will flash the LED whenever any traffic is detected on the network segment. This setup gives you a better idea of how frequently there is traffic on the entire network segment.

Of course, these indicators give you only a very general idea of the activity and collision levels; for more detailed information, you should use a network monitor that can provide actual statistics such as packets per second or bytes per second as well as collision statistics. I use the indicators on a hub to verify workstation connectivity and then as a general guide when I need to look for a collision problem.

The activity light can let you know something else about your network: the frequency of broadcasts. If you are in an area in which no computers are currently in use but you see the activity light blinking frequently, the activity probably comes from broadcast packets that occur periodically with some protocols. If you have large broadcast domains, you may see a lot of activity just from broadcasts on an otherwise little-used network. This information can clue you into the fact that you may want to either make your broadcast domains smaller or change to a protocol that is less dependent on broadcasts. Changing from NetBEUI to TCP/IP, for example, typically reduces the overall broadcasts in a network.

AUI or 10Base2 Connection

Even if your network primarily consists of twisted-pair Category 5 cabling, there may come a time when you need to connect to a different media type. For example, you may need to connect to a remote workstation using 10Base2 due to the distance limitations of twisted-pair (as discussed earlier in this chapter). Alternatively, you may need to connect to a fiber-optic segment of your network. Many hubs come with a 10Base2 connector, an AUI, or both. The AUI gives you the most flexibility, allowing you to connect a transceiver for any media type you need. Even if you do not think that you need this capability today, your requirements may change in the future. This feature is usually inexpensive, so it is best to have it even if you don't need it, rather than not have it when you *do* need it.

3

Uplink Port

An uplink port is a port on a hub through which you can connect another hub in daisy-chain fashion without using a crossover cable. Some hubs designate a port specifically for uplink connections. Other hubs come with a switch or button next to one of the ports that allows you to designate it as a normal port or an uplink port. You need a crossover cable or an uplink port to connect two hubs together because the wiring of transmit and receive pairs on a NIC differs from the wiring on a hub. The RJ45 port on a NIC is wired as a **media-dependent interface (MDI)** device, and the RJ45 port on a hub is wired as an MDI-X device, where the "X" indicates the crossover function.

Table 3-1 shows the wiring for an MDI and MDI-X port. As you can see, pins 1 and 3 on the MDI device are the two transmit pins, and pins 1 and 3 on the MDI-X device are the two receive pins. Pins 3 and 6 on the MDI device are receive, and pins 3 and 6 on the MDI-X device are transmit. This is why you can use a normal straight-through patch cable when connecting a NIC to a hub. The transmit on one side connects to the receive on the other side, which is as it should be.

Table 3-1   MDI and MDI-X wiring scheme

Pin #	MDI Wiring	MDI-X Wiring
1	Xmit +	Rx +
2	Xmit −	Rx −
3	Rx +	Xmit +
4	unused	unused
5	unused	unused
6	Rx −	Xmit −
7	unused	unused
8	unused	unused

If you try to connect two hubs together with a regular patch cable, you would be connecting two MDI-X devices, causing the receive pins on one hub to be connected to the receive pins on the other hub. (The same would happen with the transmit pins.) This situation would be analogous to talking into the earpiece of your telephone while listening to the microphone. The uplink port on a hub changes the wiring on the hub to the MDI type. When you want to connect two hubs together, plug a standard patch cable into the uplink port of one hub (MDI) and into a regular port on the other hub (MDI-X). If the hub is equipped with a switch, rather than a dedicated uplink port, the switch will likely be labeled either Normal/Uplink or MDI/MDI-X. Figure 3-19 shows a hub with a normal/uplink switch. On hubs that have a dedicated uplink port, you generally lose the use of the port next to it because only one of the ports—the uplink port or the normal port—can be used at one time. If you have a hub that has nine ports and one of them is labeled Uplink, then probably you can use only seven of the normal ports. Figure 3-20 shows an example of this type of hub. Port 8 can be used only if the uplink port is not being used.

Figure 3-19   Hubs with normal/uplink switch

Figure 3-20   Hub with dedicated uplink port

Most hubs have the features just discussed, and the hubs that are limited to those basic features can be had at a reasonable price. Some of the advanced features found on certain hubs can add substantially to the price tag but can be well worth the added cost in a large network.

Hubs—Advanced Features

The advanced features found on some hubs are designed to provide easier management, troubleshooting, reliability, or connectivity, or a combination of these features. Many hubs have several or all of the advanced features we will discuss. The features that are most commonly found on advanced hubs include stackability, 10/100 autosensing, fiber-optic ports, SNMP management, and autopartitioning. The first three features are important for ease of connectivity, and the last two aid in management and troubleshooting.

Stackable Hubs

A hub is considered **stackable** when there is a method, usually through a proprietary cable, to connect hubs together such that the entire stack of hubs counts as only one repeater in the 5-4-3 repeater rule. (The 5-4-3 rule is discussed in detail later in this chapter.) The connection used in stackable hubs differs from the use of an uplink port because with an uplink port, each connected hub acts as a separate repeater.

By using stackable hubs, you can connect many more hubs together, allowing for more stations on a network segment. The cable that is used to connect stackable hubs together is usually proprietary and can be used only with a single manufacturer's hubs. Thus the downside to stackable hubs is that all hubs in one stack must be from the same manufacturer. There is usually a limit to the number of hubs that can be stacked together, with that number being manufacturer dependent. For example, Nortel Network's Baystack hubs allows as many as ten 24-ports to be stacked. Figure 3-21 shows a stack of Nortel Baystack 250 hubs daisy-chained with proprietary cables.

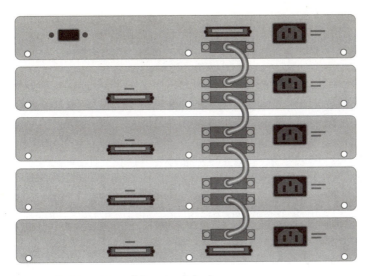

Figure 3-21   Nortel Baystack hubs

Aside from reducing the repeater count as it applies to the 5-4-3 rule, stackable hubs have a management advantage. Hubs can be managed and monitored remotely if the hub supports remote management, but that feature is usually quite expensive. Conversely, a stack of hubs can have a single hub with built-in management, allowing the entire stack to be managed through the single managed hub.

10/100 Autosensing

If a hub is 10/100 autosensing, both 10-Mbps and 100-Mbps devices can be connected to the hub and the hub will detect the speed and link at the appropriate rate. If you want to upgrade your network from an all 10-Mbps network to a 100-Mbps network, you can upgrade gradually rather than changing all network devices and NICs at once. Just start installing 10/100 hubs into the network. If the NIC in the connected workstation supports 100 Mbps, the hub will detect that speed and adjust the port accordingly. If the NIC is only 10 Mbps, the hub will run at that speed. Ideally, you should upgrade your servers to 100 Mbps first, as your network will gain the most advantage if the servers are running at a faster rate. Occasionally, a hub and NIC will fail to detect the correct speed. In this case, they usually fall back to 10 Mbps. Some hubs allow you to force a port to the 100 Mbps speed rather than relying on autosensing. If you do so, you must also force the NIC card to 100 Mbps by using the Network Control Panel and the NIC driver properties.

Fiber-Optic Ports

Some hubs come with a pair of fiber-optic ports as a means to connect the hub or hub stack to a campus backbone over a long distance. You can usually accomplish this goal by purchasing a fiber-optic transceiver and connecting it to an AUI port on the hub if available. It is more convenient to have the fiber ports be built in, however. This feature is usually found only in high-end hubs that also have some or all of the other advanced features discussed here.

SNMP Management

Simple Network Management Protocol (SNMP) is a TCP/IP standard that specifies a method for network devices such as hubs, switches, routers, and NICs to gather statistical information about the network and provide for remote management of the devices. SNMP enables network managers to configure, monitor, and even upgrade network devices from a remote management station equipped with network management software.

A hub or hub stack equipped with an SNMP module can send statistics about the network segment or even each hub port to the management station. This information, because it is based on the TCP/IP protocol, can be sent across LANs or even WANs, permitting the network manager to examine statistics such as utilization, error rates, and collision rates from across the building or across the continent. The network manager can also get a real-time graphical view of the hub or hub stack, including the status of each indicator light.

Recently, this feature was extremely helpful to me in tracking down a workstation that was sending a broadcast storm onto the network. By identifying the port from which the broadcasts were originating, I could easily instruct a technician who was posted in an area near the hub to unplug the patch panel from that particular port. What if I didn't have a technician in the area or, for that matter, what if no one was in the immediate area of the hub? The next section explains what could have been done in such a case.

Port Partitioning

Port partitioning on a hub disconnects the port from the rest of the hub, such that no data is repeated out that port and no data that goes into the partitioned port is repeated to any other port. If a port on a hub is the source of excessive error packets or broadcasts that cause your network to grind to a halt, the port can be partitioned, thereby cutting it off from the rest of the hub and the network. Ports can be partitioned remotely if the hub supports SNMP, or they can be partitioned manually through a console connection to the hub. In the previous example, I could have used SNMP to partition the port from which the broadcast storm was originating rather than calling a technician to unplug the cable. Some hubs support autopartitioning as well, in which the hub will automatically partition a port from which an excessive number of errors is originating.

Port Segmentation

Hubs that feature **port segmentation** allow an administrator to create two or more groups of ports on a hub or hub stack that operate in separate collision domains. This scheme permits you to reduce the size of your collision domains while utilizing more cost-effective, high-density hubs rather than purchasing several smaller hubs. Normally, all of the ports on a hub or hub stack belong to the same collision domain. Port segmentation allows you to break the larger collision domain into two or more smaller collision domains.

For example, imagine that you have a 24-port SNMP managed hub in which 20 of the ports are utilized. Perhaps 20 computers on one collision domain was a workable number a year ago, but the usage of that network segment has increased significantly since high-speed Internet access was installed and a client/server database was implemented. Currently, you are seeing a high rate of collisions due to the higher utilization. One way to solve the problem is to buy a second hub and connect each hub to a switch. That option is expensive, especially if you want to maintain management over the hub via SNMP, and it wastes several ports. Another option is to use port segmentation, in which you group 12 of the ports into one collision domain and the other 12 ports into another collision domain. Then, with two of the unused ports, you connect each segment into a four-port switch. Figure 3-22 demonstrates the use of a segmented hub and a switch.

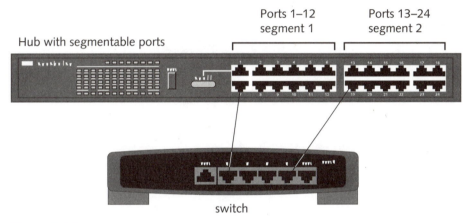

Figure 3-22 Using port segmentation

Hubs are the most common Physical layer devices, though others exist as well. We discuss transceivers next, and then examine media converters.

TRANSCEIVERS

A transceiver is used when an Ethernet device does not contain the signaling electronics for a particular media type. A transceiver has a 15-pin female connector to plug into an AUI port on one end; the other end has a connector for the media type in use. Figure 3-23 shows three transceivers for the most common media types. The 10BaseFL fiber-optic transceiver could be used to bring fiber-optic cable to the desktop if the NIC had an AUI connector. The 10BaseT transceiver is frequently used on devices such as routers that do not specify the media type, such as Cisco 2500 series routers. The 10Base2 transceiver might be used to connect a thinwire cable segment to a 10BaseT hub that has an AUI.

15-pin AUI
connector

10BaseFL optic transceiver

10BaseT transceiver

10Base2 transceiver

Figure 3-23   Fiber-optic, 10BaseT, and 10Base2 transceivers

Transceivers are relatively simple devices, and one rarely has occasion to troubleshoot a transceiver. There are some things to look for if a device with a transceiver is not working properly. Transceivers usually have a power-on LED that will be lit if the transceiver is correctly plugged into the AUI of the device and the device is turned on. If this LED is not lit, make sure that the transceiver is properly seated on the AUI connector, and, of course, verify that the device is turned on. Transceivers also have link status and activity LEDs just as NICs and hubs do, which work just like the LEDs on those devices.

One feature of an Ethernet transceiver bears special mention. An Ethernet transceiver has a switch to enable a function called **Signal Quality Error (SQE) Test**. The SQE Test finds out whether the collision detection circuitry on the transceiver is working correctly. It sends a signal on the collision detection wires to the Ethernet interface after every packet transmission, thereby testing the collision detection mechanism after every packet transmission. Because this signal is sent so regularly, it is sometimes called a heartbeat signal. The signal is sent during the required dead time between each packet transmission, so there is no ill effect on performance on most devices. However, the SQE Test must be disabled if the transceiver is used on a repeater—a repeater cannot expect to have any dead time between packets as a packet may be sent by any of the connected workstations at any time. If the SQE Test is enabled on a repeater, you may see extremely slow performance because a repeater may interpret the SQE Test signal as a collision and respond by sending a jam signal. This action will result in what looks like excessive collisions on the network. For Ethernet NICs, routers, and other internetworking devices that use an AUI, the recommendation is to enable the SQE Test on the transceiver. For simple repeaters and hubs, disable the SQE Test.

3

MEDIA CONVERTERS

Media converters contain electronics and connectors that convert the signals produced by one media type to the signals required by another media type. For example, if you use fiber-optic cable to connect two buildings together but your switch, hub, or router interfaces are designed for twisted-pair only, you can use a media converter on each side to transition from twisted-pair to fiber-optic and back to twisted-pair. Figure 3-24 depicts an example of how this conversion might work.

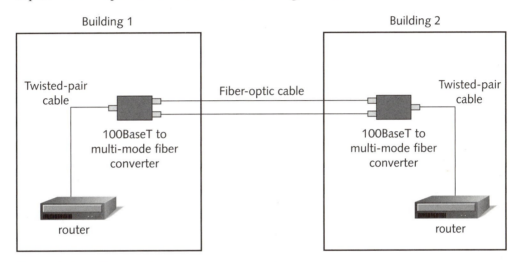

Figure 3-24   Fiber-optic to twisted-pair media conversion

Very often, a media converter is a less expensive solution—particularly where fiber is concerned—than purchasing the network device with a fiber-optic interface. The types of media converters you are most likely to run across include the following:

- 10Base2 to 10BaseT
- 10Base2 to multimode fiber-optic
- 10BaseT to multimode fiber-optic
- 100BaseT to multimode fiber-optic
- Single-mode fiber to multimode fiber

These devices are relatively reliable, and troubleshooting is primarily limited to being sure that you have connectors fastened securely. Like transceivers, these devices also have link status indicators, so you can determine whether your media conversion is occurring properly by referring to the link LEDs.

One problem that I encountered with a 100BaseT-to-multimode fiber converter had a very simple solution once the problem was identified. An entire section of the campus network was isolated from the rest of the network. This section of campus was connected via multimode fiber-optic cable, and there were media converters at each end going to a 100-Mbps switch that used 100BaseT media—much like Figure 3-24 except that the devices were switches instead of routers. The first thing I checked was the fiber-optic connections, then the patch cables that went from the media converters to the switch. Everything looked good, but there was no link status. The media converters were up on a shelf and difficult to see, so I climbed up to see their status. There was no status; in fact, there was not even a power indication. These devices draw power from a standard AC adapter plugged into a wall socket. I looked behind the rack and there was the AC adapter plug lying on the floor. Apparently a cleaning crew (or perhaps the network goblins present in almost every organization) had accidentally kicked the cable out of the socket and failed to replace it. Needless to say, I found a more secure method of plugging in the AC adapters and let the cleaning crew know that the room was no longer their responsibility.

SUPPORTING 10-MBPS ETHERNET HUBS

Now that you are familiar with the components of the Physical layer, let's discuss some of the support issues involved with building networks at the Physical layer. The rules for implementing Ethernet networks are specified in the IEEE 802.3 standard. This standard was originally designed around 10 Mbps Ethernet networks but now covers operation at 100 Mbps and, more recently, 1000 Mbps. This section covers the use of 10-Mbps Ethernet hubs and explains some of the reasons behind the rules governing their use, such as the 5-4-3 rule.

The 5-4-3 Rule

The 5-4-3 rule states that in a 10-Mbps Ethernet network, you may have a maximum of five cable segments between two stations, and a maximum of four repeaters in the path between two stations; only three of the five cable segments may be populated with network devices such as computers. The 5-4-3 rule is usually defined in this way, but some further definitions are required. The Ethernet standard defines two types of cable segment: **link segments** and **mixing segments**. A link segment is one in which there is a maximum of two **medium attachment units (MAUs)** connected together by a full-duplex medium. A MAU is a device like a transceiver that connects to an AUI; it allows the medium to attach to the network. In the case of a 10BaseT hub, each port is considered a MAU. The term "full-duplex medium" can be misleading. It does not mean that the link segment must operate in full-duplex mode, but that the medium must contain a separated transmit and receive path, as is the case with 10BaseT cabling or fiber-optic cabling. Coaxial cabling does not meet the definition of a full-duplex medium because there is only one conductor to carry both the transmit and receive signals; therefore, it cannot be used as a link segment. A mixing segment is one in which there can be more than two MDIs attached to the segment, as is possible with a coax 10Base2 segment.

We now can refine the 5-4-3 rule even more. There may be a maximum of five cabling segments between stations, with a maximum of four repeaters in the path between stations. If there are five cabling segments between stations, only three of those segments may be mixing segments. The remainder of the segments must be link segments. Let's look at two scenarios: one in which all cabling is 10BaseT and another in which the network mixes 10BaseT, fiber-optic, and coax media.

Figure 3-25 presents the first scenario in which all segments are 10BaseT, or link segments. As there are no mixing segments (that is, there are no coax or 10Base2 cables), the only restriction here is that there can be a maximum of five cabling segments between workstations and four repeaters in the path. The path between Workstation A and Workstation B, which meets that requirement, is the worst-case scenario in this network.

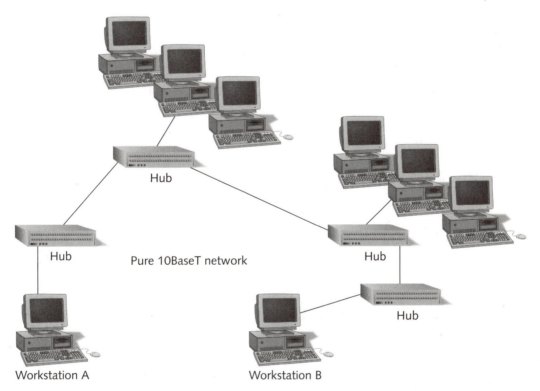

Figure 3-25   Four-repeater 10BaseT network

Figure 3-26 presents the second scenario in which fiber-optic cable is used along with 10Base2 and 10BaseT media. Fiber-optic cable can be used as a link segment because it has both a transmit fiber and a receive fiber. In this scenario, the path between Workstation A and Workstation B is still five cable segments and four repeaters. This network can range over a wider area than the one in Figure 3-25 thanks to the use of fiber-optic cable as link segments. Notice that the segment between Hub 1 and Repeater 2 consists of 10Base2 coax cable. It still counts as a mixing segment—even though there are no stations attached, a segment can be considered a link segment only if it has separate transmit and receive paths. Do not think that four repeaters is the maximum number that your network can have. This restriction applies only if four repeaters are in the path between two workstations. The network in Figure 3-26 could be extended by connecting another hub or repeater to Hub 1 in the diagram. The same is true for Repeater 2.

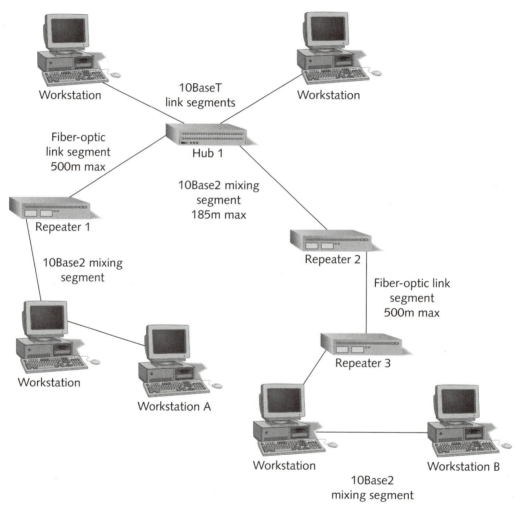

Figure 3-26   Four-repeater network with multiple media types

Fiber-Optic Cable and Repeaters

Since we mentioned fiber-optic cable, let's go over a few rules for using fiber-optic cabling in your network. Every media type has a maximum length restriction between repeaters or end stations. The length restriction on copper media types is consistent no matter what your network configuration is. In other words, 10Base2 always has a maximum length of 185 meters per segment, and 10BaseT always has a maximum segment length of 100 meters. Fiber-optic cable is not so simple. As previously discussed, the fiber-optic, 10-Mbps Ethernet standard of 10BaseF is divided into three subcategories: 10BaseFL, 10BaseFP, and 10BaseFB. The maximum segment length for 10BaseFB and 10BaseFL is 2000 meters; for 10BaseFP, it is 1000 meters. These maximums apply only in a network in which there are two or fewer repeaters in the path between end stations. To make this idea easier to understand, Table 3-2 lists the maximum lengths for fiber-optic segments between repeaters.

Table 3-2   Maximum repeater-to-repeater cable lengths

	Four Repeaters	Three Repeaters	Two or Fewer Repeaters
10BaseFB	500 meters	1000 meters	2000 meters
10BaseFL	500 meters	1000 meters	2000 meters
10BaseFP	300 meters	700 meters	1000 meters

The preceeding rule applies only to fiber-optic cable that connects two repeaters. Just to complicate matters, another set of rules applies regarding the use of fiber-optic cable. The maximum cable lengths allowed if fiber is used to connect workstations or other devices to a hub, also referred to as DTE-to-repeater links, is 500 meters in four-repeater networks in which no link exceeds 500 meters; it is 400 meters in three-repeater networks. In networks with fewer than three repeaters, the maximum length of 2000 meters for 10BaseFL and 1000 meters for 10BaseFP applies. 10BaseFB is not used for DTE-to-repeater links.

Stacked Versus Uplinked Hubs

Earlier we saw that hubs can be stacked by using a proprietary cable that acts as a backplane through the hubs which communicate. Hubs that are stacked together count as a single repeater with respect to the 5-4-3 rule. Hubs that are connected together via an uplink port, however, each count as a repeater. Clearly, stacked hubs permit you to install many more workstations in a network without violating the 5-4-3 rule. For example, you could stack three 24-port hubs together and have as many as four of these hub stacks linked together, which gives you a total of twelve 24-port hubs permitting 288 devices to be placed on the network. Figure 3-27 depicts a network using stacked hubs that complies with the 5-4-3 rule as well as one using only uplink ports, which violates the rule.

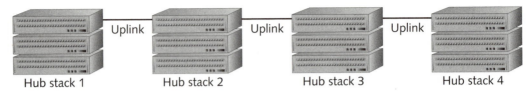

Four stacks of three hubs each
comply with the 5-4-3 rule.

Uplink   Uplink   Uplink

Hub stack 1   Hub stack 2   Hub stack 3   Hub stack 4

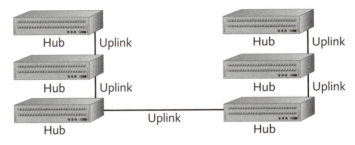

Six hubs connected with the uplink port
violate the 5-4-3 rule.

Hub   Uplink   Hub   Uplink

Hub   Uplink   Hub   Uplink

              Uplink
Hub   Hub

Figure 3-27   Stacked hubs versus uplinked hubs

Now that you have a good understanding of the rules for implementing 10-Mbps Ethernet networks, let's look at why these rules exist in the first place.

Round-Trip Collision Delay

One of the key factors limiting the length and number of your cable segments and the number of repeaters in the path between stations is a value called the **round-trip collision delay**. The round-trip collision delay is the amount of time that it takes for a sending station to send the first bit in a frame, have that bit collide with another station's attempt to send a signal, and have the first station hear the collision. Figure 3-28 shows a simple network in which Workstation A has sent a frame. Just before the first bit from that frame arrives at Workstation B, Workstation B sends a frame and a collision occurs. Workstation B will send a jam signal because it will detect the collision first. When Workstation A hears the jam signal, the round-trip collision delay time is complete. This amount of time must not be longer than the amount of time that it takes Workstation A to completely transmit 64 bytes of data—the minimum-size Ethernet frame. This time is referred to as 575 **bit-times**. A bit-time is the amount of time it takes a bit to travel about 20 meters in copper, or 0.1 μs (100 ns). But 64 bytes of data amounts to only 512 bits (64 × 8), so why is the value 575?

Every frame that is sent has bits in the beginning of the frame called the **preamble**. A preamble allows an Ethernet receiver to become synchronized with the sending station. It consists of a string of alternating ones and zeroes, which the receiver detects and prepares for the incoming frame. The preamble ends with a pair of binary ones to signal that what follows is the actual frame data. Without the preamble, an Ethernet receiver may miss the beginning of a frame. There are 64 bits of preamble in an Ethernet frame, so adding this 64 bits to the 512 bits in a minimum-size Ethernet frame gives us 576 actual bits that are contained in the minimum-size Ethernet frame. If an Ethernet device successfully sends 576 bits without detecting a collision, the device assumes that the frame made it to the destination successfully. Therefore, the maximum delay time must be one less than this value—575.

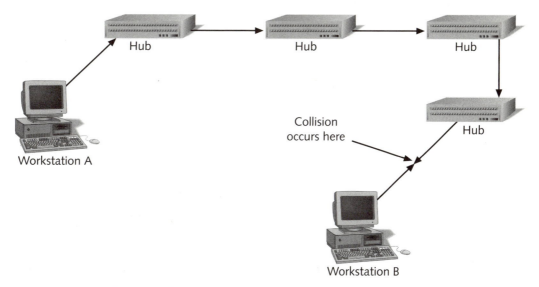

Figure 3-28   Collision at the far end of the network

The round-trip collision delay time is calculated by adding up the time that it takes for a bit to travel through all cable segments and through all repeaters to the farthest destination. The time it takes for a bit to travel this distance is called the **path delay value (PDV)**. The path delay value must be calculated from sender to receiver. If it exceeds 575 bit times, late collisions can occur. Ethernet devices are not required to resend a frame if a collision occurs after they successfully transmit the first 64 bytes of a frame. Late collisions will result in lost frames or retransmissions requested by upper-layer protocols. An excellent resource for more information on how to calculate the PDV and round-trip collision delay can be found at *www.ots.utexas.edu/ethernet/*. If you sit down with your calculator and calculate the round-trip collision delay for a proposed network topology, you may find that you can violate some of the rules with regard to segment length or numbers of repeaters. However, another requirement must be passed before a given topology is considered workable—the interframe gap.

The Interframe Gap

The **interframe gap** is the amount of time between the end of one frame on the medium and the beginning of the next frame. Remember how CSMA/CD works? A station must listen before sending a frame. The station must hear silence on the media for a minimum of 9.6 μs before the line is considered silent and safe to transmit on. This 9.6 μs comes from the fact that Ethernet devices need some time to switch their circuitry from transmit mode to receive mode, so this delay between frames guarantees that a frame will not be missed. A time of 9.6 μs allows 96 bit-times of interframe gap. This gap time is reduced somewhat with each repeater that the frame passes through because of the retiming that occurs at each repeater. This retiming usually increases the length of the packet preamble. The resulting decrease in the interframe gap is known as interframe gap shrinkage or interpacket gap shrinkage. A maximum of 49 bit-times may be lost in the interframe gap before the amount of time between frames becomes too little to guarantee that end stations will be able to properly receive all frames. The URL mentioned earlier provides information about calculating the total interframe gap shrinkage for a particular topology.

As you can see, the rules for Ethernet topologies are based on physics (the speed of a bit traveling across a medium) and electronic limitations (the speed at which a device can switch from sending to receiving mode). The length limitations stated for various media types and the number of repeaters allowed in a path are meant to provide worst-case scenarios such that, if you follow the rules, Ethernet will work. Careful calculations of a particular topology may let you break some of the rules and still allow Ethernet to work. But be careful—Fast Ethernet has considerably more stringent rules and what worked with 10-Mbps Ethernet may not work with 100-Mbps or 1000-Mbps Ethernet.

SUPPORTING 100BASET NETWORKS

The 100BaseT standard is specified in the IEEE 802.3u document. Because 100-Mbps Ethernet networks transmit bits 10 times faster than 10-Mbps networks do, many of the topology rules are more stringent. Before we go into those differences, let's examine the 100BaseT specifications. Within the 100BaseT standard are three different specifications for media: 100BaseTX, 100BaseT4, and 100BaseFX.

100BaseTX

The 100BaseTX standard specifies full-duplex 100-Mbps Ethernet over Category 5 or better UTP. The standard also permits Type 1 shielded twisted-pair cabling. Data is carried on two pairs of wires as in 10BaseT Ethernet, but is encoded on the wire differently. Whereas 10BaseT Ethernet uses Manchester Encoding, which is based on signal transitions, 100BaseTX is based on an encoding scheme called 4B/5B, which was originally developed for encoding signals for FDDI. The details of the encoding schemes are beyond the scope of this text, but for an excellent discussion of these schemes, refer to *www.optimized.com/COMPENDI/FE-Encod.htm*. For those managers wishing to upgrade from 10BaseT to a 100-Mbps network, 100BasetTX is the most logical choice because the connectors and wiring are identical to those for 10BaseT.

3

100BaseT4

The 100BaseT4 standard permits 100-Mbps bandwidth over Categories 3, 4, 5, and higher UTP cable. 100BaseT4 can achieve faster transfer rates with a lower category cable because it uses all four pairs of wire rather than only two. Three pairs of wire are used for transmitting and receiving data using an 8B6T encoding scheme, and the fourth pair is used for carrier and collision detection. Standard RJ45 connectors are used. This version of 100-Mbps Ethernet is not nearly as common as 100BaseTX but is available if, for example, you have a big investment in a Category 4 cable plant and cannot afford to replace it with Category 5 cable. The wiring of the four pairs is done according to EIA/TIA standards. Thus, if you wired your network correctly for 10BaseT Ethernet by using either 568-A or 568-B wiring, your cable plant is 100BaseT4 ready.

100BaseFX

The third 100 Mbps Ethernet standard uses two multimode fiber-optic cables. The IEEE 802.3u standard permits SC, ST, and MIC fiber-optic connector types, with SC-connectors being preferred. 100BaseFX also is based on the FDDI 4B/5B encoding scheme for representing bits.

100 Mbps Ethernet Hub and Segment Length Rules

As mentioned, the rules for 100-Mbps Ethernet are somewhat more stringent than those for 10-Mbps Ethernet. There is no 5-4-3 rule, and the length limits on fiber-optic media are significantly shorter. We will look at the rules for hubs and repeaters first and then examine some of the cable segment length limitations for a variety of topologies.

100-Mbps Repeater Rules

The 100BaseT standard, which applies to all three subcategories mentioned above, defines two classes of repeaters: Class I and Class II. The use of Class I repeaters limits the total number of repeaters in a collision domain to exactly one. This restriction is a big difference from the four repeaters in a path allowed in 10-Mbps Ethernet. You may still use stackable hubs to increase the total number of stations on a 100-Mbps network, but if the hubs are Class I repeaters, you may use only one hub stack. Class I repeaters allow different signal types such as 100BaseTX and 100BaseT4 in the same collision domain and can provide translation between these types.

Class II repeaters double the size of the collision domain to a maximum of two repeaters. They permit only a single signal type, so you may not mix 100BaseTX, 100BaseT4 and 100BaseFX in one collision domain using Class II repeaters.

Because the number of repeaters is quite limited in a 100BaseT environment, most networks employ switches to interconnect repeaters or repeater stacks, thereby increasing the number of collision domains. Recall that each switch port is its own collision domain.

Maximum Segment Lengths for 100-Mbps Ethernet

The rules for maximum segment lengths with 100-Mbps Ethernet are somewhat complicated. Rather than try to describe them, Figure 3-29 demonstrates several topologies using Class I and II repeaters and using all copper, all fiber, or mixed media types.

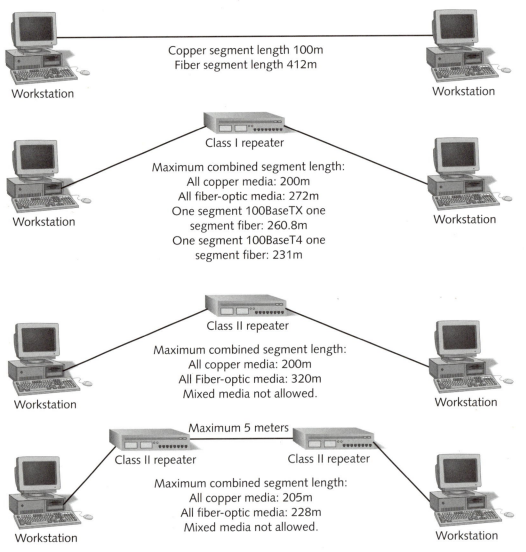

Copper segment length 100m
Fiber segment length 412m

Workstation   Workstation

Class I repeater

Maximum combined segment length:
All copper media: 200m
All fiber-optic media: 272m
One segment 100BaseTX one
segment fiber: 260.8m
One segment 100BaseT4 one
segment fiber: 231m

Workstation   Workstation

Class II repeater

Maximum combined segment length:
All copper media: 200m
All Fiber-optic media: 320m
Mixed media not allowed.

Workstation   Workstation

Maximum 5 meters

Class II repeater   Class II repeater

Maximum combined segment length:
All copper media: 205m
All fiber-optic media: 228m
Mixed media not allowed.

Workstation   Workstation

Figure 3-29   100-Mbps Ethernet topologies

To extend your network beyond these limitations, you will need to include a switch in your network. The link between a hub and a switch for 100BaseTX and 100BaseT4 is limited to the normal 100 meters. Fiber-optic media can be used to link a hub to a switch by using segment lengths up to 160 meters. Longer-distance links can be achieved by linking switches together with full-duplex fiber-optic cable at distances of up to 2 kilometers. Figure 3-30 depicts networks using switches to interconnect hubs with fiber links, thereby extending the reach of the network.

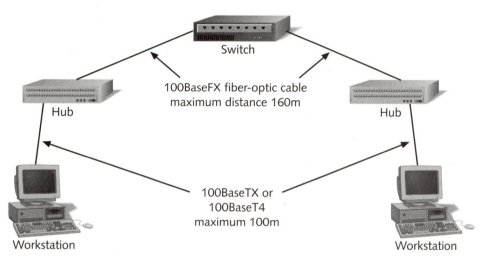

Figure 3-30   Extending the distance with switches

As you can see, there is a lot to remember when building and supporting an Ethernet network at the Physical layer. Careful consideration must be given to the devices and media types you choose when upgrading, troubleshooting, and supporting a network's Physical layer. If you take the time to study the rules and weigh the advantages and disadvantages of various media and devices, however, you will build a solid Physical layer. You will also have the knowledge necessary to make changes or recognize problems that involve Physical layer components.

CHAPTER SUMMARY

❑ The Physical layer provides the foundation for a reliable, high-performance LAN. Network media selection, installation, termination, and testing all play vital roles in determining whether your network will be able to support your organization's current and future information system needs.

❑ Physical layer components include network media, along with the associated connectors and patch panels, and devices such as NICs, hubs, transceivers, and media converters.

❑ Copper wire media can be classified into two categories: coaxial cable and twisted-pair. There are two popular coaxial cable types used in Ethernet networks, Thinnet and Thicknet. Twisted-pair cabling is classified into five grades, Category 1 through Category 5. Only Categories 3 through 5 are acceptable for Ethernet LAN applications.

- Coaxial cable is no longer used in new network installations but still has a large installed base. It is limited to 10 Mbps of bandwidth and can be difficult to troubleshoot due to the bus topology. Coaxial cable's main strengths are long cable segment lengths and good resistance to interference.

- Unshielded twisted-pair Category 5E cabling is the current standard for copper cabling. It supports bandwidths up to 1000 Mbps. The cable segment length is limited to 100 meters but can be extended with repeaters. Careful attention must be given to proper termination of twisted-pair cabling because of the lack of a shield to prevent EMI.

- Fiber-optic cabling is slowly gaining acceptance as a desktop medium. It is immune to outside interference sources and can be run over a much greater distance than can copper cabling. The bandwidth capabilities of fiber range into the gigabits, which make it an ideal medium for network backbones.

- Devices operating at the Physical layer of the network are primarily concerned with two things: How are bit signals encoded, and what should be done with the bit signals once they are received? Four of the more common Physical layer devices are network interface cards, repeaters and hubs, transceivers, and media converters.

- NICs provide computers and other devices with an interface to the network media. They also handle the details of receiving and sending bits and accessing the media. The importance of selecting appropriate network interface cards for your workstations is often overlooked. There are several options available for NICs, and the choices you make can affect your network's performance and manageability.

- A hub typically has four or more ports and some indicator lights. It has the relatively simple job of receiving a signal on one port and repeating the signal out of all the other ports that have a device connected. The advanced features found on some hubs are designed to provide easier management, troubleshooting, reliability, or connectivity, or a combination of these capabilities, as many hubs offer several or all of the advanced features. The features that are most commonly on advanced hubs include stackability, 10/100 autosensing, fiber-optic ports, SNMP management, and autopartitioning.

- A transceiver is used when an Ethernet device does not contain the signaling electronics for a particular media type. Transceivers are relatively simple devices and rarely need troublshooting. Nevertheless, there are some things to look for if a device with a transceiver is not working properly.

- Media converters contain electronics and connectors that convert the signals produced by one media type into the signals required by another media type. If you use fiber-optic cable to connect two buildings together but your switch, hub, or router interfaces are designed only for twisted-pair media, you can use a media converter.

- The rules for implementing Ethernet networks are specified in the IEEE 802.3 standard. This standard was originally designed around 10-Mbps Ethernet networks but now covers operation at 100 Mbps, and more recently, 1000 Mbps. This chapter covered the use of 10-Mbps Ethernet hubs and explained some of the reasons underlying the rules governing their use, such as the 5-4-3 rule.

◻ The 100BaseT standard is specified in the IEEE 802.3u document. Because 100-Mbps Ethernet networks transmit bits 10 times faster than 10 Mbps networks do, many of the topology rules are more stringent. The 100BaseTX standard specifies full-duplex 100-Mbps Ethernet over Category 5 or better UTP. The standard also permits Type 1 shielded twisted-pair cabling.

3

KEY TERMS

attachment unit interface (AUI) — A 15-pin interface that allows you to connect a transceiver that supports the media type of your choice.

attenuation — The loss of signal strength as a signal travels the length of the media.

bandwidth — The amount of data that a medium is capable of carrying, measured in bits per second.

bit-time — The amount of time it takes a bit to travel about 20 meters in copper, or 0.1 μs (100 ns).

cancellation — The effect that occurs when wires carrying a differential signal are twisted tightly together, resulting in the cancellation of each other's electrical field.

cleaver — A sharp ceramic or diamond-edged cutting tool used to prepare fiber-optic cables for termination.

coaxial cable — A cable type that consists of a single conductor inside a layer of insulating material, surrounded by a metal shield and plastic outer jacket.

crossover cable — A cable that has been wired purposely with transposed pairs.

crosstalk — The leaking of signals from one wire onto another wire.

daisy-chain — The connection of two or more devices with what amounts to a continuous line of cable without connecting to a central device.

Desktop Management Interface (DMI) — A standard framework for managing and tracking components in a PC or server.

differential signal — Two wires are used to send the same signal using different polarities.

electromagnetic field — The energy field that surrounds a conductor carrying electrical signals.

Electromagnetic Interference (EMI) — Interference to data signals caused by the magnetic field of nearby electrical cables or equipment.

encoding — The method used to represent a 0 or 1 bit on the physical media.

full-duplex — Allows a device to send and receive data simultaneously.

half-duplex — Allows a device to send or receive data, but not simultaneously.

impedance — The amount of resistance to the flow of electricity exhibited by a media, measured in ohms.

interframe gap — The amount of time between the end of one frame on the medium and the beginning of the next frame.

light-emitting diodes (LED) — A low-energy light source used in multimode fiber-optic cabling transmitters.

link segment — A segment in which there is a maximum of two medium attachment units connected together by a full-duplex medium.

media converter — Converts signals to a type that can be used by a specified medium.

media-dependent interface (MDI) — The IEEE standard for the interface to unshielded twisted-pair cable.

media-independent interface — A network interface, such as an AUI, that does not have a connector or transceiver for a specific media type.

medium attachment unit (MAU) — A device such as a transceiver that connects to an AUI. The MAU then allows the medium to attach to the network.

minimum bend radius — The amount of cable that must be used to circumvent a 90° angle.

mixing segment — A cable segment in which there can be more than two MDIs attached to the segment, as you have with a coax 10Base2 segment.

path delay value (PDV) — The time it takes for a bit to travel through all cable segments and through all repeaters to the farthest destination.

port partitioning — Disconnecting a port from the rest of the hub such that no data is repeated out that port and no data that goes into the partitioned port is repeated to any other port.

port segmentation — A process that allows an administrator to create two or more groups of ports on a hub or hub stack that operate in separate collision domains.

preamble — A string of alternating ones and zeroes, which the receiver detects and prepares for the incoming frame.

radio frequency interference (RFI) — Interference to data signals caused by radio broadcast sources such as radio transmitters, microwaves, and X-rays.

RJ45 — Registered jack type 45. A common connector used in twisted-pair Ethernet cabling.

round-trip collision delay — The amount of time that it takes for a sending station to send the first bit in a frame, have that bit collide with another station's attempt to send a signal, and have the first station hear the collision.

Signal Quality Error (SQE) Test — A test that ensures that the collision detection circuitry on the transceiver is working correctly.

signal reflection — The phenomenon that occurs when electrical signals travel down a wire and meet a change in impedance such as an open, short, or end of the cable.

Simple Network Management Protocol (SNMP) — A TCP/IP standard that specifies a method for network devices such as hubs, switches, routers, and NICs to gather statistical information about the network and provide for remote management of the device.

split pair — A wiring error in which the differential signals from one circuit are traveling on two different pairs of wires, negating the cancellation effect.

stackable — A hub has this characteristic when there is a method, usually through a proprietary cable, to connect hubs such that the entire stack of hubs counts as only one repeater in the 5-4-3 repeater rule.

TDR (Time Domain Reflectometer) — A device used to measure the length of a cable by measuring the amount of time needed for the signal to reflect back when it meets the end of the cable.

Telecommunications Industry Association/Electronics Industries Association (TIA/EIA) — A standards body governing, among other things, telecommunications wiring in buildings.

3

termination — The method used to end a length of network media, either with a connector or by securing the wires in a jack or patch panel.

thickwire Ethernet — 10 Mbs Ethernet running on a thick coaxial cable; also called Thicknet and 10Base5.

Thinnet — Thinwire Ethernet.

thinwire Ethernet — 10 Mbps Ethernet running on thin coaxial cable, type RG58; also called Thinnet and 10Base2.

transceiver — A device that contains the transmit and receive circuitry and the appropriate connector for the media used.

transposed pair — A wiring error where one end of a cable is terminated according to the 568-A wiring standard and the other end is terminated according to the 568-B standard.

unshielded twisted-pair (UTP) — An unshielded cable type that contains from two to four pairs of wires twisted together.

wake-on-LAN — Allows an administrator to remotely turn on the computer by sending a signal to the NIC.

REVIEW QUESTIONS

1. Which of the following are examples of Physical layer components? (Choose all that apply).

   a. NIC

   b. Protocols

   c. Operating system

   d. Media

2. When installing cable, which of the following is not a determining factor in media selection?

   a. What type of testing equipment you have

   b. The type of operating system that will be implemented

   c. The maximum number of stations you can attach to a cable run

   d. The cost of the media that you have selected

3. EMI is caused by _____.

   a. An as-yet-unexplained phenomenon

   b. Exceeding the maximum amount you can bend the cable around corners

   c. Data traveling at high speeds across the cable

   d. Fluorescent lights and electric generators

4. Which type of cable media is referred to as 10Base2?

   a. Thickwire Ethernet

   b. Thinnet Token Ring

   c. Thinwire Ethernet

   d. Unshielded twisted-pair

5. What is an advantage of using thinwire as your media selection in a bus topology?

   a. You can daisy-chain other workstations with ease.

   b. It has a minimum bend radius of 1 inch.

   c. It has a maximum length of 500 meters.

   d. You can add a workstation without disrupting the network.

6. What is the maximum cable run of a 10Base2 network?

   a. 210 meters

   b. 100 meters

   c. 90 meters

   d. 185 meters

7. What Physical layer device can be used to extend length limitations?

   a. Router

   b. Repeater

   c. Switch

   d. VLAN

8. How many hosts can be attached to a Thinnet cable segment that does not have a repeater?

   a. 25

   b. 30

   c. 35

   d. 40

9. What is the maximum number of hosts that can be attached to any cable segment in a 10Base2 network that uses repeaters?

   a. 30

   b. 60

3

c. 90

d. 120

10. What is the bandwidth specification for Ethernet over coaxial cable?

    a. 1 Mbps

    b. 10 Mbps

    c. 10 Kbps

    d. 100 Mbps

11. What is the function of a terminating resistor?

    a. It prevents an electrical signal from bouncing back after it reaches the end of the wire.

    b. It shields the transmission from EMI and RFI.

    c. It provides for continuous data flow through the LAN even if a cable has been disconnected.

    d. It transmits data along the Thinnet wire.

12. What is a disadvantage of using a 10Base2 network?

    a. The cable is not easy to install.

    b. The cable is not flexible.

    c. It is prone to EMI and crosstalk problems.

    d. It is difficult and time-consuming to troubleshoot.

13. A stub cable segment is _____.

    a. A cable segment with two pieces of cabled joined by a T-connector used to extend the bus

    b. A shorted-out cable segment

    c. A cable segment that does not meet the minimum bend radius

    d. A cable segment with a grounded terminating resistor

14. What is the maximum cable run distance of a 10Base5 cable segment?

    a. 185 meters

    b. 200 meters

    c. 485 meters

    d. 500 meters

15. Thicknet is also known as _____.

    a. 10Base2

    b. 10Base5

    c. 10BaseT

    d. 10BaseE

16. The maximum cable segment length from a hub to a workstation for UTP is
    _____.

    a. 100 meters

    b. 185 meters

    c. 90 meters

    d. 10 meters

17. Which of the following wiring errors will most likely result in crosstalk?

    a. Transposed pair

    b. Crossed pair

    c. Split pair

    d. Twisted-pair

18. EMI will most likely be caused by _____.

    a. Transposed pairs

    b. Coax and twisted-pair in close proximity

    c. Fiber-optic cable near UTP

    d. Electrical cabling in the same conduit as UTP

19. Fiber-optic cabling is most susceptible to _____.

    a. EMI

    b. RFI

    c. Crosstalk

    d. None of the above

20. The device used to measure the length of a copper cable is called a(n)
    _____.

    a. TDR

    b. CRT

    c. OTD

    d. DDT

21. When a network cable is correctly installed at the NIC and hub, you will typically
    see a(n) _____ light on the hub and NIC.

    a. Collision

    b. Attenuation

    c. Link

    d. MDI

22. Name three Physical layer devices.

23. True or False? A transceiver is used to convert from one media type to another.

24. The amount of silent time between frames is called the _____.

25. The minimum-size Ethernet frame is _____.

26. The amount of time required for a bit travel from the sending computer to a computer is _____.

3

HANDS-ON PROJECTS

Project 3-1 Examining Cable

In this activity you will examine cables and find faults. Your instructor has a variety of twisted-pair cables that have various faults. Without using a cable tester:

1. Examine each cable.

2. Make notes on suspected faults that you see.

3. Describe the problem or problems that the faults may cause.

4. Test the cable and note whether your examination and conclusions were accurate.

Project 3-2 Creating and Identifying Faulty Cables

In this activity you will create faulty cables in an effort to fully understand how such errors may occur. This project requires that you work in pairs or small groups.

1. Using UTP Cat-5 cable, make the following types of cables:

   a. Cable with split pairs

   b. Cable with transposed pairs

   c. Cable with crossed pairs

2. Give the cables to your partner or members of your group and have them identify the faults.

Project 3-3 Cable Analysis

In this activity you will use a cable performance analyzer to test Cat-5 cable for crosstalk. This project requires the use of a cable performance analyzer.

1. Get approximately 200 feet of Cat-5 cable.

2. Terminate the cable properly with RJ45 connectors.

3. Test the cable to Cat-5 standards with a performance analyzer.

4. Save or write down the results of the crosstalk test.

5. Cut the RJ45 plug off one end of the cable.

6. Connect new RJ45 plug wires so that you have split pairs.

7. Retest the cable and record the results of the crosstalk test.

8. Was there a difference? Were any other tests different?

Project 3-4 Patch-Panel Termination

1. Your instructor will give you a length of Category 5 cable.

2. Strip off about 1.5 inches of cable jacket.

3. Untwist the wire pairs, leaving the like colors together.

4. Arrange the wires in the order required for the patch panel you are using.

5. Leave at least one twist on the two end pairs, as they will have the most exposed wire.

6. Slip the wires into their appropriate slots on the patch panel, trying to get the jacket as close to the terminator block as possible.

7. Using a punch-down tool, punch down the wires.

8. Compare your work to your classmates' work. See who has the termination with the least amount of wire untwisted and out of the jacket.

Project 3-5 Calculate the Path Delay Value—Part 1

1. Using the Table 3-3, calculate the PDV for the following network:

   a. The sending station is on 100 meters of Cat-5 cable attached to Hub 1.

   b. Hub 1 is attached to Hub 2 with 700 meters of 10BaseFB fiber.

   c. Hub 2 is attached to Hub 3 with 300 meters of 10BaseFL fiber.

   d. The receiving station is on 50 meters of Cat-5 cable attached to Hub 3.

2. To make this calculation, you always start with the sending station, which is the left end segment. The base time specified is a constant value. The max time is the amount of delay that would occur if the segment length is the maximum allowable. If the segment is less than the maximum, you calculate the delay for that segment by adding the base time to the RT delay/meter value multiplied by the number of meters. For example, 50 meters of 10BaseT cable on the left segment is calculated as 15.25 (base) $+ (50 \times 0.113) = 20.9$ bit-times. The mid-segment numbers are used for repeater-to-repeater links, and the right-end segment numbers are used for the destination station link.

3. For segment a, do the calculation of the 100-meter Cat-5 10BaseT segment, which is just 26.55 bit-times because the maximum length of 100 meters is used.

4. For segment b, do the calculation: 24 (base) $+ (0.1 \times 700) = 94$ bit-times.

5. Do the calculations for segment c.

6. Do the calculations for segment d.

7. What is the final PDV? Is this network in spec?

Table 3-3   Round-trip delay values in bit-times

	Max Length (meters)	Left End		Middle Segment		Right End		RT Delay Meter
		Base	Max	Base	Max	Base	Max	
10Base5	500	11.75	55.05	46.5	89.8	169.5	212.8	0.0866
10Base2	185	11.75	30.731	46.5	65.48	169.5	188.48	0.1026
10BaseFB	2000	NA	NA	24	224	NA	NA	0.1
10BaseT	100	15.25	26.55	42	53.3	165	176.3	0.113
10BaseFL	2000	12.25	212.25	33.5	233.5	156.5	356.5	0.1
Excess AUI	48	0	4.88	0	4.88	0	4.88	0.1026

Project 3-6 Calculate the Path Delay Value—Part 2

1. Assume that 100 meters of UTP cable connects a workstation to Hub 1. Calculate the path delay value for this cable segment.

2. Assume that 500 meters of 10BaseFB fiber connects Hub 1 to Hub 2. Calculate the PDV for this segment.

3. Assume that 100 meters of UTP cable connects a workstation to Hub 2. Calculate the PDV for this segment.

4. Add all of the PDVs and write down the total. Is the network within specifications? How do you know?

CASE PROJECTS

Case 3-1 Describe Possible Causes for Common Cable Faults

Given the list of cable problems below, list the possible causes.

1. Crosstalk with Cat-5 cabling

2. Attenuation with Cat-5 cabling

3. High error rates with Cat-5 cabling

4. No connection with 10Base2 cabling

5. No connection with Cat-5 cabling

6. Working connection at 10 Mbps, no connection at 100 Mbps

7. High error rates with fiber-optic cabling

8. No connection with fiber-optic cabling

Case 3-2 Network Tour and Cable Identification

Your instructor will give you a tour of your school network. Identify as many different cabling types as you can that are used at your school. Look for potential problem areas (excessive bend, cabling near EMI sources, poor termination, and so on) and note them. Write a report describing how your school network cabling could be improved.

Case 3-3 Research Network Media Developments

New advances in networking occur all of the time. As a future network technician or administrator, it is your job to keep abreast of the latest developments. Using magazines or the Internet, research two recent developments in network media. Write a report on your findings and present it to the class.

Case 3-4 Cabling Recommendations for Sails and Snails Industries

Sails and Snails Industries is adding a new wing to its offices. It will be fully networked, running at speeds ranging from 10 Mbps to 100 Mbps. It has been determined that no cabling segment will need to be longer than 250 feet. Sails and Snails Industries wants to adhere to the latest standards in cabling. What type of cabling do you recommend? What tests should be performed on the cabling? It has been determined that approximately 30,000 feet of cabling will be required. Research the cost of the cabling. Did you find any major differences in costs among vendors? If so, why do you think the differences exist?

Case 3-5 Design a Topology That Violates the 575 Bit-Time Rule

Come up with a network topology that does not meet the 575 bit-time requirement. Sketch this topology and explain why it does not meet the requirement. Challenge the class to fix the topology in a way that will meet the requirement without decreasing the size of the network or reducing the number of stations possible.

Case 3-6 Research a Variety of Hubs

Using network catalogs or Web sites, research the available hubs. Come up with at least six different hubs that vary in number of ports and that range from having only the basic features discussed in this chapter to having many of the advanced features. Write a report about the various hubs you have researched, describing the differences in features and price and explaining under what circumstances you might use the hubs.

4

SUPPORTING THE DATA LINK LAYER

> **After reading this chapter and completing the exercises, you will be able to:**
>
> ◆ Identify the role of the Data Link layer
>
> ◆ Describe the network components that work at the Data Link layer of the OSI model
>
> ◆ Describe the components and characteristics of an Ethernet frame and understand the importance of having a thorough knowledge of these components
>
> ◆ Support network interface cards and understand the options and modes of their operation
>
> ◆ Describe the role of Ethernet switches and know how to support a network using Ethernet switches
>
> ◆ Use a protocol analyzer to capture frames and understand the situations in which a protocol analyzer may be an effective troubleshooting tool
>
> ◆ Understand the mechanics and rationale for capturing Ethernet frames

I can hear you now: "Oh no, not the Data Link layer again! How much can we possibly talk about the Data Link layer? There isn't much to see or touch; all the 'touchable' stuff is done at the Physical layer, and all of the real configuration challenges occur at the Network layer where IP addressing and routers can be found. So why don't we just skip this chapter and move on to some more interesting subjects?"

Not so fast. The Data Link layer, while seemingly uninteresting, does a lot of work that you never see. In addition, its ability to recognize data delivery errors can bail you out when a boatload of trouble results from a hasty Physical layer implementation.

Let's elaborate on this idea. In a LAN, aside from the Physical layer, it is the Data Link layer where most network problems are going to occur. After all, data that travels along the Physical layer is wrapped in Data Link layer clothing, so when problems occur here, nothing moves or, if it does move, it moves slowly. In addition, when you need to expand or upgrade your network, Data Link layer issues will become a factor. Thus your thorough understanding of the components, common problems, and troubleshooting techniques at the Data Link layer will lead to a faster, more efficient network, which means much happier users.

We begin by taking a more detailed look at the role of the Data Link layer.

THE ROLE OF THE DATA LINK LAYER

The Data Link layer performs many roles on your network. In fact, you can build a serviceable network with the Data Link and Physical layers alone if your data does not have to travel beyond a single broadcast domain. So you should make the effort to get to know the Data Link layer and, ideally, you'll learn to like it. That being said, let's look at all of the things the Data Link layer does for your network.

- It defines physical addresses: Every device has a physical address. Without one, data cannot be delivered.

- It defines and provides the Physical layer access method: Rules must be defined as to who can talk, when they can talk, and for how long they can talk. The Data Link layer defines these rules.

- It defines the network architecture: With what kind of network are you dealing? Ethernet, Token Ring, or Fiber Distributed Data Interface (FDDI)? Each network architecture has a different definition of how data is formatted, sent, and received on a network. The Data Link layer is a key component of this architecture.

- It defines the logical topology: Along with the network architecture comes the logical topology of the network. The logical topology defines how the data travels on the network. For example, on Ethernet, data travels on a bus; on Token Ring and FDDI, the data travels on a ring topology.

- It encapsulates Network layer protocols: The Data Link layer puts a final wrap around the data being sent; this "wrap" includes physical source and destination addresses and error-checking information.

- It provides error detection: If an error occurs in the transmission of your data (perhaps you placed that cable too close to the backup generator?), the **Cyclic Redundancy Check (CRC)** in the Data Link layer will detect the problem, ensuring that the upper layers do not receive corrupted data.

Is it all coming back to you now? Can you see that each task is critical in the delivery of data in any network? If you have a firm grasp of the issues involved with the Data

Link layer, you will be able to identify problems and find solutions in an orderly and efficient manner. We begin by identifying the components of the Data Link layer.

COMPONENTS OF THE DATA LINK LAYER

Before you can solve problems related to the Data Link layer, you must know the components of the Data Link layer. This way, you will not be wandering aimlessly through your network hoping to stumble on a device or piece of software labeled "Data Link layer" (by the way, there won't be any).

Any device that is responsible for receiving and *then examining* information directly from the Physical layer contains Data Link layer functionality. (Note that a Physical layer device does not examine information.) The information that is examined by the Data Link layer device is a package of bytes called a **frame**. In the following sections, we will discuss frames, network interface cards (NICs), and switches and bridges. When we are done, you will have an appreciation of the components of the Data Link layer and the ways in which they work.

Frames

A frame is the final packaging, or encapsulation, of data before it is broken into individual bits to be delivered to the Physical layer. It is called a frame for a simple reason: When the Network layer sends a packet down to the Data Link layer, the packet is "framed" with bytes on the front and back ends of the packet. These framing bytes are referred to as the header and trailer, respectively. See Figure 4-1.

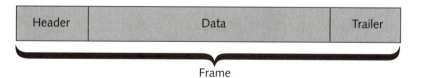

Figure 4-1   A frame has a header and a trailer

Network Interface Cards

NICs operate at the Physical layer as well as at the Data Link layer. In the Data Link layer, a NIC contains the physical address of a device and the firmware responsible for carrying out the formatting and media access procedures required of the particular network architecture. The device driver that serves as the interface between the operating system and the NIC also is part of the Data Link layer.

Firmware is software instructions within read-only memory (ROM).

Switches and Bridges

Switches and bridges receive and examine frames and make filtering or forwarding decisions based on physical addresses. Because a switch, in function, is just a multiport bridge, and because switches are more common than bridges, this book will focus on switches. Keep in mind that most of the support issues involved with switches apply to bridges as well.

Now that you have in mind the components of the Data Link layer, it is time to examine these components in detail and look at some of the support issues involved with each one.

SUPPORTING ETHERNET FRAMES

Because a frame is the unit of information with which the Data Link layer works, you need to understand the various ways in which Ethernet frames can be formatted. You will then know what to look for when tracking down problems. We begin with the basics: Ethernet frames come in four formats and range in length from a minimum of 64 bytes to a maximum of 1518 bytes. Frames shorter or longer, respectively, than these lengths are invalid frames. Thus, if the number of bytes that a station has to send is less than 64, it will **pad** the data field with extra characters, usually zeroes, to meet the 64-byte minimum.

The following list describes the four Ethernet frame formats.

- 802.3 Raw: This frame format is also called NetWare Raw and is based on an early release of the IEEE 802.3 Ethernet specification, which was a proprietary Novell NetWare frame format. The Institute of Electrical and Electronics Engineers (IEEE) added an additional header to this format to make the 802.3 Raw format incompatible with the current 802.3 standard. Table 4-1 details the Raw format.

- IEEE 802.3: The current IEEE frame format includes the Logical Link Control (LLC) header that is specified in IEEE 802.2 standards documents. Table 4-2 details this format.

- Ethernet Version II: This frame type uses the original Ethernet frame format as specified by the DIX consortium that originated Ethernet: Digital, Intel, Xerox. It is much like the 802.3 Raw format in that it contains no LLC header, but it does include a field—called the EtherType field—to specify the Network layer information that it is carrying. Table 4-3 details this frame type.

- IEEE 802.3 SNAP: This frame format extends the IEEE 802.3 frame format by adding a five-byte SNAP (Subnetwork Access Protocol) field, which provides backward compatibility between the IEEE 802.3 format and the Ethernet Version II format. See Table 4-4 for more details.

Table 4-1   The 802.3 Raw Frame Format Fields and Byte Sizes

Destination Address	Source Address	Length	Checksum (FFFF)	Data	FCS
6	6	2	2	44–1498	4

Table 4-2   IEEE 802.3 Frame Format Fields and Byte Sizes

Destination Address	Source Address	Length	LLC Header	Data	FCS
6	6	2	3	43–1497	4

Table 4-3   Ethernet Version II Frame Format Fields and Byte Sizes

Destination Address	Source Address	EtherType	Data	FCS
6	6	2	46–1500	4

Table 4-4   IEEE 802.3 SNAP Frame Format Fields and Byte Sizes

Destination Address	Source Address	Length	LLC Header	SNAP Header	Data	FCS
6	6	2	2	5	39–1493	4

After studying the preceding tables, you can see that three fields remain unchanged among all frame formats: the destination address, the source address, and the **frame check sequence (FCS).** The FCS is the 32-bit value that results from the CRC calculation that is performed on each frame and that is used to validate the frame.

In the following subsections, we will discuss physical addressing, errors that can occur in frames, and Ethernet frames that can rob you of network performance. Being less than fully conversant on these issues will hinder your troubleshooting efforts and prevent both you and your network from realizing your full potential.

Physical Addressing

For data to make it from a source computer to a destination computer, both computers must have physical addresses. In Ethernet networks, the physical address is a 48-bit value, expressed in hexadecimal, that is burned into the NIC. This address is referred to as the MAC address. Although many NICs allow this burned-in address to be overridden by a software assignment, this practice is not recommended because it can result in duplicate MAC addresses, which could have a disastrous effect on the network.

The MAC address is divided into two fields: the **Organizationally Unique Identifier (OUI)**, which is 3 bytes or 24 bits in length, and the serial number, which is the remaining 24 bits. The OUI identifies the manufacturer of the NIC. The serial number portion of the MAC address uniquely identifies that NIC. The combination of OUI and unique serial number guarantees you will not have duplicate MAC addresses on your network. If a company wants to manufacture Ethernet cards, it must purchase a 24-bit ID from the IEEE. As of this writing, the fee for your very own OUI is $1250.

 You can read about OUIs at the IEEE Web site at *www.ieee.org*.

So, how is an OUI useful? Well, most protocol analyzers keep a table of current OUIs. If you are using an analyzer to capture frames, you can have the MAC addresses displayed with a vendor alphabetical code rather than with a 12-digit hexadecimal value. For example, a MAC address displayed using the 12-digit hex value for a 3COM Ethernet card might look like this:

00-20-AF-05-37-44

You can use the OUI identifier for 3Com, 00-20-AF, to display the address like this:

3Com-05-37-44

This different format can be useful in quickly identifying the type of device to which the address belongs. If you have hundreds of devices using 3Com cards, this information may not be so useful, but it would at least give you a start. For instance, if you saw a frame that had a source MAC address of 00-00-81-53-9B-2C, the OUI code of 00-00-81 tells you that the address belongs to a device from Bay Networks (now part of Nortel Networks), a major manufacturer of hubs, switches, and routers. This information limits your search to these types of devices.

The first byte of the OUI also can tell you something significant about the MAC address when it is a destination address in a frame. The **least significant bit (LSB)** in the first byte of a MAC address is the **Individual/Group (I/G)** bit; it also is the rightmost bit in a byte. If this bit is 0, the frame is addressed to an individual station. If this bit is 1, the frame is a multicast or broadcast frame. If all bits in the destination MAC address are 1, the frame is an all-stations broadcast and will have the value FF-FF-FF-FF-FF-FF.

A multicast address will have the I/G bit set, but the states of the remaining bits will depend on the type of multicast. A multicast frame is one in which one or more stations should process the frame and typically is used for special applications such as routing protocol updates. A MAC address that corresponds to an IP multicast will look like this:

01-00-5e-xx-xx-xx

The 01 in the first byte shows that the I/G bit is set to 1, and the 5e in the third byte specifies that this frame is an IP multicast message. The remaining bytes, designated with x's, will vary depending on the specific type of IP multicast.

Why is it useful to know this information about the I/G bit? It may help you diagnose and debug problems related to multicast traffic. As you will see later in this chapter when we discuss the use of protocol analyzers to capture frames, you can capture all the information being transmitted on your network and then create searches or filters to look for specific types of data. If you are hunting down a problem with routing updates, for example, you could search for the type of multicast packet that your routing protocol uses. Applications such as video conferencing also use multicasting, and knowing what to look for in captured frames might help you resolve problems related to those types of applications.

As mentioned, it is possible to override the burned-in MAC address and assign your own MAC address to a NIC. The next least significant bit in the first byte of the MAC address is referred to as the **Universally/Locally Administered (U/L)** bit. If this bit is a 0, the MAC address is the burned-in address, it has an OUI assigned by the IEEE, and it is Universally Administered. If this bit is a 1, the burned-in address is overridden, the MAC address has been assigned locally, and it is Locally Administered.

Although this may not be a recommended practice, due to the possibility that you could duplicate an address by mistake, overriding the burned-in address may provide a clever way for you to augment your network documentation. For example, you could assign MAC addresses to users' workstations based on a telephone extension or office number, or you could combine them. Let's say you have a user who works in office 3170 and has a phone extension of 419. You could assign his or her workstation this MAC address: 02-00-00-31-70-04-19. The "02" in the first byte indicates that the U/L bit is set and the MAC address is therefore a Locally Administered address. If you are monitoring your network and see an extraordinary number of errors or other undesirable traffic patterns coming from that MAC address, you then know just where to go to solve the problem.

Errors That Occur in Frames

Ethernet provides error detection for transmitted frames by performing a CRC calculation on all bytes in the frame. The result of that calculation is 32 bits in length and is appended to a packet as the frame trailer. This trailer is called the FCS field.

When the frame is received by the destination, the destination device performs the identical calculation and compares its results with the FCS included in the frame. If the results do not match, the data was changed during transmission, and the frame is discarded.

CRC errors occur whenever data in the frame is corrupted during transmission. They can be caused by noise (Electromagnetic Interference [EMI] or radio frequency interference [RFI]), crosstalk, undetected collisions, signal reflections, and faulty hardware, to name a few.

CRC errors are not the only type of errors that can occur in an Ethernet frame. Other potential frame errors include giants, jabbers, runts, fragments, misaligned frames, and late collisions. After discussing each of these in more detail, we will look at a critical question for network administrators: How do I know when I have errors?

Giants

A **giant frame** is one in which the size of the frame is larger than the allowed maximum of 1518 bytes. A packet exceeding the maximum size will result in a Frame Too Long Error. These frames can be perfectly formed, including having a valid CRC, but still will be discarded by the receiving station due to their length. This unusual error is typically caused by the addition of extra headers on the packet before it is passed to the Data Link layer. It could be the result of an incorrectly configured or corrupt NIC driver.

Jabbers

A **jabber** is similar to a giant frame in that the size of the frame exceeds the maximum size, but a jabber frame does not have a valid CRC. Jabbers usually are caused by malfunctioning hardware, not NICs; Ethernet NICs often have built-in circuitry to control jabbers.

The jabber control circuit monitors the number of bytes sent and terminates the frame if too many bytes are attempted. If an error in hardware or software causes very large packets to be sent, and if the jabber control circuit fails, your network may be flooded with huge, invalid packets, which cause slowdowns or a complete halt to network activity. Other causes of jabbers include faulty cabling and incorrect or damaged device drivers.

A jabber problem once happened on a network managed by the author. This error manifested itself in two ways: excessively long frames and broadcasts. A network printer was the culprit. This particular printer had a built-in NIC to attach it directly to the network, plus parallel and serial interfaces. The serial interface sported an RJ45-to-serial port converter. When a user moved the printer, she inadvertently plugged the Ethernet patch cable into the RJ45-to-serial converter rather than into the NIC card. This resulted in a serial device transmitting on the Ethernet network. The result was a nearly constant stream of 1 bits, which, to all of the stations on the network, looked like a destination address of FF-FF-FF-FF-FF-FF (a broadcast). Not only was the network flooded with what looked like huge broadcast frames, which caused an enormous amount of network traffic, but also all workstations ground to a halt because their CPUs were constantly interrupted to process broadcasts.

Runts and Fragments

A **runt frame**, as you might guess, is a very small frame—less than 64 bytes, to be exact. It can have a good or bad CRC depending on how the monitoring software that detects it defines a runt. A frame of less than 64 bytes with a good CRC is often called just a Short Frame. In either case, the result is a discarded frame.

A runt can be the result of a malfunctioning NIC or NIC driver, or it can result from certain types of collisions in which part of the frame makes it to the destination without being detected as a collision. A **fragment** is a runt frame with a bad CRC and usually is the result of a collision that is not recognized as a collision, causing an incomplete frame to be processed. This type of frame also will be discarded by the NIC.

Misaligned Frames

A **misaligned frame** is one in which there are extra bits at the end of the frame so there is an incomplete **octet**. Recall that an octet is a grouping of 8 bits. A frame must have complete octets to be considered valid; any extra bits are truncated. The receiving station will continue to verify the CRC, but, usually the verification will fail. A Frame Alignment Error then is reported. Corrupt software drivers, faulty NICs, collisions, and noise on the cable cause misaligned frames.

Late Collisions

A **late collision** is a collision that occurs after the first 64 bytes of a frame have been transmitted. It is a problem because an Ethernet NIC is not required to retransmit the frame if it has successfully transmitted 64 bytes without detecting a collision. This type of collision will require upper-layer protocols to detect the missing frame and request a retransmission. Such retransmissions will slow your network down considerably if the late collisions occur frequently.

Late collisions can be caused by networks that do not meet specifications for total cable length or networks that violate the 5-4-3 repeater rule. Most likely, they result from a combination of the two violations or simply a violation of the repeater rule. For the cable length alone to be responsible for late collisions would require the cable to be more than three miles long! Late collisions also can be caused by faulty or failing hardware. Most NICs and network monitoring programs detect late collisions simply as CRC errors.

 Do not confuse error detection with error correction. The Data Link layer is not responsible for correcting errors; rather, it is responsible for detecting that the errors have occurred and for discarding the frame. The exception involves detected collisions; in this case, the sending station will automatically resend the data. Generally speaking, when a frame error occurs, the receiving station discards the frame and the upper-layer protocols must request that the lost frame be sent again.

How Do You Know If You Have Frame Errors?

So how do you know if frame errors are occurring in your LAN? If the upper-layer protocols are doing their job, your LAN might appear to be running in an acceptable manner, even if errors are occurring at a fairly high rate. Symptoms of a high rate of errors might include a slow network response, dropped network connections, and generally unhappy users. If the errors are numerous enough, your network will come to a screeching halt—so don't let it get to that point!

You can monitor your network periodically with a number of software and hardware network monitoring tools. You might already have a tool that you didn't realize was present in your network. Most routers and switches maintain statistics on errors received on each port or interface. For example, on a Cisco router, you can use the Show Interfaces command to display the status of each interface, along with various statistics regarding that interface—including error counters. Refer to Figure 4-2 to see the output of this command on a Cisco router. The highlighted part of the screen shows both input and output errors detected by the router.

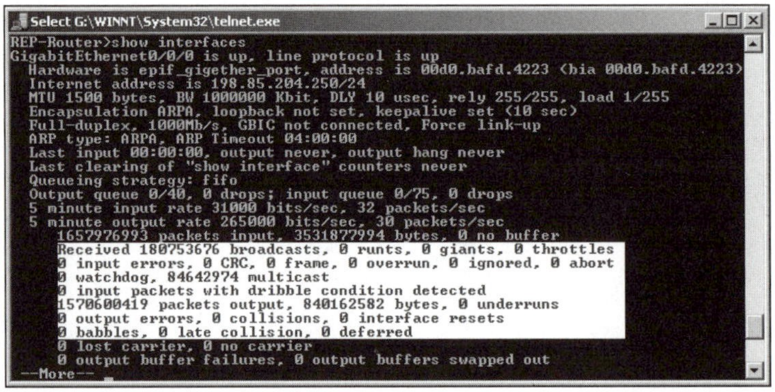

Figure 4-2 Show Interfaces command and error statistics on a Cisco router

Switches frequently show similar information on a port-by-port basis. See Figure 4-3 for the output of a Show Port Counters command on a Cisco 6506 switch module. Note that these statistics are gathered over time and do not represent the current number of errors. You can reset the counters if you want to start looking at statistics from a known beginning time.

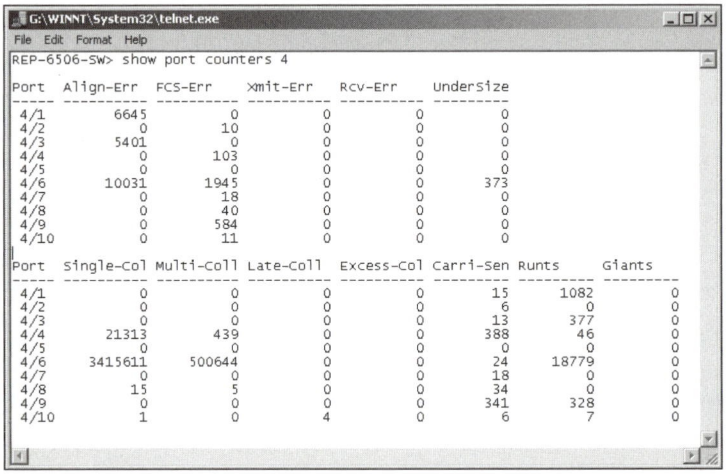
G:\WINNT\System32\telnet.exe

File Edit Format Help

REP-6506-SW> show port counters 4

Port	Align-Err	FCS-Err	Xmit-Err	Rcv-Err	UnderSize
4/1	6645	0	0	0	0
4/2	0	10	0	0	0
4/3	5401	0	0	0	0
4/4	0	103	0	0	0
4/5	0	0	0	0	0
4/6	10031	1945	0	0	373
4/7	0	18	0	0	0
4/8	0	40	0	0	0
4/9	0	584	0	0	0
4/10	0	11	0	0	0

Port	Single-Col	Multi-Coll	Late-Coll	Excess-Col	Carri-Sen	Runts	Giants
4/1	0	0	0	0	15	1082	0
4/2	0	0	0	0	6	0	0
4/3	0	0	0	0	13	377	0
4/4	21313	439	0	0	388	46	0
4/5	0	0	0	0	0	0	0
4/6	3415611	500644	0	0	24	18779	0
4/7	0	0	0	0	18	0	0
4/8	15	5	0	0	34	0	0
4/9	0	0	0	0	341	328	0
4/10	1	0	4	0	6	7	0

Figure 4-3 Output of a Show Port Counters command on a Cisco switch

When you are viewing statistics on a router or switch interface, you are viewing information only about frames that the interface actually saw. Thus only frames that were originated on or sent to the cable segment attached to that interface, along with all broadcasts on the subnetwork, will be reported in the statistics for that interface.

If you want to have a more graphical view of the network statistics, you can use a network monitor or protocol analyzer such as Wildpacket's EtherPeek, Fluke's Protocol Inspector, or Sniffer Technologies' Sniffer program. Figure 4-4 shows EtherPeek's error display screen. These types of monitoring programs give you a quick, real-time view of your network error and utilization statistics. They also provide historical information so that you can see numbers of errors over time.

Figure 4-4 EtherPeek error display

How many errors are too many errors? Every network, even a well-designed and well-managed one, will report some errors. Don't go into a frenzy trying to track down the source of a CRC or frame alignment error if *one* shows up in your counters or network monitor. Instead, look for trends. If one out of every 10,000 frames is an error frame this week, next week the error rate rises to one out of five thousand and the week after that one out of one thousand frames, it may be time to start tracking down the source of the errors. In addition, if you see bursts of error frames coming from a particular MAC address, the device with that address should be investigated for hardware or software problems. In general, if you are cruising along with one error out of five or six thousand frames, you probably do not have anything to worry about. Any more than that, and users will probably notice a slowdown in network response time.

Ethernet Frames That Rob Network Performance

One of your jobs as a network administrator is to ensure peak performance of your network. A well-performing LAN is difficult to define, but let's say that your LAN is performing well when your users are happy and you are utilizing your hardware resources and bandwidth efficiently.

One mistake LAN administrators often make is to permit upgrade creep to sabotage network performance. Upgrade creep (programmers will know it as "feature creep") occurs when a few network printers are added here and a couple of servers are added there; throw in a few dozen new workstations and soon a once-zippy network may be brought to its knees. Now you have to go to management, panic-stricken, and ask for a few days of network downtime and $20,000–$30,000 to upgrade the network.

Monitoring your network on a regular basis for the types of traffic patterns that cause problems could prevent a last-minute panic. You may still have to upgrade, but if you can do it on your own terms, before things get out of hand, the users you pass in the hall will look at you more kindly. In the following section, we will look at issues that typically cause delays—collisions and broadcasts. The fix for these issues is sometimes, but not always, increasing bandwidth.

 When considering performance issues of a network, you must look at two factors: bandwidth and delay. The bandwidth is how many bits per second the media and devices are capable of carrying. The delay is how much time the devices on the network must wait before sending data that is ready to go.

Collisions

Collisions in an Ethernet network are normal and expected, but every collision that occurs causes a delay. Because the colliding frames must be retransmitted, collisions tie up bandwidth. The more stations you have on a collision domain, and the higher the frequency that those stations need to send, the more collisions you will get.

How do you know when you have too many collisions? There is no magic number, but you typically want to keep the collision rate below 5 percent of your total traffic. There will be times when the rate spikes to a very high percentage (for example, if students in a classroom containing 25 workstations all decide to load Microsoft Word over the network simultaneously), so you need to monitor the rate over a period of several seconds at least.

At some point, probably around 15 percent, the percentage of collisions becomes critical because the number of collisions starts to snowball until nothing is being sent onto your network except collisions. If you think about it, it makes sense. Take a room full of people who all have something to say but politely wait until no one else is speaking before beginning to talk. If you start with three or four people, you will probably have good communication with everyone getting a turn. Increase that number to ten people, and now you have several situations in which two or more people have something to say, hear a pause in the conversation, and speak. This action will cause a collision.

In this scenario, a collision is not a big problem; both people pause, one begins to speak, and communication resumes until the next collision. If you increase the number of people to 100, however, you likely will have dozens of people with something to say at any given time. These dozens will all hear a pause and start to speak. A collision will be heard and those people will pause, waiting for silence. Meanwhile, a dozen different people will hear the pause and begin to speak, causing the first group to wait even longer. Before you know it, you have 100 people with something to say but every time they try to speak, a collision occurs, so no one can successfully say anything. When this scenario happens in an Ethernet network, it is referred to as multiple collisions.

Normally, when a station experiences a collision, it backs off for a period of time. If a collision occurs when the station retries after the backoff period, the backoff time is increased (up to double the time). If yet another collision occurs, the process is repeated until it has tried 16 times without success. At that point, the NIC informs the driver and a message usually is generated to inform the user that the network is unavailable.

How can you reduce collisions in a network? Take that room full of people, all with something important to say. Two approaches could resolve that problem. One approach is to teach the users to talk much faster so that in a given period of time, more people could speak (increase the bandwidth). Another approach is to break the crowd into smaller groups. If a person in one group needs to speak to someone in another group, a relay person is used who can queue up messages and deliver them when there is a break in the action (segment the network).

In the Ethernet world, you could implement the first solution by going from 10 Mbps Ethernet to 100 Mbps Ethernet. The second solution can be accomplished by replacing shared bandwidth devices, such as hubs, with switches; this action creates more collision domains, each with fewer stations on it.

Look at Figures 4-5 and 4-6. In Figure 4-5, there are 80 workstations in the collision domain. By replacing the one central hub with a switch, as in Figure 4-6, you can create four separate collision domains of 20 computers each, thereby reducing the number of collisions significantly.

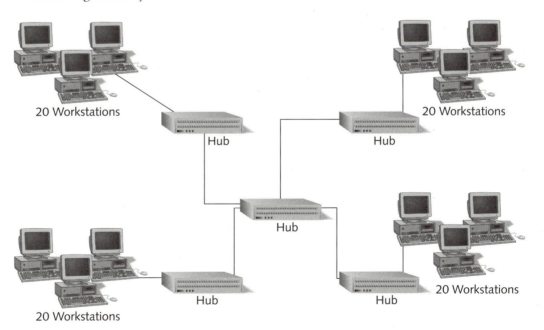

Figure 4-5   Single collision domain

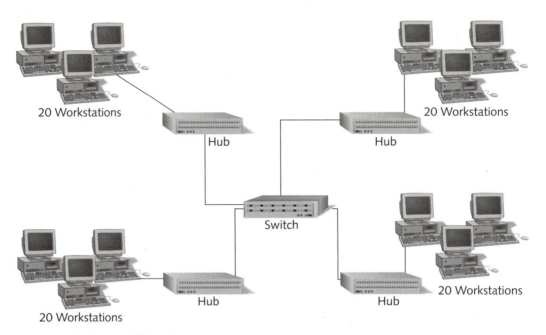

20 Workstations

Hub

Hub

20 Workstations

Switch

20 Workstations

Hub

Hub

20 Workstations

Figure 4-6   Four collision domains

Another solution to the problem may be to upgrade from 10 Mbps to 100 Mbps Ethernet, assuming you are not already running 100 Mbps Ethernet. However, this could be a considerably more expensive solution. You would have to be sure that the workstation and server NICs supported 100 Mbps and, if they do not, replace them. In addition, your media must be Cat-5 compliant or better, and you would have to replace the hubs.

The type of collision we have been discussing is an ordinary collision that occurs early in the transmission of a frame and that is recognized by all stations in the collision domain. The problem can become much worse if you have late collisions. As noted earlier, a late collision occurs when a workstation sends a message, but has sent more than 64 bytes of the message before a collision occurs. In this case, the workstation does not acknowledge that a collision occurred, but goes about its business happily thinking the message was received successfully. Not only does this type of collision cause the upper-layer protocols to request that the data be re-sent, slowing things down, but it also probably means you have a problem in your network.

Cable length standards and maximum repeater rules were created for a reason. Although the signals that travel on copper media and fiber-optic media travel very fast, they do not travel infinitely fast. It takes time for the data to travel the length of the media and even more time for it to travel through repeaters. The longer the cable and the more repeaters that are in the path, the longer it takes.

The standards are set such that if you use the longest allowable cable runs and have the most allowable repeaters between end stations, a workstation will still be able to detect that a collision has occurred on the farthest end of the network before it can send more than 64 bytes. If a station does send 64 bytes or more and a collision occurs after that point, one of two things has occurred: either your network does not meet specifications or it includes faulty equipment.

Unfortunately, network monitoring tools cannot detect late collisions in 10BaseT networks because it would be necessary for the monitoring station to send information at the time the collision occurred. However, switches and routers that keep error statistics will keep track of the late collisions that occurred while their interfaces were sending. The bottom line is this: If you pay strict attention to the cabling and repeater standards, then these collisions likely will not be a problem for you, barring faulty hardware.

Although too many collisions are frequently a problem for a growing network, and segmenting the network with switches often can solve a significant part of this problem, switches cannot do anything for a problem related to broadcasts.

Broadcasts

A **broadcast** is a frame whose destination address is set to all 1s and that is processed by all stations that hear the frame. By themselves, broadcasts are not an indication of any specific error occurring in your network.

Broadcast frames are a common method of communicating in the network; workstations and servers use them to announce their presence on the network and to find out information about the network. Broadcast frames are just like any other frame except that they must be processed by every workstation in the broadcast domain. This means that switches forward them out all ports just as a repeating hub does with all traffic, and the broadcast is propagated throughout the network until it comes to a router or the end of the network, where it stops.

When a frame is sent on a network with a **unicast** address, only the workstation with that particular address processes the frame. A unicast frame is addressed to a particular MAC address, with the intention that only one station will process it. Because a broadcast requires all stations to process the frame, the CPU of each and every workstation in the network must stop what it is doing and service the interrupt generated by the NIC so that the frame can be processed. If several hundred broadcasts per second are generated, the result is called a **broadcast storm**. This usually leaves workstations frozen or operating very slowly because all the CPU time is going into processing broadcasts.

A broadcast storm can be the result of a bad NIC or a misconfigured device. Broadcast storms also can result from protocols such as IPX, which are very broadcast-oriented. For instance, a problem can occur on Windows 95 machines running Internetwork Packet Exchange (IPX) when the machines first boot and try to locate network resources with an incorrect MAC address. This problem is discussed on Microsoft's Web site under article number Q149448.

Even valid broadcasts can be so numerous as to slow workstation response time to a crawl. If you are using a broadcast-oriented network protocol such as NetBEUI or IPX/SPX, a significant percentage of your traffic can be broadcasts.

How many broadcasts are too many? This question is more difficult to answer than the same question about collisions. On a network in which no users are requesting network services, your broadcast percentage may be 100 percent because broadcast frames are often sent automatically and periodically by various network protocols. Rather than use a percentage as compared to unicast traffic, you may want to look at the percentage of broadcast traffic as compared to network utilization. If the network utilization is 1 or 2 percent, a high percentage of broadcasts may not be a problem. Of course, if network utilization is 25 percent and broadcasts make up half of that, that is an awful lot of broadcast traffic.

Another way to measure broadcasts is in terms of broadcasts per second. Four or five broadcasts per second is a tolerable number for most workstations. However, if you increase that number to 80 or 100 broadcasts per second over a sustained period of time, you are likely to see significant slowdowns in network and workstation response. The long and short of it is this: If the broadcasts affect network or workstation performance, they are a problem; otherwise, they are okay.

What do you do about broadcasts? If a large number of broadcasts also carry CRC errors, you probably have a jabber problem and need to track down the faulty hardware. If the broadcasts are valid, you can reduce them by making additional broadcast domains—that is, by creating more subnets separated by router interfaces.

Alternatively, you can reduce the number of network protocols you are using. Many workstations and printers come preconfigured with two or three protocols enabled; uninstall them if you do not need them. You also can turn off features such as the Spanning-Tree Protocol on switches, if it is unnecessary. In addition, you can change the protocol to one that is not as dependent on broadcasts; for example, you can use TCP/IP with WINS name resolution rather than TCP/IP with NetBIOS name resolution. NetBEUI and IPX/SPX are very broadcast-oriented and should be used only if necessary.

SUPPORTING NETWORK INTERFACE CARDS

Ideally, a network interface card should play an unobtrusive role in your network. The card comes with the workstation; you plug it in and hope never to put much thought into what it is doing or how it is doing it. This is the approach most administrators take and it is often a reasonable approach. However, there are some considerations to keep in mind when selecting and configuring a NIC—considerations that can make the difference between a network that works so-so and one that works like a well-oiled machine. In this part of the chapter, we'll discuss network architecture, NIC drivers, and

NIC modes of operation so that you can get a good feel for the options available to you when selecting or supporting a NIC.

Match the Network Architecture

First and foremost, you need to make sure that the type of NIC you select matches the network architecture you are using. This may seem like an obvious consideration, and indeed it is—so obvious that in at least one case known to the author, it was not even a second thought when a key system was purchased at one company. The system, an IBM AS/400, was being installed in an Ethernet network. When the system arrived, a patch cable was plugged in, network protocols were installed and configured, and nothing happened. After a few hours of checking and rechecking the configuration, the packing list for the system was consulted. Lo and behold, the system shipped with a Token Ring NIC! Of course, this was an IBM system, the first and one of the last major supporters of Token Ring, so this choice made sense. Perhaps this case involves an uncommon problem, but it once again shows you what kind of trouble you can get into when you assume something about a configuration.

NIC Drivers

A **driver** is software that interfaces between the operating system and a hardware device. The NIC driver is one part of the Data Link layer that you can actually see in the Network Control Panel and over which you have some control. Most of the Data Link layer work is done with chips on the NIC or inside switches. However, the device driver is part of the Data Link layer and serves as the interface between the NIC and the next-higher layer, the Network layer. Thus it is very important that the NIC driver be configured correctly and optimized for operation in your network.

If a high rate of errors such as jabbers, misaligned frames, or runts can be tracked to a particular workstation, the NIC driver is one key suspect. A corrupted driver, an outdated driver, or a driver that is simply wrong for the NIC can cause any number of errors on the network. In particular, if you have recently changed network protocols, changed operating system versions, upgraded from 10 Mbps to 100 Mbps, or changed out your hubs with switches, you'll want to verify that your drivers are the most recent versions. Drivers that worked in one environment may fail or exhibit flaky behavior in another, so if you suddenly have an increase in errors, check your drivers.

NIC Modes of Operation

Some NICs can operate in a variety of modes. A NIC that has this capability usually is designed to automatically select the optimal mode depending on the device to which it is connected. The common modes of operation of which a NIC may be capable are as follows:

- 10 Mbps half duplex
- 10 Mbps full duplex

- 100 Mbps half duplex

- 100 Mbps full duplex

See Figure 4-7 for the Windows 2000 Network Control Panel settings related to a NIC's operational modes. The manner in which this information is displayed is manufacturer- and operating system–dependent, so your system may look somewhat different. Note that Network Control Panel will not show this information if the NIC does not support multiple modes.

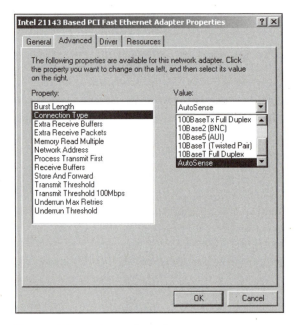

Figure 4-7   NIC modes of operation

There are two terms that you may hear in relation to NICs and switches: AutoSense and autonegotiation. **AutoSense** means that the device automatically detects the speed of the device to which it is connected. **Autonegotiation** allows two devices to decide whether the connection should be established as half duplex or full duplex. For autonegotiation to work properly, the NIC card, driver, and the device to which the NIC is connected must all properly implement the IEEE 802.3u NWAY autonegotiation specification. If both devices correctly implement this specification, the autonegotiation process should work.

Occasionally, problems may arise from options such as autopolarity or cable integrity checks that vendors implement on their NIC drivers. If autonegotiation does not work, be sure to turn these nonstandard options off. If autonegotiation still does not work, one of the following problems could result:

- Speed mismatch: One device attempts to run at 10 Mbps and another device attempts to run at 100 Mbps. This mismatch will result in no data link, which can be seen by the absence of a lit LED on the switch and NIC.

- Duplex mismatch: This problem is more troublesome because you may believe that everything is working correctly but one device is actually trying to run at full duplex and the other is running at half duplex. This mismatch will result in very slow performance, dropped connections, or complete loss of connectivity.

If autonegotiation does not appear to select the optimal speed and duplex mode for the connection type (the optimum is 100 Mbps at full duplex), verify that both the NIC driver and the switch port support autonegotiation. If they do, try configuring both the switch port and the NIC to 100 Mbps/full duplex. Do not configure only the NIC or the switch port, as it may result in a speed or duplex mismatch.

If configuring both devices to the optimal setting does not resolve the problem, verify your Physical layer. If the media tests correctly, try a different switch port and check whether there is a NIC driver upgrade. If none of these solutions works, try different hardware.

NICs are the workstation side of Data Link layer puzzle. A workstation has to connect to something, and at the Data Link layer, the most common device is a switch.

SUPPORTING ETHERNET SWITCHES

Until the mid- to late 1990s, Ethernet networks operated almost exclusively in shared media environments, with workstations connected together by hubs to create large collision domains. If you needed to segment your network by creating more collision domains, you added a bridge, which at the time was quite expensive and fitted with only two ports.

As is typical in the computer industry, parts became cheaper and faster, and prices came down, so faster bridges were being manufactured that offered more ports for less money. The industry needed a new name to market these better, faster, cheaper bridges—and so the Ethernet switch was born. Almost everything that is said in this book about switches applies equally to bridges.

This book will focus on the type of switching or bridging used in an Ethernet environment: transparent bridging. **Transparent bridging** simply means that Ethernet frames pass through the switch unaltered; what goes in is what comes out. Transparent bridging operation, which covers the details of how switches learn MAC addresses and forward frames, is described in detail in the IEEE 802.1D standard document. This standard also describes the spanning-tree algorithm, which is used to prevent loops in a switch environment with multiple paths to one destination.

This book will cover the operation and features of switches that are most important to supporting and troubleshooting networks. The next several pages discuss the roles that switches can play in your network, the methods switches use to move frames from the incoming ports to the appropriate outgoing ports, the prevention of bridging loops, and an advanced switch feature called VLAN, which allows you to break your network into multiple broadcast domains.

The Role of Switches

A switch in an Ethernet network can play a variety of roles. It can be used as a high-speed backbone for your network through which the traffic of hundreds or even thousands of workstations and servers pass. It can be used to segment large collision domains, as shown in Figures 4-5 and 4-6. In addition, it can be used in place of a hub so that every workstation has its own collision domain. Many organizations, when moving to upgrade their networks from a traditional, shared media environment, will gradually introduce switches into the network until switches fill all these roles.

There are a number of things you need to know about the operation and features of switches so that you can effectively troubleshoot a switched environment. Your knowledge of switches also will help you decide when the use of hubs, which create a shared media environment, is causing problems that can be solved by using switches instead.

Deciding Between Switches and Hubs

Recall from Chapter 1 that a hub takes bit signals in one port, cleans up the signals, amplifies them, and then repeats them out all other ports. A hub doesn't know anything about the data those signals represent. In contrast, a switch actually processes the frame that it receives, examines the destination address, and decides to which port the frame should be forwarded to reach its destination. It sounds like a lot of work, and it is.

The switch does this extra work so that frames are forwarded only out the port where the intended destination can be found. This means less traffic on every cable segment and many fewer collisions. However, this extra work comes at a price—latency. A frame will take longer to get from source to destination if the devices are connected to a switch as compared to a hub, provided that the hub environment does not slow things down due to collisions.

How does this information figure into a "hub or a switch" decision? Switches are twice as expensive as hubs, so where money is an issue (and where isn't it?), you may want to opt for hubs if they will provide satisfactory performance. In addition, you may want to replace your hubs with switches in the following circumstances:

- Your network is currently experiencing considerable collisions, and particularly multiple collisions, that will severely affect performance.

- You have a mixed speed environment—for example, 10 Mbps workstations and 100 Mbps servers.

- Your network performance would benefit from full-duplex communications.

- You are seeing a lot of error frames (some types of switches can reduce the effects of certain types of errors).

- You want to have better control over your network traffic patterns.

- You expect to expand the network, thereby increasing traffic.

4

The first item in the list is fairly obvious. Switches will reduce the number of collisions in your network, particularly if you use a switch to break up a large collision domain into several smaller domains. On the other hand, if you have 10 workstations and 1 server, and 95 percent of all traffic is going to the server or coming from the server, the area of contention will be the server cable segment. Merely replacing the hub with a switch is unlikely to provide a major performance gain.

If your environment is a mixed 10/100 environment, in which your workstations are running at 10 Mbps and your server is running at 100 Mbps, a switch that accommodates dual speeds likely will help. With this configuration, the switch can theoretically forward 10 simultaneous workstation requests to the server in the time it takes to forward one request in a hub environment.

A switch is required to operate your NIC in full-duplex mode. If your NICs have this capability, the advantage of being able to receive data at the same time that data is transmitted has clear performance implications. Both the NIC and the switch must support this feature, as well as your server NIC, to gain any benefit.

The fourth item mentioned earlier requires additional explanation. The presence of significant runt, fragment, CRC, or other error frames is a condition that should be addressed separately from the issue of whether to use switches or hubs. Although a hub will always forward all signals that it hears, thereby affecting the entire network segment, some switches (as we will discuss later) can be configured to ignore invalid frames. This means that the error frames will not be delivered to the destination, saving bandwidth on the collision domain on which the destination resides. This is particularly helpful with error broadcast frames. If a switch does not forward a broadcast frame that has an error condition, bandwidth is conserved on all collision domains throughout the broadcast domain.

Switches typically have the ability to more finely control traffic patterns. Because they are frame-filtering devices, many switches have features that allow an administrator to program custom filtering decisions. For example, an administrator could program a switch to always filter certain source MAC addresses from reaching particular destinations. Many switches also have the ability to maintain statistics on a port-by-port basis, allowing the administrator to have a better view of the network traffic patterns and the frequency of errors.

If your network is always in growth mode, switches are probably the best option for connectivity. Even if your traffic is light today with few collisions and none of the circumstances discussed previously applies, a switch gives you more room to grow and more options when making network enhancements.

In discussing the question of whether to use a switch or a hub, our focus has primarily been on whether to use a hub or switch to connect individual workstations—that is, one station per port. In many cases, a switch is clearly the best choice, but hubs do have their place, particularly in smaller networks or networks with fairly light traffic. Cost will often be a determining factor in these cases.

Switches as Concentrators for Hubs

As your network grows, you typically add more cable, more workstations, and more hubs. Before you know it, you are dealing with the question of how to add another hub without violating the 5-4-3 repeater rules. Even if you are successful with that venture, you will start to see the familiar collision LED on your hubs with alarming frequency. The network is slowing to a crawl and users are starting to get impatient.

This scenario of impatience and frustration is a common one for businesses and schools that have had a network in place since the early to mid-1990s and that have kept adding to it and spending just enough to accommodate the number of workstations and servers in operation. Pretty soon, they have 50, 100, or even 300 workstations on a single collision domain! Ouch! Take a look at Figure 4-8 to see what this might look like.

Yes, you have heard of switches, but it would take tens of thousands—perhaps hundreds of thousands—of dollars to replace all your hubs with switches. Many switch marketers and salespeople would like you to take this step, of course. However, upgrading from a shared hub environment to a switched environment can be done gradually. For instance, that collision-infested, slowed-to-a-crawl network shown in Figure 4-8 can be made quite tolerable with the addition of a few switches, as shown in Figure 4-9.

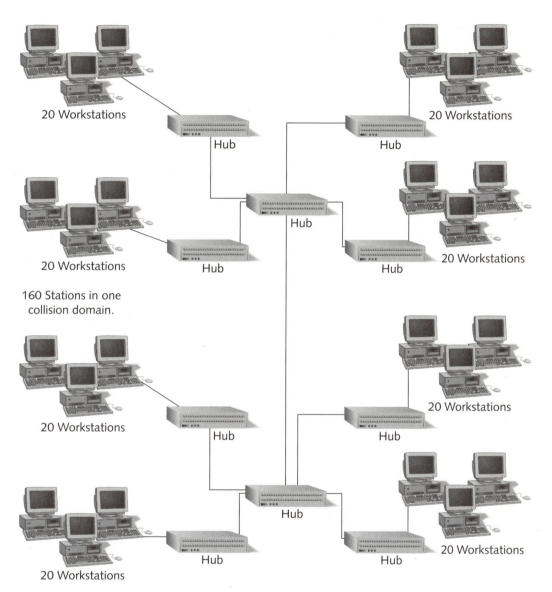

20 Workstations

Hub

20 Workstations

Hub

20 Workstations

Hub

Hub

20 Workstations

Hub

160 Stations in one collision domain.

20 Workstations

Hub

20 Workstations

Hub

20 Workstations

Hub

Hub

20 Workstations

Hub

20 Workstations

Hub

Figure 4-8   Really big collision domain

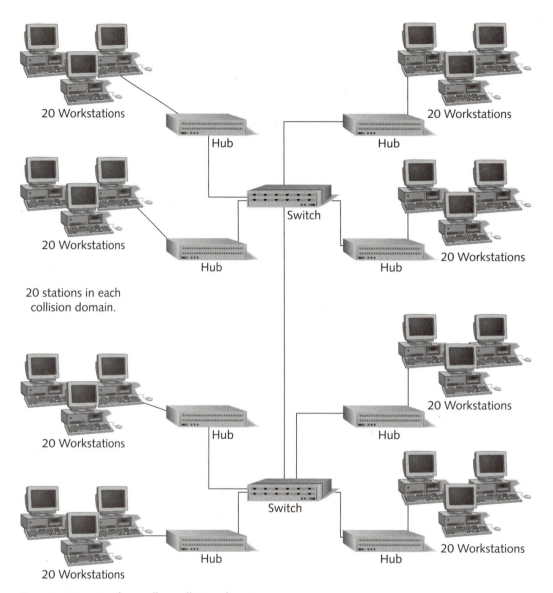

Figure 4-9   Much smaller collision domains

The switches are concentration points for your hubs, with each hub or hub stack becoming its own collision domain. Furthermore, each switch has a 100 Mbps port that connects two switches for fast transport of traffic between them.

Switches in Your Network Backbone

A switch is the device of choice for a network backbone. Today's switches can transfer huge numbers of frames quickly across the switch backplane, and the ports can be configured from 10 Mbps to 1 Gbps. These types of switches are usually chassis-based and include several slots to add cards that have the number and type of switch ports you require. You usually can add more modules for network management and layer 3 switching and routing operations. Figure 4-10 shows a switch in a typical network environment. Note that this type of switch is beyond the scope of this text because its use and configuration is highly specialized and vendor dependent.

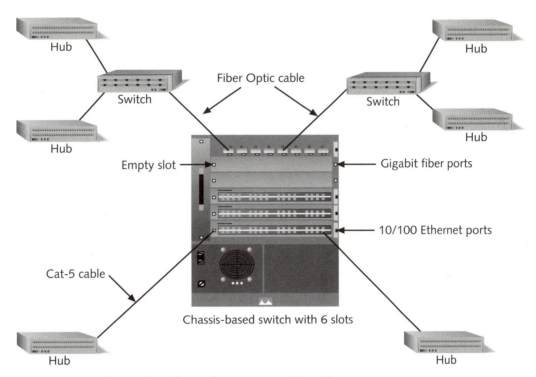

Figure 4-10   Chassis-based switch as a network backbone

We have discussed how you can use switches in your network to solve various problems; now we need to take a closer look at the various methods that switches use to get network frames from source to destination. You can use this information to make intelligent decisions when you configure and implement switches in your network.

How Switches Do What They Do—Switching Methods

The basic operation of all switches is essentially the same: receive a frame, look up the port for the destination address, and forward the frame. Switches keep a table of MAC addresses and port number pairs. When a switch is first powered on, the table is empty. As a workstation sends a frame, the switch reads the source and destination address of the frame and notes from which port it was received.

The source address and port number are used to build the switching table, which is stored in **content addressable memory (CAM)**. If the switch already has the source MAC address in its table, it simply updates an aging timer that keeps track of how long the address has been in CAM since that source has sent a frame. The destination address of the frame is checked against the table and forwarded out the appropriate port.

Some switches can provide a little extra assistance to your network by examining more of the frame than just the source and destination address before forwarding the frame. We will take a look at four common switching methods and the circumstances in which you may want to use them.

Cut-Through Switching

Cut-through switching is the fastest of the three methods of switching. It provides no added protection against frame errors. As soon as the switch looks up the destination address and its related port, the frame is forwarded to the destination port or, in the case of a broadcast, to all ports, without further examination. This type of switching is sometimes referred to as cross-point switching.

The problem with cut-through switching is that error frames can be propagated throughout the network, only to be discarded by the destination devices. This needlessly uses bandwidth. The upside to cut-through switching is that latency is minimized. If your network is very reliable and has few frame errors, cut-through switching is probably a sound choice because it will provide the best performance.

Keep Your Runts to Yourself—Fragment-Free Switching

As the name suggests, **fragment-free switching** minimizes the effects of runts and frame fragments. If a switch operating in fragment-free mode receives a frame less than 64 bytes in length, it will discard the frame. This prevents the forwarding of these error frames. Thus the errors travel only on the cabling segment on which they originated, and they do not needlessly traverse additional segments. Latency is increased by using this method, but the extra latency is probably worth it because overall bandwidth is conserved.

Taking Care of Everything—Store-and-Forward Switching

Store-and-forward switching provides the most error checking and allows additional checking and manipulation of the frame because the entire frame is read and held in memory before it is forwarded to the destination. The main advantage of this method is that the number of frames forwarded that contain errors drops to zero. In addition, because the entire frame is read into a buffer, the switch can do a CRC check on the frame. If there is a CRC error, the frame will be discarded. Of course, this also means that frames that are too long will also be discarded.

Storing the entire frame in memory comes at a price: more latency and a higher price. Store-and-forward switches require considerably more memory than cut-through switches or fragment-free switches because more data must be stored. However, the assurance that a store-and-forward switch will not, for example, take down your entire network by forwarding jabber frames to all ports may make the extra cost worth it. Also, if a switch has the entire frame in memory, additional functions can be performed.

Store-and-forward switches can translate between network architectures such as Ethernet to Token Ring by modifying the frame headers after the frame is in the buffer. These kinds of switches are commonly referred to as **translation bridges**. Less common are store-and-forward switches that allow an administrator to filter based on information other than the destination address. For example, he or she may be able to filter based on the protocol type field of an Ethernet Version II frame.

The Best of All Worlds—Adaptive Switching

Which switch should you use? After all, you want your network to be fast, so cut-through switching sounds pretty good. But you don't want one station or cabling segment that starts acting flaky to contaminate the rest of the LAN. If only the switch would use cut-through switching most of the time and then switch to store-and-forward or fragment-free switching if there are a lot of errors. Ask and you shall receive: Some switches have just that capability. Such a switch will operate in cut-through mode normally, but if a high number of errors occurs on a port, the switch will change that port to store-and-forward operation. Additionally, some switches will always process broadcast frames using the store-and-forward mode, thereby minimizing the more damaging effects of bad broadcast frames.

 Mid- to high-end switches can operate in a variety of modes that you can configure to suit your environment.

Now that you know what options are available in terms of switch methods, you can make intelligent choices based on your LAN environment and your budget as to which types of switches to use and where to use them. Because a switch is potentially such a critical element of your network, what happens if a critical switch port, or the entire switch, fails? Wouldn't it be nice to provide more than one path for your data when a failure occurs? Once again, switch manufacturers have come to the rescue.

Expanding Your Options with the Spanning-Tree Protocol

Some switches, unlike hubs, are designed to accommodate redundancy, or multiple paths, in the network. However, using redundant switches can also cause a network administrator's worse nightmare: a bridging loop. A **bridging loop** occurs when switches are connected in such a way that it is possible for frames to be forwarded endlessly from switch to switch in an infinite loop. Figure 4-11 shows a network configuration in which this situation could happen.

Because a bridge forwards broadcast frames out every port except the port on which the frame was received, a broadcast frame originating from a computer attached to Switch A will be forwarded to Switches B and C. Switches B and C will forward the frame to Switch D. Switch D will forward the frame received from Switch B to Switch C, and the frame received from Switch C will be sent to Switch B. Switches B and C will then forward the frame to Switch A, which will start the process again. On and on it goes until all that these switches are doing is forwarding the same broadcast frame over and over again, while at the same time causing every computer in the network to process the frame.

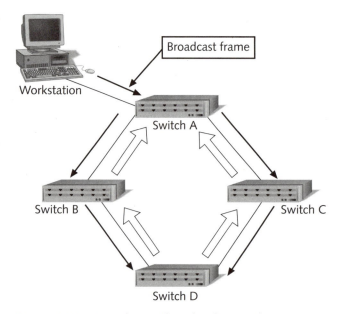

Figure 4-11   Switches with redundant paths

Luckily, this doesn't usually happen. IEEE 802.1D, as mentioned, specifies an algorithm, known as the spanning-tree algorithm, that prevents this behavior. The spanning-tree algorithm requires that switches communicate with one another. The protocol used to communicate among bridges is, not surprisingly, the **Spanning-Tree Protocol (STP)**.

STP allows switches to detect when there is a potential for a loop. When a potential loop configuration is detected, one of the switch ports goes into **blocking mode**, preventing it from forwarding frames that would create the loop. If the loop configuration is broken, perhaps due to a switch failing or due to the connection between two switches failing, the switch port that was in blocking mode resumes forwarding frames. In this way, redundancy is achieved, allowing frames to reach their destination in the event of a switch or media failure but preventing the disastrous effects of bridging loops.

STP is an integral part of most mid-range to high-end switches. Beware of the so-called SOHO (Small Office Home Office) products, as most of these lower-end switches do not support STP. Before using a switch in a configuration that could form a loop, be certain that all of the involved switches support the 802.1D standard, which provides for STP.

Some switches divide the switch ports into separate broadcast domains. This feature allows a single switch to be broken into two or more separate LANs that will not communicate with one another unless connected by a router. You can create virtual LANs (VLANs) with this feature. We discuss them next.

The Value of VLANs

A switch that allows you to create multiple broadcast domains can bring considerable value to your network. Look again at Figure 4-9, in which a large collision domain is broken into several smaller collision domains. A switch that has VLAN capability could further optimize that configuration by creating two or more broadcast domains without having to add a new switch. This setup could benefit your network because it allows you greater management and security of the network, plus control of broadcast frames.

Although the discussion of VLANs is more of a network design issue, which is beyond the scope of this book, we'll discuss enough here that you'll be able to handle an encounter with a VLAN environment.

What You Need to Know Before You Use VLANs

Because a VLAN breaks the network into more broadcast domains, devices on switch ports that belong to different VLANs must have logical addresses (IP addresses, for example) on different networks. Furthermore, if the devices on one VLAN are to communicate with devices on another VLAN, a layer 3 device (typically a router) is required to route packets between the VLANs.

Because routers are slower devices than switches or hubs, you should plan your network so that the majority of resource accesses occur within VLANs. Figure 4-12 shows a multiple-collision domain network divided into two VLANs, with a router communicating between VLANs. Notice that there is a server on each VLAN so that workstation traffic need not cross the router for access to a server.

You must consider carefully the ramifications of moving a workstation from one switch port to another. When adding a workstation to your network, you must know in which VLAN the workstation should belong before choosing a switch port to connect the station and a logical address to assign to the workstation.

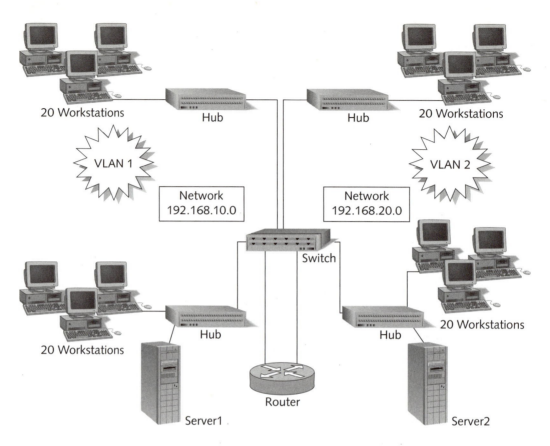

Problems with VLANs

You might be tempted to utilize VLANs because the prospect of optimizing your network is enticing. However, the overuse of VLANs can end up costing you much more than any benefits provided. In addition, because more VLANs mean more layer 3 networking, your network will be more complex. Furthermore, they can actually slow down your network when your intention is to increase performance. All of these things can combine to mean more headaches for IT.

Because VLANs require a router to communicate among them, every VLAN you create requires a corresponding router interface, which usually means more expense. More router interfaces means additional IP networks, which is likely to require subnetting of your existing network, which can become quite complex. If you need to change your existing network address scheme, you will probably have to reconfigure many devices to reflect the new addressing scheme, and that step can take lots of time. Lastly, more, smaller VLANs can slow your network unless the workstations and the network resources they access the majority of the time are within the same VLAN.

Remember, for a workstation to communicate outside its VLAN, it must go through a router. Communication through a router will always be slower than communication through a switch.

Take another look at Figure 4-12. Figure 4-12 shows a network with VLANs; it makes sense because there is a network resource in both of the VLANs. Figure 4-13, on the other hand, shows a network in which it was probably better to leave the network without VLANs; with only one server, the workstations in VLAN 2 will need to cross the router for every access to the server.

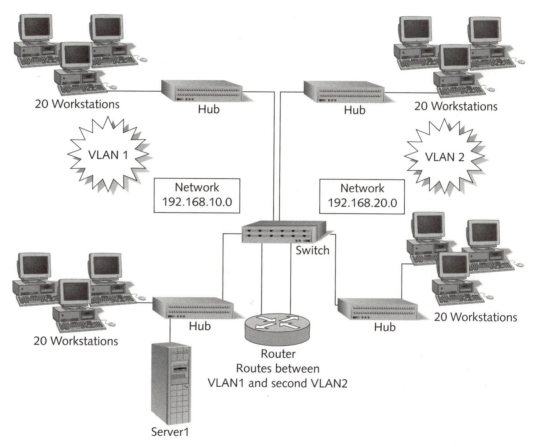

Figure 4-13   VLAN configuration that will slow your network

Now that you know some of the features and functions of switches, what do you need to know to effectively troubleshoot a switched network? Plenty. We'll discuss troubleshooting next.

TROUBLESHOOTING A SWITCHED ETHERNET NETWORK

Because switches have more work to do than layer 1 devices such as repeating hubs, there is also more that can go wrong with a switch and more that you have to know to solve the associated problems. We'll divide our discussion in this part of the chapter by looking first at the learning curve of a switch and then examining the use of tools in a switched environment.

The Learning Curve of a Switch

Switches, unlike repeating hubs, have to learn about your network before they can be effective. When a workstation or group of workstations is connected to a switch port, it takes time for the switch to learn about any devices that are connected. First, there is the negotiation process for a switch to determine what mode of operation each connected device requires. Next, the switch must learn the MAC addresses of all devices connected to each port so that frames can be forwarded properly. This takes time.

Some things of which you must be aware during this learning curve include the switch's MAC address learning process and its implications for your LAN, the effect of a power loss on a switch in a large LAN, and the capacity limitations of a switch. You also need to understand the limitations of the use of network monitors and protocol analyzers in switched environments. We discuss these issues in the following sections.

Patience Is Required When Troubleshooting

If you have experience with using hubs in your network, you probably expect to be able to transmit and receive data as soon as you plug the cable into the hub. In contrast, a switch that has advanced connectivity features, such as autonegotiation of line speed and duplex mode, requires a little more time to get settled, often as long as 10 seconds.

Whenever a NIC or router interface is changed such that the interface is reset (such as an IP address change or similar configuration modification), the switch to which the device is attached must go through the autonegotiation process to determine line speed and duplex mode. Similarly, if a cable is plugged into the switch, this process must take place. Again, this takes time.

Many people try to make a change in the configuration of a router or NIC and immediately test the configuration by using the ping command, only to receive timeout results from the ping command. Alternatively, they may plug in the network cable, sit down to try their communication, and get timeout errors. They then question the configuration or start looking at other causes of the problem—when all they really had to do was wait a few more seconds and try ping again.

I once observed a group of students troubleshoot, change configurations, and reboot workstations and routers for more than a half an hour because of their impatience. They were so busy looking for problems they may have caused that they didn't look for one simple thing: a link light on the switch.

If they had taken a moment, the students would have remembered that all switches have at least one LED for each switch port to indicate the port's link status. Often, these switches have two color modes, amber and green. Unfortunately, there is no standard for the meaning of the LED indicators. An amber LED on a Cisco switch indicates that a station is plugged into the port and that a link has been established, but that the port is not forwarding data. This amber state usually persists for several seconds after a station has been plugged into a port until the switch has configured itself for the appropriate speed and the STP has learned of this new connection. A green LED indicates that a link has been successfully established and that the switch is ready to receive and send data. Many switches also have LEDs that indicate the mode in which the port is operating. See Figure 4-14 for a look at a switch with a variety of LED indicators.

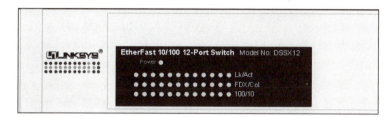

Figure 4-14   LED indicators on a switch

After a switch has successfully negotiated the data link, data can be transferred.

When a Switch Loses Its Way

Your switch has been up and operating for three weeks and things are humming along nicely, when suddenly a power failure occurs. The power comes on after a few seconds, but because you didn't put an uninterruptible power supply (UPS) on your switch, it takes a little longer before things are back to normal.

Of course, there's a reason for the delay. When a switch learns MAC addresses, it stores them in memory, along with the port number from which the MAC addresses were learned. If a frame arrives at the switch with a destination MAC address that is not in its table, the switch forwards the frame to all ports, just a like a repeater. This process is referred to as **flooding** the frame. Because the switch forwards every frame out every port, each frame in a sense acts like a broadcast, causing a considerable amount of unnecessary traffic until the switch rebuilds the MAC address table. Don't be surprised, then, when your network traffic patterns increase dramatically for a period of time (usually only a few minutes) shortly after a loss of power to the switch.

What's the moral of the story? Keep your switches on UPS, and be cautious about powering down a switch for even a second.

When Your Switch Encounters Too Many Stations

A switch does not have a limitless capacity to store MAC addresses. If you plan to use a switch to break up collision domains by connecting hubs to the switch ports or if you plan on using it as a network backbone, you need to consider the MAC address capacity of the switch.

For smaller networks, the address capacity is not much of an issue because even today's low-end products are typically designed to accommodate nearly 1000 MAC addresses. However, if you have an older switch or are using a switch in a very large network, the maximum number of addresses may be a consideration. If a switch does fill the MAC address table and more MAC addresses are introduced, all frames for the addresses that are not in the table will be forwarded to all ports. Thus, although connectivity will still be available, network performance will suffer.

To counteract this performance problem, you can age out MAC addresses. After some period of time (usually minutes or even hours), if a switch does not see a MAC address that is in its table, the switch can remove the address, thereby freeing table entries. In the event that a workstation NIC was replaced or a computer was moved to a different switch, the MAC address is prevented from remaining in the switch memory indefinitely.

A switch usually functions as expected and makes your network support job easier. However, as with any complex piece of hardware, failures do occur, and sometimes these failures can go undetected and be disastrous. We discuss that problem next.

How a Switch Can Introduce Undetected Errors

Transparent switches operate by forwarding frames unaltered from one port to another. When a store-and-forward switch checks the FCSig field to make sure no CRC error exists, the FCS field is checked when the frame is entering the switch. However, all layer 2 and higher-layer devices must calculate the FCS before the frame is sent to its destination. Although rare, memory errors or some other hardware problem could potentially cause the frame data to be changed after the frame has been received and, in the case of a store-and-forward switch, after the FCS is checked. Thus, when the frame is forwarded to the destination, the FCS field is recalculated and appended to the frame, and it will reflect any changed data. When the destination receives the frame, it will not know that data has been corrupted because the FCS field will match the altered data.

Again, these undetected errors are not an extremely common problem. Because this problem happened to me in a live network, causing numerous data corruption problems and taking several long weekends to identify the problem, you should be aware of it.

We're now at the point that we can discuss monitoring a network and capturing and analyzing frames. These are two ways to find and resolve insidious problems like the one just described.

Network Monitors and Protocol Analyzers in a Switched Environment

We have already considered some of the ways in which network monitors and protocol analyzers can be useful. These programs or hardware devices work by listening to all of the frames on the wire as they go by. They gather statistics on the frames or store them in a buffer to be analyzed later. On a shared media network that uses hubs, this process works well because all frames that are sent are seen by all stations, regardless of whether they are the destination address. The key here is that although all frames are seen by all devices, only the device with the matching destination address actually processes the frame.

Don't Let the Switch Fool You

Workstations running network monitoring or protocol analysis software process every frame so that they can gather statistics or capture frames for analysis. Unfortunately, a switch gets in the way of this process. Because a switch forwards frames only to the port where the destination MAC address can be found, the workstation running a protocol analyzer or network monitor will see only those frames that are broadcast frames or that are addressed to that particular workstation.

I hate to admit it, but this characteristic of a switched network once fooled me, albeit for only a few minutes. Some weeks after a network with which I was involved was upgraded from a totally shared media network, like the one in Figure 4-8, to a network with a switched backbone, like the one in Figure 4-10, a network technician ran up to me in an highly excited state. This technician exclaimed that the network was operating really slowly and that the network monitor (Fluke LanMeter) was showing nearly 100 percent broadcasts! Oh boy, that sounded like a broadcast storm. We checked the LanMeter and expected to find a particular device sending lots and lots of broadcast frames or a great deal of jabber errors. Neither was found. In fact, the distribution of frames coming from different devices appeared quite ordinary. After a few minutes of head scratching and checking various servers and router statistics, the answer struck me. Of course the broadcasts were nearly 100 percent! The LanMeter was showing the statistics on frames that it could see, and the only frames it could see were frames that were forwarded out the switch port on which the LanMeter was attached—that is, the broadcast frames.

It turned out the error was not network related at all, but a particular server that needed to be rebooted; however, it was a good lesson. I don't feel too bad; since then, several network technicians have described to me "problems" with a high rate of broadcasts, and I now know to ask them whether the monitor is connected to a switch port. As a teacher, I now can coax them into figuring out the problem for themselves.

So what do you do when you want to monitor all of the traffic on all of the ports on your switch? Luckily, switch manufacturers have thought of this too.

Seeing It All with a Port Monitor Function

Distributed monitoring programs are available that can be installed on a device in each collision domain to forward the statistics to a monitoring station. You even can use a managed switch that can collect data for you and send it to a network management program, but these options are usually expensive and tedious to set up.

Fortunately, a quick and easy way to accomplish your goal is to use a switch's port monitor function. A switch port running in port monitor mode will forward all frames to that port as well as to the appropriate destination port. You have to specifically turn on this function, and usually it can be activated only on a single port—namely, the port to which you would connect your network monitor or the workstation running the monitoring software.

This type of functionality is not available on all switches, so you need to check your switch's user manual to determine whether a port monitor is a feature of your switch. Further consider that some switches allow the monitoring of only one port at a time, so you still cannot get an overall picture of network traffic. Other switches allow you to monitor several ports at one time, giving you a broader picture of what is happening on the network.

Because this monitoring feature degrades switch performance somewhat, you should use it only for troubleshooting purposes and disable it when not troubleshooting. For long-term monitoring, you need to use a more comprehensive tool such as a distributed network management program that is able to gather statistics using Simple Network Management Protocol (SNMP). The use of such tools is beyond the scope of this discussion.

CAPTURING ETHERNET FRAMES

Imagine that you have exhausted all other avenues of troubleshooting a particular network problem and now sit wide-eyed, staring at the initial screen of your protocol analyzer software, hoping it will magically pop up a window telling you what is wrong. I'm afraid it doesn't quite work that way—well, not always, at any rate. Some companies have done an excellent job of building intelligence into their network analysis software so that it can tell you what is wrong. However, you still have to know why you want to capture the frame and what the captured frame can tell you. We discuss these issues next.

Why Do You Want to Capture Frames?

Your average networking day will not be focused on capturing and analyzing Ethernet frames. Although a network monitor that simply gathers and displays statistics will be a far greater part of your life than a frame capture and protocol analyzer program, there are certain situations in which an analysis of the actual data being sent and received is the fastest or perhaps the only way to solve a problem.

What types of problems can be tackled with a protocol analyzer? For one thing, you can solve network application configuration problems. You also can solve frame-formatting problems caused by incompatible frame types or misconfigured or corrupt NIC drivers.

The first time I used a protocol analyzer to solve a problem was also the first time I tried to configure a DNS server. I didn't read or understand (I forget which) the server installation instructions, and my DNS server was not working. Sure, I could have read or reread the manual, but using our new protocol analyzer seemed like a more entertaining idea. I figured we could kill two birds with one stone: learn how to use the analyzer and solve the DNS problem. Using the analyzer, I captured frames related to DNS, and I could clearly see my mistake in the DNS configuration. Because of my ignorance about configuring DNS, I had mistakenly configured the domain name with "www." in front of the domain; requests for hosts on that domain therefore looked like www.www.mycompany.com instead of simply www.mycompany.com. I saw this error immediately while analyzing the frame. When you can actually see the data that the computer processes, errors sometimes jump out at you, allowing you to solve them quickly and easily.

Another problem that was hunted down with a protocol analyzer was a rogue DHCP server. In this case, when workstations booted, they received IP addresses that were not the addresses configured in the DHCP server. I started the protocol analyzer and configured it to look at only DHCP-related frames. Within seconds, it was discovered that someone had set up an unauthorized DHCP server on the network, which was serving invalid IP addresses. Because the protocol analyzer provides such information as the IP address of the sending station, the server was quickly tracked and shut down.

Now that you know why you might want to capture frames, let's look at a frame and check out each of its fields.

Anatomy of a Captured Frame

Let's dissect a frame captured by Wildpacket's EtherPeek protocol analyzer to see what information it has to offer. Figure 4-15 shows the summary screen of a group of captured frames.

Packet	Source	Destination	Size	Time-Stamp	Protocol
1	00:04:4D:1C:FD:45	Mcast Cisco Discovery	139	21:33:35.008790	Discovery
2	00:04:4D:1C:FD:45	Mcast 802.1d Bridge group	64	21:33:35.107462	802.1
3	00:04:4D:1C:FD:45	Mcast 802.1d Bridge group	64	21:33:37.110221	802.1
4	00:04:4D:1C:FD:45	Mcast 802.1d Bridge group	64	21:33:39.115994	802.1
5	00:04:4D:1C:FD:45	Mcast 802.1d Bridge group	64	21:33:41.118931	802.1
6	00:04:4D:1C:FD:45	Mcast 802.1d Bridge group	64	21:33:43.122048	802.1
7	00:04:4D:1C:FD:45	Mcast 802.1d Bridge group	64	21:33:45.123256	802.1

Figure 4-15   EtherPeek frame capture summary

Note the highlighted line in Figure 4-15. We will examine the source address, destination address, and size fields. Note that the packet number, time-stamp, and protocol are not part of the frame, but are merely information that the protocol analyzer provides.

The source address here is 00:04:4D:1C:FD:45. Recall that the first 24 bits or 3 bytes of a MAC address is the OUI that identifies the vendor of the device. The OUI, therefore, is 00:04:4D. EtherPeek attempts to display the vendor name if it has the OUI in its list; in this case, it does not. If you go to *www.ieee.org* and search for this OUI, you will see that it belongs to Cisco Systems. (EtherPeek was updated so that you will see this name in the next figure.)

The next field is the destination address. EtherPeek recognizes this address as a Multicast 802.1D Bridge Group. Recall from our discussion about physical addresses, that the least significant bit of the first byte of the address is the I/G bit. If this bit is 1, the frame is destined for multiple stations. Thus this particular address specifies a multicast frame to all bridges or switches running the 802.1D Spanning-Tree Protocol.

The size of the frame is next. You can see that it is the minimum frame size for Ethernet; that is, it is 64 bytes. The time-stamp is shown in an hours:minutes:seconds:microseconds format and can be helpful in determining how far apart frames were sent. These frames appear to come every two seconds. The last field of interest is the Protocol field, which shows that this is an 802.1 frame.

Figure 4-16 shows one frame from Figure 4-15 in more detail.

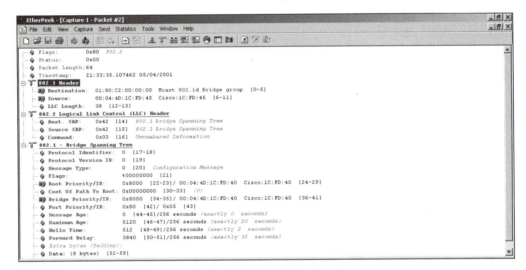

Figure 4-16   Detailed look at a captured frame

The frame data actually starts at the highlighted line titled 802.3 Header. The bracketed numbers to the right of the data on subsequent lines are byte offsets into the frame. For example, the Destination field shows an offset of [0–5], meaning that the destination address occupies bytes 0 through 5 in the frame; the Source field occupies bytes 6 through 11.

EtherPeek has identified this frame as an 802.3 format frame. Recall the format of an Ethernet 802.3 frame, shown again in Table 4-5.

Table 4-5   IEEE 802.3 Frame Format Fields and Byte Sizes

Destination Address	Source Address	Length	LLC Header	Data	FCS
6	6	2	3 or 4	42–1497	4

4

Let's look at the fields one at a time. The destination address comes first and is six bytes in length. Note that the frame in Figure 4-16 shows all six bytes of the MAC address and beside it the vendor ID—in this case, the frame type of Multicast 802.1D Bridge Group. As expected, the first bit of the first byte is set to 1 to indicate a multicast address. The source address comes next and shows the vendor ID of Cisco. (Can you guess what kind of device sent this frame?) The last field is the 802.3 header, with an offset of [12–13] as the length. The length field in an 802.3 frame is the length of the data in the frame, not including the 32-bit FCS, the source and destination addresses, or the length field itself. The length field in our frame has a value of 38. If you add to it the 12 bytes of the source and destination addresses, the 4 bytes of the FCS, and the 2 bytes of the length field itself, you arrive at a total of 56 bytes.

Hey, wait a minute! An Ethernet frame must be at least 64 bytes in length! Correct. If you jump down to offset [52–59], you will see what an Ethernet driver does if the frame is less than 64 bytes of data. It simply pads the rest of the frame with bytes of value 0 until the minimum is reached. In this case, 8 bytes were added before the FCS to create a 64-byte frame.

Look at the next header, the 802.2 LLC header. This header provides important information to the receivers of the frame. The first byte of this header is the **Destination Service Access Point (DSAP)**, which informs the receiver what type of information is in the frame; in this case, it is an 802.1 spanning-tree frame. The **Source Service Access Point (SSAP)** tells the destination from which application the information originated. In this case, the DSAP and the SSAP are the same. The third byte of the LLC header is a control byte and contains no useful information in this frame.

The rest of the frame up to the FCS is considered data and is identified as 802.1 STP information. The last field of note is the FCS. The FCS is shown in Figure 4-16 as all zeroes because the NIC on the station running EtherPeek is not capable of capturing the actual FCS.

You can easily see how capturing frames with a protocol analyzer can be an aid in troubleshooting. We will look at more examples of frame captures, along with upper-layer protocol information, when we discuss the Network and Transport layers in later chapters.

CHAPTER SUMMARY

- The Data Link layer performs many roles on your network. In fact, you can build a serviceable network with the Data Link and Physical layers alone if your data does not have to travel beyond a single broadcast domain.

- Before you can solve problems related to the Data Link layer, you must first know the components of the Data Link layer. They include frames, NICs, and switches and bridges.

❑ A frame is the unit of information with which the Data Link layer works. Consequently, you need to understand the various ways in which Ethernet frames can be formatted so that you will know what to look for when tracking down problems.

❑ When selecting and configuring a NIC, consider network architecture, NIC drivers, and NIC modes of operation so that you can get a good feel for the options available when selecting or supporting a NIC. These factors can make the difference between a network that works so-so and one that works like a well-oiled machine.

❑ Switches are valuable tools, but you must be a knowledgeable user of them. In particular, you must know the methods that switches use to move frames from the incoming ports to the appropriate outgoing ports, STP, and VLANs. In addition, to effectively troubleshoot a switched Ethernet network, you need to know the learning curve of a switch and recognize how to use tools in a switched environment.

❑ You can use protocol analyzers to solve network application configuration problems. You also can solve frame-formatting problems caused by incompatible frame types or misconfigured or corrupt NIC drivers.

KEY TERMS

autonegotiation — An approach used for two devices to decide whether the connection should be established as half duplex or full duplex; specified in the IEEE 802.3u standard.

AutoSense — A method by which a device automatically detects the speed of the device to which it is connected—for example, 10 Mbps or 100 Mbps.

bandwidth — The number of bits per second that media and devices are capable of carrying.

blocking mode — A mode in which a switch port will not forward frames to avoid a bridging loop.

bridging loop — A condition that occurs when switches are connected in such a way that it is possible for frames to be forwarded from switch to switch in an infinite loop.

broadcast — A frame whose destination address is set to all 1s and that is processed by all stations that hear the frame.

broadcast storm — A network condition in which several hundred broadcasts per second are generated.

content addressable memory (CAM) — Memory that contains the switching table, which itself contains source addresses and port numbers.

cut-through switching — A method of switching in which a frame is forwarded to the destination as soon as the destination address is determined.

Cyclic Redundancy Check (CRC) — A calculation performed on the data in a frame that results in a 32-bit value that is used for checking the integrity of transmitted data.

delay — The amount of time that the devices on a network must wait before sending data that is ready to go.

Destination Service Access Point (DSAP) — The first byte of an 802.2 LLC header; used to inform the receiver what type of information is contained in the frame.

driver — Software that serves as an interface between an operating system and a hardware device.

flooding — A situation that occurs when a switch does not know the port for a destination address, and the switch forwards the frame out all ports.

fragment — A runt frame with a bad CRC; it usually results from a collision that is not detected.

fragment-free switching — A switching method in which a switch will discard the frame if the length is not at least 64 bytes.

frame — The final packaging, or encapsulation, of data before it is broken into individual bits to be delivered to the Physical layer by the Data Link layer.

frame check sequence (FCS) — The 32-bit value that results from the CRC calculation performed on each frame and that is used to validate the frame.

giant frame — A frame that is larger than the allowed maximum of 1518 bytes, but that does have a valid CRC.

Individual/Group (I/G) — The first byte of a MAC address; it is used to determine whether the frame is addressed to an individual station or multiple stations.

jabber — A frame that exceeds the maximum frame size and that does not have a valid CRC.

late collision — A collision that occurs after the first 64 bytes of a frame have been transmitted.

least significant bit (LSB) — The rightmost bit in a byte.

misaligned frame — A frame that contains extra bits at the end of the frame that do not form a complete octet.

octet — A grouping of 8 bits.

Organizationally Unique Identifier (OUI) — The first 24 bits of a MAC address; it is used to identify the manufacturer of the NIC.

pad — Extra characters added to a frame or packet as required to meet the minimum frame size.

runt frame — A frame that contains fewer bytes than the minimum frame size of 64 bytes.

Source Service Access Point (SSAP) — Informs the destination from which application the information contained in the frame originated.

Spanning-Tree Protocol (STP) — A protocol used by switches to ensure that a bridging loop does not occur when switches are connected in a redundant fashion.

store-and-forward switching — A switching method in which the entire frame is buffered on the switch until the CRC can be checked.

translation bridges — Bridges that can translate between network architectures by changing the frame header before passing the frame on to the destination.

transparent bridging — A situation in which Ethernet frames pass through a switch unaltered.

4

unicast — A frame that is addressed to a single MAC address with the intention that only one station will process the frame.

Universally/Locally Administered (U/L) — Used to determine whether a MAC address is burned in or assigned locally.

REVIEW QUESTIONS

1. The Data Link layer is responsible for all of the following except _____.

   a. providing encapsulation for Network layer protocols

   b. defining the network architecture

   c. checking each frame for corrupted data through the use of error detection

   d. allowing filtering on logical addresses

2. A MAC address is a _____-bit value that is expressed in hexadecimal format.

   a. 32

   b. 48

   c. 64

   d. 128

3. What type of internetworking device operates at the Data Link layer and makes forwarding decisions based on physical addresses?

   a. switch

   b. router

   c. hub

   d. repeater

4. Which of the following is true about switches? (Choose all that apply.)

   a. Switches forward frames based on the logical address.

   b. Switches operate at the Data Link layer.

   c. Switches help to segment a network.

   d. Switches do not forward broadcast messages.

5. Which of the following is not an example of a physical address?

   a. 04-00-FF-6B-BC-2D

   b. 8C-4C-00-10-AA-EE

   c. 4G-2E-18-09-B9-2F

   d. 00-00-81-53-9B-2C

4

6. A _____ is a frame that is larger than 1518 bytes and that contains a valid CRC.

   a. jabber

   b. giant

   c. misaligned frame

   d. runt

7. A _____ occurs when an excessive amount of broadcast messages are generated, causing extreme slowdowns or failure of the network.

   a. collision domain

   b. multicast cyclone

   c. broadcast storm

   d. unicast storm

8. Which of the following is not an advantage of using a switch? (Choose all that apply.)

   a. Switches can reduce the effects of error frames.

   b. Switches reduce the number of collision domains.

   c. Switches minimize the number of collisions on any given segment.

   d. Switches increase the probability of a collision.

9. A(n) _____ or _____ internetworking device may be used to increase the number of collision domains on the network.

10. A(n) _____ occurs when more than one station tries to transmit at the same time on the same segment.

11. _____ and _____ are frames smaller than 64 KB. They are discarded, regardless of the CRC.

12. Ethernet frames ensure that data is not corrupted during transmission by using _____.

13. A hexadecimal value of _____ indicates a broadcast frame.

14. A(n) _____ refers to the logical grouping of data sent as a Data Link layer unit over a transmission medium.

15. After _____ collisions in a row, a sending NIC stops trying to send a frame and sends an error to the targeted NIC driver.

16. Briefly describe three fields common to all frame formats and explain what they do.

17. How are late collisions handled by the Data Link layer?

18. Speed mismatch and duplex mismatch are symptoms of _____.

   a. improper LSI bit settings

   b. collisions occurring after the first 64 bytes are broadcast, but before the frame is complete

   c. autonegotiation not working

   d. feature creep

19. You would not receive any significant benefit from replacing your hub with a switch if _____.

    a. you have a mixed speed environment

    b. broadcast messages are consuming too much bandwidth

    c. your network performance would benefit from full-duplex communications

    d. you need to filter frames based on MAC addresses

20. The autonegotiation specification is IEEE _____.

21. You have traced a large percentage of your network's jabbers, misaligned frames, and runs to a particular workstation. Which troubleshooting methods should you use next? (Choose all that apply.)

    a. Check the currently selected driver to make sure that it is the correct driver and that it is functioning properly.

    b. Verify that station's TCP/IP settings.

    c. Investigate the local office environment to make sure there are no sources for EMI interference.

    d. Connect the workstation to a different hub.

22. What is the definition of bandwidth?

    a. the number of bits per second the media and devices are capable of carrying

    b. the number of members of the band who play an instrument

    c. the number of devices that can be placed on a segment

    d. the frequency of collisions

24. What is the OUI and what is it used for?

25. The consortium that originated Ethernet, DIX, was named after

    _____.

    a. the base that DARPA used to house the Ethernet studies, Fort Dix

    b. the goal of the project, Duplex Internet Xmit

    c. the three companies that formed the consortium: Digital, Intel, Xerox

    d. its founder, Henri Shault St. Dix

HANDS-ON PROJECTS

Project 4-1 Identify Data Link Layer Components in the Network Control Panel

In this project, you will look at the Network Control Panel in Windows 95 or 98 and identify the Data Link layer components found there.

1. Right-click **Network Neighborhood**.
2. Select **Properties** from the context menu, and then click the Configuration tab, if necessary.
3. Click the adapter next to the icon. If more than one adapter is visible, do not click Dial-up Adapter; Click the name of the other adapter.
4. What type of NIC is installed in your machine?
5. Select the **NIC driver component**.
6. Select **Properties**.
7. What properties can be set for your NIC?
8. Click **Cancel** until the Control Panel is closed.

Project 4-2 Examine LEDs to Determine Whether Collisions Are Present

In this project, you will create network traffic, along with your classmates, to try to create collisions. You will watch the hub LEDs to determine whether collisions are present.

1. Click **Start**, click **Run**, and then type **command**.
2. Your instructor will give you the IP address of his or her workstation. Write it down. You will use it in Step 3 in place of *instructor-ip-address*.
3. At the DOS prompt, type **ping –n 100 –l 1400** *instructor–ip–address*.
4. Observe the LEDs on the hub to which your workstations are attached. Do you see the collision indicator? Is it flashing? Flashing means that collisions are occurring.
5. Write a short explanation of the –n and –l parameters used in the ping command and discuss how these parameters can be useful in troubleshooting.
6. Close the DOS box by typing **Exit**.

Project 4-3 Determine the Switching Method Used by a Switch

This lab requires a Cisco 1900 series switch or another switch that can be configured for different switching methods.

1. Connect your PC to the console port of the Cisco 1900 switch. This step requires a terminal adapter for your Com1 port and a rollover cable.
2. Open Hyperterminal by clicking **Start**, pointing to **Programs**, pointing to **Accessories**, pointing to **Communications**, and then clicking **HyperTerminal**.
3. In the Name text box, type **Console**, and then click **OK**.
4. In the Connect Using text box, select **Com1**, and then click **OK**.
5. In the Bits Per Second text box, select **9600**, and then click **OK**.
6. Press **Enter**. You should see a menu with three choices, M, I, and P.
7. Type **M** to get to the Main menu.

8. Type **S** to get to the System menu. In the Settings section, beside the line that says "[S] Switching Mode," you should see either Fragment Free or Store and Forward.

9. Write down the Settings listed for Address Aging Time and Action Upon Address Violation. The Address Aging Time is the number of seconds that the switch keeps a learned MAC address in its address table if the switch does not hear any more frames from that address. The Action Upon Address Violation is a security measure. If the switch sees a MAC address that is not valid, the switch will take the prescribed action.

10. Type **X** to get back to the Main menu.

Project 4-4 Determine Latency Between a Switch and a Hub

This project requires a switch and a hub and at least two workstations, preferably with 10 Mbps NICs. You will work with a partner.

1. Connect two workstations to a hub.

2. Both workstations should be configured with TCP/IP with different addresses on the same network. Write down your partner's IP address. You will use it in Step 4 in place of *partner-ip-address*.

3. You or your partner (not both) should open a DOS box by clicking **Start**, clicking **Run**, and then typing **command**.

4. At the DOS prompt, type **ping –n 10 –l 1400** *partner-ip-address*.

5. Record the response time of all 10 pings.

6. Have your partner repeat the process starting at Step 3.

7. Connect the two stations to a switch. The hub and switch should both operate at the same speed and at half-duplex mode for a fair test.

8. Repeat Steps 3 through 6.

9. What were your findings? Which device appeared to provide a faster response, the hub or the switch?

10. Repeat the process again, this time with both you and your partner running the Ping command at exactly the same time. Were there any differences?

Project 4-5 Capture Frames with EtherPeek

EtherPeek should be installed on the workstations according to the instructions that came with the program for you to do this project.

1. Click **Start**, point to **Programs**, and then click **Wildpackets EtherPeek**.

2. From the Capture menu, select **Start Capture**. If a Capture Options dialog box is displayed, uncheck the **Show this dialog when creating a new capture window** check box, and then click **OK**.

3. In the window that opens, click the **Start Capture** button.

4. If no frames appear in the capture window, double-click **Network Neighborhood**; otherwise, go to Step 6.

5. You should start to see frames appearing in the capture window. After 8 or 10 frames appear, click the **Stop Capture** button.

6. Double-click one of the frames to get a detailed view.

7. Use the tables explaining the four frame formats (Tables 4-1 through 4-2) to figure out which format you are looking at. How can you tell?

8. Close all windows, and then close EtherPeek.

Project 4-6 Determine Frame Sizes and Statistics in Your Network

This project uses EtherPeek to display a graph of the various frame sizes seen on your network and a table of the protocol mix used in your network. This project works best if the workstation running EtherPeek is attached to a live network.

1. Click **Start**, point to **Programs**, and then click **Wildpackets EtherPeek**.

2. Click the **Statistics** menu and select **Size**. A pie chart appears. Note that the smallest frame size shown is 64 bytes and the largest is 1518 bytes. These are the minimum and maximum frame sizes for Ethernet.

3. Click the **Statistics** menu again and select **Protocols**. A table appears showing the protocols seen on the network.

4. At the top of the Protocol Statistics window, click the **Protocols Seen** list arrow, and then click **2s**. This sets the screen refresh time to two seconds.

5. In the Protocol column, click the box with the minus sign in it to the left of the protocol Ethernet Type 2. This collapses the protocols displayed under Ethernet Type 2.

6. Click the box again to expand the protocol display.

7. Close the Protocol Statistics and Size Statistics windows.

8. Close EtherPeek.

CASE PROJECTS

Case 4-1 Describe a Capture

Take a look at Figure 4-17. This capture is the result of a single command typed at a workstation. Which command was used? Write down as much information as you can think of that this frame capture tells you.

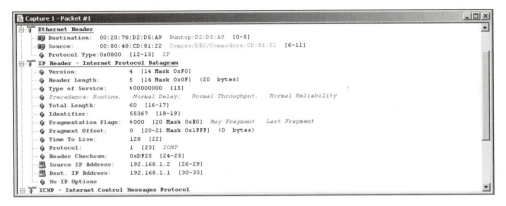

Figure 4-17   Capture of a workstation command

Case 4-2 Researching Errors

Research an error related to the Data Link layer. Use the Internet or magazines to conduct the search. Try to find a unique error and the solution used on the problem. Write a brief report on your findings.

Case 4-3 Network Problems

Describe three network problems that replacing a hub with a switch could help solve. Describe two network problems that replacing a hub with a switch probably would not solve.

Case 4-4 Monitoring a Network

You have been monitoring a network for the past 10 minutes. Your network monitor gives you the following information on a 10 Mbps, hub–based network:

- Average utilization: 35%
- Percent broadcasts: 5%
- Percent collisions: 15%
- Total number of frames: 1,800,000
- CRC errors: 150

Given this information, what do you conclude about the operation of this network? Is everything okay? If so, why do you come to that conclusion? If not, what problems do you see and how would you go about fixing them?

Case 4-5 Determine Speed and Duplex Mode

In this case, you will examine the LEDs on your workstation NIC. Find the NIC on the back of your PC. Which LEDs are visible? Can you determine the speed or duplex mode from the LEDs? Describe the information the NIC LEDs provided.

4

5

SUPPORTING THE NETWORK AND TRANSPORT LAYERS

> **After reading this chapter and completing the exercises, you will be able to:**
> ♦ Understand and describe the roles of the Network and Transport layers of the OSI model
> ♦ Identify the components of the Network and Transport layers
> ♦ Support the TCP/IP protocol, understand why UDP is an unreliable protocol, and support IPX/SPX
> ♦ Understand NetBEUI
> ♦ Support routers

Networking professionals find the Network and Transport layers interesting because they are where the majority of the configuration and fine-tuning of network devices occurs. It is the Network layer of the OSI model that makes internetworks work, and it is the Transport layer that makes them reliable.

Your mastery of the use and support of these two layers of the OSI model can transform you from just a face in the network-technician crowd to the go-to person when big internetworking problems arise. To begin your ascension to network mastery, we start with the roles of the Network layer.

THE ROLES OF THE NETWORK LAYER

The Network layer is where you will likely do the most network configuration. There are network addresses and subnet masks to assign, default gateways and name servers to add, and routers to install and configure. Of course, the Network layer is also where the most errors in network configuration occur, and in a large internetwork, a lot of your time is likely to be spent unraveling its intricacies.

The tasks involved in supporting the Network layer are not numerous, but you must have a thorough understanding of the roles the Network layer plays to effectively maintain and troubleshoot networks at this level. The Network layer deals in logical addresses; using these addresses, network protocols move your data packets from one network to another efficiently.

We frame our discussion of the Network layer in three parts: defining logical addresses, providing path selections, and working with connectionless delivery of packets.

Defining Logical Addresses

A **logical address** is the address assigned to devices that provide both network and host information and that operate at the Network layer. Logical addresses, unlike the physical addresses that the Data Link layer defines, give your network structure. For a networking protocol to move data from one network to another, it must utilize two-part logical addresses: one part to identify the network and one part to identify the host.

Many, but not all, network protocols utilize logical addresses in this manner. TCP/IP, IPX/SPX, and AppleTalk do meet this requirement, for example, but NetBEUI and Data Link Control (DLC) do not. Because of the dominance of TCP/IP in today's networking environment, and the complexity of its addressing, our focus will be on the TCP/IP protocol when discussing logical address issues.

 For more information on IPX/SPX and AppleTalk, visit these two URLs: *www.protocols.com/pbook/novel.htm* for IPX/SPX and other Novell protocols, and *www.protocols.com/pbook/appletalk.htm* for AppleTalk and related protocols.

Logical addresses must have both a network and host portion so that large networks can be built with hosts in the thousands (a corporation) or even in the millions (the Internet) and each host can be quickly located within the network. Routers find an individual host by first concentrating on finding the network in which the host resides. After the network is found, a router on that network locates the individual host by mapping the logical address to the Data Link layer physical address. Each protocol uses a different method to map the logical host address to the physical address after the packet has arrived at the correct network. TCP/IP's method is to use the Address Resolution Protocol (ARP).

One of the more complex aspects of the Network layer is determining the best way to get a packet from network to network as it moves toward its destination. We discuss that issue next.

Path Selection in an Internetwork

If there were only one way to get from here to there, the Network layer's job would be pretty ho-hum. However, much like the nation's road system, most large networks have multiple paths to get from location A to location B. It is not always a clear-cut decision as to which path to take. Some paths are heavily traveled, and some are lightly traveled; some have construction or accidents, and still others are clear sailing.

The Network layer, using routing protocols, can select the best path to the destination. If a once-good path becomes unavailable or congested, an alternate path can be selected. Routing protocols depend on logical addresses that have both Network and Host Address fields. Protocols that have this type of logical addressing scheme are said to be routed or routable protocols. When routers are discussed later in this chapter, we will look in more detail at how routing protocols are configured and watch for some problem areas.

The Network layer has plenty to do in trying to get a packet from one network to another efficiently. The secret to this efficiency is low overhead. In other words, the Network layer has a specific job to do, and issues such as reliability and flow control are left to other networking layers.

Connectionless Delivery of Packets

The Network layer relies on the upper layers of the OSI model to provide advanced features such as reliability and flow control. The Network layer's responsibility is to deliver packet Y from a source network to a destination network, with no concern as to whether packet X or packet Z also made it to the destination. In fact, after the Network layer component on one network has sent a packet to the next network along the path to the packet's destination, there is no confirmation as to whether it actually arrived safely. This approach is called **connectionless communications**.

In connectionless communications, there is no connection made from source to destination. The Network layer protocol relies on faith (or an upper-layer protocol) to ensure the packet's safe journey. This system is much like the delivery of a first-class letter using the U.S. mail. You drop the letter in the mailbox and hope that it makes it. Usually it does, but when you want to be certain that it was received (or notified that it was not), you must add a layer of complexity to the letter (and pay a few more dollars) and send the letter by certified mail. Certified mail requires an acknowledgment from the receiver, and a notice of receipt is sent back to the sender. In networking, this is the role of the Transport layer—and the topic of the next section of this chapter.

ROLES OF THE TRANSPORT LAYER

Without the Transport layer in networking protocol suites, the Internet would be in big trouble. So many things can go wrong with complex, ever-changing networks that without some safeguards, it would be a miracle if you successfully transferred any information at all.

In the following sections, we discuss the many roles that the Transport layer fills. The first four roles are important, no doubt. The fifth role—determining quality of service—is the role that makes the whole network hum.

Segmenting Data

The Transport layer segments data before sending it to the Network layer, and it reassembles the data before sending it up to the Session or Application layers. When the Transport layer receives data from the upper layers of the OSI model, the size of the data may be too large to send to the Network layer in one piece. In such a situation, it is the job of the Transport layer to break the data into smaller pieces called **segments** before handing each piece to the Network layer. Each segment is labeled with a sequence number so that, if the segments arrive at the destination out of order, they can be reassembled in the correct order using the sequence number.

Flow Control with Acknowledgments

Another role of the Transport layer is to provide flow control, which prevents a destination from becoming overwhelmed by data; such an event would cause packets to be dropped. The Transport layer accomplishes this goal by establishing a maximum number of bytes that may be sent before the destination must acknowledge the receipt of the data. In TCP/IP, this maximum number of bytes is referred to as the window size. If a sending machine has not received an acknowledgment before it has sent the number of bytes established by the window size, it stops sending data. If no acknowledgment is received within a specified timeout period, the sender retransmits the data from the point at which an acknowledgment was last received.

Providing a Checksum

Many Transport layers provide a checksum to protect data integrity. Remember the Cyclic Redundancy Check (CRC) discussed in the Data Link layer? The checksum in a Transport layer segment provides a function that is similar to the function provided by the CRC.

The checksum is a 16-bit value that is calculated based on data bytes in the segment.

Note that the CRC is not always a perfect mechanism to ensure that data did not become corrupted en route to its destination. Routers and switches have been known to corrupt data, recalculate the CRC, and send the corrupted data on its way. Because the CRC is calculated after the corruption, the receiver would have no way of knowing that the data was corrupted.

Intermediate devices do not recalculate the checksum in the Transport layer. Thus, if data corruption occurs along the way, the final receiving station will detect the checksum error and discard the data. A checksum can be implemented by both connection-oriented and connectionless Transport layer protocols. (These protocols are discussed later in this section.)

Identifying Data

The Transport layer can indicate to the receiving computer what kind of data is contained in the message. This information ensures that the proper application processes the data.

When a computer receives a packet of data, it is received by the NIC and then sent up to the Data Link layer, the Network layer, and finally the Transport layer. Then what? Eventually, data that is received must go to an application, but the computer might have one, two, three, or a dozen applications waiting for data. Fortunately, the Transport layer header provides the information to determine to which application the received data should be sent. With TCP/IP, port numbers are used to specify the destination application. The NetWare protocol IPX/SPX uses a similar method, but—just to confuse you—in IPX/SPX the destination application information is contained in the Network layer.

 An IP application that does not use a Transport layer protocol may rely on the Network layer to provide application information. Examples of such applications are the Ping utility and routing protocols. As you will see later in this chapter, the IP packet header provides a Protocol field for just this purpose.

Determining Quality of Service

In networking, **quality of service (QoS)** determines how reliable data transfers will be and at what performance level the transfer will occur. The protocols that operate at the Transport layer help determine the QoS that will be available to an application that is transferring data. If an application requires a sound, reliable method of transferring data, it will use a Transport layer protocol that provides the desired reliability, but usually at a somewhat reduced performance level. If an application does not require a high level of reliability, a Transport layer protocol that is less reliable but more performance-oriented may be used.

In this part of the chapter, we divide the discussion into two parts: connection-oriented protocols, which provide more reliability, and connectionless protocols, which skimp on reliability in favor of less overhead and more performance.

Connection Oriented Equals Reliable

The need for QoS becomes particularly acute in situations such as data transfers across unpredictable environments like the Internet. Applications that require reliability use a Transport layer protocol that provides an end-to-end **virtual circuit** that uses flow control, acknowledgments, and other methods to guarantee delivery of data. Such protocols are referred to as **connection-oriented protocols**. The establishment of a conversation session, or a data-transfer session between two network nodes, is an integral part of the reliability that the Transport layer provides.

 A virtual circuit is much like a human telephone conversation in which conversation (data transfer) occurs only when a connection has been established. The caller dials the number, the phone rings, and someone answers. After the called party answers, the caller identifies himself or herself, the called person acknowledges the caller, and the conversation begins.

Connectionless Equals Unreliable

Not every application needs the benefit of a Transport layer that provides a reliable QoS. Some applications are meant to run primarily in LANs as opposed to large internetworks, and reliability, although still important, is taken for granted. In these applications, the overhead and complexity of a transport system that provides a high degree of reliability are neither required nor desirable. In such situations, the application uses a connectionless Transport layer protocol because it consumes less overhead in the form of network bandwidth and processing.

If the whole idea of the Transport layer is to provide a layer of reliability for the Network layer, why is there an "unreliable" Transport layer protocol? Your first step to answering that question is remembering that the Transport layer does more than just provide reliability through connection-oriented sessions. It can also protect data using a checksum and provide valuable information to applications. Thus, if an application requires a Transport layer protocol but does not want the extra overhead that a connection-oriented protocol requires, perhaps because reliability is not a major concern, a connectionless protocol can be used, which still offers many advantages of the Transport layer. TCP/IP implements just such a pseudo-Transport layer protocol called UDP. We discuss UDP in more detail later in this chapter.

COMPONENTS OF THE NETWORK AND TRANSPORT LAYERS

When you think of the Network and Transport layers, two things should come to mind: protocols and routers. Protocols are integral to these layers because they define the rules and syntax of data transfer sessions. Routers are critical to the Network layer because they utilize the logical address defined at the Network layer to determine how best to get data from here to there in an internetwork. In addition, the Network and Transport layers are integral to your career because expertise in these areas is in high demand and frequently pays quite well.

Next, we discuss each of these components in detail.

Networking Protocols

Although the Physical layer is the foundation of your network, protocols working at the Network and Transport layers are the heart and soul of the network. Most protocols come as a package deal, combining a suite of functions into one protocol installation. For example:

- TCP/IP carries with it the IP Network layer protocol and the TCP and UDP Transport layer protocols, not to mention a nice collection of applications and troubleshooting tools such as the FTP and Ping utilities.

- IPX/SPX carries with it the IPX Network layer protocol, the SPX Transport layer protocol, and the NetWare Core Protocol (NCP), which handles some Transport layer and upper-layer functions.

- NetBEUI is a lightweight, performing only at the Transport and Session layers.

Although many networking protocols are available, this text concentrates on the most pervasive protocol around the world, TCP/IP. IPX/SPX and NetBEUI are discussed as well, based on their popular use in small to medium-size NetWare networks and Windows peer-to-peer networks, respectively.

Protocols are the language of the network, and typically, the more complex your network is, the more complex your protocol needs to be. Simple networks that require only some file and print sharing among a few Windows-based computers work fine with NetBEUI. In addition, networks that rely on dedicated NetWare servers without the use of Internet technologies have worked well with IPX/SPX for years. However, complex networks spanning areas ranging from a large campus to the entire globe and providing a myriad of services and Internet technologies require a correspondingly complex protocol—TCP/IP. Get used to TCP/IP; you'll be seeing a lot of it.

Routers Get Your Data Where You Want It to Go

Without routers working hard, primarily at the Network layer, we wouldn't have wonderful resources such as the Internet. Imagine a postal system in which we address our mail with a street address only—no city, no state, and no ZIP code. The complete hopelessness of such a system is what large networks would be like without routers.

Routers, along with the protocols that contain logical addresses, provide some order and structure to large internetworks. A router's job is to receive a network packet, determine the network number of the destination address, and send the packet in the direction of the destination network. If the router receiving the packet happens to be directly connected to the destination network, the router delivers the packet to the destination host. In small internetworks with only a few network numbers, this is not a complicated task. In an internetwork with dozens or thousands of networks, however, the proper configuration of routers, the selection of routing protocols, and the implementation of security measures is a highly sought-after skill.

SUPPORTING TCP/IP WITH THE INTERNET PROTOCOL

If you want to be known as a networking expert, you need to know the ins and outs of the protocol that runs the Internet. The TCP/IP protocol suite consists of many components and encompasses the top five layers of the OSI model.

At this time, review Figure 5-1, which shows the TCP/IP protocol suite in relation to the OSI model. Notice the Network Interface layer, which corresponds to the Data Link and Physical layers of the OSI model. TCP/IP does not have a protocol or component that works at these two layers, but it does work with any Physical and Data Link specification, provided that appropriate Data Link drivers are used.

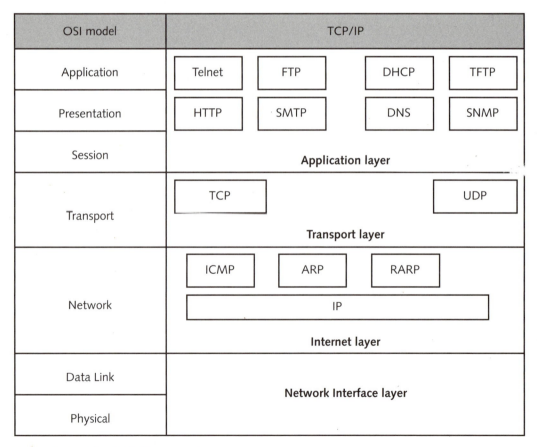

Figure 5-1   The TCP/IP protocol suite

In the next section, we will concentrate on the components of the TCP/IP suite that operate at the Network and Transport layers. We will look at IP and study IP addressing and packet formats. In addition, we will examine ICMP and ARP, two of the IP routing protocols. Last, we will study the nuances of TCP, concentrating in particular on ports, handshaking, and segments.

IP at the Network Layer

That global wealth of information and misinformation known as the Internet is named after the now–ubiquitous networking protocol that is Internet Protocol (IP). Who would have guessed that a communications technology developed almost 30 years ago could have such a tremendous effect on our everyday lives today? The staying power of IP is a testament to the forethought of those who developed it. Of course, it has been enhanced over the years to accommodate the tremendous growth the Internet has undergone, but fundamentally the IP protocol remains the same today as it was 30 years ago.

 If you would like to read about some of the enhancements and clarifications made to IP and the TCP/IP protocol suite over the years, there is a set of published documents called Requests for Comments (RFCs) that are as close to a published standard as you will find. They can be accessed at *www.rfc-editor.org/rfc.html*.

The key to supporting IP is understanding the addressing scheme. After the addressing is understood, it is easier to support the operation and configuration of network hosts and routers. For this reason, addressing is where we will start.

IP Addressing

There is plenty of information available on IP addressing, and it is expected that you have some training in this area already. But, as students are fond of saying, if you don't use it, you lose it. This section will serve as a refresher for those of you who have not been using it.

An IP address is a 32-bit number, broken into four 8-bit values called **octets**. Each octet can have a value in the range 0 to 255. Traditionally, IP addresses are written in dotted decimal form, although you may occasionally run into an application that requires hexa-decimal. A typical IP address might look like:

192.168.254.17

where 192 is the first octet and 17 is the fourth octet.

Contained in every IP address is a network number and a host number. That is, some of the 32 bits specify the network on which the host can be found. The rest of the bits specify a particular computer or device on that network.

Three classes of IP addresses can be assigned to a host: class A, class B, or class C. The class to which a particular IP address belongs is determined by the value of the first octet of the address, as shown in Table 5-1.

Table 5-1   IP Address Classes

Value of First Octet	Class
1–127	A
128–191	B
192–223	C

 Class D and E IP addresses also exist. Class D addresses have a first octet value in the range 224–239 and are used for multicast applications. Class E addresses have a first octet value in the range 240–255 and are reserved for experimental use.

The class of the address determines the default number of bits that are used to specify the network number; the remainder of the bits specify the host. The network bits are always allocated starting with the first octet. Table 5-2 shows this relationship.

Table 5-2   Network Bits and Default Subnet Masks in Address Classes

Class	Number of Network Bits/Octets	Default Subnet Mask
A	8/1	255.0.0.0
B	16/2	255.255.0.0
C	24/3	255.255.255.0

To specify a network number, you write the value of the network number, followed by zeroes for the host portion of the address. For example, a class A network might look like 10.0.0.0, a class B network might look like 172.15.0.0, and a class C network might look like 192.168.1.0. From this information, it is easy to see that a class A network can have plenty of hosts, whereas a class C network is limited to a single octet's worth of hosts.

When assigning IP addresses to hosts, there are some rules to remember:

- All hosts on the same physical network must share the same network number.

- All host IDs on the same network must be unique.

- You cannot assign a host ID in which all of the host bits are zero. Such a host ID is reserved for the network number.

- You cannot assign a host ID in which all host bits are 1. Such a host ID is reserved for the network broadcast address.

Hopefully, it is all coming back to you now. It's time delve a little deeper. Let's take a look at a class A address again. The first octet, 8 bits, specifies the network number, and the last three octets, or 24 bits, specify the host address. Twenty-four bits! How many hosts can we assign to a class A network? That's 2^{24}, or 16,777,216 hosts. Even if we take away the all-0s and all-1s host, we still have 16,277,214 hosts.

What do you call the group of computers and devices that are on the same network? A **broadcast domain**. If you try to put 16 million hosts on a single broadcast domain, the only traffic you will ever see is broadcasts—and not many of those either, because the broadcasts will be too busy colliding with each other! That is why we don't simply go with the class rules to determine the number of bits in the network number. Instead, we need a way to break up these huge class A and B networks, and sometimes even the comparatively small class C networks. That's where subnetting and the subnet mask come in.

Subnetting and the Subnet Mask

Everybody has his or her own unique way of explaining the subject of subnetting. I will explain it my way and if that does not work for you, ask a friend or a teacher or try *www.howtosubnet.com* until you find an explanation that clicks for you.

Subnetting is the breaking up of a particular class of address into more networks. The **subnet mask** defines which part of the IP address is the network portion and which part is the host portion. The subnet mask is called a mask because it hides, or masks, the host portion of the address when a logical AND operation is done between the subnet mask and IP address.

 You must *always* use subnet masks. The subnet mask is a partner with the IP address. Neither one can stand alone, so when you assign one, you must assign the other.

The host uses the subnet mask, along with the assigned IP address, to identify its own network. The router uses it, along with the destination address in an incoming packet, to determine to which network the packet should be forwarded.

A logical AND can be looked at as multiplication on a bit-by-bit basis. Because we are working with bits, the product of the multiplication can be only a 1 or a 0. Because anything multiplied by 0 is also 0, the only way you can get a 1 is if both values are 1.

Confused yet? Let's look at a simple example using a class C address, 192.168.1.10. A class C address uses the first three octets to specify the network number. The default subnet mask for a class C address is 255.255.255.0. Again, the purpose of the subnet mask is to hide the host ID so that a device knows the network on which it belongs. Let's break the address and mask into binary and do the logical AND operation:

$$11000000.10101000.00000001.00001010 = 192.168.1.10$$

$$11111111.11111111.11111111.00000000 = 255.255.255.0$$

If you AND these two values together, you simply multiply each bit in the IP address with the corresponding bit in the subnet mask, giving you the following:

11000000.10101000.00000001.00001010

AND

11111111.11111111.11111111.00000000

11000000.10101000.00000001.00000000

This yields 192.168.1.0, which is the network number for the class C address. The host ID is effectively hidden by performing the AND operation. This approach permits a device to quickly determine to which network the address belongs.

Now imagine that we want to take this class C network and break it into six smaller networks. We need to borrow some of the 8 host bits in the fourth octet and make those bits into network bits. For n bits borrowed, there is the potential to create 2^n networks. Consequently, you have fewer hosts on each network because you have fewer bits in the Host field. Let's see why. Imagine that you have taken 2 bits from the Host field and moved them to the Network field. How many different values can you make with 2 bits? Well, you can make the following:

00, 01, 10, 11

Four different values are possible ($2^2 = 4$). If we borrow 3 bits, we can make the following values:

000, 001, 010, 011, 100, 101, 110, 111

That's eight different values ($2^3 = 8$). Now you have the idea. As mentioned, you have the potential to create 2^n networks. This ability is potential only because, as with the assignment of host addresses, rules govern the assignment of subnet numbers. You cannot use a subnet in which all of the subnet bits are 1 because the broadcast address of the subnet would be the same as the full-class, network broadcast address and that is not allowed. Additionally, on some routers, you cannot use a subnet that is all 0s. Thus you may have to subtract as many as two networks to arrive at the actual maximum number of subnets.

After you have determined the number of networks into which you want to break the larger network, you simply change the default subnet mask by changing 0s to 1s in the Host field. Look at the previous network and subnet mask of 192.168.1.0 and 255.255.255.0. If I want to break this network into six networks, I need to use 3 bits from the Host field and make them into network bits ($2^3 = 8$; subtract the 2 we cannot use, which leaves 6). Now, turn 3 of the 0 bits in the subnet mask into 1 bits (always starting from the left), and you get the following subnet mask in binary:

11111111.11111111.11111111.11100000

This yields 255.255.255.224 in decimal. What are the potential network numbers when you use the class C address of 192.168.1.0 with that mask? The way to determine that information is to take the 3 bits used previously, place them in the network number, and cycle them through the possible combinations of values they represent. Here we show only the last octet of the network number in binary, as it is the only thing that changes here. The 3 bits we used from the host are shown in boldface.

192.168.1.**000**00000	192.168.1.0
192.168.1.**001**00000	192.168.1.32
192.168.1.**010**00000	192.168.1.64
192.168.1.**011**00000	192.168.1.96
192.168.1.**100**00000	192.168.1.128
192.168.1.**101**00000	192.168.1.160
192.168.1.**110**00000	192.168.1.192
192.168.1.**111**00000	192.168.1.224

Let's eliminate the network with all 0s in the subnet bits and the network with all 1s, leaving the middle 6 of the 8 subnetworks. The host numbers for each network can be found by cycling the remaining 5 host bits, being sure to omit the all-0s host and the all-1s host. Now, if you assign a host computer with an address of 192.168.1.45 and a subnet mask of 255.255.255.224, the host computer will do this logical AND operation:

$$192.168.1.00101101$$

$$\text{AND}$$

$$\underline{255.255.255.00100000}$$

$$192.168.1.00100000$$

The result is the network number 192.168.1.32.

So, why does a computer need to know what network it is on? To answer that question, we need to look at what is needed to configure a workstation.

IP Host Configuration

After you have figured if and how you need to subnet your network beyond the default mask, it's time to configure hosts and devices. One of the rules of IP address assignment is that all hosts on the same physical network must share the same network number. Because an IP address cannot be assigned without a subnet mask, this requirement implies that they must share the same subnet mask as well.

To visualize what it means to be on the same physical network, take a look at Figure 5-2. Each area in the figure with a circle around it denotes a separate physical network. In essence, a separate physical network is any part of a network that is separated from other parts of the network by a router interface. The router interfaces within each physical network must also be assigned an address with the same network number as the hosts in that network.

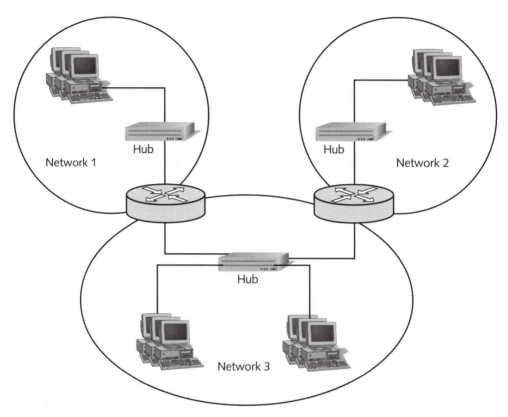

Figure 5-2   Three physical networks bounded by router interfaces

Besides an IP address and subnet mask, most host configurations also require a default gateway address. The **default gateway** is the address of the device, usually a router, to which all packets should be sent if the destination IP address of the packet is not on the same network as the host sending the packet.

When a host has a packet to send to a destination, the host ANDs the destination IP address with its own subnet mask. If the resulting network number is not the same as the host's network number, the packet is sent to the default gateway in hopes that the default gateway can find the destination network. Because the default gateway is used to locate hosts on different networks, it follows that it must be on the same network as the sending station.

One common problem with host configurations is specifying the wrong subnet mask. Suppose that two PCs are on the same physical network. Computer A has the address 192.168.1.34 with a subnet mask of 255.255.255.224. Computer B has an address of

192.168.1.60 with a subnet mask of 255.255.255.0. If Computer A attempts to ping Computer B, the following occurs: Computer A ANDs the destination address 192.168.1.60 with the subnet mask 255.255.255.224, resulting in a network number of 192.168.1.32. Because Computer A is in network 192.168.1.32, you will find that Computer A will send an ARP broadcast to retrieve the MAC address of Computer B, and in fact, the ping will be sent and replied to as if no configuration error occurred.

OK, now it's time to add to the fun. Suppose that a third computer, Computer C, is on the network with an address of 192.168.1.67 and a subnet mask of 255.255.255.0. If Computer A attempts to ping Computer C, the following occurs: Computer A ANDs 192.168.1.67 with Computer A's own subnet mask 255.255.255.224. In this case, the resulting network is 192.168.1.64. Computer A, thinking that the destination is on a different network, will erroneously attempt to send the packet to its default gateway.

Such situations can be difficult to troubleshoot. When configuring IP addresses, the importance of carefully checking the configuration cannot be overstated; typos are often the chief cause of configuration errors. It is not good enough to simply verify that the workstation can communicate with another PC, as the preceding example illustrates.

IP Packets

The unit of data with which the Network layer deals is the packet. When troubleshooting configuration or performance problems, you need to understand how IP packages the data that it receives from the upper layers. There are many fields in an IP packet, and understanding the purpose of some of the fields will help you understand what is occurring in your network if you capture packets with a protocol analyzer. It can also help you pinpoint problem areas that are causing performance degradation.

IP packets (sometimes referred to as IP datagrams) are the final encapsulation of your data before the data is sent to the Data Link layer. When the Data Link layer receives an IP datagram from the Network layer, the frame is formatted as an Ethernet Version II frame. If you recall from the earlier discussion about the Data Link layer (Chapter 4), the Ethernet Version II frame contains a two-byte field called EtherType. The Data Link layer sets the EtherType field to 0x800 to indicate to the destination that an IP datagram is contained in the frame. Figure 5-3 shows the format of a frame containing an IP datagram.

Destination Address	Source Address	EtherType 0x800	IP Header	Data	FCS

Figure 5-3   Ethernet II frame with IP datagram

The IP header length can vary between 20 and 60 bytes. The data can have a variable length. The length of the IP header plus the data in an Ethernet frame will vary from a minimum of 46 bytes to a maximum of 1500 bytes. This is because the Data Link header plus FCS in an Ethernet II frame is 18 bytes, whereas the minimum Ethernet frame is 64 bytes and the maximum is 1518 bytes.

To show these header fields more clearly, let's examine the IP header in Figure 5-4 more closely.

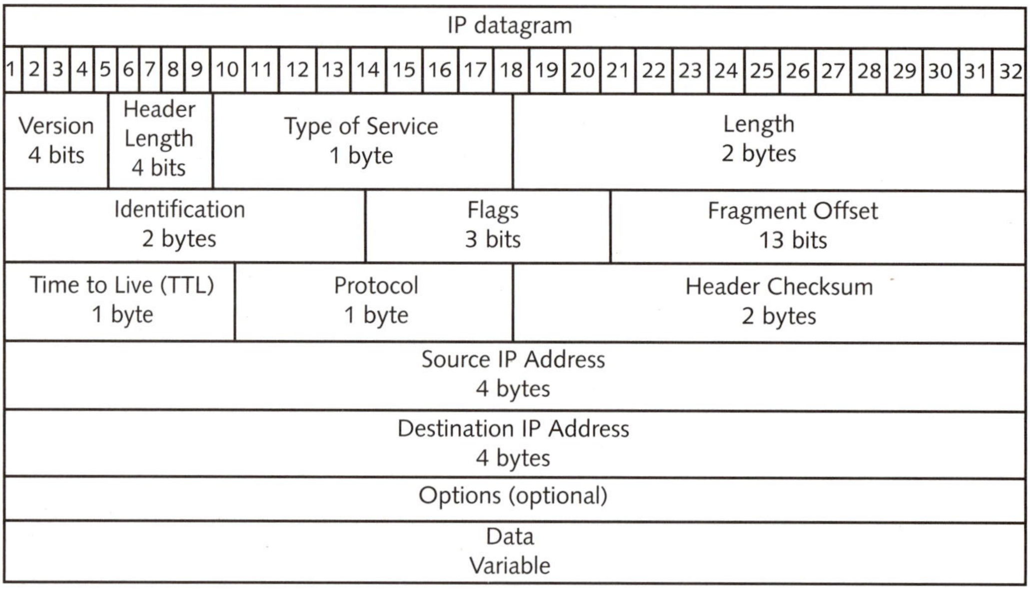

IP datagram																															
1	2	3	4	5	6	7	8	9	10	11	12	13	14	15	16	17	18	19	20	21	22	23	24	25	26	27	28	29	30	31	32

Version 4 bits	Header Length 4 bits	Type of Service 1 byte		Length 2 bytes	
Identification 2 bytes		Flags 3 bits	Fragment Offset 13 bits		
Time to Live (TTL) 1 byte		Protocol 1 byte	Header Checksum 2 bytes		
Source IP Address 4 bytes					
Destination IP Address 4 bytes					
Options (optional)					
Data Variable					

Figure 5-4   IP datagram

The Version field, 4 bits in length, indicates what version of IP packet follows. The current version of IP is 4, which you will typically see expressed as IPv4. The next version, currently under development, is IPv6, which in many respects—particularly regarding addressing—is a whole new ballgame. Although IPv6 is currently employed in the Internet II project, it will not be discussed here because it is not yet in widespread use.

The Header Length field follows the Version field and is also 4 bits in length. The Header Length is expressed as a number of 32-bit words, or 4 bytes. In other words, if the Header Length contained a value of 10, the total number of bytes in the IP header would be 10 * 4 bytes, or 40 bytes. Because the Header Length field is only 4 bits, the maximum IP header can be 15 * 4 bytes, or 60 bytes. This is normally sufficient, though some commands can exceed that number of bytes.

The Type of Service (TOS) field is next and is 1 byte in length. Bits 0–2 make up the Precedence bits and are ignored in most IP networks. Bits 3–7 define the TOS and are mutually exclusive, meaning that only one of the bits can be set to 1. To read more about the TOS bits and their meaning, see RFC 1349. You can experiment with the TOS bits using the ping command with the −v option. The last bit is unused and should always be set to 0.

The 16-bit Length field specifies the total length of the IP datagram including the header. This value plus the 18-byte Frame header in an Ethernet Version II frame should indicate the total frame size.

Following the Length field is the Identification field. This field normally contains a value that is incremented by one for each datagram sent. However, it is also useful when a datagram has been fragmented. In this case, the Identification field remains the same for each packet that makes up the fragmented datagram. The packets can then be reassembled at the destination by matching Identification fields and by using the fields in the next byte of the IP header, the Flags field, and the Fragment Offset field.

The Flags field controls whether an IP datagram can be fragmented. A datagram fragment occurs when a datagram larger than the maximum size allowed for the media or for the receiving station is broken into smaller pieces. The Flags field is 3 bits in length, and the first bit is always 0.

The second bit is the Don't Fragment bit. When this bit is set to 1, fragmentation of the datagram is not allowed, whereas a 0 value indicates that the packet may be fragmented. The default setting in a Windows environment is Don't Fragment. Windows uses this setting to adjust the datagram size to match the **Maximum Transmission Unit (MTU)** of the receiving station or routers in between. The MTU defines the largest datagram size considered acceptable by the media or Network layer protocol. When a device receives an IP datagram larger than the MTU of the media to which the datagram must be forwarded, or larger than the MTU of the receiving device, the forwarding device normally fragments the datagram to match the MTU. If the Don't Fragment bit is set, an ICMP message is returned to the sender, indicating that the packet was dropped due to the need to fragment. If Windows receives this type of ICMP message, it adjusts the datagram length downward and resends the datagram until no more ICMP messages are received. In this manner, Windows automatically discovers the MTU of the destination.

IP datagram fragmentation can hurt performance and reliability. If a datagram is fragmented into multiple packets, and one packet is lost or has a CRC error and is therefore discarded, all packets making up the entire datagram must be resent, because IP does not have a method to recover from a lost packet.

Datagram recovery is handled at the Transport layer. Performance can also be degraded by fragmentation, because the fragmentation and reassembly of datagrams are expensive in CPU cycles. A router that must fragment large datagrams to meet the destination MTU is taken away from its primary job of packet switching. In addition, a host CPU that must reassemble fragments will lose time that could be better spent on application processing.

The third bit in the Flags field tells the receiving device if more fragments are coming. A value of 1 indicates more fragments are coming, and a value of 0 indicates this is the last fragment (if the datagram was not fragmented, this bit will always be 0). The 13-bit Fragment Offset bit indicates where the fragment belongs in the datagram.

The Fragment Offset is in 8-byte units, where a value of 100 would mean the fragment is at offset 800 into the datagram.

The Time to Live (TTL) field determines the number of router hops over which a packet may travel before being discarded. It is set to an initial value by the originating host and decremented by one by each router the packet encounters. If this value reaches zero, the packet is discarded and usually an ICMP Time Exceeded message is sent to the originator. The initial value of this field depends on the operating system. In Windows 98 and Windows NT 4.0 and higher, the default is 128. In Windows 95 and NT 3.51, the default is 32.

The TTL also provides a method for a destination to inform a source when not all packet fragments were received. The TTL can be used as a timer, decremented once for each second. If a destination does not receive all fragments related to a datagram, the TTL of the received fragments will be decremented down to zero and the destination will send an ICMP message indicating the problem.

The 8-bit Protocol field is next. This field indicates which upper-layer protocol or Network layer subprotocol (such as ICMP) is embedded in the IP datagram. Some of the more common protocols and their values are listed in Table 5-3. My research shows 133 protocols are defined; the maximum possible is 256.

Table 5-3   Common IP Protocols

Protocol	Description	Protocol Field Value
ICMP	Internet Control Message Protocol	1
IGMP	Internet Group Management Protocol	2
IP in IP	IP in IP encapsulation	4
TCP	Transport Control Protocol	6
EGP	Exterior Gateway Protocol	8
UDP	User Datagram Protocol	17
IPv6 over IPv4	IPv6 Encapsulated in IPv4	41

The next field in the IP header is the Header Checksum. This 16-bit value is meant as an integrity check on the IP header only. The data is not protected with this checksum. Data protection is done with an upper-layer protocol.

The next two fields are the 4-byte Source and Destination IP addresses. The final header field is the variable-length Options field. The Options field may be from 0 to 40 bytes and is frequently 0 bytes, meaning no options are specified.

IP does not stand on its own. An IP datagram always contains another protocol as specified by the Protocol field. In addition, IP needs a helper protocol, called ARP, to translate IP addresses into physical addresses. The next section takes a look at both of these ideas in more detail.

IP Protocols

TCP/IP has a few Network layer protocols that typically fall under the general heading of IP. Two of these subprotocols—ICMP and ARP—bear additional discussion, as they can be useful in the troubleshooting process.

 There are actually a considerable number of IP-related protocols, most of which are protocols encapsulated in an IP header. RFC 790 has a partial list of these but a more current list can be found at *www.networksorcery.com*.

ICMP: The Ping and Trace Protocol

ICMP is used to transmit status and control messages in an IP environment. It is most often used to verify the ability to communicate to a particular host using the ping command. Routers also use it to send status messages regarding the availability or reachability of a destination host or network.

The trace command also uses ICMP, although in a slightly different manner than does the ping command. ICMP is an encapsulated IP protocol, which means that it is wrapped in an IP header. If you use a protocol analyzer to capture all IP packets, ICMP packets will be included in the capture.

ICMP has many functions, but the two most people know best are ICMP Echo and ICMP Reply. These messages are sent by a ping command and replied to by the target of the ping, respectively. Architecturally, the ICMP message has the format depicted in Figure 5-5.

Data Link Header	IP Header	ICMP Header	ICMP Data	FCS

Figure 5-5   ICMP message format

As you can see, just as a Data Link header always wraps around a Network layer header (in this case, an IP header), the IP header encapsulates the ICMP header. This is because ICMP cannot stand alone.

Let's examine the ICMP header in more detail by studying Table 5-4. Table 5-4 shows the ICMP header consisting of three fields that occupy 4 bytes. The most important of these fields is the Type field. The Type field tells the receiving station what type of ICMP data is enclosed. The Code field further qualifies the Type field if necessary. For example, the Type field may indicate the message is a "Destination Unreachable" message, and the Code field may indicate more specific information such as that the network is unreachable or the host or port is unreachable. (Table 5-5 shows the value and meaning of the more common Type and Code fields.)

Table 5-4 ICMP Header

Type	Code	Checksum	Identifier	Sequence #
1 byte	1 byte	2 bytes	2 bytes	2 bytes

Table 5-5 Common ICMP Header

Type	Code	Description
0	0	Echo reply
3	0	Destination unreachable
3	0	Net unreachable
3	1	Host unreachable
3	2	Protocol unreachable
3	3	Port unreachable
3	4	Fragmentation needed but don't fragment bit set
3	5	Source route failed
4	0	Source quench
5	0	Redirect
5	0	Redirect datagrams for the network
5	1	Redirect datagrams for the host
5	2	Redirect datagrams for the type of service and network
5	3	Redirect datagrams for the type of service and host
8	0	Echo
11	0	Time exceeded
11	0	Time to live exceeded in transit
11	1	Fragment reassemble time exceeded
12	0	Parameter problem
13	0	Time-stamp
14	0	Time-stamp reply
15	0	Information request
16	0	Information reply

The Checksum field is used to protect the ICMP message. Much like a CRC, the checksum is a 16-bit value calculated from the data bytes of the message starting from the Type field. It detects data corruption that may occur in a switch or router. The Identifier and Sequence Number fields are used to match requests with replies. These fields may be zero for many ICMP message types.

The ICMP data follows the Sequence Number field and can be of variable length. For ICMP echo requests, the data is usually a recognizable pattern such as the letters of the alphabet or, in some cases, simply zeros. Windows uses the letters of the alphabet in ping ICMP requests and zeros in trace route ICMP requests.

Figure 5-6 shows the results of an ICMP request and the successful reply. Packet #1 is the ICMP request and Packet #2 is the reply. Notice that the Identifier and Sequence Number fields in the reply match those in the request. The ICMP data is just 32 bytes, which, in this case, is the letters of the alphabet. You can vary the amount of data in the ping command by specifying the size on the command line.

Figure 5-6   ICMP request and successful reply

The trace route command (tracert.exe in Windows) uses ICMP to elicit a response from each router between the source and the destination. To do so, the Trace Route utility sends an ICMP echo request to the destination repeatedly with an increasing value of the TTL field in the IP header, starting with 1. When a packet reaches a router, the router decrements the TTL field in the IP header.

If the TTL is zero after the router decrements it, the router sends back an ICMP message type 11 with a code 0, which means "Time to live exceeded in transit." When the router responds with this message, it must also send its IP address to the source of the echo request. When the Trace Route utility receives the message, it displays the router's IP address and the amount of time it took the router to respond. The utility then sends another ICMP request message to the destination with one added to the TTL.

The just-described process is repeated until the destination is finally reached and a normal ICMP reply is received from the destination. In this way, each router hop along the way from source to destination is discovered, along with the response time. Most Trace Route utilities will send several ICMP messages with the same TTL value so that the same router responds each time. This approach provides a better gauge of the response time than does a single message.

ICMP messages that indicate an error or problem of some sort, such as the "Time to live exceeded" message, sometimes contain the original packet that caused the error. Using an analyzer, you can capture ICMP messages that contain ICMP errors messages and view the packet that caused the error.

Figure 5-7 shows results of an ICMP "Time to live exceeded" message returned by a router. Notice the highlighted line that states "Header of packet that caused error follows." The data you see there is the original ICMP request. Note the TTL field, which is set to 1. When the responding router received the message, the TTL was decremented to 0, which caused the TTL-exceeded error.

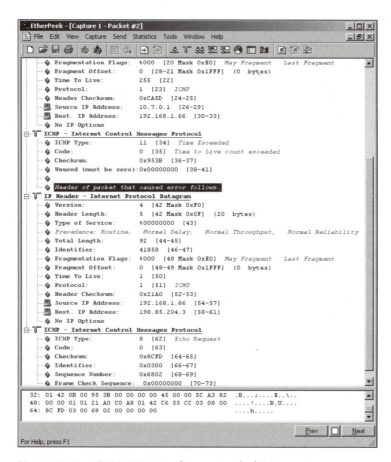

Figure 5-7 ICMP "Time to live exceeded" message

ARP: The MAC Address Protocol

The Address Resolution Protocol (ARP) is actually considered a separate Network layer protocol in TCP/IP. In fact, because of its function, ARP is more like a layer between the Network layer and Data Link layer.

As the name implies, ARP resolves addresses. Specifically, it finds the MAC address of a destination after an IP packet addressed to that destination reaches the network on which it resides. As you know, a message cannot be delivered to a host until the physical address of the host is added to the Data Link frame header.

When a computer using the TCP/IP protocol wants to communicate with another computer, it must know the IP address of the destination. The IP address is usually known by the application sending the message or it is resolved using the computer name. If the IP address of the destination is on the same network as the source, the source computer sends an ARP request in the form of a Data Link broadcast. The ARP request is processed by all computers in the broadcast domain; the computer with the IP address that is being queried sends back an ARP reply that contains the computer's MAC address. After the MAC address is received, the frame header can be constructed, and the frame is delivered to the destination.

If a computer has to send an ARP broadcast every time it wants to send an IP packet to a particular destination, the network would have one broadcast ARP frame for every frame that carries actual data. That is a big waste of bandwidth. To avoid sending an ARP request every time an IP packet is to be delivered to a particular destination, PCs and other devices store the learned MAC addresses in an **ARP cache**. A computer or router then has to send an ARP broadcast only once for each destination host on its network with which it communicates. That solves the too-many-broadcasts problem, but unfortunately it can cause another problem, depending on how long the device stores the learned MAC address in its cache. Let's look at this problem.

First, remember that networks are dynamic entities. Computers are installed and uninstalled, IP addresses get changed (particularly if you are using dynamic IP address assignment), NIC cards get replaced or swapped from one machine to another, and so forth. Consider the nuances of such a dynamic environment. Let's say device A wants to send a file to device B using IP. Device A sends an ARP broadcast request and device B responds with its MAC address, which device A promptly stores in its cache for current and future communication. Just after the file is sent, Technician X comes along and upgrades the NIC on device B from 10 Mbps to 100 Mbps. Device A wants to send another file to device B, but the attempt times out. Why? When the NIC was changed, so was the MAC address. Device A has the old MAC address in its cache for device B.

Fortunately, operating system designers thought of this potential problem and ARP cache entries are routinely expired. On Windows 2000, ARP entries expire in 2 minutes if the entry has not been used again. If the entry is used within the first 2 minutes after having been created, the entry will stay longer, up to 10 minutes. On some devices and operating systems, the time the entry remains in cache could be significantly longer, up to hours.

If you suspect an ARP cache problem, you have a few choices. You can simply wait until the entry expires. You also can force the device whose address changed to communicate with the other device, thereby causing the entry to be replaced with the new value. In addition, you can simply flush the ARP cache, which causes the device to relearn the address.

Most devices and operating systems have a method of creating static ARP cache entries. Neither flushing the cache nor waiting will make the entry go away; you have to manually delete it. Although creating static entries seems like a nice way to reduce broadcasts, the potential problems it can cause are probably not worth the slight efficiency advantage that static entries might provide.

Our discussion so far has focused on the structure of IP packets and some of the protocols and features that structure makes possible. As mentioned before, IP does not stand alone. The vast majority of IP datagrams encapsulate one of two Transport protocols: TCP or UDP

TCP: The Reliable Transport Protocol

The Transmission Control Protocol (TCP) has been a key reason the Internet has thrived using the TCP/IP protocol suite. Although the features and functions of IP get your data from here to there, TCP makes sure that it gets there in one piece. TCP also makes sure that the destination host knows what to do with the newly arrived data. It accomplishes these tasks with three mechanisms: ports, handshakes, and segments. We discuss them in the following sections, after a brief digression into the details of the TCP header.

TCP Header

Figure 5-8 shows an Ethernet frame carrying an IP datagram encapsulating a TCP header. The entire unit of information that includes the TCP header and data is referred to as a **TCP segment**. The TCP segment is shown in detail in Figure 5-9.

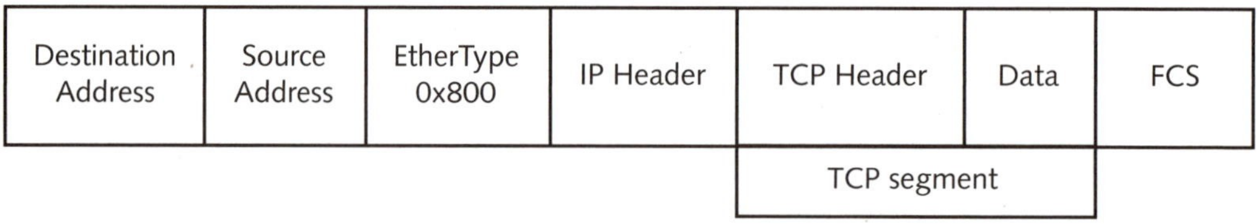

Destination Address	Source Address	EtherType 0x800	IP Header	TCP Header	Data	FCS
				TCP segment		

Figure 5-8   Ethernet frame carrying a TCP segment

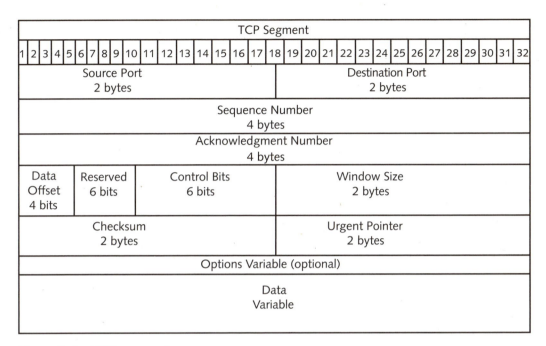

Figure 5-9   TCP segment

Now that the format of a TCP segment is in hand, we can look at the fields and see how each plays a part in the three important functions of TCP.

TCP Ports: Tell the Application What's Coming

The first two fields of the TCP header are the Source Port and Destination Port. The Source Port is used to identify the sending application when a response is sent back to the originator of the segment. The Destination Port identifies the TCP process or application to which the segment should be sent once it arrives at the destination computer.

TCP/IP has defined a number of well-known ports that are specific to different types of applications. Because the Port fields are 16 bits in length, the value of the port can range from 1 to 65,535. Note that the use of 0 is not allowed. The well-known ports, which are in the range 1 to 1023, define such applications as HTTP, FTP, and SMTP, to name a few.

The next range of ports is from 1024 to 49,151. The ports in this range are called **registered ports** and can be used by private applications within an intranet or extranet. Ordinary user processes and programs can use ports in this range, provided this use does not conflict with a registered application. The **Internet Assigned Numbers Authority (IANA)**, an organization that maintains a variety of numbering schemes used in the Internet, assigns the ports in the range from 1 to 49,151.

The last range of ports, from 49,152 to 65,535, is for dynamic assignment and private use. These port numbers are used, for example, to dynamically assign a source port number to a Web browser process when it requests an HTTP resource.

A complete listing of all registered ports can be found at *www.iana.org/assignments/port-numbers*.

Figure 5-10, shows the packet decode of an HTTP request, followed by an HTTP reply. The request is shown in the capture titled Packet #4. Notice the source port number of 1623, which is in the range of registered ports. This port number was assigned at random by Windows 2000 for the Internet Explorer application. Although unlikely, it is possible that this assignment could cause a conflict because this is a registered port number to a private application.

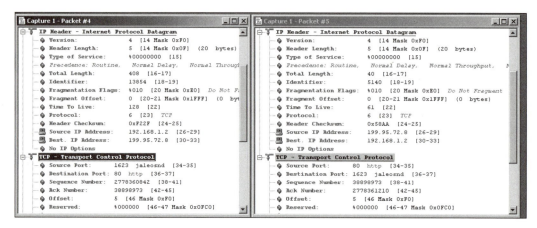

Figure 5-10   TCP headers in an HTTP request and reply

Aside from letting a receiving computer know to which application the packet should be forwarded, port numbers are used to keep track of multiple conversations by a single application. For example, you may have two Web browser windows open at the same time, looking at different Web sites. Each of the TCP sessions associated with the Web browser windows will have a different source port number assigned.

Port numbers are a convenient way to filter packets that are being captured. Rather than having to sift through dozens or even thousands of packets in a packet-capture session, a user can specify that only packets containing a specific port that belongs to a particular application being debugged should be captured. In addition, if you are interested in just one conversation, you can specify both the source and destination ports involved in the conversation.

TCP Handshaking: Establish a Valid Connection

One strength of a connection-oriented protocol like TCP is that a connection or session is established between sender and receiver before data transfer begins. TCP uses a three-way handshake to accomplish this connection. The TCP header fields involved in the handshake include Sequence Number, Acknowledgment Number, Control Bits, and Options.

Your understanding of the three-way handshake is critical to successful troubleshooting of slow or unsuccessful connections as well as to your understanding of common security threats to your network. Our first step on the road to understanding is expanding the Control Bits field so that you know the meaning of each bit in this field. Figure 5-11 shows the bits, from left to right, as they appear in the byte that makes up the Control Field.

Bit #	5	4	3	2	1	0
Description	**URG** Urgent	**ACK** Acknowledgment	**PSH** Push Function	**RST** Reset Connection	**SYN** Synchronize	**FIN** End of Data

Figure 5-11   TCP Header Control Bits field

A TCP session begins when a client sends a TCP synchronization (SYN) segment to the destination device, usually a server. The SYN bit is set in this segment. The client also sends the initial Sequence Number that will be used by the server to respond to the SYN segment. A destination port number for HTTP is specified (the port number is typically one of the well-known ports, such as 80). Then, a source port number is dynamically assigned. One option that is almost always included is the **Maximum Segment Size (MSS)**, which tells the server the maximum number of bytes that can be received by the client in a single TCP segment.

When the server receives the SYN segment, it usually responds in one of two ways: by sending an acknowledgment-synchronization (ACK-SYN) segment or by sending a reset connection (RST) segment. If an RST segment is returned, the server refused the request to open a session, possibly because the destination port is unknown. If an ACK-SYN segment is returned, the Acknowledgment Number field has a value equal to the client's initial Sequence Number plus one and the Sequence Number field contains the initial sequence number for the server. The server may also send the MSS to specify the maximum segment size it is prepared to receive.

To complete the three-way handshake, the client sends an ACK segment back to the server acknowledging the server's ACK-SYN segment. The client is now ready to begin sending or requesting data.

Figure 5-12 shows the TCP headers of the three packets involved in the three-way handshake to start an HTTP session. Packet #1 shows the initial client request, which is a SYN packet, called Synch Sequence in the analyzer. Notice that the Sequence Number is an apparently random number and the Acknowledgment is 0. The other parameters sent include a MSS of 1460 and a Window Size of 8760. Packet #2 is the response from the server. Both the Acknowledgment bit and the Synchronization bit are set; this is the ACK-SYN packet.

Take a note of the Acknowledgment Number. This value is one greater than the Sequence Number in Packet #1. Packet #2 sends its own Sequence Number, MSS, and Window Size. This is a request to the Course Technology Web server; this server appears to be based on Windows NT 4.0, as the MSS and Window Size match NT 4.0 server parameters. Packet #3 completes the handshake and is from the client back to the server, acknowledging the server's Synch packet. Notice that the Acknowledgment Number is one greater than the Sequence Number in Packet #2.

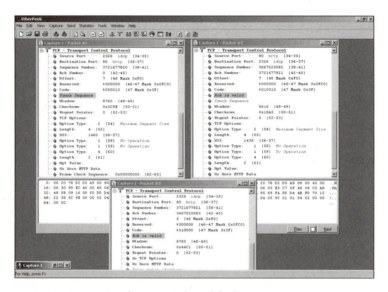

Figure 5-12   TCP three-way handshake

There are a few important things to point out regarding the three-way handshake sequence. The completion of a three-way handshake usually indicates that the server being contacted is alive and well and ready to communicate. If a server responds with a reset connection segment, it probably means that the server is alive and well but unable to respond to the requested port number.

One trick that hackers use to create havoc in a network is to send SYN packets to a valid server and port number, but with an invalid source address. The server will attempt to respond to this SYN packet with a SYN-ACK segment and then wait for the final ACK packet to complete the sequence. However, if the source address specified in the original SYN packet did not actually send the SYN packet, the server will have to wait until a timeout occurs. (Servers can maintain only a finite number of open sessions, and although the server is waiting for the final ACK, it is still considered an open session.) Hackers can inundate a resource by sending thousands of these bogus packets to a server and thus cause too many open sessions. This flood of data renders the server unable to respond to real requests for its resources. It is referred to as a **Denial of Service (DOS) attack** because real clients are being denied service while the server is overwhelmed waiting for fake three-way handshakes to complete.

Another use of the information contained in the three-way handshake relates to the MSS value. If this value is set too low, the network will be inefficient because it must send more segments than necessary. If it is set too high, there will be packet fragmentation, which also causes inefficiency. This issue is discussed in the next section.

TCP Segments: Keep the Data in Order

When a computer requests a file from or sends a file to an Internet host, the file is often too big to send as a single transmission. To counteract this problem, the file is broken into smaller pieces, called segments, which are more manageable. Eventually, the files leave the source computer as several, or even thousands, of packets. When the data arrives at the other end, the segments are reassembled into the original data before being sent up to the higher layers.

Each segment created by the Transport layer is tagged with a Sequence Number. If the segments arrive out of order, the Sequence Number is used by the Transport layer to reassemble them correctly. Additionally, if a segment is lost, the Transport layer detects this fact and a retransmission occurs.

The segmenting of the data is important. If the Transport layer does not segment the data, the Network layer is obligated to break the data into a size agreeable to the network architecture in use; for Ethernet, this means 1518 bytes minus the Data Link layer headers, which, conveniently enough, is the size of the MTU.

When the Network layer breaks up segments that are too large for the MTU, the resulting packets are called **fragments**. Because the Network layer does not have any recovery methods for lost or out-of-order packets, any errors resulting from fragments that are lost require retransmission of all the data. To avoid this problem, reliable transport protocols typically segment the data so that the segment size matches the MTU, minus the Transport, Network, and Data Link layer headers. In this way, the Network layer is relieved from having to fragment information sent to it from the Transport layer.

Figure 5-13 shows the progress of information as it is sent from the application down to the Transport, Network, and then Data Link layers. Notice how the Transport layer, in this example, segments the data so that by the time all applicable headers have been added, the size of the datagram equals the maximum frame size for Ethernet, which is the MTU. In general, this approach offers the most efficient way to reliably transfer the information, putting no additional burden on the Network layer and ensuring that all datagrams sent have Transport layer headers with sequence numbers.

Application	Data 5840 bytes		
Transport: Segment 1	TCP header is 20 bytes	Data is 1460 bytes	
Segment 2	TCP header is 20 bytes	Data is 1460 bytes	
Segment 3	TCP header is 20 bytes	Data is 1460 bytes	
Segment 4	TCP header is 20 bytes	Data is 1460 bytes	
Network: Packet 1	IP header 20 bytes	TCP header 20 bytes	Data is 1460 bytes
Packet 2	IP header 20 bytes	TCP header 20 bytes	Data is 1460 bytes
Packet 3	IP header 20 bytes	TCP header 20 bytes	Data is 1460 bytes
Packet 4	IP header 20 bytes	TCP header 20 bytes	Data is 1460 bytes
Data Link: Frame 1	Data Link header is 18 bytes + 1500 bytes = 1518 bytes MTU		
Frame 2	Data Link header is 18 bytes + 1500 bytes = 1518 bytes MTU		
Frame 3	Data Link header is 18 bytes + 1500 bytes = 1518 bytes MTU		
Frame 4	Data Link header is 18 bytes + 1500 bytes = 1518 bytes MTU		

Figure 5-13 Segmentation of data

What happens if a segment never arrives? The receiving side knows this fact because it will be missing a segment Sequence Number. Furthermore, it won't have to wait too long to get the missing segment because, during the initial establishment of the data transfer, the receiver and sender agreed how many segments should be received before the receiver must send back an acknowledgment. When the sending computer does not receive an acknowledgment on recently sent data, it will retry all segments sent since the last acknowledgment.

A TCP retransmission timer governs how long before a retry occurs. The sending station will continue to retry a configurable number of times (a default of 5 in Windows) until an acknowledgment is returned or the retry count is exceeded. If the retry count is exceeded, the upper layers are informed, and eventually the application displays an error message.

The number of segments before a receiver is obliged to send an acknowledgment is defined in the Window Size field. The Window Size is a 16-bit value that represents the maximum number of bytes that can be received before sending an acknowledgment. The Sequence Numbers in the TCP header are based on bytes, not numbers of segments sent. As a consequence, TCP is often called a **byte stream protocol**.

When data transfer begins, the Sequence Number is increased with each segment sent. The increase is based on the number of bytes in the segment minus the header. When an acknowledgment is returned to the sender of data, the Acknowledgment Number equals the last Sequence Number sent plus the number of data bytes in the last segment. In other words, the Acknowledgment Number tells the sender, "I have received all bytes of the segment up to this point." If an acknowledgment is missing, the sender will know where to start resending data.

Figure 5-14, shows the TCP header for three segments. In particular, concentrate on the highlighted lines.

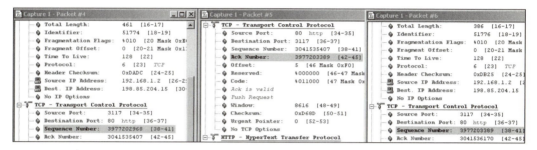

Figure 5-14   Sequence and Acknowledgment Numbers

Packet #4 starts off the sequence by sending a segment of 421 bytes, which is listed as 461 bytes in the Total Length field in the IP header. We have to subtract 20 bytes for the IP header and 20 bytes for the TCP header to get the segment size of 421. When the destination receives this information, it responds with Packet #5, an acknowledgment with an Acknowledgment Number equal to Packet #4's Sequence Number plus the segment size of 421. This number should equal the next Sequence Number from the sender, which is Packet #6. Basically, the acknowledgment sent in Packet #5 tells the sender that it expects the next packet to start with data byte 3977203389.

The Window Size value is ideally a multiple of the segment size. In Windows 98, the initial value is fixed at 8760, six times the default MSS of 1460. The Window Size is dynamic and is called a sliding window because it can change during a connection. If a server sends three segments of 1400 bytes each to a client and the client acknowledges the 4200 bytes sent, the client may send back a new Window Size—perhaps 7360, if 1400 bytes are still in the receive buffers, making the amount of information that can be received 1400 bytes less. The Window Size will probably increase again to 8760 if there is a pause in the data stream.

Windows 98 clients will send an acknowledgment for every two to four segments received, even though the Window Size value allows for as many as six full-sized segments between acknowledgments. This is not a tunable TCP parameter and is not very efficient. Windows 2000, however, has an initial window size of 12 times the MSS, and Windows 2000 may wait to receive 10 or 12 segments before sending a series of acknowledgments. This is considerably more efficient, so you can expect better performance with data transfers with Windows 2000.

The Window Size and MTU are tunable parameter in Windows, but MSS is not. The MSS is based on the MTU of the media and can be made smaller only by changing the MTU value. You must be careful when changing these values, because you can adversely affect performance if you make unwise changes. For example, if the MTU is changed to a value less than 1500 on an Ethernet network, you will send frames that are less than the maximum size of 1518, which is an inefficient use of bandwidth. You cannot increase the value of the MTU to higher than that of the default media MTU.

The Window Size is a parameter that may be worth changing in some circumstances. A system can benefit from a higher Window Size if it is on a high-bandwidth, low-delay link because bursts of many segments can be sent before an acknowledgment would be required, increasing overall throughput. A very busy or unreliable link would not benefit from this change. An example of a situation where the Window Size may be changed is on a server that is on a dedicated 100 Mbps or 1 Gbps network segment. To change the Window Size from the default, you need to add a key to the Registry and assign the value. This issue is covered in Hands-on Project 5-7 at the end of this chapter.

The last three parameters of the TCP header are Checksum, Urgent Pointer, and Options. The Checksum parameter does what checksums do—that is, protect data. The TCP checksum, unlike the IP checksum, protects not only the header, but also the data, thereby allowing TCP to detect data corruption. The Urgent Pointer points to the last byte of urgent data if the Urgent control bit is set. The processing of urgent data is application-dependent but is typically used to send interrupt signals to Telnet applications—for example, when someone presses the Esc (escape) key in a Telnet session. TCP Options are optional and are generally used to send parameters to receiving devices to change the way TCP operates. Examples include keep-alive intervals and TTL timers.

The last thing to cover in the TCP header is the remaining bits in the Control Bits field. We have talked about the SYN and ACK bits already. Bit 0 is the FIN bit that is set when there is no more data to send for the current request. Bit 2 is the RST bit that is used to terminate or reset a connection. When a communication session is over or if the initial SYN packet is rejected, the RST bit closes the connection.

The PSH bit tells TCP to send the data in the segment to the destination application. Several segments may be buffered by the receiving host and sent as a group when TCP receives a segment with the PSH bit set. If it is desirable for the application to receive each segment as it arrives, as may be the case with a Web browser, the PSH bit can be set with each segment of data that is sent. Bit 5, the URG bit, signifies that the segment contains urgent data.

What does this vast knowledge of TCP header fields do for you? A few of the ways you can put this knowledge to use have already been mentioned, such as tuning TCP for better performance. In addition, understanding the control bits can help you see what is happening in a data transfer. For example, you can determine whether a three-way handshake was ever completed between a source and destination if you are having trouble communicating with a device. Or, if an application hangs when communicating with a device, you may be able to see whether a FIN segment or PSH segment was ever sent. If not, the application may be waiting forever for TCP to send the data.

You'll also find your knowledge of the TCP header fields useful when a network appears sluggish. By examining the Sequence and Acknowledgment Numbers of sent and received packets between two parties, you can tell whether segments are being resent for some reason, possibly because of CRC or checksum errors. Of course, if you are sitting back with your feet up on the desk because your network is humming along smoothly, you can always take a few packet traces just to see how things work.

Speaking of seeing how things work, let's turn our attention to the other Transport layer protocol used in IP networks—UDP.

5

UDP: THE UNRELIABLE TRANSPORT PROTOCOL

As previously discussed, TCP is not the only Transport layer protocol found in the TCP/IP protocol suite. The **User Datagram Protocol (UDP)** is a protocol that provides limited functionality compared to TCP. UDP provides Application layer information via port numbers in the UDP header as well as a checksum to protect data integrity.

Much of the complexity of TCP—complexity that makes TCP so reliable—is not included in UDP. This was done so that you would have a fast, simple, low-overhead—but unreliable—Transport layer protocol. In fact, UDP is often expanded to mean Unreliable Datagram Protocol. Because of the simplicity of UDP, the discussion of it here will be short and to the point. We will discuss the UDP datagram format and then discuss common applications for the UDP protocol.

The UDP Datagram

The UDP datagram consists of a header and data. The UDP header contains four 16-bit fields: Source Port, Destination Port, Length, and Checksum. Following the header is the Data field, which can be of varying lengths. The Data field contains the data required by the application and nothing more. There are no Sequence Numbers, no Acknowledgment Numbers, no flags, and no Window Sizes. The Source and Destination Port fields convey the same information as do the port fields in the TCP header—identification of the sending and receiving applications.

The Length field specifies the length in bytes of the datagram, which consists of the 8-byte header plus the length of the data. If there is no data, the value for the field is 8. The Checksum field protects the integrity of the data in the same way that the TCP checksum does. UDP is simple, but it is effective in applications where reliability is not the overriding concern.

Applications for UDP

Applications that use UDP are typically not concerned with using a reliable Transport protocol because of one of the following reasons:

- The application runs on a LAN, where data reliability is usually taken for granted, as opposed to over a WAN, where reliability is more questionable.

- The application requires only small data transfers so segmentation of the data and windowing are not considerations.

- The small amount of data being transferred or the relatively infrequent use of the application makes it acceptable to place the burden of error recovery on the application rather than the Transport protocol.

Applications that use UDP in a LAN environment include Trivial File Transport Protocol (TFTP), Boot Protocol (BOOTP), and Dynamic Host Configuration Protocol (DHCP). Diskless devices such as routers, switches, or diskless workstations often use TFTP and BOOTP to load configuration or operating system information when the device powers on.

A TFTP or BOOTP server is usually on the same LAN as the device requiring its services. DHCP is used by workstations to request a dynamically allocated IP address. DHCP is a broadcast-based protocol, and the DHCP server and the devices requiring its service are frequently in the same broadcast domain. All of these applications are responsible for error recovery should errors occur.

An example of an UDP application whose data transfers are usually quite small is DNS. DNS is often used in WAN environments (for example, the Internet), but DNS requests and replies are short in length. If a DNS client does not receive a response from the server, the DNS client is responsible for error recovery, usually relying on a backup DNS server to complete the query.

Most of the applications mentioned, and the majority of UDP-based applications, are used infrequently when compared to TCP-based applications. For example, DHCP and BOOTP requests usually only occur at most once per day when a device is started for the first time. TFTP transfers, used by routers or switches for configuration or operating system updates, might occur only once in several months or less frequently. This comparatively infrequent use of the application makes the use of a complex, reliable Transport protocol such as TCP unnecessary. The burden of reliability falls to the application itself, which is an acceptable burden for this type of application.

Our discussion of TCP/IP has been fairly thorough and detailed because TCP/IP is by far the dominant network protocol used worldwide. However, the protocol developed by Novell, IPX/SPX, can still be found in thousands of networks, and it is to this protocol suite that we now turn our attention.

SUPPORTING IPX/SPX: THE NETWARE PROTOCOL

Novell NetWare has been around for a long time and, despite rumors to the contrary, it is not dead yet. IPX/SPX is the proprietary protocol that Novell designed when NetWare was just getting started, and it has been a mainstay in many networks since the mid-1980s. However, even its creator has abandoned IPX/SPX as the primary protocol in the latest releases of Novell NetWare, starting with version 5.0. Because IPX/SPX is still so prevalent in many small to medium-size networks, it bears some detailed description. But fear not, this text will not go into the detail that it has with TCP/IP. We will discuss only IPX addressing and frame types, a little bit about SPX, and a few packet traces.

5

IPX Addressing

IPX, like IP in TCP/IP, is the Network layer component in the IPX/SPX protocol suite. IPX is a routable protocol so it can be used in fairly large networks. There are no such things as subnet masks or address classes, and IPX cannot be used except in private networks because no outside agency (like the InterNIC) oversees the use of network addresses to prevent conflicts. Thus it is up to the administrator of the network to decide on the network number and to ensure that no conflicts exist.

IPX addresses have two parts, as do IP addresses, but the two parts are a fixed length, which is why you do not have to worry about subnet masks. The network part of the address is 32 bits in length and the host part of the address is 48 bits, totaling 80 bits in an IPX address. IPX addresses are expressed in hexadecimal and may be written in a variety of ways, such as with a period or a colon between the network and host portion.

Consider these examples of IPX addresses: 123.123456789ABC and 44C2:55789BCFE4C2. Notice that the network numbers do not actually seem to use 32 bits. In reality, they do: There are just leading zeroes, which are normally not shown. The host portion of the address is always 48 bits and will always show leading zeroes if they exist.

The host portion of the address is also the host computer's MAC address. This fact is convenient in a couple of ways. First, network administrators do not have to spend time assigning the host addresses. Second, no logical-to-physical address mapping mechanism (like IP's ARP) is needed. The physical address is built into the logical address.

IPX is easy to configure. As discussed, because the MAC address is the host logical address, there is no need to assign IPX host addresses to stations. Furthermore, the network number can be created from your imagination. For example, you can make the network number F00D or BEEF if you happen to have lunch on your mind, or you can make the network number more documentary, such as B18022, which might stand for Building 1, 802.2 frame type. The sky's the limit, at least within the confines of the eight hexadecimal characters you have to play with for the 32-bit number. The network number usually has to be configured only on the NetWare servers. The host client software automatically detects the network number from broadcast frames that the NetWare servers frequently send.

One of the few concerns with IPX addresses is that, as with IP addresses, the network numbers assigned must be the same for all servers on the same broadcast domain and different for servers located on different broadcast domains. This requirement is easy to forget when installing a NetWare server, because the default NetWare installation simply assigns a random number for the network number. If you do not change the network number for the second or third server you install on the same network, the servers will start beeping at you as soon as you plug in the network cable. The beeping is nice because it alerts you to your blunder and the message more or less points out your mistake. Nonetheless, I've still had administrators come to me and explain that they cannot see a newly installed server on the network. They report, "The servers started beeping and printing a message about Server X claiming Network 123 should be Network ABC." At that point, I remind them that this message is the server telling them that they have two servers with two different network numbers on the same physical network segment.

IPX Frame Types

IPX addresses are fairly straightforward, but IPX frame types are less so. As discussed in Chapter 4, Ethernet supports four frame formats, and NetWare also supports four frame formats. In fact, if you are running NetWare 3.11 and NetWare 4.0 and supporting IPX/SPX plus TCP/IP and AppleTalk clients, there is a good chance you are using all four frame types in your network. The frame types, as named by Novell, are as follows:

- Ethernet_802.2: Corresponds to the IEEE 802.3 frame format and is the default frame format for IPX used in NetWare versions 3.12 and above.

- Ethernet_802.3: Corresponds to the 802.3 Raw frame format and is the default IPX frame format for NetWare versions prior to 3.12.

- Ethernet_II: Corresponds to the Ethernet Version II frame format and is used when TCP/IP is loaded on NetWare versions prior to version 5.0.

- Ethernet_SNAP: Corresponds to the IEEE 802.3 SNAP frame format and is used for AppleTalk compatibility to support Macintosh clients.

One of the "gotchas" with IPX frame types occurs when you install a NetWare 3.12 or higher server in the same network as a NetWare 3.11 or lower server. If the default frame types are not changed, the two servers will not be able to communicate with each other. Even worse, because Windows clients detect and use the first frame format they see on the wire, Windows clients will see only one of the two servers.

The simple solution to this dilemma is to change the default frame type on one of the servers to match the other. Unfortunately, that choice can get you into trouble. Certain devices—most notably, some older print servers—support only one frame type and that frame type is fixed. I ran into this problem in a network in which NetWare 4.0 servers were installed and the default frame type of Ethernet_802.2 was used. The network also had a NetWare 3.12 server running with the Ethernet_802.3 frame type (this NetWare 3.11 server had been upgraded, so the frame type remained the default for NetWare 3.11). Rather than run multiple frame types on the same server (which you can do), the solution seemed to be to change the NetWare 3.12 server to the Ethernet_802.2 frame type.

Well, everything was well and good until people started calling because they could no longer print. The print servers supported only Ethernet_802.3, so they no longer communicated with the NetWare servers. There were two choices: replace the print servers with newer versions that supported more frame types (which was eventually done) or add the Ethernet_802.3 frame type to both servers. The latter solution was chosen in the short term.

5

 Another cautionary note on changing frame types: If DOS clients are used, the client software may be set to support only one frame type. Thus, even if there are no old print servers on your network, beware of old DOS clients.

The IPX/SPX Transport Layer

SPX is a reliable Transport layer protocol that requires a connection be established before data is transferred and acknowledgments are sent to verify the safe arrival of data. Unlike TCP, which is considered a byte-stream protocol and which sends Sequence Numbers and acknowledgments based on numbers of bytes sent and received, SPX uses sequential numbers in its packets. Furthermore, SPX packets are acknowledged only when the sender sets a request-for-acknowledgment bit in the packet.

As an example of the SPX acknowledgment method, consider this scenario: If station 1 sends a packet to station 2 with a Sequence Number of 100 and the request-for-acknowledgment bit is set, station 2 replies with an acknowledgment number of 101. This method has drawbacks, because to have truly reliable delivery of packets every packet must be acknowledged. That is, for every data packet sent, an acknowledgment packet must be returned, which is an inefficient use of bandwidth.

Another drawback of SPX is its limited segment size. SPX defaults to the minimum segment size that matches the smallest MTU found in today's networks, which is 576 bytes. With headers totaling up to 64 bytes, this leaves a mere 512 bytes of actual data that can be transferred with every packet. On an Ethernet network that can handle frames up to 1518 bytes, this limitation is extremely inefficient.

Fortunately, SPX has a successor in SPX II, which fixes many of these deficiencies. SPX II probes the network for the maximum MTU size by sending large and then progressively smaller packets until the packet is acknowledged, indicating a suitable size. SPX II also incorporates a form of windowing in which multiple segments may be sent before an acknowledgment is required. The default setting is eight segments before acknowledgment is expected.

The SPX Transport layer protocol, strangely enough, is not used for the majority of communication with a NetWare file and print server. Instead, the **NetWare Core Protocol (NCP)** is used over IPX. NCP is really an Application layer protocol, but it does provide Transport layer-type services such as Sequence Numbers and replies that act as acknowledgments. Conversations using NCP are actually series of NCP request and NCP reply pairs, with the NCP request containing a Sequence Number and the NCP reply containing the matching Sequence Number in acknowledgment of the request. Sequence numbers are incremented by one for each NCP request sent.

Figure 5-15 shows an NCP request and NCP reply that was captured at the beginning of a directory listing. The NCP request is coming from a Windows 2000 Professional computer running the Novell Client over NWLink, which is the Windows implementation of IPX/SPX.

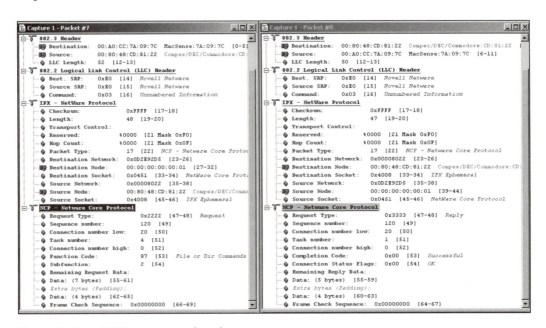

Figure 5-15   NCP request and reply

Notice in the figure that IPX encapsulates NCP, just as IP encapsulates TCP. Packet #7 contains an NCP request for a directory listing and a Sequence Number of 120. Packet #8 is an NCP reply that returns the Sequence Number of 120, along with a status of successful. This request–response sequence can have problems. When an NCP request is sent, no additional packets can be sent until a reply is received. Older NetWare clients would wait about one-half second and, if no reply was received, send the request again. In computer terms, one-half second is a long time to wait before retrying a packet. In networks that were prone to CRC or other errors that cause packets to be dropped, NetWare could seem awfully slow.

An easy way to determine whether packets are being dropped is to simply look for two NCP requests in a row from the same source to the same destination. If packets are not received continuously, the NetWare client will give up and send an error to the user, usually after about 10 retries. Newer 32-bit NetWare clients have a sliding retry timer rather than a fixed one-half second retry timer, with retries occurring as quickly as a few milliseconds.

Another enhanced feature of NetWare 32-bit clients is **packet burst mode**, in which acknowledgments are not required for each packet sent. A client can make an NCP burst request when copying a large file. The burst request is followed by as many as 10–15 NCP burst packets containing the file data. This is clearly a more efficient way to transfer data but reliability is compromised, particularly in error-prone networks. I have seen client stations hang while transferring files using burst mode due to damaged files on the server or dropped packets. You can turn off burst mode in the client properties windows in Windows Network Control Panel.

As promised, this chapter has kept the details on IPX/SPX to a minimum. The NetBEUI protocol is the next subject to tackle. Because of its relative simplicity and lack of configurable parameters, the discussion will be short and sweet.

NETBEUI: THE WINDOWS PROTOCOL

NetBIOS Extended User Interface (NetBEUI) is really not a Network or Transport layer protocol. Instead, it exists at the Session layer and runs directly on top of the Data Link layer. Because there is no Network layer information included in NetBEUI, it cannot be used to communicate over routers. A short explanation of NetBEUI is provided here only because it is installed in Windows environments as a networking protocol and we normally think of such protocols as running at the Network and Transport layers of the OSI model.

NetBEUI was originally developed for use in IBM-DOS environments running over Token Ring. It was then adapted to OS/2 and Windows environments for simple but effective networking in small LANs. Its primary function is to provide name resolution services for the Data Link layer. NetBEUI and its major component, NetBIOS, are discussed in more detail in Chapter 6, which covers the Session layer and the rest of the upper layers of the OSI model.

SUPPORTING ROUTERS

A router used to be seen and touched only by the most elite of network gurus in the largest of corporate networks. Routers have since become ubiquitous, however, and they can now be seen almost anywhere a network can be found. For instance, my little home network consists of six computers of various configurations and operating systems, but included with this small network is a router that allows all of my computers to access the Internet via cable modem. It is a simple router with few configuration parameters, but I have to know just enough about how routers work to get it to do the things I require of it.

Of course, it's not that simple with larger networks. Such networks require routers not only to put the workstations in touch with the Internet, but also to connect with remote offices around town or across the country. In addition, networks with many hosts and servers require routers to break the network into smaller broadcast domains.

One of the greatest strengths of the TCP/IP protocol is its ability to scale. It is effective on a small LAN with just a few computers and yet just as effective on a global network with millions of computers. One of the reasons for that flexibility is the ability of IP datagrams to be routed efficiently. Much of this ability is due to the hierarchical structure made possible by the combination of IP addresses and subnet masks.

IP routing is a vast and often complicated subject that can fill volumes. For the purposes of this book, we will look at only the major components of a router configuration and some of the tools available for troubleshooting a router configuration.

IP Router Configuration

A router is designed to receive packets on one interface, look up the destination address in its routing table, and switch the packet out of the interface that will best get the packet to its destination. As a network administrator whose job it is to configure and maintain routers, you must be able to accomplish two tasks:

- Properly configure router interfaces to accept incoming and outgoing packets
- Properly configure the router so that its routing table is accurate for your network

In a comparatively small internetwork with just a few physical networks, this task is not too terribly difficult. With dozens or hundreds of networks and a variety of network architectures including LANs and WANs and multiple protocols, however, the job can be difficult and stressful. The key to solving the big picture is always to remember that the big picture in a large internetwork is made up of much smaller pieces all connected together. If all of your smaller pieces are working, the big picture usually comes together. So, again, you need to focus on what is required for a router to work.

A router interface requires a proper data-link connection and a correct address assignment to be operational. The connection can be as simple as a patch cable that connects the Ethernet interface on the router to a hub or switch. Without such a connection, the data link never comes up and the interface is considered down from the router's perspective. On a serial link, such as in a WAN environment, the data-link connection requires not only a physical connection to another device such as a CSU/DSU or another router, but also proper encapsulation. The encapsulation tells the router how to format packets that are sent on the serial line and includes such types as HDLC, Frame Relay, and PPP, to name a few.

The address assignment is the IP address assigned to the router, along with the subnet mask. If the router has a proper data-link connection and the address assignment is correct, there is a good chance the interface part of your router is not going to give you problems.

The next part of the router equation is the proper configuration of a routing protocol to ensure that the router knows about all of the other networks to which it may need to send packets. The subject of routing protocols is too extensive to go into here, but suffice it to say that the routing protocols build the routing table. If you are unable to reach a particular network destination, the first place to look is in the routing table. If the destination network or default network are not listed in the table, your packets are not going anywhere. If these things are in place, then you need to look somewhere other than that particular router.

Router Troubleshooting

This section looks at three router commands that can help you troubleshoot myriad router problems and misconfigurations. The examples here use a Cisco 6500 series route switch module, but the information could be applied to almost any router.

The first command deals with the interfaces on your router and is quite simple: show interfaces. Figure 5-16 shows the output of the show interfaces command. Notice the first line of the output: "GigabitEthernet0/0/0 is up, line protocol is up." This is perhaps the most critical piece of information, but is often overlooked when someone configures a router. When things are not working, show interfaces is always the first command to try. If the interface were not plugged into a hub or switch, the line would say "GigabitEthernet0/0/0 is up, line protocol is down." That is your first clue to check the cabling. The line protocol on an Ethernet port will be up only if it is plugged into a device correctly. Another possibility is "GigabitEthernet0/0/0 is Administratively Down," which simply means that the interface was never enabled, also a common problem.

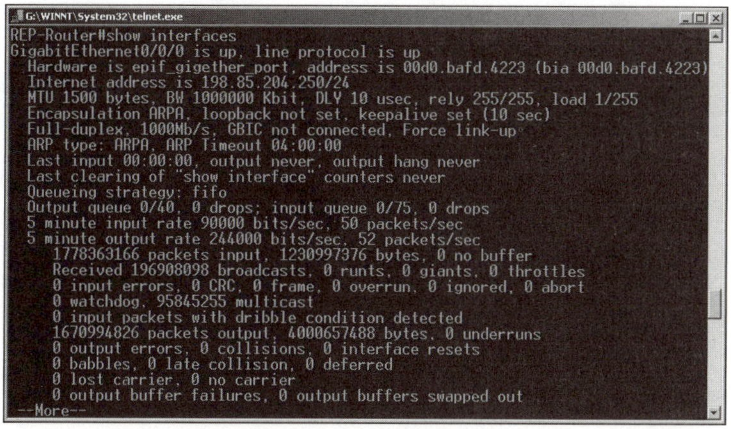

Figure 5-16   Show interfaces command

Another command with which you should become well acquainted is the show ip route command, which lists the current routing table. If the hosts on a network are not able to reach the hosts on another network, the routing table can be consulted to determine whether the router has an entry for the network in question. If the routing table does not have an entry for a network you are trying to reach, you have found your problem. The exception occurs when the router has its own default gateway or "gateway of last resort." The gateway of last resort is the network to which the router can forward packets that have destination addresses for which there is no routing table entry.

Figure 5-17 shows the output of the show ip route command. It is not very interesting, as it merely shows networks directly connected to the router, but it makes the point nonetheless.

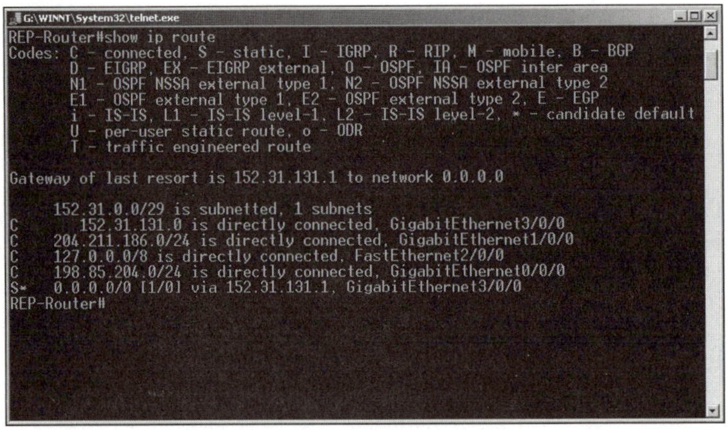

Figure 5-17 Show ip route command

You can see from the routing table in Figure 5–17 that this router knows how to get to three different networks (127.0.0.0 is a loopback address and is used only for management purposes). Packets addressed to all other destinations are forwarded to the address listed as the gateway of last resort, which is typically used to send packets to the Internet.

You can see at a glance which networks in the entire internetwork are available. If your internetwork included more than the three networks listed in the output, you would know that something is amiss. That brings us to the next command, the show ip protocols command. It tells you which routing protocols are active, which networks are included with each routing protocol, and from which other routers this router is receiving information. Figure 5-18 shows the output from this command.

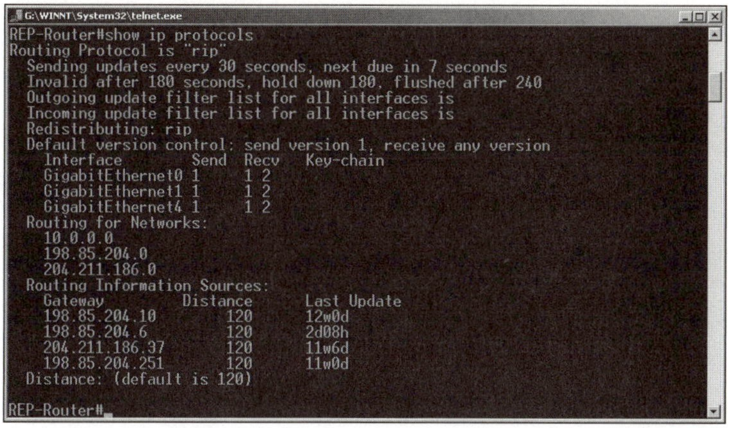

Figure 5-18 Show ip protocols command

The first line in Figure 5-18 indicates that the active routing protocol is RIP. If more than one protocol is active, each is listed on a separate screen. If no protocol is listed, then no routing protocol is running, which is likely your problem.

About halfway down the screen, you see the line "Routing for Networks:", followed by a list of the networks that are utilizing the RIP protocol. Typically, you will see a network listed for each network number that has been assigned to an active router interface. A common mistake is to configure and address all interfaces correctly, but forget to include all networks in the routing protocol.

Below the list of networks is the line "Routing Information Sources:". The IP addresses listed under that heading are the other routers in the network that have sent routing information to this router. If everything looks good on this router, but no routing information sources are listed or some are missing, the problem may be with another router in your network.

The three commands just described can tell you a good deal about the current state of your routed network. Many more commands are available for troubleshooting routers, but these three commands are usually the place to start to verify a new router configuration or to check an existing one. Whether I am teaching basic router configuration or the advanced routing courses, I have my students use these three commands over and over again when their configurations do not work. In the majority of cases, the information found in one of the three commands points out the problem or at least guides the student as to where to look next.

CHAPTER SUMMARY

❑ The tasks involved in supporting the Network layer are not numerous, but you must have a thorough understanding of the roles the Network layer plays to effectively maintain and troubleshoot networks at this level. The Network layer deals with logical addresses. Using these addresses, Network protocols get your data packets from one network to another efficiently. Specifically, you need to know how to define logical addresses, provide path selections, and work with connectionless delivery of packets.

❑ Without the Transport layer in networking protocol suites, the Internet would be in big trouble. It is at this layer that you segment data, provide flow control, provide a checksum, identify data, and determine quality of service.

❑ Protocols and routers are important to the Network and Transport layers. Protocols are integral to these layers because they define the rules and syntax of data transfer sessions. Routers are critical to the Network layer because they utilize the logical addresses defined at the Network layer to determine how best to get data from here to there in an internetwork.

❑ You should know how the TCP/IP protocol suite relates to the OSI model. For instance, the Network Interface layer corresponds to the Data Link and Physical layers of the OSI model. TCP/IP does not have a protocol or component that works at these two layers, but it does work with any Physical and Data Link specification, provided that the appropriate Data Link drivers are used.

❑ The User Datagram Protocol (UDP) provides limited functionality compared with TCP. UDP provides Application layer information via port numbers in the UDP header as well as a checksum to protect data integrity.

❑ IPX/SPX is the proprietary protocol Novell designed when NetWare was just getting started; it has been a mainstay in many networks since the mid-1980s. As a network administrator, you should know IPX addressing and frame types, a little bit about SPX, and the key packet traces that you can perform.

❑ NetBEUI exists at the Session layer and runs directly on top of the Data Link layer. Because no Network layer information is included in NetBEUI, it cannot be used to communicate over routers. NetBEUI was originally developed for use in IBM-DOS environments running over Token Ring. It was then adapted to OS/2 and Windows environments for simple but effective networking in small LANs. Its primary function is to provide name resolution services for the Data Link layer.

❑ A router is designed to receive packets on one interface, look up destination addresses in its routing table, and switch the packets out of the interface that will best get them to their destinations. To effectively use a router, you need to know how to use the show interfaces command, the show ip route command, and the show protocols command.

KEY TERMS

ARP cache — A storage area, usually in RAM, where MAC address-to-IP address mappings are kept.

broadcast domain — A group of computers and devices that reside on the same network.

byte stream protocol — A protocol, such as TCP, that sends and acknowledges data based on the number of bytes sent rather than the number of packets sent.

connectionless communications — A form of communication in which there is no confirmation to the sender as to whether the data arrived at the destination.

connection-oriented protocols — Protocols that use flow control, acknowledgments, and other methods to ensure the reliable delivery of data.

default gateway — The address of the device, usually a router, to which all packets should be sent if the destination IP address of the packet is not on the same network as the source.

Denial of Service (DOS) attack — A problem that occurs when real clients are being denied service because the server is overwhelmed waiting for fake three-way handshakes to complete.

fragment — A part of a datagram that has been broken into sections by the Network layer.

Internet Assigned Numbers Authority (IANA) — An organization that maintains a variety of numbering schemes used on the Internet.

logical address — The address assigned to a device that provides both network and host information and operates at the Network layer.

Maximum Segment Size (MSS) — The maximum number of bytes that can be received by a client in a single TCP segment.

Maximum Transmission Unit (MTU) — The largest datagram size accepted by the media or Network layer protocol.

NetWare Core Protocol (NCP) — An Application layer protocol that is part of the IPX/SPX protocol suite and provides some Transport layer services.

octet — A grouping of 8 bits that represent a byte.

packet burst mode — A mode of transferring IPX data in which acknowledgments are not required for each packet.

quality of service (QoS) — A factor that determines the reliability of data transfers and the performance level of those transfers.

registered ports — TCP and UDP ports in the range 1024 to 49,151 that may be used by private applications within an intranet or extranet.

Request for Comments (RFCs) — An open forum for creating documents that describe networking processes or procedures.

segment — A data portion created when the Transport layer breaks data into smaller pieces prior to hand-off to the Network layer.

subnet mask — Defines which part of the IP address is the network portion and which part is the host portion.

subnetting — The act of dividing one large IP address space into two or more smaller address spaces.

TCP segment — The entire unit of information that includes the TCP header and data.

User Datagram Protocol (UDP) — An unreliable Transport layer protocol that is part of the TCP/IP protocol suite.

virtual circuit — A communication method in which a connection is established between the sender and receiver before data transfers begin. Once the transfer is finished, the circuit is broken.

REVIEW QUESTIONS

1. Which two parts does a routable logical address define?

   a. network and host

   b. network and subnet

   c. host and MAC address

   d. host and subnet

2. What are the responsibilities of the Transport layer? (Choose all that apply.)

   a. Provides for the physical transmission of data

   b. Provides for flow control and a checksum to protect the data

   c. Segments data before sending it to the Network layer

   d. Handles routing information for determining the source and destination addresses

3. Which of the following protocols operate at the Network layer? (Choose all that apply.)

   a. TCP

   b. IP

   c. UDP

   d. IPX

   e. SPX

4. Which of the following protocols operate at the Transport layer? (Choose all that apply.)

   a. TCP

   b. IP

   c. UDP

   d. IPX

   e. NetBEUI

5. Which of the following is a reason for using a connectionless protocol?

   a. To keep data from being corrupted

   b. To provide reliability when getting data to a desired destination

   c. To provide information to application programs

   d. To provide for fast delivery of data without extra overhead

6. Given the network number 162.12.0.0 with a subnet mask of 255.255.255.224, which of the following is a valid subnet?

   a. 162.12.0.0

   b. 162.12.172.66

   c. 162.12.3.128

   d. 162.12.256.96

7. Which field in an Ethernet frame can tell you that IPv4 is being used?

   a. Version

   b. Length

   c. Identification

   d. Flags

8. Which ICMP command verifies that a particular host is able to communicate?

   a. tracert

   b. arp

   c. ping

   d. winipcfg

9. If a source knows the IP address of its destination but not its MAC address, which protocol can it use to determine this information?

   a. RIP

   b. ARP

   c. IGRP

   d. RARP

10. _____ protocols define a logical address so that packets can be sent from one network to another.

11. The Transport layer uses the feature of _____ to prevent a destination from being saturated with data packets.

12. _____ provide a method for specifying to which application received data should be sent.

13. The IP address 126.3.145.7 is a standard class _____ address.

14. Given the IP address 191.152.39.97 using the default subnet mask, what is the network portion of the address? What is the host portion of address?

15. The _____ is the address of the device to which all packets should be sent if the destination IP address of the packet is not on the same network as the host sending the packet.

16. How many bits are in the network portion of an IPX address? The host portion?

17. Connectionless protocols do not require an acknowledgment to determine whether the packet was delivered to a destination. True or False?

18. The Network layer of the OSI model is concerned with the assigning of physical addresses. True or False?

19. TCP provides guaranteed delivery of data through the use of Sequence Numbers and acknowledgments. True or False?

20. Describe a problem that can arise from the use of static entries in an ARP cache.

21. Explain why a valid CRC in a frame does not always guarantee that data has not been corrupted.

22. What information is sent between communicating computers in the TCP three-way handshake?

23. What problems can arise when employing NetWare servers that use different frame types?

24. If you see a message similar to "Server X claims Network 123 should be Network ABC" on a NetWare server, what is the problem?

25. On a Cisco router, what are three of the more important troubleshooting commands?

HANDS-ON PROJECTS

Project 5-1 The Windows ARP Cache

In this project, you will learn about the Windows ARP cache.

1. Click **Start**, click **Run**, and then type **command**.

2. Type **arp –?** at the DOS prompt and examine the options.

3. Type **arp –a** to view the current ARP cache. Are any entries listed? If so, write them down and explain to which device the IP address belongs if you know it.

4. Ping the IP address of a classmate's computer.

5. Type **arp –a** again and view the entries. What does the word "dynamic" under Type mean?

6. Wait about four minutes and type **arp –a** again. Has anything changed? Why?

7. Your instructor will give you the IP address of a computer on a different network (or you can use the URL of an Internet computer). Ping this address.

8. Type **arp –a**. Do you see the address that you just pinged? Why or why not? What address do you see?

9. Close the DOS box by typing **Exit**.

Project 5-2 Creating a Filter EtherPeek

In this project, you will create an address filter in EtherPeek that you can use to limit your packet captures to only your workstation. You will need EtherPeek on your computer to complete this exercise.

1. Click **Start**, point to **Programs**, and then click **WildPackets EtherPeek**.
2. From the Capture menu, select **Start Capture**. If a Capture Options dialog box is displayed, uncheck the **Show this dialog when creating a new capture window** checkbox, and then click **OK**.
3. Click the **Filters** tab at the bottom of the window that opens.
4. Click the **Insert** icon at the top-left corner of the Filters window.
5. The Edit Filter window opens. Type **My IP Address** in the Filter box.
6. Click the **Address Filter** check box.
7. In the Type: box, select **IP**.
8. In the Address 1 box, type the IP address of your workstation.
9. Click the **Both directions** button, and then click **Both Directions**.
10. Click the **Any address** option button. The dialog box should look like Figure 5-19.
11. Click **OK**.
12. Close EtherPeek. You now have a filter you can use to capture packets that have your IP address in the source or destination.

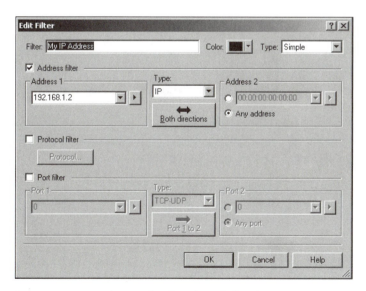

Figure 5-19 EtherPeek Edit Filter dialog box

Project 5-3 Tracing a Ping

In this project, you will learn the nuances of tracing a ping command. You will need EtherPeek on your computer to complete this exercise.

1. Open a DOS box.

2. Type **arp −a** to list the ARP cache. If there are any entries, delete them by typing **arp −d** *address*, where *address* is the IP address of the entry. Delete each entry displayed by using this method.

3. Leave the DOS box open, but minimize it.

4. Open the WildPackets EtherPeek program.

5. From the Capture menu, select **Start Capture**. If a Capture Options dialog box is displayed, uncheck the **Show this dialog when creating a new capture window** checkbox, and then click **OK**.

6. Click the **Filters** tab at the bottom of the window that opens.

7. Find the My IP Address filter you created in Project 5-2 and click the **checkbox** next to it. Also, click the **IP** filter checkbox.

8. Click the **Packets** tab at the bottom of the window, and then click the **Start Capture** button.

9. Open the DOS box you minimized earlier.

10. Ping the instructor's computer.

11. Close the DOS box by typing **Exit**.

12. Click the **Stop Capture** button in EtherPeek. Notice that the first packet is an ARP request and the second is an ARP reply. (Depending on your network setup, these two packets may not be consecutive. Other packets may be inserted between the ARP request and the ARP reply.)

13. Why are these the first two packets captured and why do they appear before the ping packets?

14. Close all windows.

Project 5-4 Viewing the IP Options Field

In this project, you will create a ping packet using the record route option and capture the packets generated. This exercise will demonstrate the use of the Options field in the IP header. You will need EtherPeek on your computer to execute this project.

1. Open the WildPackets EtherPeek program.

2. From the Capture menu, select **Start Capture**. If a Capture Options dialog box is displayed, uncheck the **Show this dialog when creating a new capture window** checkbox, and then click **OK**.

3. Click the **Filters** tab, and then check the **checkbox** to the left of the My IP Address filter that you created in Project 5-2.

4. Click the **Packets** tab, and then click the **Start Capture** button.

5. Open a DOS box.

6. Ping an IP address that you know is less than nine hops away (you may need to use the tracert command first to ensure that the destination meets this criterion). Use the **–r** option—for example, ping –r 9 www.course.com.

7. Close the DOS box.

8. Click the **Stop Capture** button in EtherPeek.

9. Double-click one of the reply packets and find the Route Data field in the IP header. This field contains data that is part of the optional Options field in the IP header.

10. What does the information in the Route Data field signify?

11. Exit all programs and close all windows.

Project 5-5 IP Packet Fragment

In this project, you will see what happens when an IP packet is too big for the MTU. You will need EtherPeek on your computer to complete this exercise.

1. Open the WildPackets EtherPeek program.

2. From the Capture menu, select **Start Capture**.

3. Click the **Filters** tab, and then check the **checkbox** to the left of the My IP Address filter you created in Project 5-2.

4. Click the **Packets** tab, and then click the **Start Capture** button.

5. Open a DOS box.

6. Ping a classmate's computer using the command **ping –l 1700** *address* (note that the character after the minus sign is the letter "l," not the number "1"), where *address* is the IP address of your classmate's computer. What does the –l 1700 option in the ping command mean?

7. Close the DOS box.

8. Click the **Stop Capture** button in EtherPeek.

9. Inspect the captured packets. Why is one packet 1518 bytes and the other 266 bytes? The ping command output shows only four replies; why are eight packets sent and eight packets returned?

10. Double-click one of the packets that is 1518 bytes.

11. Inspect the Fragmentation Flags and Fragment Offset fields. What do the values signify?

12. Double-click a 266-byte packet. What do the Fragmentation Flags and Offset fields signify in this packet?

13. Exit all programs and close all windows.

Project 5-6 See the Effects of Fragmentation on Performance

This project demonstrates the performance degradation when sending packets that are fragmented compared to nonfragmented packets.

1. Open a DOS box. Ping the Internic using the following command:
   ping –l 1472 www.internic.net. In Ethernet, this will generate the maximum size frame of 1518 bytes. Record the average round-trip time. Perform the same ping again, except this time use the following command:
   ping –l 1473 www.internic.net. You are sending only one additional byte. Record the average round-trip time.

2. Was the ping with a packet size of 1473 slower? Should one byte in the packet size make such a difference? Why do you think the size-1473 ping was slower?

3. Close all windows.

Project 5-7 Change the Default TCP Window Size

In this project, you will change the default Window Size in Windows NT or Windows 2000.

1. Click **Start**, click **Run**, and then type **regedt32**.

2. Select the **HKEY_LOCAL_MACHINE** window.

3. Double-click the **System** key, the **CurrentControlSet** key, and then the **Services** key.

4. Scroll down to and double-click the **Tcpip** key.

5. Double-click the **Parameters** key.

6. With the Parameters key open and selected, click **Edit** on the menu bar and select **Add Value**.

7. In the Value Name dialog box, type **TcpWindowSize**.

8. In the Data Type drop-down list, select **REG_DWORD**.

9. Click the **OK** button.

10. In the Dword Editor dialog box, select the **Decimal** option button.

11. Enter **17520** in the Data field.

12. The default value for Windows 2000 is 17520. You can experiment by making this value larger or smaller and then doing some traces of file transfers to see whether a smaller size increases the number of acknowledgments per data packets sent. If you do not want to change the Registry, click **Cancel** in the Dword Editor dialog box.

13. Close any remaining open windows.

CASE PROJECTS

Case 5-1 Determine the MTU on a Network

There is a way that you can determine the MTU on a network, if you did not already know it—by utilizing some options of the ping command. See if you can figure out how this can be done. Think about packet fragmentation and why it must be done in some circumstances.

Case 5-2 Create a Filter for Web Traffic

Now that you know how to create filters in EtherPeek, create a filter that will allow you to capture only packets related to Web browser requests to and from your workstation. Save and try out the new filter by starting a capture session and then using Ping and other utilities to create traffic. Verify that the packets created by these requests were not captured. Next, open a Web browser and see whether the packets are captured.

Case 5-3 Explain the Do Not Fragment Bit

Windows sets the Do Not Fragment bit on most packets that it sends. How can this choice help find the smallest MTU between the source and destination computers? Explain in detail what occurs to allow this information to be discovered.

Case 5-4 Web Filter Traffic

Using the Web Traffic filter that you created in Case 5-2, capture a Web browser session involving a Web site of your choice. Study the first six packets in detail by double-clicking them and examining the headers and data. Write a summary of what you think is occurring with each of the six packets. Include information on the handshaking, Window Sizes, options, and data.

CHAPTER

6

SUPPORTING THE UPPER LAYERS

After reading this chapter and completing the exercises, you will be able to:

♦ Understand the roles that the upper layers play in a network environment

♦ Identify and describe the network components that work at the upper layers

♦ Troubleshoot and identify services that work at the Session layer

♦ Describe the common functions associated with the Presentation layer

♦ Support Application layer software in a TCP/IP environment

♦ Understand network clients and their role within the Application layer

The top three layers of the OSI model—Session, Presentation, and Application—are the upper layers. They are grouped in this manner because the most common network protocol suites, such as TCP/IP and IPX/SPX, combine the functions of these three layers into a single software component.

This combining of the three layers makes identifying the components of an individual layer less obvious when troubleshooting. Still, as a network technician, you must be able to identify when a network support issue involves the upper layers and know where you should start looking to resolve the problem. This chapter looks at some of the problems and solutions associated with components of the upper three layers.

We begin with a review of the roles played by the upper layers.

ROLES OF THE UPPER LAYERS

The three layers under discussion in this chapter are frequently referred to as the application layers (lowercase "a") because these layers are so closely tied to computer applications. Some of the functions that occur at these layers include network security via login and logout, name resolution, data translation, and network resource location.

These layers, which are all implemented in software, can be described collectively as a client, a server service, or, in some cases, simply an application such as FTP or Telnet. However, certain functions performed by these components can be tied to individual layers. For example, resolving a computer name to its TCP/IP or physical address is typically considered a Session layer duty.

 Note that "Application layer" and "application layers" are *not* the same thing.

Network security is provided by the Session layer in the form of user login and authentication, which establishes the communication session between a user's workstation and a network resource. The termination of the communication session is done through the Session layer logout procedure. The Session layer also provides name resolution. If a user wishes to access a network resource, a computer name or **Universal Resource Locator (URL)** can be used rather than a physical or logical address. (Recall that a URL is the standard naming convention for Internet resources.) The Session layer is assigned the task of resolving these user-friendly names to computer-friendly physical or logical host addresses.

"Data translation" is a catch-all phrase describing the job of the Presentation layer. As the name of this layer implies, data that is received is presented to the Application layer in a form that the Application layer expects. If data were compressed or encrypted before being sent, the Presentation layer has the job of decompressing or decrypting the data before sending it up to the Application layer. In addition, the Presentation layer is concerned with the structure of data and the syntax used to transfer and process different data types. Files such as graphics, sound, or video are all composed of binary data but have different structures and require different handling. It is the Presentation layer's responsibility to coordinate with the application regarding how these data types should be handled for proper processing.

The Application layer provides an interface to network resources for user applications. In the user-oriented computing environments of today, the Application layer is expected to provide users and applications with access to network resources in a transparent manner. That is, we should be able to save or copy a file from a network resource without any special knowledge of how the network works or without even knowing that the resource is on a network. Other tasks occurring at this layer are e-mail, Web browser functions, and network terminal functions such as Telnet. Remember that the

Application layer does not include user applications such as word processing and spreadsheets, but rather these programs gain access to network resources through the Application layer.

COMPONENTS OF THE UPPER LAYERS

Before we can start troubleshooting and supporting the upper layers, we need to identify the components and services in our network and computers that work at these layers. As I mentioned, this endeavor is not as clear-cut as identifying the components of the lower four layers. Nonetheless, we'll start by looking at the Session layer and work our way upward through the Presentation and Application layers. In each layer, we'll identify specific functions and then list the software or process that supports each function.

The Session Layer Components

One of the primary jobs of the Session layer is to resolve computer names to addresses, which is the first step in establishing a communication session between two computers. The next step is usually the negotiation of a login or authentication procedure. After a communication session has been established, data transfers can begin. Once the session is finished, the session is closed, often by a logout procedure.

To fully illustrate these Session layer procedures, we first look at the processes involved in the resolution of names and then examine the components involved in the session establishment and termination.

Name Resolution

A pure TCP/IP environment is one in which only TCP/IP protocols and services are used. That being said, in pure TCP/IP environments, the service that resolves names is the **Domain Name Service (DNS)**. DNS resolves host computer and domain names to IP addresses. I say "pure" TCP/IP environments in my opening sentence because Windows client/server environments prior to Windows 2000 may use a service called **Windows Internet Naming Service (WINS)** to resolve Windows computer names to IP addresses. In addition, Windows environments can use NetBIOS to resolve computer names to IP addresses in an implementation called NetBIOS over TCP/IP.

 The naming service you are most likely to encounter in a corporate network depends largely on the operating system used. In a Windows 2000, Windows XP, or UNIX environment, you are most likely to see DNS as the naming service. With earlier versions of Windows, you may see WINS and NetBIOS as the principal name service.

NetWare environments using IPX/SPX resolve network resource names to IPX addresses by using **Service Advertising Protocol (SAP)**. SAP is a special IPX packet that is broadcast by NetWare servers to inform the network of the resources that the server has available. NetWare clients also use SAP to find NetWare resources. Windows environments using IPX/SPX use NetBIOS over IPX to resolve computer names.

NetBIOS can stand on its own in addition to being used within IPX/SPX and TCP/IP. Small Windows networks can use the NetBEUI protocol, which is simply NetBIOS running as a Session and Transport layer on top of the Data Link layer. NetBIOS is responsible for resolving Windows computer names to physical addresses.

Session Establishment and Termination

In a TCP/IP environment, each Application layer protocol has its own syntax for beginning and ending a session. For example, in FTP, the FTP client sends a command called USER to the FTP server, followed by the user name, and then a PASS command, followed by the user's password. When the FTP session is over, the FTP program sends a QUIT command. While all of these functions are part of the FTP client and server programs, one could argue that they fulfill the functions specified by the Session layer. Other applications that are part of the TCP/IP protocol suite have similar session establishment and termination command sequences. We will look at some of them later in this chapter.

Client/server environments utilize login and logout procedures to begin and terminate a session. The login procedure may include a process that determines the hours of the day during which the user may log in, the stations from which the user may log in, and the resources to which the user has access. When a user logs out of the resource, open files are closed, network processes supporting the session are terminated, and the session is closed. Network clients initiate the login and logout sequences, and network servers process the requests appropriately.

Windows environments use a series of broadcast packets that contain NetBIOS commands to locate the server to which the workstation wishes to log in. The server responds if it is available, and then a series of Server Message Block (SMB) packets are transferred back and forth to negotiate the details of the connection. After establishing suitable session parameters, data transfer can begin.

Although each protocol, whether TCP/IP, IPX/SXP, or NetBEUI, has its own details regarding the session negotiation process, the process goal is always the same—to create a communication session between computers for the purposes of data transfer. When a user logs out of a computer or shuts a computer down, the connection is closed with a series of SMB packets. All of this functionality is built into **Client for Microsoft Networks**, which is the client software you install if you wish to communicate from one Windows computer to another. The Windows server component is **File and Print Sharing for Microsoft Networks**. Later in this chapter, we will look at some of the details involved in session establishment and termination in a Windows environment.

NetWare environments use NCP packets to begin and end sessions. NCP can run over IPX or IP. When a NetWare client finds a NetWare server using SAP packets, as previously discussed, the client then sends an NCP login request. Once the login is processed, connection details are negotiated between the client and the server, a connection is established, and login scripts are run, if necessary. The client and server are now ready to begin a data transfer session. When a user logs out, an NCP logout request is sent, open files are closed, and the session is terminated. In Windows client stations, the Client for NetWare Networks or Novell Client handles the client side of the login equation and the NetWare server handles the server side. Later in this chapter, we will look at some of the details of this process.

Presentation Layer Components

The Presentation layer, as we have seen, is responsible for making sure that the user application receives data in a format that the application expects. Most Presentation layer functions are built into the applications that actually need the services provided by the Presentation layer. However, a formal Presentation layer protocol does exist: **Abstract Syntax Notation Number One (ASN.1).** ASN.1 is an **International Standards Organization (ISO)** standard, and it is gaining support for use in many network applications. ASN.1 is already used in network applications such as **Simple Network Management Protocol (SNMP)**, which is a TCP/IP network management protocol, and it is under consideration for use in a new version of HTTP, called HTTP-NG (Next Generation).

 The ISO, if you recall, is the author of many standards, including the famous OSI networking model.

At the present, the Presentation layer is somewhat difficult to nail down in most systems. Probably the best example of a Presentation layer activity is the HTML code in a Web page document. The HTML code specifies the information (such as a movie or a sound file) that is to be embedded in the document. It also identifies the appropriate application or Web browser plug-in required to process the file. Because of the vague nature of the Presentation layer, it will be discussed only briefly in this chapter when upper layer support issues are presented.

Application Layer Components

The Application layer is the layer closest to the user applications and therefore provides those applications with an interface to the network. This interface is important because it saves authors of user applications the necessity of knowing the details of how the network works. However, this can also cause problems—if an application uses network resources inefficiently, slow performance can result.

Application layer components in an operating system such as Windows usually consist of a set of **application programming interfaces (APIs)**. A network API is a set of operating system subroutines that an application developer can call from a program to request a network service. For example, Windows includes the **Winsock API**, which allows applications to use TCP/IP services, and the **NetBIOS API**, which allows programs designed for NetBIOS to access network resources.

The NetBIOS API comes in three flavors: **NetBIOS over IPX (NBIPX)**, **NetBIOS over IP (NetBT)**, and **NetBIOS Frame Protocol (NBF)**, which is better known as NetBEUI. While our focus here is not to understand how to write applications, it is important to understand the terminology used and the Application layer components that are used in a Windows environment.

Aside from APIs, Application layer components found in a Windows environment include **network redirectors**, which are built into the network client and server components. The redirectors determine whether a requested resource is local to the application or a network resource. If the resource is local, the request is sent to the local service or driver that handles the resource. If the request is for a network resource, the redirector passes the request down to the lower layers. This functionality allows commonly used applications such as word processors and spreadsheets to access network files and printers without being specifically written to work in a network environment.

When a user opens a file in a word processor, the word processor does not know or care whether the file is located on the local hard disk or on a network server. The file request is simply sent to the redirector, and the redirector determines how to get the request to the appropriate machine. File and Print Sharing for Microsoft Networks and Client for Microsoft Networks are redirectors in a Windows environment.

When a file operation is requested for a network resource, the request is sent over the network in the form of a **Server Message Block (SMB) datagram**. The SMB datagram is a protocol developed by Microsoft, IBM, and Intel that contains commands used by redirectors to indicate what type of request or response is contained in a packet. SMB is analogous to a NetWare client NCP request for resources.

In a TCP/IP environment, the Application layer components we will discuss include DHCP, FTP, Telnet, and HTTP. These services are all defined at the Application layer in the TCP/IP model and correspond primarily to the Application layer in the OSI model. However, because the Application layer in the TCP/IP model covers all three upper layers of the OSI model, these services naturally include functions performed at the Presentation and Session layers.

Table 6-1 provides a view of many of the networking components found at these three OSI model layers. After you review them, we can get down to the business of troubleshooting and supporting what goes on at these layers.

Table 6-1   Upper layer protocols and components

	Operating Environment		
	Windows	NetWare	TCP/IP
Application layer components	Winsock and NetBIOS APIs, SMB, and redirectors	NCP	FTP, Telnet, HTTP, DHCP, and others
Presentation layer components	SMB and redirectors	NCP	FTP, Telnet, HTTP, DHCP, and others
Session layer components	NetBIOS and WINS	SAP	DNS and RPC

6

SUPPORTING THE SESSION LAYER

Before two computers can start a data transfer session, there must be a convenient method for one computer to locate another. Once located, the parameters of the communication session must then be established, and once the communication session is complete, the session must be terminated. The Session layer is responsible for these tasks, and different protocols and even different applications within the same protocol accomplish the tasks differently. Supporting these functions, therefore, is not always a straightforward proposition.

In this section, we will examine the name resolution services, which describe the method used to locate another computer, and then we will look at session establishment and termination. We will start by examining DNS, which is the name resolution service employed in TCP/IP environments such as the Internet; we then discuss the IPX/SPX Session layer protocols and, finally, the NetBIOS Session layer services.

Name Resolution Services

Name resolution is accomplished in a variety of ways depending on the network operating system in use and the protocols employed. TCP/IP environments use DNS, NetWare environments use SAP, and Windows environments use NetBIOS, WINS, or DNS, depending on the version of Windows running and the protocol in use. DNS is the most pervasive naming service because it is used to locate resources on the Internet. We discuss it in detail next.

Supporting DNS

In this section, we will discuss the basic structure of DNS and take a quick look at DNS operation. Then we will discuss the packet structure and look at some troubleshooting issues associated with DNS and DNS servers. By the time you finish this section of the chapter, you should be able to understand and support DNS with confidence.

The Structure of a DNS Name

The DNS system used throughout the Internet is organized as a tree-like hierarchy. The tree consists of several domain levels: root, top, second, subdomain, and host. Below the root level, each level has branches, each of which has a name. When you put all of the names of the branches together, separated by a period, you have the **Fully Qualified Domain Name (FQDN)** of the network resource—for example, www.course.com.

The top-level domains are organized into categories such as commercial interests (.com), nonprofit organizations (.org), government (.gov), educational institutions (.edu), or country of origin (a two-letter country code). The second-level domain is usually the name of a company or institution. The subdomain level can consist of several names separated by a period and is optional. An example might be a department or branch of an organization. Finally, the host level represents individual computers that host network services. An example might be server1.marketing.xyzcorp.com, where com is the top-level domain name, xyzcorp is the second-level domain, marketing is the subdomain, and server1 is the host. Figure 6-1 shows a diagram of the tree structure.

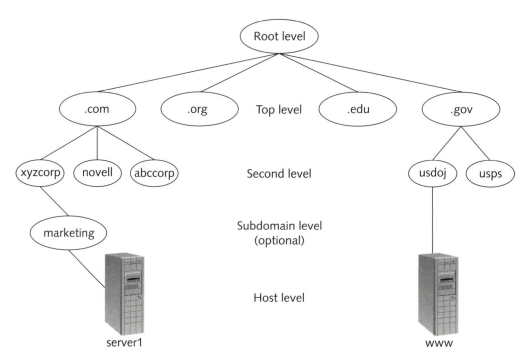

Figure 6-1   DNS hierarchical tree structure

 A company maintaining a private DNS server need not conform to the Internet top-level domain names as long as its DNS server is to be used solely within the organization. For example, a private DNS server could have a FQDN such as server1.mycompany.

The DNS Database

DNS servers maintain a database of information that consists of a variety of record types called **resource records**. A resource record contains information about DNS resource types maintained by the server. Examples of resource types are host names, other name servers in the domain, and mail exchange servers.

 For a complete description of DNS and resource records, refer to RFC 1035 at *www.networksorcery.com/enp/rfc/rfc/rfc1035.txt*.

Resource records consist of several fields, three of which are most important: Name, Type, and Data. The most important type of resource record is an **Address (A) record**. The A record consists of a host name/IP address pair. For example, an A record might look like Table 6-2.

Table 6-2   Address record format

Name	Type	Data
www	A	192.168.1.15

A client that is attempting to resolve a name to an IP address makes a DNS request to retrieve an A record. DNS server administrators manually enter A records for each host in the domain in case the host needs to be located by name. The host would need to be located by name if it were providing services to other network devices.

Another resource record type is the **Start of Authority (SOA) record**. The SOA record lists information for a **DNS zone**. DNS zones are the second-level and top-level domains, as pictured in Figure 6-1. Each zone has a primary DNS server that maintains the master copy of the DNS record information, and the SOA record lists the name of that server. The SOA record also contains important information such as the zone administrator contact information, a serial number, and refresh and expiration time values. This information is common to all DNS servers in the zone. An SOA record is created when an administrator creates a new zone for the DNS server, typically when a new domain or subdomain is created.

A third resource record type is the **Name Server (NS) record**. The NS record specifies the name of a server that is authoritative for a domain. A server is authoritative if the organization in which the server is maintained has control of the domain name for which it is maintaining A records. For example, if you own a company called Netbiz, Inc., and you register a domain name of Netbiz.com, your DNS server (assuming you maintained your own DNS server) would be the authoritative server for Netbiz.com.

You would be free to add host names and subdomains as you wished. Any information about Netbiz.com would be considered authoritative information if it came from your DNS server.

Now you know the basic organization of a DNS server. So, if you have a DNS server on your network and your network is connected to the Internet, do you have to enter domain names and host names for every computer on the Internet? It would be a lot of work if you did, so perhaps you'll want to hunt down a master file somewhere that you can download to your DNS server rather than entering everything manually. That approach would be a little better, but you must have a lot of disk space if you plan to hold every host name and IP address for every computer on the Internet! Fortunately, the DNS system is organized as a hierarchy and that hierarchy will save you from a great deal of typing. We discuss it next.

The DNS Hierarchy

Because of the hierarchical nature of DNS, it is not necessary for every DNS server to maintain a database of all domain and computer names and addresses for the entire Internet. Instead, most DNS servers maintain the addresses for only those domains under their control. The domain might be a single secondary-level domain such as xyzcorp.com, or, if your business hosts Web sites for other companies, you might maintain hundreds or thousands of domains. Of course, even thousands of domains and their associated hosts is a small number when compared to the entire Internet.

When a DNS server is installed, the administrator creates one or more domain names or zones and then creates the A records for each host. That is not all that the DNS database contains, however. A DNS server database comes preloaded with a list of NS records that point to a list of A records; these A records contain the addresses of servers that maintain the top-level domains throughout the Internet. The NS and A records usually can be found in a section of the DNS database called Cached Lookups or something similar. Figure 6-2 shows the Windows 2000 Server DNS service. The NS records shown point to A records that are contained within the gtld-servers folder.

The Windows 2000 Server DNS service maintains a folder called Cached Lookups, and the NS records can be found in a subfolder called net. These NS servers are referred to as gtld-servers, where "gtld" means generic top-level domain. The gtld-servers are maintained by Verisign Global Registry Services, formerly Network Solutions.

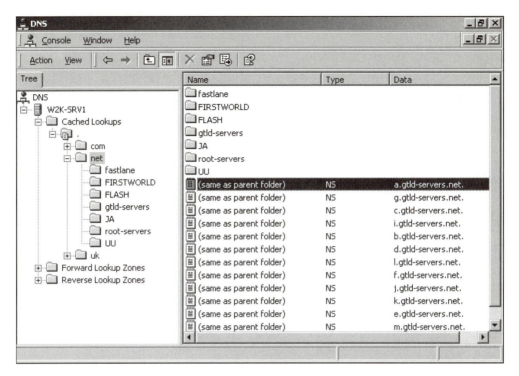

Figure 6-2   Windows 2000 Server DNS service

When a DNS server receives a request to look up a host name that is not maintained by that DNS server, it can do one of two things: It can send the address of a top-level domain server back to the host so that the host can query the top-level server, or it can do a **recursive lookup**. A recursive lookup requires the DNS server to query a top-level domain server for the name. If the name being resolved has several subdomain names, it is possible that the top-level domain server will return the address of another server that should be queried. In turn, that server could return the address of a subsequent server that should be queried, and so forth.

Figure 6–3 shows a trace of a DNS query that resulted in four queries and four responses before the IP address of the requested host was finally returned. Luckily, this situation does not happen too often. Once a DNS server has learned of a host or domain, it caches that information for a period of time so that it can respond directly the next time a query for that host or domain is received.

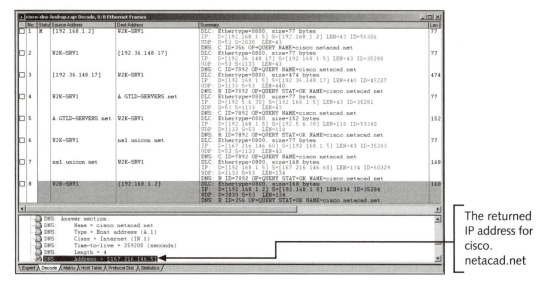

The returned IP address for cisco. netacad.net

Figure 6-3   Recursive DNS lookup

The packet trace shown in Figure 6-3, and the packet traces described in the rest of this chapter, are done with Sniffer Pro from Network Associates. Sniffer Pro's packet summaries show more information in the initial capture screen than do EtherPeek's summaries, so it is easier to show an entire sequence of packets without having to go to the packet detail screens. The actual information captured is the same with either program.

Let's examine what occurs in Figure 6-3. The DNS client is address 192.168.1.2, and the primary DNS server for this station has an address of 192.168.1.5. The first packet capture shows a DNS query (UDP destination port 53) from the client to the server. The query is attempting to look up the address for cisco.netacad.net. The second packet shows the DNS server sending a DNS query to 192.36.148.17, which is a root-level domain server. The third packet shows the root-level domain server returning a response, but the response contains information on the next DNS server that should be queried. The fourth and fifth packets show the local DNS server querying the gtld-server and the subsequent response. The sixth and seventh packets show the local DNS server querying the authoritative DNS server for netacad.net and the subsequent response by that server. Finally, the eighth packet shows the local DNS server returning the IP address to the DNS client. Graphically, the exchange looks like the diagram in Figure 6-4.

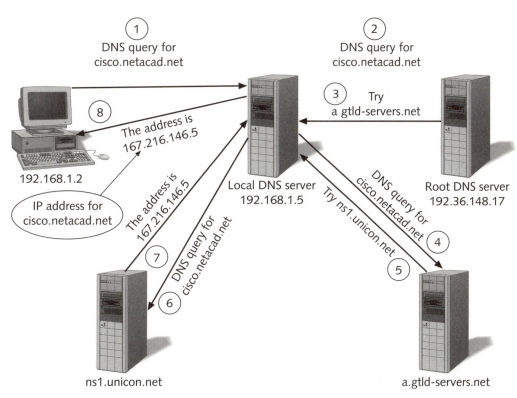

Figure 6-4 DNS recursive query

DNS Caching

DNS servers will normally cache information for a period of time, so eight–packet queries like the one described in the previous section are not the norm. Networks benefit from caching because DNS queries are answered more quickly and the amount of network traffic is reduced.

Most networks have both primary and secondary DNS servers, which maintain zone information for the domains registered for the network. This setup provides fault tolerance in the event that one of the DNS servers fails or needs to be taken offline for maintenance.

In large networks with many subnets, it is a good idea to place **caching DNS servers** on several subnets. A caching DNS server does not contain a copy of the zone file; instead, it simply passes on requests to either the primary or secondary DNS server and then caches responses. After a while, the caching servers can directly respond to most DNS queries from workstations in their subnet or nearby subnets. This ability can significantly improve performance on the network because it eliminates or reduces the number of router hops along which DNS queries and responses must travel, plus it reduces the load on the primary and secondary servers.

Figure 6-5 shows the same DNS query as Figure 6-3, but, here only two packets are involved. The first packet is from the DNS client to the local DNS server, and the second packet is the response from the local DNS server. Because the local server cached the response from a previous DNS query, there was no need to send additional queries to outside DNS servers.

Figure 6-5 DNS cached query

Windows 2000, Windows NT, and Windows XP all have the ability to do client DNS caching. That is, a local computer keeps a cache of recent DNS lookups, much as it maintains an ARP cache. The local client cache is checked for a domain name before a name resolution request is sent to a DNS server. We will take a look at this type of caching more closely in Hands-on Project 6-1.

DNS caching, for the most part, has a positive effect on networks. However, because DNS names and IP addresses change from time to time, stale entries in a DNS cache can prevent a successful name resolution. Fortunately, a stale entry quickly turns into a timed-out entry, which is an entry that is removed from the DNS cache. Thus, you can simply wait until a particular entry expires so that the DNS server is forced to retrieve the correct entry from an authoritative server.

To counteract stale entries, you can also clear your server's DNS cache manually. Most DNS servers have a utility that allows the cache to be cleared. Before you undertake this task, you need to understand that clearing the DNS cache will cause a temporary degradation in name lookup performance and an increase in network traffic.

 You can do very little about stale DNS entries in servers you do not manage. If your DNS server is retrieving a domain entry from another server that has the name cached, you will just have to wait until the entry expires in that server.

The DNS server in Windows 2000 has a default expiration time (expressed as TTL, not to be confused with an IP packet TTL) of one day.

DNS Packet Format

DNS packets use UDP as the transport protocol; they also use the port number of 53. A DNS packet begins with a 12-byte header, followed by a data section that consists of one or more questions and answers and, optionally, a number of name server records and resource records. The simplest of DNS packets will contain a single question record such as when a computer queries for the IP address of a host. Figure 6-6 shows the header format.

DNS packet																															
1	2	3	4	5	6	7	8	9	10	11	12	13	14	15	16	17	18	19	20	21	22	23	24	25	26	27	28	29	30	31	32
ID 2 bytes																Q	Query			A	T	R	V	B				RCode			
Question count 2 bytes																Answer count 2 bytes															
Authority count 2 bytes																Additional count 2 bytes															
Questions: variable length																															
Answers: variable length																															
Authoritative servers: variable length																															
Additional records: variable length																															

Figure 6-6 DNS packet format

The 16-bit ID field is used to match questions with answers. When a DNS server responds to a question, the ID field of the response should match the ID field of the query. The Q bit is set to 0 if the packet contains a DNS question; it is set to 1 if it is a response. The 4-bit query field can have one of three values: 0 for a standard query, 1 for an inverse query, and 2 for a server status request. Note the following facts about the remaining bits:

- The A bit will be set to 1 if the response is from an authoritative server. If the response is from a cached entry, the A bit will be 0.

- The T bit is set to 1 if the DNS answer is longer than 512 data bytes, which is the maximum number permitted in a UDP datagram. When a DNS answer longer than 512 bytes occurs, the message is truncated.

- The R bit is set to 1 if the inquiring computer wants the query to be carried out recursively.

- The V bit is set to 1 in a response if the server can perform recursive lookups.

- The 3-bit B field is reserved and must be set to 0 (zero).

- The 4-bit RCode is returned by a server to indicate the status of a response.

The response by a DNS server to a DNS query may be one of those listed in Table 6-3.

Table 6-3   DNS response codes

Response Code	Description
0	No error condition
1	Unable to interpret query due to format error
2	Unable to process due to server failure
3	Name in query does not exist
4	Type of query not supported
5	Query refused

The next four header fields are 16-bit values specifying the number of questions, answers, authoritative name servers, and additional records that follow in the data section of the packet. These counters provide the information necessary to properly decode the data fields of the DNS packet.

If your network is having difficulty receiving DNS information, the DNS response codes can tell you a considerable amount of information about what is wrong. For example, a response code of 3 indicates that the query name does not exist. An authoritative server will provide this response if, for example, you tried to ping a host whose name does not exist but whose domain name *does* exist. A response code of 2 indicates that the query was unable to be resolved and that there was no authoritative server in charge of the domain specified. This situation might happen if, for example, you typed a domain name incorrectly.

A response to an unknown host on a known domain usually will be returned more quickly than an attempt to look up a host on a domain that does not exist. The difference in response times occurs because, in the former case, the DNS server keeps attempting to find the domain by querying additional top-level servers. In the latter case, the query stops after an authoritative name server responds with a code of 3, which indicates that the host does not exist.

DNS Troubleshooting

Problems that occur with DNS are usually the result of a misconfigured server, a stale entry in a DNS cache, or authoritative servers for a domain becoming unsynchronized. (Yes, more than one server can be authoritative. Often several servers will provide fault tolerance and redundancy, and they can become unsynchronized.)

Misconfigured servers can result from something as simple as a typo. If an administrator types the domain name or host name entry incorrectly, the correct name will never be found. A stale entry can result as described earlier in this chapter. Servers can become unsynchronized when a server goes down, misses DNS updates, and later comes back up, or if the communication fails between two servers for a period of time.

When a computer performs a **reverse DNS lookup**, it receives the FQDN for a given IP address. Although the vast majority of DNS lookups are queries for an IP address based on a domain and host name, reverse lookups are used when a destination device needs to verify the identity of a source IP address. This procedure might be done for additional security. For instance, an Internet resource may want to exclude access from particular domains or perhaps ensure that the packet can be traced to a domain in the event the sender is into mischief such as hacking.

 When a Web server can't do a reverse DNS lookup for a particular IP address, the server may deny access to the host requesting its resources. This problem can be solved by ensuring that all hosts have DNS entries and associated reverse DNS entries.

A **PTR record** is a DNS entry that makes reverse lookups possible. A PTR record contains the IP address in reverse dotted decimal notation in the Name field, the text "PTR" in the Type field, and the host name of the specified computer in the Data field. Normally, when you create A records, you have an option of automatically creating the associated PTR record for each host you enter. If you choose not to create the PTR record, a reverse DNS lookup will not be possible for that host. If users on your network complain about an inability to access certain Internet resources because their host name was unable to be resolved by the destination, the problem may be due to missing PTR records.

Stale DNS cache entries have already been discussed in this chapter. If you suspect that a problem with DNS lookups is related to invalid cached entries, don't forget about the local workstations DNS cache. Not all operating system versions have the ability to clear the local cache; thus, if you suspect the local cache is the problem, you may have to reboot the computer to clear it.

Most organizations that manage one or more domains have at least one primary DNS server and one secondary DNS server. The primary server holds the master copy of the zone file, and the secondary server holds a replica of the zone file. When changes are made to the domain, the changes are applied to the primary server. The SOA record on

6

the primary server contains a serial number that must be incremented for the secondary server to know that a change in the database occurred and to synchronize with the primary server. If the secondary server does not receive the new zone file, workstations that are configured to use the secondary server will not be able to correctly look up the changed or added host or domain names.

Troubleshooting DNS with the Nslookup Utility

Nslookup is a standard TCP/IP utility that comes with the various versions of the UNIX operating system and with Windows NT, Windows 2000, and Windows XP. The nice thing about this program is that you can send DNS queries directly to the name server of your choice without having to change the default name-server settings in your client operating system. This approach allows you to bypass your local name servers to look up an address that your servers might not have cached correctly.

For Windows 9x versions, you can download a freeware or shareware program that does the same thing as the Nslookup utility.

Besides looking up host names, you can retrieve other types of resource records with the Nslookup utility. For instance, you can find MX records, (the mail servers in a domain) and NS records to get a list of all name servers for a domain. Another option of the utility allows you to list all records for a given domain, provided the name server queried is authoritative over the domain whose records you want to list.

Nslookup is particularly valuable if you do not have administrative capabilities over your name server, such as when you use a Web hosting company that maintains your domain information. In such a situation, you can use the Nslookup utility to verify whether hosts have been added to your assigned DNS server. You can even query the root servers to see whether your domain information has been propagated throughout the Internet. This feature is especially useful when you first register a domain and begin adding hosts.

Nslookup is run from a Windows NT or Windows 2000 command prompt. When you run the utility, you can specify a name to look up, followed by an optional DNS server to query. If you omit the DNS server, the default DNS server listed in your TCP/IP settings is used. If you simply type the nslookup command at the command prompt, you will enter interactive mode, in which a variety of options is available. Hands-on Project 6-4 lets you practice using the nslookup command.

The information presented in this section and the Hands-on Projects should give you sufficient understanding of DNS to be able to find and resolve problems related to DNS. For a more in-depth look at DNS, refer to RFC 1034 and RFC 1035. For a look at managing DNS in a Windows 2000 environment, see Course Technology's *MCSE Guide to Microsoft Windows 2000 Networking*.

Supporting NetWare IPX Session Layer Protocols

The Session layer in an IPX environment is vastly different than the analogous layer in a TCP/IP environment. Although the mechanisms may be different, the goals remain the same: find resources, gain access to the resources, and establish a communication session with those resources. This section examines the mechanisms used in a NetWare IPX environment to accomplish those goals.

Finding Resources Using NetWare SAP Packets

Whereas TCP/IP environments require a client workstation to know the address of a DNS server so as to retrieve the address of a resource, NetWare IPX environments depend on network broadcasts of SAP packets to find network resources.

Finding such network resources requires three steps:

1. The client must find a server, and then session parameters such as packet size must be agreed upon.

2. The client station must log in to the server.

3. A data transfer session begins in the NetWare IPX environment.

When a NetWare client attempts to log in to a NetWare server, that client broadcasts a SAP packet called a **Get Nearest Server (GNS) query**. NetWare servers that are in the broadcast domain respond with their names and addresses. The client then attempts to find the network ID specified in each server's reply. This network ID is the internal network number for the NetWare server. After the client finds the network ID, it creates a connection, and other session parameters are exchanged. Finally, a login is attempted. After a successful login, data transfer can begin.

Using a GNS query to find resources does have its drawbacks. For instance, because the GNS query is a broadcast packet, it needs a device on the same subnet to respond to it; routers do not, by default, pass along broadcasts to other subnets. Because of this limitation, router manufacturers that support IPX also support handling SAP packets.

Two main types of SAP packets are involved in the name resolution process. We have discussed the first type—GNS. The other type of SAP packet is a broadcast generated by the NetWare server to advertise to all other SAP-enabled devices the services that the NetWare server can offer.

Here is where the router comes into play. Routers that are running the IPX protocol listen for the SAP broadcasts generated by NetWare servers. When a router receives a SAP, it stores the information in a table. When a client sends a GNS request on a subnet that lacks NetWare servers, the router responds with the address of a NetWare server on another network.

Of course, there is a problem with these broadcasts from the NetWare servers: The router will always respond with the first server in its SAP table. There may be one, two, or ten servers available, but the router always chooses the first one in the table. Not only will this practice inundate one NetWare server at 8:00 A.M. when everyone turns his or her PC on to log in, but it can also cause servers to run out of connection licenses. Even if the server whose address with which the router responded is not the server the user will ultimately log into, the initial sequence to prepare for login requires a connection license. An additional problem with this name resolution method is the extra burden placed on the network due to broadcasts and the burden placed on routers to maintain the SAP table and to respond to GNS requests.

 The connection license issue is no joke. I ran into it once. The server's connection screen showed many NetWare connections, but no logins. Unfortunately, NetWare considers any connection to the server to be a licensed connection even if the connection was made only as a response to the GNS request and even if no login or sharing of resources was attempted.

Figure 6-7 shows the six-packet sequence required for the GNS request and reply, the location of the network ID, and the connection establishment. Notice that there is no login sequence yet. A connection is created before the login occurs and will persist until the client asks to detach from the server or the client reboots.

Packets 3 and 4 in Figure 6-7 bear some additional explanation. After the workstation receives the server name and network ID, a RIP broadcast request is sent out to locate the network ID. The server responds, telling the workstation how many hops there are to the requested resource. As you see, SAP and RIP are tightly coupled in a NetWare IPX environment.

No.	Status	Source Address	Dest Address	Summary	Len
1	M	8023.005004B3E823	0.FFFFFFFFFFFF	NSAP: C Find nearest File server	60
2		8022.00A0CC7A097C	8023.005004B3E823	NSAP: R CONSTELLATION	11
3		8023.005004B3E823	0.FFFFFFFFFFFF	RIP: request: find 1 network, 0D2E92D5	60
4		8022.00A0CC7A097C	8023.005004B3E823	RIP: response: 1 network, 0D2E92D5 at 1 hop	60
5		8023.005004B3E823	CONSTELLATION	NCP: C Create service connection N=0 Cx=255	60
6		CONSTELLATION	8023.005004B3E823	NCP: R OK	60

Figure 6-7   NetWare and GNS connection

NetWare Login Procedure Using NCP Packets

Before a data transfer session can begin on a NetWare server, the client must be logged in. After the sequence shown in Figure 6-7, a series of negotiations occurs using NCP packets. (Recall that NCP is NetWare's upper-layer protocol that covers the Session, Presentation, and Application layer functions.)

Figure 6-8 shows the complete sequence from the GNS packet through the login. Packet 7 starts the negotiation process. The first thing the client needs to do is get information about the server. Packet 8 is the server's response, which includes information such as the server name, operating system version, maximum number of connections, and file system details. Packets 9 through 12 negotiate data transfer parameters. The client requests and receives an encryption key needed for login in packets 13 and 14. Packets 15 through 18 complete the login by sending the user name and the encrypted password; the server responds with a successful login.

```
Snif7: Decode, 1/18 Ethernet Frames                                                          _ □ ×
No.  Status  Source Address        Dest Address          Summary                              Len (Byte Re
  1    M      8023.005004B3E823     0.FFFFFFFFFFFF        NSAP: C Find nearest File server      60
  2           8022.00A0CC7A097C     8023.005004B3E823     NSAP: R CONSTELLATION                113
  3           8023.005004B3E823     0.FFFFFFFFFFFF        RIP: request: find 1 network, 0D2E92D5  60
  4           8022.00A0CC7A097C     8023.005004B3E823     RIP: response: 1 network, 0D2E92D5 at 1 hop  60
  5           8023.005004B3E823     CONSTELLATION         NCP: C Create service connection N=0 Cx=255  60
  6           CONSTELLATION         8023.005004B3E823     NCP: R OK                             60
  7           8023.005004B3E823     CONSTELLATION         NCP: C Get file server info           60
  8           CONSTELLATION         8023.005004B3E823     NCP: R OK for CONSTELLATION (v5.0)    183
  9           8023.005004B3E823     CONSTELLATION         NCP: C Get big packet max size 1494    60
 10           CONSTELLATION         8023.005004B3E823     NCP: R OK, accepted max size 1494     60
 11           8023.005004B3E823     CONSTELLATION         NCP: C Negotiate buffer size of 1444   60
 12           CONSTELLATION         8023.005004B3E823     NCP: R OK, Accepted buffer size of 512  60
 13           8023.005004B3E823     CONSTELLATION         NCP: C Get Login Key                   60
 14           CONSTELLATION         8023.005004B3E823     NCP: R OK, Got key                     63
 15           8023.005004B3E823     CONSTELLATION         NCP: C Get bindery object ID for GTOMSHO  67
 16           CONSTELLATION         8023.005004B3E823     NCP: R OK, Received GTOMSHO          109
 17           8023.005004B3E823     CONSTELLATION         NCP: C Keyed Object Login             75
 18           CONSTELLATION         8023.005004B3E823     NCP: R OK                             60

IPX:  ----- IPX Header -----
IPX:
IPX:  Checksum = 0xFFFF
IPX:  Length = 34
IPX:  Transport control = 00
IPX:          0000 .... = Reserved
IPX:          .... 0000 = Hop count
IPX:  Packet type = 17 (Novell NetWare)
IPX:
IPX:  Dest   network.node = 0.FFFFFFFFFFFF, socket = 452 (NetWare Service Advertising)
IPX:  Source network.node = 8023.005004B3E823, socket = 400E (Unknown)
IPX:
NSAP: ----- NetWare Nearest Service Query -----
NSAP:
NSAP: Service type = 0004 (File server)
DLC:  Frame padding= 9 bytes

00000020: ff 04 52 00 00 80 23 00 50 04 b3 e8 23 40 0e 00   y.R..#.P.³è#@..
00000030: 03 00 04 98 04 98 04 98 04 98                    ......

Expert  Decode  Matrix  Host Table  Protocol Dist.  Statistics
```

Figure 6-8   NetWare login procedure

One of the difficult aspects of troubleshooting NetWare Session layer transactions is that you must catch the sequence starting from the initial GNS packet. This procedure normally occurs at boot time for NetWare clients. Thus, if a Presentation layer problem is suspected and requires a packet trace, you will likely have to tell the user to reboot the station after you have set up the analyzer.

NCP also performs the logout, which terminates a communication session. The logout procedure is quite straightforward: A logout request by the client is followed by an OK status from the server. A request is then made by the client to destroy the connection, and the server sends an acknowledgment response.

A final note about IPX Session layer components. SAP packets, as you have learned, are broadcasts. A NetWare server broadcasts SAP packets to advertise its services once every minute. Each server may need to send several packets each minute. In a very large network with many servers, this amount of broadcast traffic can saturate slower WAN links and even affect LAN links. NetWare offers an answer to this problem in the form of **NetWare Link State Protocol (NLSP)**. NLSP, which is Novell's proprietary link-state routing protocol, is much more efficient than SAP and RIP because it broadcasts service advertisements only once every two hours and when a service changes. NLSP is turned on by default in NetWare 4.11 and above and is backward compatible with RIP/SAP so that you can migrate from a RIP/SAP network to an NLSP network as time and resources allow. For more on NLSP, see Novell's documentation on its Web site at *www.novell.com*.

Supporting NetBIOS

NetBIOS is more of a service than a protocol. In LAN environments, NetBIOS is typically used on top of one of three protocols (NetBIOS over TCP/IP, NetBIOS over IPX/SPX, or NetBEUI) or directly on top of the Data Link layer. In the context of this discussion, "on top of a protocol" means that the protocol is encapsulated with a NetBIOS header.

While NetBIOS does perform some functions beyond the description of the Session layer, two of its more important functions in LAN environments are the location and registration of computer names and session establishment. We discuss each of these duties in turn.

NetBIOS Name Registration

One key feature of NetBIOS is its dynamic name resolution. When a computer running NetBIOS comes on the network, it attempts to register its NetBIOS names to whomever will listen. In addition, it registers the names using every protocol for which NetBIOS is configured. This task is carried out through a series of broadcasts or multicasts. In a sense, it is much like a NetWare SAP broadcast because the computer registers not only the NetBIOS names but also the services provided.

Names that are registered include the computer name, workgroup name, messenger service name, and domain name, if applicable. After a successful login, the user name is registered as well. Not only are all of these names registered with each protocol running NetBIOS, but each name is registered three or four times depending on the protocol. The names are registered multiple times to ensure that there is no conflict with another machine with the same name.

What does all this name registration mean for your network at 8:00 A.M. if you have two or three protocols running? Lots and lots of broadcasts. On a Windows 95 computer with TCP/IP, IPX/SPX, and NetBEUI loaded, I have counted 44 broadcast packets sent just for the process of registering NetBIOS names, querying for a server, and logging into a Windows 2000 server. The packets sent for a single Windows 95 login could total 121.

You may think that having three protocols loaded is unusual, but it is not. Many manufacturers ship workstations that include a NIC loaded with all three protocols, plus both Windows and NetWare clients. A recent customer of the author received four such computers.

When NetBIOS runs over TCP/IP, the NetBIOS name registration packets will be in the form of a WINS packet. The information in a WINS packet is the same as that sent with a NetBEUI or a NetBIOS over IPX packet. This is a great example of the benefit of a layered architecture. The underlying Network and Transport layer protocol can be TCP/IP or IPX/SPX, which differ significantly, but the NetBIOS information, working at the Session layer, can remain the same and work with either of these protocols.

Figure 6-9 shows a series of packets generated by a Windows 95 computer when it first boots up. The first three packets shown, packets 16–18, are NetBEUI packets so there is only NetBIOS over the Data Link layer shown. Packets 19–21 are the NetBIOS over TCP/IP name registration packets and are shown as WINS packets. Packets 22–24 are the NetBIOS over IPX/SPX packets.

> The next several figures that contain packet traces show a source address that sometimes reads "GLT_DELL" and other times reads "Laptop-MAC." These names are registered in the analyzer's name table. GLT-DELL indicates that the IP address is being used as the source address; Laptop-MAC indicates that the MAC address is being used.

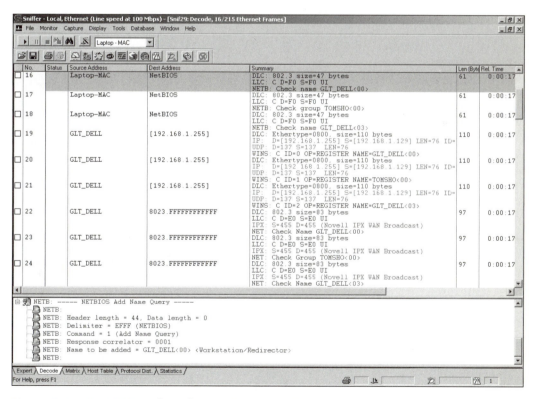

Figure 6-9   NetBIOS packets during Windows 95 boot

Note packets 16 and 18, which contain the text "NETB: Check name GLT_DELL," and packets 19 and 21, which contain the text "OP=REGISTER NAME=GLT_DELL"; these lines of information tell you that the names are registered. In all three protocols, the name GLT_DELL appears to be registered twice, but there is a difference. The number that comes after each name is a NetBIOS code indicating the type of NetBIOS name it is. GLT_DELL is registered with <00> and <03> codes. These codes are called NetBIOS name suffixes.

Two types of suffixes are possible: a Unique Name suffix, as for a computer name, and a Group Name suffix, as for a workgroup name. Table 6-4 lists the suffix codes and their descriptions for both types. In the table, U indicates a Unique name type and G indicates a Group Name type. This list is incomplete, but it contains the suffix codes you are most likely to encounter; for a complete list, refer to Microsoft's Web site.

Table 6-4   NetBIOS name codes

Name	Number	Type	Usage
<computername>	00	U	Workstation Service
<computername>	01	U	Messenger Service
<_MSBROWSE_>	01	G	Master Browser
<computername>	03	U	Messenger Service
<computername>	20	U	File Server Service
<computername>	30	U	Modem Sharing Server Service
<computername>	31	U	Modem Sharing Client Service
<computername>	BE	U	Network Monitor Agent
<computername>	BF	U	Network Monitor Application
<username>	03	U	Messenger Service
<domain>	00	G	Domain Name
<domain>	1B	U	Domain Master Browser
<domain>	1C	G	Domain Controllers
<domain>	1D	U	Master Browser
<domain>	1E	G	Browser Service Elections

This information in Table 6-4 can be useful for the administrator who wants to keep track of which computers are offering which services. For example, a Unique Name service code of 20 indicates that the machine is providing file-sharing services. It is clear from this trace that it is desirable to limit the protocols in use and to limit services offered by each computer to only those necessary. Your users will thank you for the improved network response.

NetBIOS Session Establishment

After the NetBIOS name is registered, the booting computer sends a request to log on. The logon request is also sent with each protocol supporting NetBIOS because the client doesn't know which protocol the server might be running.

Figure 6-10 shows three logon requests in packets 88, 90, and 91—one for each protocol. Packet 93 shows the server responding with a "Response to LOGON Request." The server that responded to the logon request is running only TCP/IP, so the requests using the other two protocols are ignored. You can see that the logon requests are broadcast or NetBIOS multicast packets because the Windows 95 client does not know yet which server will respond to the logon request. If the client did know which server would respond, you would see destination addresses with a specific MAC address in the figure.

6

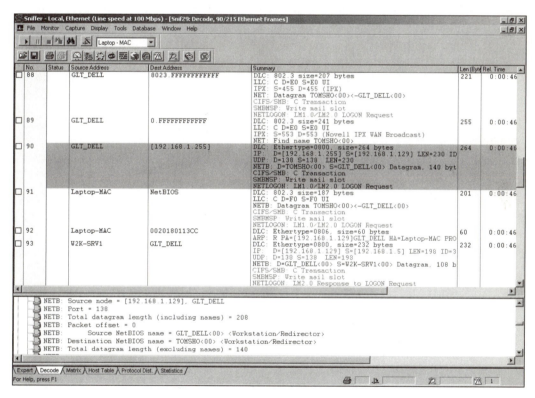

Figure 6-10   NetBIOS name registration and session establishment

Figure 6-11 shows the next packet sequence during the logon process. The client attempts to register the login name (in this case, GTOMSHO) in packets 94–96, again using all three protocols. The client has the name of a server that responded to the logon request; packet 97 shows the attempt to find that name, with packet 98 being the response from the server.

Up to this point, almost all of the packets generated by the client have been broadcast and multicast packets. Starting with packet 99, we finally get a one-on-one conversation going between the client and the server. Packets 99 through 102 are an interesting group of packets. There is no network or higher-layer protocol involved. The packets are simply Data Link layer packets implementing a Type II Logical Link Control (LLC) communication session. They actually set up a connection-oriented Data Link layer communication session. A Type II LLC is a very-low-overhead, acknowledgment-based protocol that allows 128 frames between acknowledgments. You will see these frames scattered throughout traces.

Packets 103 and 105 establish a NetBIOS session between the client and the server. Packets 107 through 117 negotiate session parameters. A logon is finally performed in packet 113, with a positive status being returned by the server in packet 117. Take a close look at packet 105. The D= and S= correspond to remote and local session numbers, respectively. These session numbers are used in the exchange of SMB packets that follows. They allow a client and a server to keep track of multiple sessions occurring simultaneously. The session numbers can also help the administrator keep track of which packets belong to which conversations during the troubleshooting process.

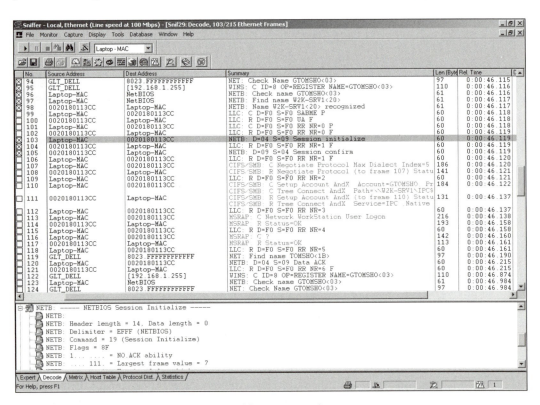

Figure 6-11   Session establishment and logon completion

What can this advanced knowledge of NetBIOS packets and session establishment do for you? To tell you the truth, the knowledge is not very useful when everything is working right. However, when everything is working correctly is the time to take some network traces that you can use later when things go *wrong*. You can save traces of various working procedures such as logons to Windows and NetWare servers, boot-up procedures, DNS queries, and so forth. Then, when something stops working, you can compare the nonworking trace to the working trace to determine where the problem lies.

SUPPORTING THE PRESENTATION LAYER

6

As previously mentioned, it is difficult to pinpoint a particular component or function of the Presentation layer, so our discussion here will be brief. Each network application includes the necessary programming to handle the types of data that the application is expected to process. Any data translation that may occur is typically handled internally by the application and would not be seen in a packet trace. The usual result of a failure of the Presentation layer is scrambled data on the screen or in transferred files. Usually, little can be done except to contact the manufacturer of the application and see if a fix is available.

In some cases, a user may be able to "fix" a Presentation layer problem if the application has configuration options that permit the translation of data. For example, a common data translation example is that of ASCII encoding versus EBCDIC encoding of character data. ASCII is the method used by PCs for representing printed characters, but EBCDIC is used in some IBM environments. If you transfer a text file from an IBM machine that uses EBCDIC to a PC that uses ASCII, your data will look strange indeed—unless the codes are translated. Some file transfer programs may have a configuration option that can be set to perform this translation if the translation does not occur automatically.

SUPPORTING THE APPLICATION LAYER

We're there! The top layer of the OSI model! You may have noticed throughout the past several chapters, particularly when viewing packet traces demonstrating activities at the various layers, that the higher we go in the OSI model, the more complex and less clear-cut each function becomes. This happens because the higher we go in the model, the closer the activities are to dealing with humans, and with humans come complexity and ambiguity.

Let's think about this point for a minute. We initiate and terminate most network communications, so we need a Session layer. We don't think in binary, so we need data presented to us and to our application in a way that it can be understood; thus, we need a Presentation layer. In addition, we need a user interface and don't want to know about the details of accessing a network resource, so we need an Application layer. As you can see, the need for humans to interact with a computer system adds a lot of complexity to the network and operating system software.

Humans are unpredictable and want things to be easy to use. Many writers of user application software (note that this does not mean Application layer software) do not have a detailed understanding of networking and therefore may write applications that do not use network services efficiently. To accommodate all of these aspects of applications, the Application layer has become very complex.

This section of this chapter discusses the Application layer as it applies to TCP/IP Application layer components. Later chapters discuss troubleshooting and supporting clients and servers in a Windows or NetWare environment.

Specifically, we'll see that the TCP/IP protocol suite includes a host of useful applications, each of which has its own way of doing a fairly narrowly defined job. There is File Transfer Protocol (FTP) for uploading and downloading files, Telnet for terminal-like communications to remote hosts, HTTP for Web page browsing, and DHCP for IP address management. There are other Application layer programs and functions, but this book looks at these four because they are commonly used.

Before jumping into the four applications, we need to review some facts about the Application layer first.

Application Layer Fast Facts

TCP/IP defines a set of protocols for accomplishing a particular Application layer function, such as FTP for transferring files, and there is actually a user application that goes along with this function. Its availability makes the support and troubleshooting of TCP/IP Application layer functions easier than the support of the Application layer in a client/server operating system environment. You can focus on one application, so as to understand what that application is supposed to do and how to hone in on it.

TCP/IP applications use TCP or UDP port numbers to identify an application for which a packet is intended. If the application requires reliable delivery of data, error checking, and recovery mechanisms, then it uses TCP as the transport protocol. Examples include FTP and HTTP. If the application is a simple, LAN-based application or one in which the majority of data transfers are composed of just a single packet, then UDP may be used. You can put this knowledge to good use when analyzing TCP/IP applications because you can restrict packet captures to particular transport protocols and particular ports.

Supporting FTP

FTP has one job to do—transfer files. It does this job efficiently and, because it has only one job, the protocol is comparatively simple. FTP, like most Application layer components, has a client side and a server side. The client might be an inconspicuous command-line program such as FTP.EXE that is included in the Windows TCP/IP protocol stack, or it might be a fancy graphical user interface (GUI) program with a few more bells and whistles.

FTP gets its job done by sending simple text-based commands to the server component to process. The server component in the UNIX world is called a daemon, as are the server components for most TCP/IP applications. Because TCP/IP applications originated in the UNIX world, you will hear terms such as FTP daemon or HTTP daemon regardless of whether you are working in a UNIX environment. On the other hand, they may just be called servers, depending on with whom you are speaking.

An FTP server, by default, uses TCP ports 21 and 20. Most FTP server programs allow you to change the port numbers, which is useful if you want to hide the server and make it available to only a chosen few. To keep things simple in this text, we will examine FTP using the standard port numbers.

FTP uses two ports. Port 21 is the command port and is the port on which an FTP session is initially established, and it is the port that is used for sending FTP commands. Port 20 identifies the default data port, which is used for the transfer of file data. When you look at an FTP conversation, you will see two TCP three-way handshakes: one to establish a connection with port 21 and, after a successful login and transmission of a file transfer command, another to establish a connection with port 20. In a sense, the two functions of initiating a connection and logging in are Session layer functions, but they are built into the FTP client application and server application so they are discussed here.

Many of the problems you are likely to see with FTP are of the ho-hum variety, such as an incorrect user name or incorrect password. There isn't much to examine with those errors. Either the administrator of the server has to change account information or the user has to remember the password! There is one thing to be aware of, however, with the login procedure: The password is sent in **clear text**. With clear text, the password is not encrypted and someone capturing packets on the network can easily see the password when it is sent. Obviously, this issue has implications in network security, particularly if you use one user name and password for most of your accounts; if an enterprising hacker captures one of your FTP sessions, your user name and password may be revealed to give the user access to many of your accounts. It is therefore a good idea to use a different password for applications that do not encrypt the password by default.

Figure 6-12 shows an FTP connection and logon. This entire exchange uses the server port 21 and the client port 2158. This FTP logon was accomplished with a freeware FTP client from IPSwitch called WS_FTP. The server is Microsoft's FTP server that is part of IIS 4.0. Note the following pieces of information about the packets in the figure:

- Packets 1–3 are the familiar TCP three-way handshake. The destination port is 21 and the source port is a random port number selected for the FTP client.

- Packet 4 is a greeting sent by the FTP server.

- Packet 5 contains the FTP command USER followed by the user name ftpuser.

- Packet 6 is the server's response indicating that a password is required for this user.

- Packet 7 shows the client sending the PASS command followed by the clear text password letmein.

- Packets 8 and 9 are the server's acknowledgment and a message indicating a successful login.

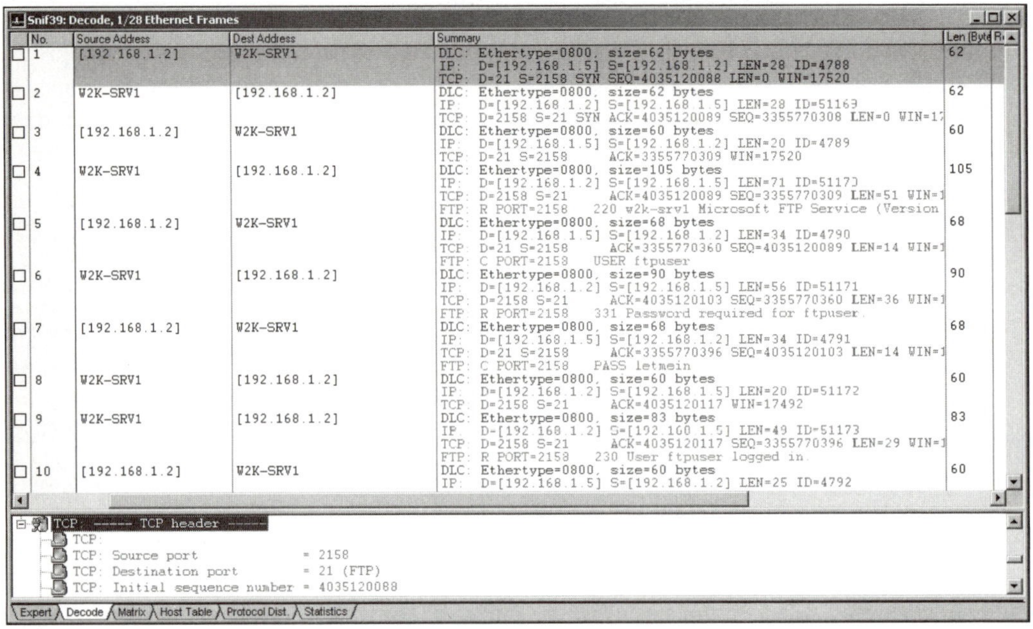

Figure 6-12 FTP connection and login

After a login, users can list files, upload files, and download files. Figure 6-13 shows the packets involved in an ftp list command, which lists the contents of the directory. Packet 16 is the client's transmission of the list command, and packet 17 is the server response indicating that an ASCII mode data connection is opened. Packets 18–20 show the three-way handshake to open a new communication session for server port 20 and client port 2159. The server sends the directory listing in packet 21, and a FIN TCP packet in packet 22 indicates the end of the data transfer. Packets 23 and 24 are ACK packets sent by the client. Packet 23 is an ACK to packet 22 in the port 20 session, and packet 24 is an ACK to packet 17, which is part of the port 21 TCP session.

You can tell that packet 24 is an ACK to packet 17 based on the ACK number. If you look at the SEQ number in packet 17 and add to it the length of the TCP data specified as 53, you arrive at the ACK number found in packet 24. Two final packets (not shown) complete the data transfer by closing the port 20 session with a FIN ACK sent by the client and a final ACK by the server. The command port session, port 21, stays open until the user logs out of the FTP server.

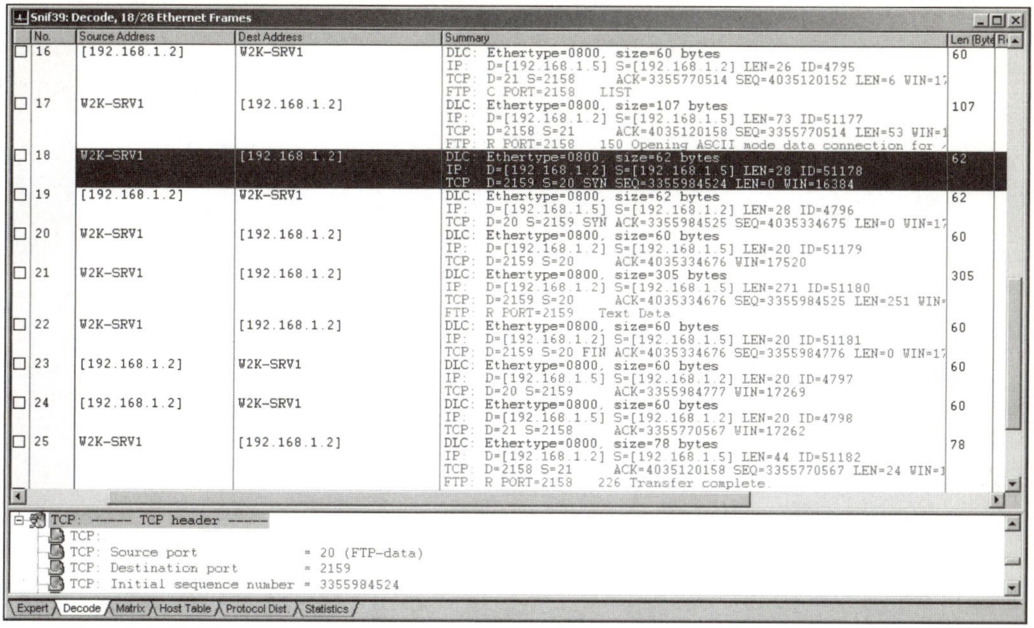

Figure 6-13   FTP data transfer

The exchanges in Figure 6-12 and 6-13 show how a typical FTP session works. It's pretty simple—not a lot that can go wrong. Sometimes, however, things do go wrong. In such a case, knowing how an FTP session is supposed to work can help you track down an errant session.

One problem that does occur from time to time is the result of an FTP transfer being initiated behind a firewall. Many firewalls are set to allow FTP transfers to be initiated from inside their network, but not from outside the network. In other words, someone may download or upload files from the Internet to his or her workstation, but someone on the Internet should not attempt an FTP transfer with a server inside the company network.

Refer again to Figure 6-13 and take a look at packet 18. Packet 18 shows the FTP server initiating a TCP three-way handshake with the FTP client to open the data port 20. Many firewalls on the client side will stop this type of communication because administrators do not want TCP sessions initiated from outside the network. The problem here is that the client initiated the FTP transfer, which your firewall may permit, but only port 21 is opened on the server side. It is the server that initiates the port 20 data transfer session. Many firewalls will block this procedure because TCP sessions may not be initiated from outside servers.

Fortunately, there is a way around this potential problem. Many FTP clients can be set to use **passive transfer mode**, and most FTP servers support this mode. Passive transfer mode requires the client to send a message to the server using port 21 and request passive transfer mode. The server will respond with an acknowledgment and a message if passive transfers are allowed. The client then initiates the TCP three-way handshake using a pair of random ports, over which the data such as files and directory listings will be transferred. So, you see, this avoids the problem of having the FTP server initiate a TCP connection that many firewalls will reject.

Refer to Figure 6-14 and compare the sequence there to the sequence in Figure 6-13. In Figure 6-13, the three-way handshake to open port 20 begins at packet 18 and is initiated by the server; in Figure 6-14, using passive transfer mode, the three-way handshake to open the data port connection begins at packet 15, after the pasv command is sent by the client and acknowledged by the server. If you ever receive an error indicating a failed data connection, try using passive transfer mode and see if it solves the problem.

Another possibility for solving the problem of a failed data connection is to configure the firewall to allow connections inside the network from source port 20. Note, however, that this choice can compromise the network's security because it circumvents a common precaution of disallowing TCP sessions from being initiated outside the network.

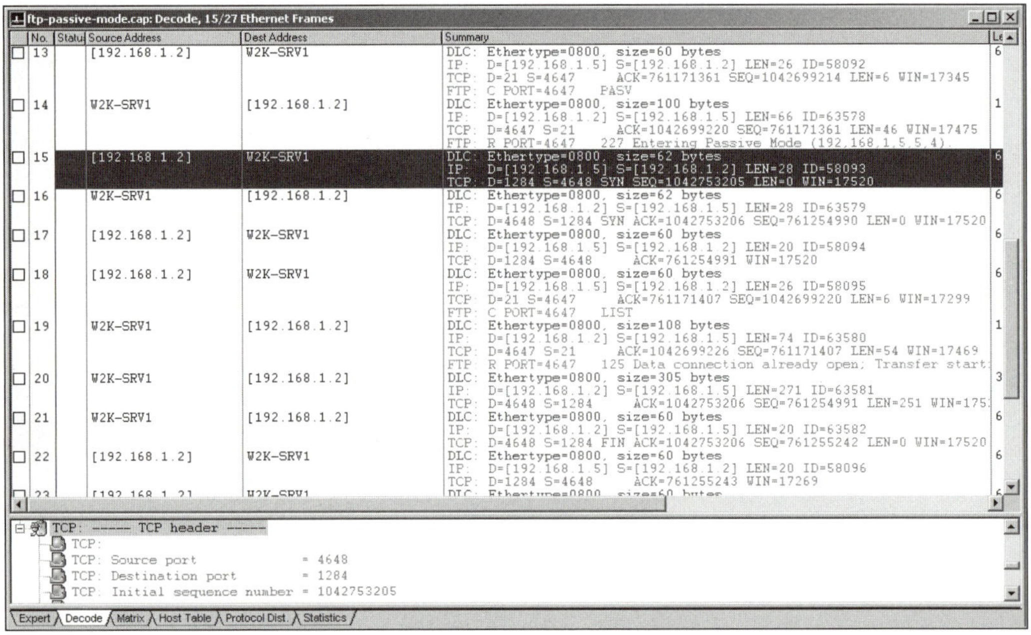

Figure 6-14   FTP passive transfer mode

Supporting Telnet

The first thing you should notice about Telnet is that it is practically the only TCP/IP component that does not use an acronym. Aside from that, Telnet is a client/server Application layer service that allows terminal-like connections over a network. It is an extremely inefficient application in that few data bytes are transferred for every packet sent, which translates into high network overhead. This is the nature of the program. If your network users make significant use of Telnet, you'll just have to get used to seeing a lot of small packet transfers when you do network monitoring.

A Telnet session is begun with an exchange of parameters to determine the mode of operation. Most of these parameters are Presentation layer-type items such as the character encoding and terminal emulation type. Figure 6-15 shows a packet trace of a Windows Telnet client establishing a Telnet session with a Windows 2000 server. This tool can prove useful for remote administration of your Windows servers. The first three packets are the familiar TCP three-way handshake. The next three packets are unique to a Windows 2000 Telnet server and client. Why? As you know, the Windows 2000 Telnet server application requests authentication. Most systems that run Telnet have a login procedure that is conducted after the Telnet connection is established. Windows 2000, however, requires that the Telnet client provide NT Lan Manager (NTLM) authentication before connecting. The client that comes with Windows 2000 supports NTLM authentication, but Windows 9*x* clients do not and neither do most readily available Telnet clients.

Packets 7 through 16 set up parameters such as echo and the terminal type. The last two packets show the server sending a screen prompt and the client responding with an ACK.

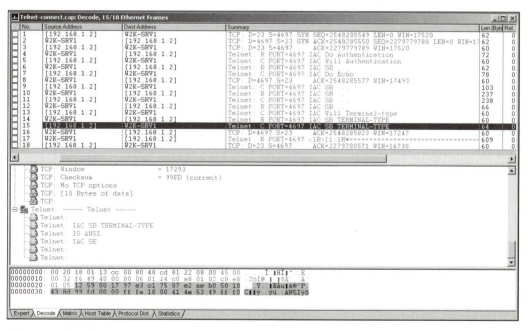

Figure 6-15   Telnet connection

Figure 6-16 shows a simple command being performed on the Telnet connection: a dir command to print out a directory listing. Packet 1 shows the letter "d" being sent from the client to the server, and packet 2 shows the server responding echoing the letter "d" and showing ANSI display characters. Packet 3 is the client's ACK to packet 2. Each character typed creates three separate packets, giving a total of 12 packets for a simple command. Packet 10 is the character generated by pressing the Enter key, and packet 11 contains significant data. In the figure, notice that packet 11 has a length of 1233 bytes. It is the directory listing being sent to the Telnet client.

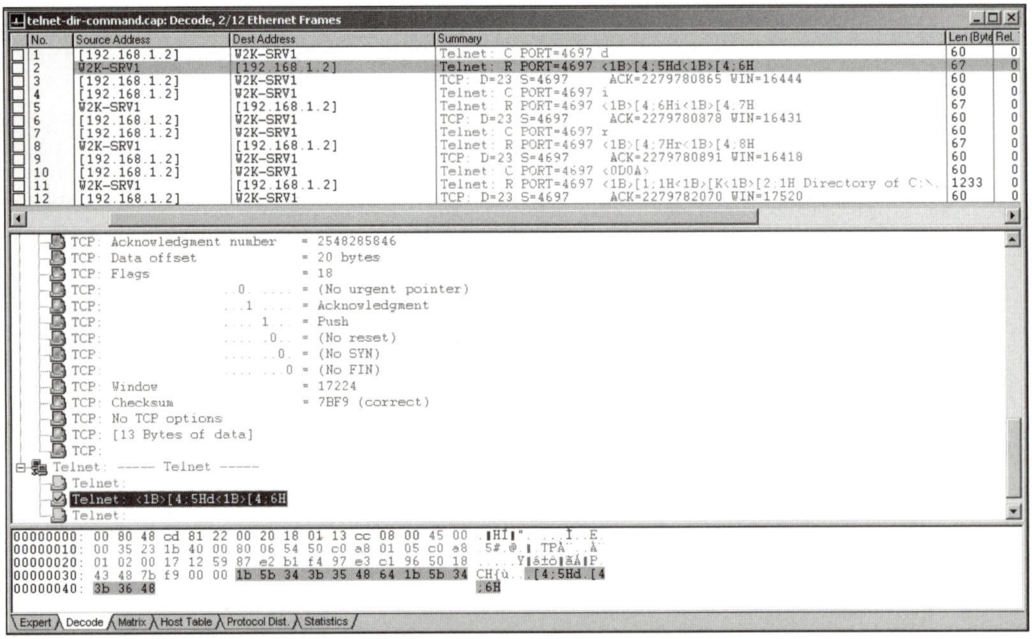

Figure 6-16   A dir command in a Telnet session

A Telnet client and server that deal with complete lines before sending the packets would have reduced the number of packets to three. Thus, if Telnet is a major part of your business operation, it may pay to find a client and server that can reduce the network overhead by dealing with lines of input *as a unit* instead of keystroke-by-keystroke. If Telnet is used only occasionally or by a mere handful of people, it's probably not a cause for worry.

Of course, there are always things to watch out for as a network administrator. For instance, because Telnet is a character-based terminal emulation program, input by the user typically occurs one keystroke at a time. A single keystroke can create as many as three packets, totaling nearly 200 bytes of data. All that from one keystroke! The first packet is the transmission of the keystroke from the client to the server, the second packet is the server echoing the keystroke back to the Telnet client, which the client then displays for the user, and the third packet is the client's ACK packet. It sounds like a lot of wasted bandwidth and it is, but luckily, a single user typically cannot generate hundreds of packets per second unless the user is a pretty fast typist. As a consequence, the inefficiency of Telnet is a problem only if you have hundreds of users on a single network segment all using Telnet continually at the same time.

If you do have multiple users in such a situation, you can take some steps to lessen the problem. Telnet has a mode in which characters are not sent until an entire line of data is entered and the Enter key is pressed. In this case, the Telnet program must echo the characters typed locally and handle special characters such as tabs or backspaces. This mode reduces the number of packets generated for each line of text from three packets for each character typed to three packets for each line of data typed. In an environment that has significant reliance on Telnet, that is a big saving on network overhead. In fact, there is an algorithm called the Nagle algorithm that addresses this very issue. Information about this algorithm is published in RFC 896 and can be found at *www.networksorcery.com/enp/rfc/rfc896.txt*. The generic Telnet application that comes with Windows does not include such advanced features, so a commercial product is required.

Supporting HTTP

HTTP traffic may eventually become the dominant Application layer protocol in most networks. This dominance may occur because we have the Internet, intranets, and extranets all using HTTP in the form of Web browser traffic. Some companies are even starting to use Web browsers as the primary user interface for access to all of their network resources. Why? Because the public at large knows how to use a Web browser. If the browser remains the primary user interface when the operating system is upgraded, there is no necessity to retrain employees to use the network.

In fact, Microsoft has already begun to use the browser as the primary interface with the Windows operating system. Windows Explorer and Internet Explorer are tightly coupled, starting with Windows 98. This coupling means that you can type a Web address into a Windows Explorer address line and display a Web page, or you can type a drive path in Internet Explorer and display a directory listing for that drive. In light of these trends, this section of the chapter concentrates on what happens when we connect to a Web site and transfer information using the HTTP protocol.

HTTP was designed to allow a Web browser to request pages of information, including multimedia content, from Internet servers. The pages are formatted in **Hypertext Markup Language (HTML)**, which specifies the formatting of the page and allows words and pictures to be linked to other HTML documents. These linked words are hyperlinks. Hyperlinks may be selected, usually via a mouse click, to easily navigate from one Web page to another. Because the HTML code tells the Web browser what type of content should be loaded and how it should be formatted, HTML might be considered the Presentation layer portion of the HTTP protocol.

HTTP, like FTP, is a client/server protocol. The client is the Web browser and the server is the Web server software, which is sometimes referred to as an HTTP daemon. A client initiates a Web browser session by specifying a URL. A URL specifies a Web resource with the syntax *protocol://host.domain*. The protocol for displaying a Web document is HTTP, so you have the familiar http://www.mydomain.com.

Most Web browsers support other protocols, such as FTP and gopher. HTTP clients will usually send one of two requests—a GET or a POST—to a server. A GET asks the server to send the contents of a particular file, usually to be displayed by the Web browser. A POST allows the browser to send information to the server for processing. For example, an online form that a user fills out is sent to the server using a POST request.

Figure 6-17 demonstrates a typical Web browser session with a server. The client station must first resolve the domain and host name to an IP address. A Web browser accepts an IP address for the URL, but using a domain name is much simpler. There is one very good reason for using an IP address to request a Web page—for example, http://192.168.1.5. If your page does not load using the host and domain name, you can try the IP address if you know it. If the page loads using the IP address, you know that the problem is related to the domain name server.

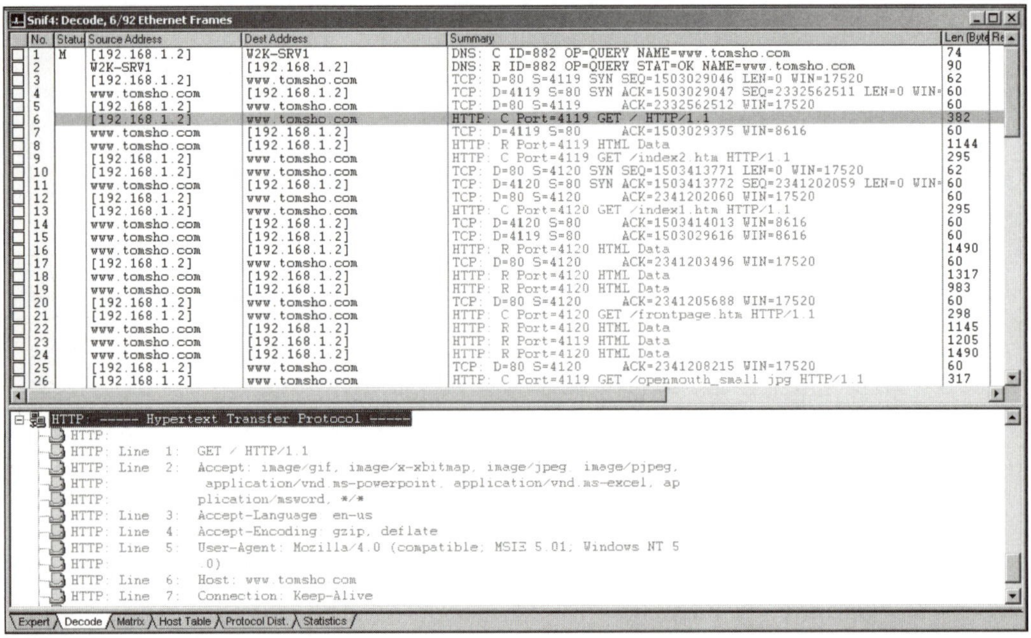

Figure 6-17 An HTTP session

In Figure 6-17, packets 1 and 2 are the DNS request. By now, you should recognize packets 3 through 5 as the TCP three-way handshake; in this case, they open a session with the Web server on port 80. Port 80 is the default port for HTTP servers. Packet 6 is the first packet to use the HTTP protocol, and an HTTP GET is executed.

Notice the HTTP section of packet 6 at the bottom of the figure. The client informs the server which version of HTTP the browser supports (in this case, version 1.1) as well as the type of data that the browser is able to accept. The browser specifies that it can accept various image types and several document types such as Excel, PowerPoint, and Word. Again, this capability might be considered Presentation layer functionality, but it is built into the Application layer HTTP protocol because TCP/IP does not specify a separate Presentation layer.

Line 6 of the HTTP data specifies the host that is being requested—www.tomsho.com. It is an enhancement of HTTP version 1.1. Because the host is specified in the HTTP data, a single server with a single IP address can support multiple hosts. The server must also support HTTP 1.1 for this feature to work.

Packet 8 is the HTML data returned by the server in response to the client's GET request. Packet 9 is another GET request by the client, this time specifying a particular document— index2.htm. The HTML data that the server returns in packet 8 indicates that index2.htm is embedded in the document, much as a graphic file might be embedded in a word processing document. In this case, index2.htm is a file that is displayed inside a frame.

You might think that packets 10, 11, and 12 are strange. Why is another three-way handshake occurring? It turns out that HTTP is a multitasking protocol. That is, multiple TCP sessions can be open at the same time to handle requests for multiple files within the same HTML document. Packets 10 through 12 open another session with the server so as to request the next document, which is index1.htm. The rest of the packets shown in Figure 6-17 are HTTP GET packets, HTTP data packets, and TCP acknowledgments.

The entire Web page, along with graphics or other multimedia files, is loaded until the entire page is displayed. When all of the data has been transferred, the server sends a TCP FIN packet and the client sends a TCP FIN packet (not shown). In all, it took 92 packets to request and send one reasonably simple Web page. No wonder your network has gotten so much slower since you connected to the Internet!

Problems with HTTP are usually a result of incompatibilities between the content in a Web page and the capabilities of the browser. For example, Web browsers from Microsoft and Netscape may support slightly different versions of HTML code. In addition, older browsers may not support many of the newer features in recent versions of HTML. Not much can be done to fix those problems, aside from upgrading the software.

6

Sometimes bad HTML can trip up your Web browser, but capturing the HTTP session can help you find exactly what is causing the problem. Of course, if the problem is someone else's Web page, you may not be able to do anything about it. If the problem involves your own Web page or one that you manage, however, you can eliminate or edit the offending code. For instance, if you are designing Web pages, take a few traces when you access your Web site. You might find out that the pages you designed cause an excessive number of TCP sessions to be open simultaneously. If you don't change your code, your server might run out of available TCP sessions. In addition, you will experience slower loads because of the excessive number of packets that is generated to load the page.

Supporting DHCP

Dynamic Host Configuration Protocol (DHCP) is an IP address management tool. It allows host computers to request an IP address when they boot rather than have an address statically assigned. This approach allows for centralized, and generally easier, management of a network's IP address pool. Of course, it is not without its drawbacks. For one thing, if the DHCP server goes down, workstations cannot be assigned an IP address, which prevents those stations from communicating. For another thing, because some devices, such as servers and routers, require a static IP address, you must be careful to exclude those addresses from the DHCP server to prevent conflicts.

DHCP, like the TCP/IP Application layer protocols discussed earlier, is a client/server protocol. A device running TCP/IP can be configured to automatically request an IP address upon booting. DHCP relies on the UDP transport protocol and is largely broadcast-oriented. The DHCP process begins with a client station sending a DHCP Discover broadcast packet. The DHCP Discover packet is basically a probe to see whether a server is listening. If a DHCP server hears the message, it replies with a DHCP Offer packet.

The DHCP Offer packet contains an IP address and subnet mask that the server is offering to the client. The client replies with a DHCP Request packet, indicating its acceptance of the offered IP address. The last packet is the DHCP Acknowledgment packet sent by the server. It serves as the final agreement between the client and server to accept the IP address. This packet contains any additional IP address parameters that the DHCP server has been configured to provide, such as a default gateway, DNS servers, and WINS servers. Figure 6-18 shows the four-packet sequence.

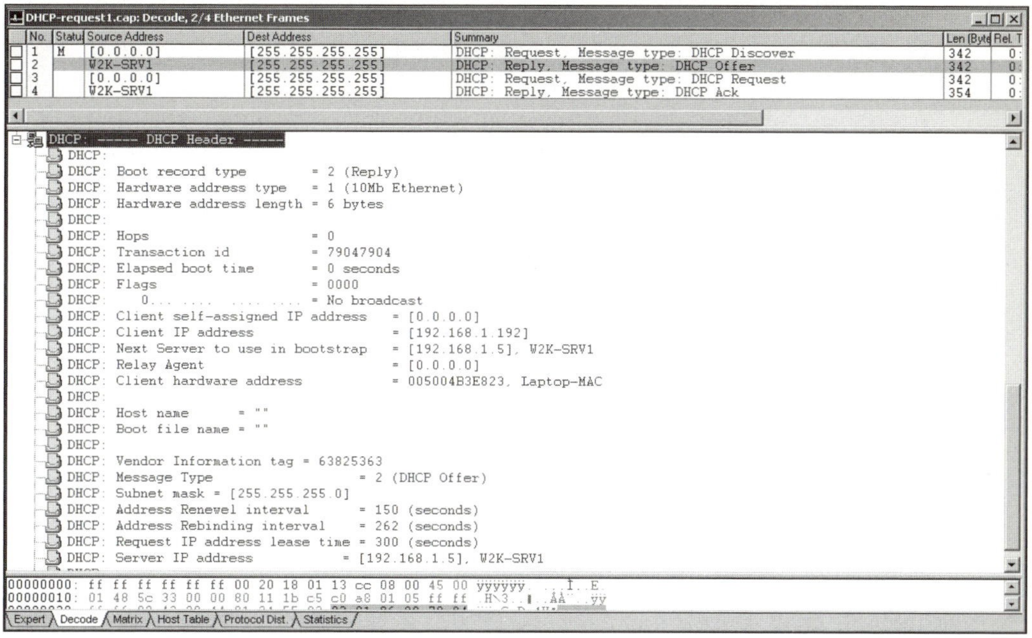

Figure 6-18   Initial DHCP request

An IP address is only leased from a DHCP server. The lease time is measured in seconds, but it can be unlimited if this option is selected. When the lease time reaches its halfway point, a client attempts to renew the lease with the original DHCP server. If the renewal is successful, the total lease time begins again. If the server does not respond to the lease renewal, the client tries again when one-eighth of the lease time remains.

Renewal attempts are unicast packets rather than broadcast packets, so only the original DHCP server is asked to renew the address. If the server does not respond to the second attempt at renewal, the client sends a broadcast DHCP request to locate any DHCP server. If the lease expires without a successful renewal, the client attempts to get a new IP address using the four-packet sequence described earlier.

In packet 2 in Figure 6-18, you can see the DHCP header information of the DHCP Offer packet. Note the IP address lease time of 300 seconds (5 minutes). The default lease time for a Windows 2000 DHCP server is eight days. You may want to shorten the lease time if you are running out of IP addresses, but be careful not to make the lease time too short. In a large network, the number of packets that are created by lease renewals can be significant.

When a workstation has been leased an address and then shuts down, the address is not given back to the DHCP server pool. This situation is somewhat unfortunate because it wastes IP addresses. Only after the lease time expires without a renewal request from the workstation does the IP address become available for lease to other workstations. For this reason, if you have an IP address pool that has fewer addresses than the number of workstations in your organization, you may want to set the lease time to some amount of time less than a day. If you count on the fact that not all workstations will be operating at the same time, make sure that each user shuts his or her machine off when it is not in use so that the IP address is returned to the lease pool as soon as possible. Alternatively, you could implement a shutdown procedure in which a station sends a DHCP release before shutting down.

If a workstation that was shut down reboots before its lease expires, it sends a DHCP request for the IP address it had when it was last running. The server will usually respond with a DHCP acknowledgment, which completes the transaction. While the packets are still broadcasts, the number of packets is reduced to two, a saving as compared to the four packets required to obtain an address after the lease has expired. Even if the lease has expired, the workstation will request the last IP address it was assigned. If the server has not assigned the address to another station, it will return the requested address. Thus, in a network in which there are plenty of IP addresses to go around, even though the addressing is dynamic and you cannot be certain that you will always have the same address, there is a strong likelihood that a workstation will keep its address from boot to boot. However, in a network that has more stations than IP addresses, you can never be sure about the station IP address from one boot to the next, particularly if the lease times are short.

DHCP is a broadcast-based protocol except when a renewal occurs. For DHCP to work in a network that has many subnets or broadcast domains, one of two things must be in place: (1) a DHCP server on every subnet or (2) a DHCP relay agent on every subnet that passes the requests from one subnet to a subnet that has the DHCP server. Windows 2000 Server has a DHCP relay agent that can be configured from the Routing and Remote Access Management Console. This feature requires that the server be connected to two different network segments, one of which has a DHCP server installed. Another option is to configure your routers to pass on DHCP broadcast requests.

Another feature of DHCP is the ability to reserve an IP address for a particular station, which guarantees that the station will always receive the same address. The reservation is based on the station's MAC address. This strategy can be useful for assignment of certain devices such as printers and servers that must always have the same IP address. It can offer an advantage over static addressing because if your IP addressing scheme ever changes or certain parameters such as DNS servers ever change, you need not go to the device to make the assignment changes. You can implement all changes from the DHCP server, and the changes will take effect when the next renewal occurs.

There is one caveat to using the address reservation feature in a multi-subnet network. If the device is moved to a different subnet and then tries to request its IP address, it will be denied. The denial occurs because the DHCP server can identify the subnet from which the request came. Because the IP address was reserved for the device based on its MAC address, which did not change, the IP address that was reserved for the device belongs to the subnet on which the device once resided. If you use address reservation, it is necessary to change the address reservation if the device is moved to a different subnet.

There is one last thing to watch out for with DHCP: Because of its broadcast orientation, every DHCP server on the same network will respond to the same request. If another DHCP server is running without your knowledge, your stations may very well be assigned addresses from a server that was not intended. For this reason, if you are testing a new server or you work in an environment where others may do so, be sure to have those servers isolated from the rest of the network to avoid conflicts.

What happens when a workstation requests a DHCP address but no server responds? Windows 95 clients send an error message to the screen indicating a DHCP error and the IP address remains all 0s. On the other hand, Windows 98 and Windows 2000 clients assign the workstation an address from the **Automatic IP Addressing (APIPA)** range of addresses defined by the Internic. This range is 169.254.0.0 to 169.254.255.254. This can be troublesome if you are not aware of it. Personally, I would like the computer to tell me if a DHCP server was unable to be contacted so I can resolve the problem. Nonetheless, be aware that if ever a workstation is having connectivity problems, you should check the IP address. If the address is in the APIPA range, something is wrong with the workstation's connectivity to the network, its IP stack, or your DHCP server.

6

Network Clients and Servers and the Application Layer

A primary goal of the Application layer is to make use of the network transparent to users and applications. In other words, a user should see a network resource as simply an extension of local computer resources. Accessing a file on a server should be no different than accessing a file on the local C: drive. The components that provide such transparency are network clients or redirectors and their server counterparts, such as Novell's NetWare Core Protocol (NCP) and Windows' Server Message Block (SMB).

Most of the problems between systems at the Application layer involve either a poorly written application that utilizes network resources inefficiently or an incompatibility between the client component and the server component with which it is trying to communicate. The next chapter deals specifically with problems relating to clients of various types interacting with servers of various types.

Chapter Summary

- One of the primary jobs of the Session layer is to resolve computer names to addresses, which is the first step in establishing a communication session between two computers. The next step is usually the negotiation of a login or authentication procedure. After a communication session has been established, data transfers can begin. Once the session is finished, the session is closed, often by a logout procedure.

- The Presentation layer, is responsible for making sure that the user application receives data in a format that the application expects. Most Presentation layer functions are built into the applications that actually need the services provided by the

Presentation layer. However, a formal Presentation layer protocol does exist: Abstract Syntax Notation Number One (ASN.1).

❏ The Application layer is the layer closest to the user applications and therefore provides those applications with an interface to the network. This interface is important because it saves authors of user applications from having to know the details of how the network works.

❏ Before two computers can start a data transfer session, there must be a convenient method for one computer to locate another computer. Once located, the parameters of the communication session must be established. Then, after the communication session is complete, the session must be terminated. The Session layer is responsible for these tasks, and different protocols and even different applications within the same protocol accomplish the tasks differently.

❏ At the Application layer, the TCP/IP protocol suite includes a host of useful applications, each of which has its own way of doing a fairly narrowly defined job. There is FTP for uploading and downloading files, Telnet for terminal-like communications to remote hosts, HTTP for Web page browsing, and DHCP for IP address management.

KEY TERMS

Abstract Syntax Notation Number One (ASN.1) — A formal Presentation layer protocol.

Address (A) record — A DNS resource record that consists of a host name/IP address pair.

application programming interface (API) — An operating system subroutine that an application developer can call from a program to request an operating system service.

Automatic IP Addressing (APIPA) — A range of IP addresses that is automatically assigned to a host when no DHCP server is available.

caching DNS server — A DNS server that does not contain any DNS zone information but that passes DNS requests along to primary or secondary DNS servers while caching the responses.

clear text — An unencrypted method of transferring data.

Client for Microsoft Networks — The client software required to communicate from one Windows computer to another.

DNS zone — The top- and second-level domains in an internet.

Domain Name Service (DNS) — A TCP/IP service that resolves host computer and domain names to IP addresses.

Dynamic Host Configuration Protocol (DHCP) — An IP address management tool that permits IP hosts to request an IP address dynamically instead of having an address statically assigned.

File and Print Sharing for Microsoft Networks — The Windows Server software component that permits a Windows computer to share resources.

Fully Qualified Domain Name (FQDN) — The name of a resource that includes the host name followed by the domain name, including the top-level domain, separated by a period.

Get Nearest Server (GNS) query — A broadcast packet sent by a NetWare client looking for a NetWare server to respond to a login attempt.

Hypertext Markup Language (HTML) — The syntax used to create Web page documents that include special formatting and multimedia content.

International Standards Organization (ISO) — An international organization composed of national standards bodies from more than 75 countries.

Name Server (NS) record — A DNS resource record that specifies the name of a server that is authoritative for a domain.

NetBIOS API — An API that allows programs designed for NetBIOS to access network resources.

NetBIOS Frame Protocol (NBF) — The NetBIOS API used by NetBEUI applications.

NetBIOS over IP (NetBT) — One of the NetBIOS APIs that permits NetBIOS applications to run over the IP protocol.

NetBIOS over IPX (NBIPX) — One of the NetBIOS APIs that permits NetBIOS applications to run over the IPX protocol.

NetWare Link State Protocol (NLSP) — Novell's proprietary link-state routing protocol.

network redirector — An Application layer client component that determines whether a requested resource is local to the requesting application or a network resource.

passive transfer mode — An FTP mode of operation that requires the FTP client to establish the data transfer session with the server using a random port number.

PTR record — A DNS entry that make reverse lookups possible.

recursive lookup — A DNS lookup that starts with the top-level domain server and returns the address of another DNS server, which is then queried, and so forth.

resource records — Information about DNS resource types maintained by a DNS server.

reverse DNS lookup — A DNS query that returns an FQDN.

Server Message Block (SMB) datagram — A protocol developed by Microsoft, IBM, and Intel that contains commands used by network redirectors to indicate what type of request or response is contained in a packet.

Service Advertising Protocol (SAP) — A protocol that creates a special IPX packet that is broadcast by NetWare servers to inform the network of the resources that server has available.

Simple Network Management Protocol (SNMP) — A TCP/IP network management protocol.

6

Start of Authority (SOA) record — A DNS resource record that lists information for a DNS zone.

Universal Resource Locator (URL) — The standard naming convention for Internet resources in the form *protocol://host.domain*.

Windows Internet Naming Service (WINS) — A Windows service that resolves Windows computer names to IP addresses.

Winsock API — An API that provides TCP/IP services to applications.

REVIEW QUESTIONS

1. Network security is provided by the Session layer in the form of user login and _____.

2. _____ is the standard naming convention for Internet resources.
   a. URL
   b. HTTP
   c. HTTP
   d. ADP

3. The Presentation layer is concerned with the structure of data and the syntax used to transfer and process different data types. True or False?

4. In pure TCP/IP environments, which service resolves names?

5. NetWare environments using IPX/SPX resolve network resource names to IPX addresses by using _____.

6. When an FTP session is over, the FTP program typically sends a QUIT command. True or False?

7. Client/server environments utilize a login and logout procedure to begin and terminate a _____.
   a. command sequence
   b. session
   c. layer
   d. component

8. What do you install if you want to communicate from one Windows computer to another?

9. The UNIX server component is File and Print Sharing for Microsoft Networks. True or False?

10. NetWare environments use NCP _____ to begin and end sessions.

11. ASN.1 is under consideration for use in a new version of HTTP, called
    _____.

    a. HTTP Forward

    b. SNMP+

    c. HTTP-NG

    d. NG of XP

12. Application layer components in an operating system such as Windows usually consist of a set of application programming interfaces. True or False?

13. _____ determine whether a requested resource is local to the application or a network resource.

14. _____ and Client for Microsoft Networks are the network redirectors in a Windows environment.

    a. File and Print Sharing for Microsoft Networks

    b. File Request for Microsoft Networks

    c. Hard Disk Replicator

    d. Presentation Synchronization

15. The DNS system used throughout the Internet is organized as a tree-like hierarchy. True or False?

16. The subdomain level can consist of several names separated by a period and its use is mandatory. True or False?

17. In packets, D= and S= correspond to remote and local session numbers. True or False?

18. TCP/IP applications use TCP or UDP datagram numbers to identify an application for which a packet is intended. True or False?

19. FTP, like most _____ layer components, has a client side and a server side.

20. The server component in the UNIX world is called a(n) _____.

HANDS-ON PROJECTS

Project 6-1 Use ipconfig to Manage the Local DNS Cache

In this project, you will learn the nuances of ipconfig.

1. Log into Windows 2000 or Windows NT.

2. Click **Start**, click **Run**, type **cmd.exe**, and then press **Enter**.

3. Type **ipconfig/?** at the command prompt. If the output scrolls off the screen, repeat the command using **ipconfig/? | more**.

4. Find the option that displays the contents of the DNS Resolver cache.

5. At the command prompt, type the command to display the cached DNS entries.

6. If there are no DNS entries, open a Web browser and go to any Web site; repeat the command you typed in Step 5.

7. Write down the format with which the cached DNS entries are displayed. What does the Time to Live entry mean? How can DNS entries that are cached by your PC be helpful to your network? How might they cause a problem?

8. How can you delete the cached DNS entries? Write down the command and then enter the command at the command prompt. Next, verify that the entries were deleted. Which command did you use to verify that the entries were deleted?

9. Close the command prompt window by typing **Exit**.

Project 6-2 Edit a DNS Filter to Capture DNS Packets

In this project, you will explore the usefulness of capturing selected packets.

1. Click **Start**, point to **Programs**, and then click **Wildpackets EtherPeek**.

2. From the Capture menu, select **Start Capture**. If a Capture Options dialog box is displayed, uncheck the Show this dialog when creating a new capture window checkbox, and then click **OK**.

3. Click the **Filters** tab at the bottom of the window that opens.

4. Find and click the filter titled **DNS**.

5. Click the **Duplicate** button (it has a yellow and blue icon). A new filter is created above the DNS filter called Copy of DNS.

6. Right-click **Copy of DNS**, and then click **Insert** to open the Edit Filter dialog box.

7. Change the Filter name from Untitled Filter to **DNS – My Workstation**.

8. Click the **Address** filter checkbox.

9. In the Type list box, select **IP**.

10. In the Address 1 text box, type the IP address of your workstation.

11. Click the button under the Type list box, and select **Both directions**.

12. Click the **Any Address** option button under the Address 2 text box.

13. Click **OK**, and then click the checkbox next to the filter you just created.

14. Click the **Packets** tab.

15. Click the **Start Capture** button.

16. Open a Web browser and go to the Web site you visited in Project 6-1.

17. Were any packets captured? Why or why not?

18. Go to **www.course.com**.

19. Were any packets captured? Why or why not?

20. Stop the packet capture and quit the Web browser.

21. Go back to the Web browser.

22. Start the packet capture again (if Etherpeek prompts you to save changes to the capture, click **No**).

23. From the Web browser, go to **www.course.com** again.

24. Were any DNS packets captured? Why or why not?

25. Write down the port number and the transport protocol that DNS uses.

26. Exit all applications and close all windows.

Project 6-3 Local Name Resolution

In this project, you will learn the benefits of name resolutions.

1. Click **Start**, point to **Programs**, and then click **Wildpackets EtherPeek**. Click **OK**.

2. From the Capture menu, select **Start Capture**. If a Capture Options dialog box is displayed, uncheck the **Show this dialog when creating a new capture window** checkbox, and then click **OK**.

3. Click the **Filters** tab at the bottom of the window that opens.

4. Find the filter titled **DNS – My Workstation**, which you created in Project 6-2, and click the check box next to it.

5. Open Internet Explorer.

6. Open the **EtherPeek** window, click the **Packets** tab, and then click the **Start Capture** button.

7. In the Internet Explorer Address bar, type the name of a classmate's or the instructor's computer in the following format: *computer-name*. Press **Enter**.

8. Did EtherPeek capture any packets? Why or why not?

9. Click the **Stop Capture** button to stop the capture.

10. Select the **Filters** tab in EtherPeek, uncheck the **DNS – My Workstation** filter, and check the filter named **My IP Address** that you created in Chapter 5.

11. Click the **Packets** tab, and then click the **Start Capture** button.

12. From Internet Explorer, type the name of a classmate's or the instructor's computer again and press **Enter**.

13. Open the **EtherPeek** window. What types of packets were captured? Can you find the packets that resolved the computer name? Describe as best you can the upper-layer protocols used to find the computer name you tried to open.

14. Exit all applications and close all windows.

Project 6-4 Using the Nslookup Utility

In this project, you will learn about the benefits of using the Nslookup utility.

1. Log into a Windows 2000 or Windows NT computer.

2. Open a command prompt.

6

3. Type **nslookup** and then press **Enter**.

4. With what output did the nslookup command respond?

5. You are now in Nslookup interactive mode. Exit from this mode by typing **Exit**.

6. At the command prompt, type **nslookup www.course.com**.

7. With what output did the nslookup command respond?

8. Explain how the use of this command can be helpful.

9. Close the command prompt by typing **Exit**.

Project 6-5 Using Advanced Nslookup Utility Commands

In this project, you will learn the benefits of using Nslookup utility commands.

1. Log into a Windows 2000 or Windows NT computer.

2. Open a command prompt.

3. Type **nslookup**, and then press **Enter**. You are now in Nslookup interactive mode as noted by the > prompt.

4. Type **www.msn.com**, and then press **Enter**.

5. With what did the nslookup command respond?

6. Type **?** at the command prompt, and then press **Enter**.

7. Find the command that allows you to display all records for a domain.

8. Type **ls −d** *mydomain.com*, where *mydomain.com* is the domain name for which your default DNS server is configured.

9. How might the ls −d command be helpful in troubleshooting DNS?

10. Exit the command prompt.

Project 6-6 Using the DHCP APIPA Feature in Windows 98

In this project, you will learn about the benefits of APIPA.

1. Right-click **Network Neighborhood**, and then select **Properties**.

2. Double-click **TCP/IP** to bring up the properties. If there is more than one TCP/IP listed in the Configuration tab of Network dialog box, be sure to select the TCP/IP entry that is associated with your workstation's NIC adapter, not the Dial-Up Adapter.

3. Make sure that the **Obtain an IP Address Automatically** option button is selected.

4. Click **OK**, and then click **OK** again. If your computer asks whether you want to restart it, click **No**.

5. Unplug your computer from the network.

6. Shut down and restart your computer.

7. When you are back in Windows, click **Start**, click **Run**, and then type **winipcfg**.

8. What is the IP address assigned to your computer? Why? Will this address work in your network?

9. Change your IP settings back to their original configuration, if necessary.

10. Reconnect your computer to the network and restart your computer.

11. When the computer reboots, verify the IP address settings are correct by running the **winipcfg** command.

12. Exit all applications and close all windows.

Project 6-7 Using ipconfig or winipcfg to View DHCP Addresses

6

This lab assumes that the student has access to a station that is running DHCP.

1. From a Windows 9*x* station, click **Start**, click **Run**, type **winipcfg**, and then press **Enter**. (For Windows 2000 or NT, open a command prompt and type **ipconfig /all**, and then skip to Step 3.)

2. Click the **More Info** button.

3. Write down the address of your DHCP server.

4. Write down the time that the IP address was leased and note when it expires.

5. Make a note of your IP address settings, including the IP address, subnet mask, and DNS servers.

6. Click the **Release** button. (For Windows 2000 or NT, type **ipconfig /release** at the command prompt.)

7. What is your IP address now? (Type **ipconfig /all** if you are using ipconfig.)

8. Click the **Renew** button. (Type **ipconfig /renew** if you are using Windows 2000 or NT.)

9. Did you get the same address as before? Why or why not?

10. Exit all programs and close all windows.

CASE PROJECTS

Case 6-1 Research Your Network

You can find out which TCP/IP Application layer services are running on a particular machine by using a port scanner. Run the Wildpackets' iNetTools program that is included with EtherPeek. Select the Port Scan tool. In the Host field, enter the IP address or name of a server on campus. Under Ports, click the TCP option button to select the TCP transport protocol. Make the starting port 1 and the ending port 150; then click the Start button. Write down as many ports as you recognize that the server supports and describe the function each provides. How can this tool be useful in securing your network?

Case 6-2 DHCP Versus Static Addressing

You are the network administrator for Sails and Snails Industries, which is starting to grow beyond the capabilities of the NetBEUI protocol. You have decided that TCP/IP is the best protocol for the firm, especially given that the company requires Internet access. Currently, there are 15 computers on the network but it is expected that there will be 50 within a year. You have heard that DHCP can be used to manage the IP address assignment, but a colleague told you that her network just uses static addressing. Compare and contrast DHCP and static addressing, and explain under what circumstances you might prefer one over the other. Which method would you use for Sails and Snails?

Case 6-3 DHCP in a Routed Environment

Sails and Snails Industries is using DHCP as you suggested. You have implemented a DHCP server on Windows 2000. The growth of the company has required that the network be split into two subnets connected via a router. Explain the options available for managing DHCP with this network configuration. Research how you might configure a router to be part of the solution.

SUPPORTING NETWORK OPERATING SYSTEMS

After reading this chapter and completing the exercises, you will be able to:

◆ Understand how a user interacts with a network operating system

◆ Understand issues and problems related to Windows peer-to-peer networking environments

◆ Troubleshoot and identify problems related to Windows client/server environments

◆ Identify issues related to locating Windows resources

◆ Understand the issues involved with a NetWare server environment

Analyzing IP headers, examining frame formats, and dissecting DNS request and reply packets may be interesting and sometimes necessary, but at the end of the day, we just want our networks to do what they were designed to do: facilitate resource sharing and enhance corporate communication and collaboration. To this end, we need a network operating system (NOS).

In this chapter, you will learn how an end user's actions affect Windows networking, peer-to-peer networks, and client/server networks. In addition, we'll cover some important details of Windows resources and name resolution and networking with Novell products. When you are done with this chapter, you will have made another step on your journey to becoming a proficient network administrator.

User Interaction with a Windows NOS

An operating system is software that controls the resources of a computer and that provides an interface to the user. In contrast, a **network operating system (NOS)** facilitates the sharing of network resources and runs and manages network applications. One network can have access to multiple NOSs. Having multiple NOSs allows the network administrator to choose the best NOS for the required applications. The trick, however, is to get the NOSs to communicate with one another so that applications can run and resources can be shared.

When an end user interacts with a network, he or she usually wants to locate a resource or service, gain permission to access that resource or service, and then access it. In a Windows environment, locating the resource or service may involve the use of Network Neighborhood to display the computers and printers that are currently available on the network. On the other hand, the user may have entered the network path of the resource into a network application.

While the end user is interacting with the network, Windows (behind the scenes) performs a name resolution function to resolve the name of the resource to an address. When the user tries to access the resource by double-clicking on a computer, for example, an authentication procedure occurs. It may involve requiring the end user to enter a user name and password or perhaps simply a password. The authentication procedure ensures that the user has permission to access the resource. If there is no password set for the resource, access is permitted without authentication. Finally, the file operation, print job, or other network function proceeds. If all of the previously mentioned functions are working properly, your client and server computers, along with the network equipment in between, are probably working correctly. If these functions are not working properly, it's time to do some investigating.

To effectively investigate networking problems, you need to know that you will encounter three types of Windows operating systems. All three types have built-in networking capabilities, but the implementation and management of networking services differ somewhat among the types. The three categories are as follows:

- Windows desktop operating systems, which include Windows 95, Windows 98, and Windows ME

- Windows workstation operating systems, which include Windows NT Workstation, Windows 2000 Professional, and Windows XP Professional

- Windows server operating systems, which include Windows NT Server, Windows 2000 Server, and Windows XP Server

You will encounter these different types throughout the remainder of the chapter as we discuss the nuances of supporting the modern network.

PEER-TO-PEER NETWORKING WITH WINDOWS OPERATING SYSTEMS

Peer-to-peer networking or, in the Windows world, workgroup networking is a viable, inexpensive, and fairly simple way to share resources in a small business environment. Small businesses that simply need the ability to share some files, a few printers, and perhaps a database application find Windows' built-in networking capabilities to be a quick and easy solution. Peer-to-peer networking is also frequently combined with client/server networking when small groups of people need to share a printer but do not want the expense of buying a networked printer.

Although a peer-to-peer network does not typically require the same level of expertise to set up and manage as does a client/server network, there are still some tasks that must be carried out along the way. For instance, there are protocols to install and clients to configure, and resources must be shared and located. Plus, you must understand and operate within the limitations that exist in a peer-to-peer network, so that you know when it may be time to upgrade to a client/server model.

7

Because peer-to-peer networks are often the best choice for small businesses with fewer than 10 users, and because businesses of this size are predominant throughout the world, your time is well spent in learning how to solve the problems that occur with this type of network.

The discussions ahead focus on some of the issues involved with peer-to-peer sharing on Windows desktop and workstation operating systems. We also examine some of the problems you can expect when a peer-to-peer operating system goes down. Last, we identify the special care that must be taken when working with older applications.

Sharing Resources with Windows Desktop Operating Systems

Desktop operating systems were designed to provide users with a comfortable user interface, a built-in network client, and reasonable file and print sharing capabilities for small office or workgroup environments. Network security and network performance took a back seat to ease of use and application performance. Nonetheless, this environment is popular due to its relative ease of configuration and management.

The desktop line of operating systems supports most of the basic file and print sharing features, but the advanced features are left to the workstation and server versions.

This section of the chapter covers the installation of the components necessary for file and print sharing; the methods used to secure resources, drive mapping, printer sharing, and troubleshooting; and the management and optimization of the installed services.

The File and Print Sharing Service

Windows desktop operating systems are configured as network clients by default. The File and Print Sharing Service adds the necessary functionality to allow the system to act as a server.

The File and Print Sharing Service is added using the Network Control Panel. Once installed, you can select among a few configuration options. You must specify what types of resources you would like to share: printers, files, or both. You can also specify how you would like to control access to the shared resources. In a peer-to-peer environment with only desktop operating systems, your only option is password protection. A few additional properties can be configured using the Properties button in Network Control Panel, as we will see shortly. Figure 7-1 shows the options for enabling the type of resources you wish to share.

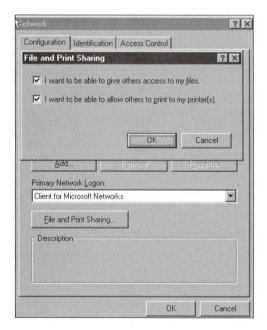

Figure 7-1   File and Print Sharing Service options

After you have installed the File and Print Sharing Service and specified the type of resources you will share, you must share each resource individually. With file sharing, you can share an entire drive or individual folders. For security reasons, you should share only those folders that contain files that must be available to the network. You will explore the File and Print Sharing Service installation and configuration in Hands-on Project 7-1.

The File and Print Sharing Service need be installed on a workstation only if the workstation has resources that need to be shared. In other words, it does not need to be installed on computers that will act only as network clients. A workstation without the File and Print Sharing Service installed on it can still access another computer's resources but that workstation will not be listed in Network Neighborhood if the computers are relying on NetBIOS for name resolution.

Sharing Folders

If the File and Print Sharing Service is installed and the option to give other computers access to files (as depicted in Figure 7-1) is enabled, a new tab appears in the Properties dialog box for folders and drives.

Figure 7-2 shows the Properties dialog box for a folder called PublicDocs with the Sharing tab selected. Notice the Shared As option button. When that button is selected, the folder is shared and you have the option to give the shared resource a different name than the default name, which is the same as the folder name. The name you provide and any comment you include in the Comment field is displayed in the Network Neighborhood browse list.

7

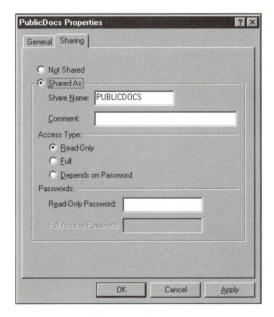

Figure 7-2   Sharing tab

One thing to keep in mind when sharing folders is that once a folder is shared, all files and subfolders are available to network users. There is no way to restrict users to just some of the files or subfolders. One mistake that I frequently see in small businesses that do not have a knowledgeable network technician on staff is that an entire drive will be shared and then individual folders within the drive also shared. While this configuration is possible, it makes little sense to go through the motions: If a drive is shared, all folders on that drive are also available.

If an individual folder is shared within a drive, network users have two ways to get to the same folder. The Network Neighborhood screen shot in Figure 7-3 depicts this scenario. The window on the left shows the list of shares available on a computer called Gt-166. The window on the right shows the list of folders underneath the share called c-drive. Notice that the folder public-docs is listed under the c-drive share. The same folder can be found in the Network Neighborhood window.

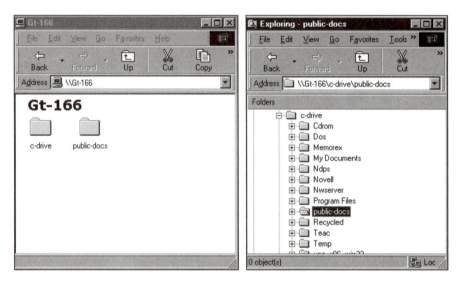

Figure 7-3 Sharing a folder inside a share

How can this double-pronged method of sharing be a problem? If you understand that the share public-docs in Network Neighborhood is the same as the folder public-docs found under the c-drive share, there is really no problem. Sadly, most users are not as well informed as you are. I know of one user who, thinking that the share in Network Neighborhood was just a copy of the folder listed under the c-drive, deleted the entire folder and its contents. Fortunately, we had a backup copy.

There is one justification for sharing an entire drive as well as some of the folders located on that drive: Network administrators sometimes need to access the entire drive on a user workstation to perform updates or replace missing or deleted files remotely. The administrator can carry out this operation safely by setting permissions on the share that accesses the entire drive so that only the administrator has access. This way, the average user will see the share for the entire drive but will not be able to access it.

Securing Resources

The Windows desktop operating systems have limited security options when it comes to restricting access to shared resources. If you look back at Figure 7-2, you can see the security options available listed under Access Type. You have three options: Read-only access, Full access, or either, depending on the password entered. You can leave the password blank to allow all users to access the resource with whichever access type you have selected. Unfortunately, you cannot restrict access on a user-by-user basis, so all users to whom you give the password have equal access.

As mentioned, you cannot enforce different access restrictions to the files and subfolders within a share. The access type assigned to the share applies to all files and folders within that share. Referring back to Figure 7-3, if you want to share the entire c-drive for administrative purposes and want users to be able to access the files in the public-docs folder, you should set the access type to Full on the c-drive share and set the password to a value only you know. Then set the access type for the public-docs share to Read-only or Full and inform users of the password. This way, you, as the administrator, can access all files on the entire drive, but other users can access only public-docs. As you will see, the Windows workstation line of operating systems provides a more sophisticated access control system.

Mapping Drives

Mapping a drive means creating a drive letter designation such as F: that refers to a network share. The drive letter is displayed in My Computer just as if the drive were a local disk such as the C: drive.

When you are instructing a user over the phone how to access a file or application, it is easier to have the user double-click a drive letter than to use Network Neighborhood to first find the computer that contains the file, and then find the appropriate share. Of course, using Network Neighborhood to find and access network resources is fine if you know what you are looking for and where to look, but many users are used to accessing files and programs by specifying a drive letter. In addition, there are still many applications in use that require a drive letter to operate properly. This restriction exists because these (usually older) applications have the use of a drive letter hard-coded into the program when constructing the path to data and configuration files.

Most peer-to-peer networks designate just one or two computers as the primary servers that hold the applications and files that are shared among the whole office. Ideally, each user will have a drive letter mapped to each share that the user frequently accesses.

There are two methods of mapping a drive. The first method uses Network Neighborhood. The user finds the computer containing the share and then double-clicks the computer to see the share. Next, the user right-clicks the share and selects Map Network Drive from the context menu; he or she is greeted with a dialog box like the one shown in Figure 7-4. The user can select the drive to map. Notice the Reconnect at logon check box. Checking this box causes the workstation to attempt to map the drive every time the computer boots and the user logs on to Windows.

Figure 7-4   Mapping a drive through Network Neighborhood

The second way to map a drive is by entering the net use command at a DOS prompt. Figure 7-5 shows the net use command used to map a drive letter to the public-docs share on the computer named glt_Win95. The syntax \\glt_Win95\public-docs is called the **Universal Naming Convention (UNC) path**. A UNC path can be used to access most types of network resources, including Windows shares and NetWare volumes. The second command in Figure 7-5, which is the net use command without any parameters, lists the current network resources that have been assigned a drive mapping along with the status of the connection. The nice thing about using the net use command to map drives to network resources is that the command can be run in a batch file, which can come in quite handy, as we will see later.

Figure 7-5   The net use command

A batch file is a text file containing one or more commands, one per line, which can be executed by simply typing the name of the batch file. The batch file name has the BAT extension.

If you are charged with setting up a peer-to-peer network and you assign drive mappings on each user's computer, you should assign drive letters in a consistent manner throughout your network. In other words, if Mary's computer uses drive letter P: to access the public-docs share, it is best to map the P: drive to the public-docs share on every user's computer. This strategy makes support easier, and some applications require it.

I had the pleasure of setting up an accounting program for a small business that used Windows 98 workgroup networking. There were only five computers, so a peer-to-peer network made sense. The accounting program was located on the newest computer, and every other computer had drive letter L: mapped to the share in which the application was located. Most applications such as this one access a database of information, and there is usually a configuration file specifying where the database is located. This application required that a drive letter be used to specify where the database was located—in this case, L:\accounting\data. This approach worked quite well except for one problem. The computer that contained the application was used by one of the employees to run the application as well. The application was physically stored on the C: drive. Because the configuration file specified the database location as the L: drive, however, when the user attempted to run the application, the database could not be found.

The story gets even more complicated. Normally, if a folder is located on the local workstation, you don't map a drive to the folder because your local drive already allows you to access the folder with a drive letter. In this case, because the configuration file specified the L: drive for the database file, we wanted to map the L: drive to the workstation's own share. At first, this choice might not seem like a problem. If you go to Network Neighborhood, you can see your own computer and your own shares, so you should be able to map a drive letter to the share. However, Figure 7-6 shows what happens when you try to do just that. Although this error occurred on a Windows desktop operating system, you can map a drive to a local share using Windows NT, 2000, or XP.

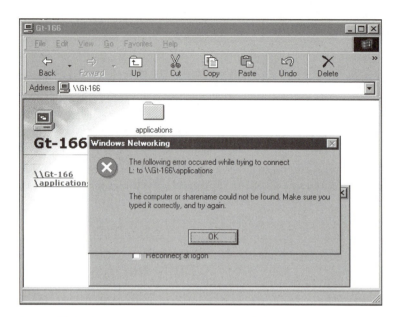

Figure 7-6   Error trying to map to a local share

Fortunately, there was a solution. It required going back to the world of the DOS command line (and you thought DOS was dead!). The subst command allows you to assign a virtual drive letter to a local resource. To accomplish what we hoped to do by mapping a drive to a local share, we used the subst command instead.

Figure 7-7 shows the use of the subst command to assign drive letter L: to the C:\applications folder. The syntax of the command is also shown in the figure. From now on, when the L: drive is invoked, the contents of the applications folder on the C: drive are accessed. The second use of the subst command in Figure 7-7 lists the virtual drives currently in use.

Figure 7-7   The subst command

Printer Sharing

The sharing of printers is often the reason that a peer-to-peer network is installed in the first place. A small business or workgroup may have several computers but only one or two printers. When a user on a computer that has no printer attached to it needs to print a document, sneakernet is the only solution. With a network in place, however, the printers can be shared and made available to all users.

 For those of you new to networking, "sneakernet" is not networking at all, but rather sharing files and printers by copying files to floppy disks and carrying the disk from computer to computer.

Sharing a printer is as easy as sharing a folder. The option in the File and Print Sharing Service must be checked to allow users to access the locally attached printers, and then the Sharing tab in the Printer Properties dialog box can be accessed to configure how the printer will be shared. Once shared, other computers can access the printer through the UNC path syntax of *\\computername\printer-sharename*. Having access to the printer is not sufficient to print to the printer with a Windows application, however. Every workstation that prints to the shared printer must also have the appropriate drivers installed.

Once a computer has the appropriate drivers installed and the printer is created in the Printers Control Panel, all that is necessary to print to the shared printer is to specify the UNC path as the port in the Printer Details dialog box.

Figure 7-8 shows the printer port pointing to a shared printer called HP-Laserjet on a computer named GLT_Win95. Figure 7-9 shows the network diagram for which this shared printing is configured. When a user on workstation Gt-166 wants to print to the LaserJet printer, the workstation submits the print job to the UNC path \\GLT_Win95\HP-Laserjet, which finds its way to the GLT_Win95 computer. Once the job is received, GLT_Win95 sends it out its LPT1: port to the physical printer.

7

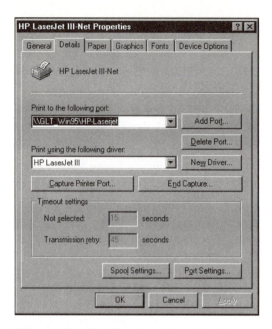

Figure 7-8   Pointing to a shared printer

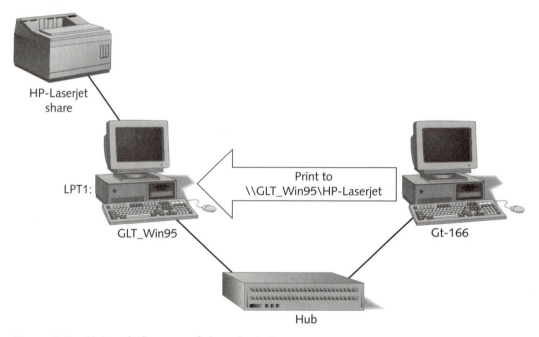

Figure 7-9   Network diagram of shared printing

This method of sharing printers in a peer-to-peer network is easy and inexpensive, but it is not without problems.

Troubleshooting Shared Printers

One problem with peer-to-peer networks in general, and with sharing printers in particular, is that the computer to which the resource is attached must be turned on and functioning properly before other computers can access the resource. If the workstation to which the print device is attached is rebooted or turned off, no one can access the shared printer.

 When you are speaking of printers in a Windows environment, it is important to understand the terminology used to differentiate the physical printer from the printer icon you see in the Printers Control Panel. The physical printer is referred to as the print device; the printer icon, which represents the print driver, is referred to as the printer.

If a user sends a print job to a network printer and the network printer is not available, the user receives an error message. This message tells the user that Windows cannot access the computer that has the shared print device, so Windows sets the printer to the Work Offline mode. The average user will typically click OK or Cancel without reading the error message or understanding the message. Frequently, he or she may attempt the print job again and again with no success. Even after the computer to which the print device is attached has been turned on or otherwise returned to a functioning status, the user still cannot print. The lack of printing occurs because the printer has been set to the Work Offline mode.

This problem is one of the easiest to fix, but it nonetheless occurs frequently in peer-to-peer environments in which the users are not well informed about little details like Work Offline mode. The solution, of course, is to go to the Printers Control Panel, right-click the printer, and uncheck the option that says Work Offline. Beware of taking this step with a user who has been trying to print for several hours or days! There may be several or several dozen print jobs in the local print queue that will be sent to the network printer as soon as you uncheck the Work Offline option. Check the print queue first, delete all pending documents (or at least those that are easily reproduced), and then bring the printer back online.

Managing Network Bindings

Network bindings are the logical connections between network components. They determine which installed protocols work with the installed network adapters as well as which installed protocols work with installed client and server components. Windows allows multiple clients, multiple protocols, and multiple network adapters to be installed and working at the same time.

By default, every protocol runs on every adapter and is bound to every client and server component. However, this configuration may not be what is needed in your network environment and may actually hamper network performance. Figure 7-10 shows a Network Control Panel in which two adapters are installed: the Ethernet NIC and the Dial-Up Adapter. You will see this setup frequently in small office or home office networks that depend upon dial-up Internet access. The protocols installed are NetBEUI and TCP/IP and, as you can see, there are two entries in the Network Control Panel for each protocol.

In the Network Control Panel, each entry represents a binding to each adapter. The problem is that your dial-up adapter probably uses only TCP/IP, so the binding with NetBEUI will just cause unnecessary traffic over the dial-up connection. Likewise, if the LAN is running only the NetBEUI protocol, the TCP/IP binding to the Ethernet NIC will cause considerable network traffic in the form of TCP/IP name resolution queries and attempts to register NetBIOS names via TCP/IP, as we saw in Chapter 6. Fortunately, this problem is simple to solve. Simply remove the entry in Network Control Panel that has the unnecessary protocol binding.

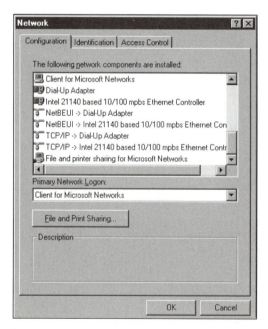

Figure 7-10   Network Control Panel with multiple protocols

Another area where bindings exist is between the protocol and the upper-layer components such as the client and the File and Print Sharing Service. By default, all protocols are bound to all clients and other upper-layer services. Again, this setup is not always what you want. If you have a dial-up connection that uses TCP/IP, you probably do not want the TCP/IP binding to be bound to the File and Print Sharing Service as well. This configuration creates a significant security risk because it is possible for Internet hosts to access your shared files with that binding. By the same token, you do not want IPX/SPX to be bound to Client for Microsoft Networks if the Windows hosts in your network use only TCP/IP.

Figure 7-11 shows the bindings dialog box for the IPX/SPX protocol, which is bound to a dial-up adapter. The dialog box on the right shows the next level of bindings from the protocol to the clients and File and Print Sharing Service. Windows desktop operating systems provide a check box for each installed client or service. In this environment, you probably want to disable the binding for Client for Microsoft Networks and the File and Print Sharing Service for Microsoft Networks, leaving IPX/SPX bound to only the NetWare client. Of course, if you do not have any NetWare servers in your network, you would want to remove the NetWare client and IPX/SPX protocol altogether.

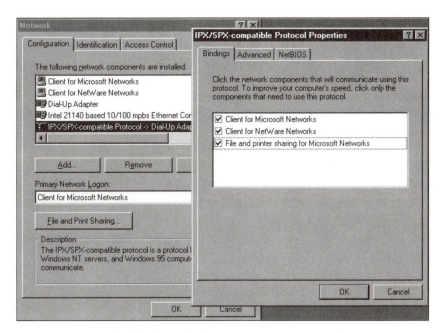

Figure 7-11   Multiple client bindings

The problem of multiple protocol bindings is not restricted to computers with multiple adapters. Many PC manufacturers ship systems with a NIC installed and two or even three protocols installed with each protocol bound to the NIC. One company I worked with had purchased several new PCs from a well-known manufacturer. I was called to troubleshoot sluggish network performance. Browse lists and network shares were very slow to display and this was a network of only about 10 computers. I found that NetBEUI, IPX/SPX, and TCP/IP were all installed and bound to the NICs of the new PCs. To make matters worse, both Client for Microsoft Networks and Client for NetWare Networks were installed. The only client and protocol required by the workstations were Client for Microsoft Networks and TCP/IP, respectively.

Manufacturers tend to ship computers configured like this in the hopes that one of the protocols and one of the clients will work in the environment in which the workstation is installed. This strategy means that the manufacturer will not have to field the inevitable technical support call if the workstation does not work on the network.

The simple solution to the situation that I was troubleshooting was to remove the NetWare client, the IPX/SPX protocol, and the NetBEUI protocol, leaving only the Windows client and TCP/IP, which was all this network required. The response time of its Network Neighborhood browse lists improved dramatically, and everyone was happy. In a network that requires multiple protocols and multiple clients, rather than removing components, simply disable the bindings for services that are not used in each protocol.

Optimizing File and Print Sharing

Reducing the number of protocols in a network and eliminating unnecessary bindings is one way to increase the performance of any network, whether it is a peer-to-peer network or a client/server network. There are other ways to boost performance, particularly in a peer-to-peer network. For instance, desktop operating systems are designed to optimize memory usage for running applications. If a particular PC is to be used heavily for file and print sharing, you can increase the amount of memory that the PC uses for file and folder caching. To do so, go to the Performance tab under the System Properties Control Panel. Click the File System button, and you can change the role of the computer in the resulting dialog box.

Figure 7-12 shows the File System Properties dialog box with the Network server role selected. (The default is Desktop Operating System.) Changing the role to Network server allocates more RAM for caching the most recent files and folders accessed. The additional cache memory allows twice as many folders and four times as many file accesses to be cached. The performance increase is achieved because Windows will not need to consult the file allocation table (FAT) as frequently when responding to disk requests from network clients. This change can improve the performance of a stand-alone system as well. Be warned that you should not make this change unless the system has at least 16 MB RAM installed.

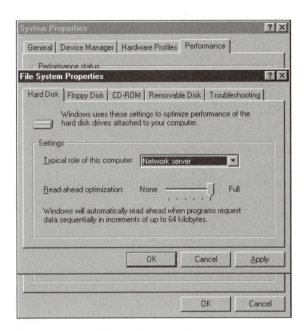

Figure 7-12   File system performance options

Another performance-enhancing tactic is to make sure that only those computers that will be sharing files or printers have the File and Print Sharing Service installed. Every service and protocol that is installed takes up memory and causes additional network traffic. As we will see later in this chapter, some additional methods of increasing network performance apply to the workstation operating systems.

Limitations of Peer-to-Peer Networking

I'll say it again: Windows desktop operating systems are designed to run local applications and run as network clients. As a result, while using these operating systems in a peer-to-peer network environment is perfectly fine and makes sense in some situations, there are clearly limits to what the Windows 9x and Windows ME File and Print Sharing Service can do. Windows desktop operating systems should never be used for critical network applications that require continual uptime and high performance. Strangely enough, there is no actual limit to the number of connections that may be made to a Windows 9x file and print server as there is with Windows NT and Windows 2000 Professional. But, I assure you, performance will not be satisfactory if you try to use one of the desktop operating systems in an environment in which more than a few computers are connected simultaneously.

Most often a desktop operating system is used as a server because the business cannot afford a dedicated server. This setup probably means that a user will be running applications on the machine that is serving files. If one of those applications happens to freeze up or perform an illegal operation that requires a reboot, down goes the server.

My experience with the Window 9*x* File and Print Sharing Service in a moderate-use network with five or six client computers is that a system reboot is necessary about every three to four days at the minimum.

The longer the server runs, the slower it becomes. This slowdown likely is caused by system resources slowly diminishing; a reboot returns resources to their original levels. If this sort of behavior from your servers is acceptable, then Windows desktop operating systems may be a good solution. If not, you can turn to one of the Windows workstation operating systems or a dedicated server environment.

Sharing Resources with Windows Workstation Operating Systems

The Windows workstation line of operating systems includes Windows NT 4.0, Windows 2000 Professional, and Windows XP Professional. Many of the qualities and procedures described in the previous section apply to these versions of Windows as well, but there are some important differences. This section will examine the use of these operating systems in a peer-to-peer environment. I will be careful to point out the areas that differ between them and the desktop line of operating systems.

 The first thing that may strike you about Windows NT Workstation is that the names of the network components are different. In Windows NT Workstation, Client for Microsoft Networks is called the Workstation Service, and the File and Print Sharing Service is called the Server Service. The names may be different, but the functions are still the same. The Workstation Service is used to access network resources and the Server Service is used to share files and printers.

Administrative Shares

All the workstation versions of Windows provide some default shares that are used for administrative purposes. Each fixed disk is shared by default with the name $X\$$, where X is the drive letter. The dollar sign in the name indicates that the share is hidden. These shares will not be displayed in a Network Neighborhood browse list and are accessible only by users with administrative privileges. If you want to access one of these shares, go to the Start menu, click Run, and then type the UNC path to the share. For example, if the computer name is WKS1 and you want to access the C: drive's administrative share, you would use the syntax \\WKS1\C$.

Administrative shares are useful for providing support to users. They allow an administrator to access each disk partition with full control, thereby permitting remote file updates and other support activities. Like the root of each drive, the \WINNT folder is shared administratively. The share name given to that folder is ADMIN$. Administrative shares cannot be permanently removed. If a user removes an administrative share, the share will be recreated the next time the system boots.

Securing Resources

The workstation line of Windows operating systems offer considerably more control in securing resources. Windows NT, Windows 2000, and Windows XP all provide a local user manager that can create and manage user accounts. A user account is required to gain access to any of these operating systems. Users and groups can be assigned permissions to access each shared resource, and different users can be assigned different levels of access, ranging from no access to full control. This flexibility differs from the password-only security available with the Windows desktop line.

Besides permitting user-level access control to shared resources, these three operating systems support the NTFS file system. The NTFS file system allows you to fine-tune your security in detail, down to individual files. The details of managing users and configuring NTFS file security are beyond the scope of this book, but this section will point out some possible problem areas and offer some tips for maintaining resource security.

 For an excellent treatment of the NTFS file system, see *MCSE Guide to Windows 2000 Professional* (published by Course Technology), or visit the Web site *www.windowsitlibrary.com/Content/592/toc.html*.

The first thing to remember about resource security when working with one of these three operating systems is that there are two places where permissions can be set for users accessing resources over the network. If a folder is shared, you can assign a set of permissions to the share called Sharing Permissions. If the shared folder resides on a partition that is formatted for NTFS, you can set NTFS permissions to the folder as well as to the files and subfolders underneath the shared folder. Sharing permissions are applied only to users accessing the share from the network.

 NTFS permissions affect both network access and local access to the folder and files. Furthermore, if both sharing and NTFS permissions are used, the most restrictive set of permissions apply to network users.

In Figure 7-13, the box on the left is the NTFS permissions dialog box, which you can reach by selecting the Security tab in the folder properties. User1 has been given permissions in both dialog boxes. User1's sharing permissions, as shown in the dialog box on the right side of the figure, are Change and Read but the NTFS permissions are restricted to Read & Execute and List Folder Contents. If this user attempts to access this folder over the network, he or she will be subject to the more restrictive permissions specified in the NTFS permission. Because NTFS permissions affect access both locally (when the user is logged on to the local machine) and over the network, it is recommended that you set only NTFS permissions. When a folder is shared, its default permissions allow Everyone Full Control. Thus, if you ignore the sharing permissions and set the NTFS permissions to be more restrictive, the NTFS permissions will take effect.

7

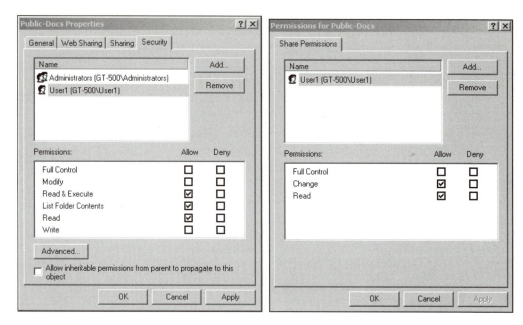

Figure 7-13   NTFS and sharing permissions

Managing Network Bindings on Windows NT/2000/XP

Network bindings on the workstation line of Windows operating systems serve the same purpose that they do on the desktop Windows versions. There is one important difference in that the workstation versions allow bindings to be placed in priority order if there is more than one protocol bound to a NIC or if there are multiple clients. This option allows the administrator to select the protocol or client that is used most frequently for network accesses.

Figure 7-14 shows the bindings order dialog box for Windows 2000 and XP, including the protocol binding order. When two or more protocols are bound to the same service, you can move the protocols up or down in priority order. On a different screen, you can change the order in which clients will be queried when a network resource is requested.

It is worth mentioning that the bindings order is important only for computers that will act as clients or as both client and servers. It is the client requests that are sent according to how the installed clients and protocols are ordered. The server that receives a request will process it according to how it was received, regardless of the order of the bindings on the server.

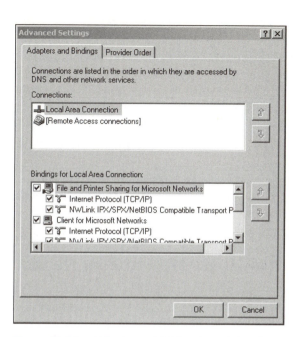

Figure 7-14   Windows 2000 network bindings order

Connection Limitations

Unlike the desktop operating systems, the workstation Windows versions have a clear limit to the number of simultaneous connections. This limit is set at 10 connections. In other ways, the workstation operating systems are designed to be almost identical to the server versions. As a consequence, network performance on a one- or two-CPU system running Windows NT Workstation can equal the performance with Windows NT Server on the same system. With this knowledge in hand, many administrators who did not require some of the additional applications that come with the server versions were, therefore, inclined to install Windows NT Workstation instead of Windows NT Server. Workstation is less expensive than Server, and no license fee is required for each network connection. (The same holds true for the Windows 2000 Professional versus Windows 2000 Server versions.) To avoid losing revenue, Microsoft established a software-based connection limitation on the Windows NT Workstation version of the operating system. Now you see why Microsoft recommends no more than 10 computers in a peer-to-peer network!

Optimizing File and Print Sharing

A peer-to-peer operating system's primary job is to run user applications, and network operations tend to take a back seat with respect to CPU priority. This caveat holds true for Windows NT Workstation, Windows 2000 Professional, and Windows XP Professional. However, as with the desktop versions, some methods exist to tilt the performance edge toward the network applications.

The System Properties Control Panel has a performance option that allows the administrator to select either applications or background services to receive CPU scheduling priority. If a workstation is going to be heavily used for file and print sharing purposes or perhaps as a small-business intranet server, the background services option will provide better performance for network access. As you might expect, this option is selected by default on the server versions of Windows.

When the Computer Goes Down in a Peer-to-Peer Network

Peer-to-peer networks have a higher reliability risk than do client/server networks because users are frequently running applications on the same computers that provide shared network resources. Applications can cause the system to crash, forcing a reboot, and users can turn the computer off unexpectedly. Such an event can cause data loss, and lost connections sometimes require more than just rebooting the workstation to resolve the problem.

One solution to the high risk of down computers in peer-to-peer networking is not allowing users to work at the most critical file and print serving computers.

If a computer goes down for some reason, there is not much you can do to stop the possible loss of data. If file corruption occurs, you will need to resort to a recent backup. But what about the annoying loss of mapped drives that sometimes occurs? If your applications and users rely on mapped drives, and the drive mapping becomes disconnected when the resource to which it is mapped goes down, the applications no longer runs and users will not be able to find their files even after the workstation comes back up.

To solve this problem, you can either train your users to map their drives to the necessary resources when needed, tell your users to reboot their computers, or save yourself and your users some frustration by placing a simple shortcut on their desktops. The shortcut should point to a batch file that runs the net use command described earlier. The batch file simply runs this command for each drive mapping that the workstation requires. A sample batch file might look like the following:

```
net use J: \\accounting\ar
net use P: \\server1\pubdocs
```

You can put a shortcut to the batch file on the desktops that require it, giving the shortcut a descriptive name such as "Reconnect to Servers." Tell your users that whenever they get errors indicating a lost drive mapping, they just have to double-click the shortcut.

While we are on the subject of the computer going down, two other aspects of reliability should not be overlooked in a peer-to-peer network: power failure protection and regular backups. It is easy to forget about these items because they are more obviously associated with dedicated servers than with workstations that also happen to be providing server services. If a workstation in a peer-to-peer network is providing file sharing, it should be linked to an uninterruptible power supply (UPS) to prevent data loss and corruption from power failures. In addition, regular backups should be performed on all critical stations that hold data that cannot be easily reproduced.

Working with DOS and Older Applications

DOS and older Windows applications require special consideration in any network environment. These applications typically do not support UNC path names, which means that mapped drives are a necessity, not simply a convenience. It also means that network printing requires **printer redirection** rather than a UNC path to the printer. Printer redirection occurs when a print job is sent to a local port, such as LPT1 or LPT2, but then redirected via network software to a network printer. Printer redirection can be configured from the Printer Details tab of the Printer Properties dialog box or via the net use command.

When the Details tab of the printer's Properties dialog box is open, click the Capture Printer Port button to access printer redirection. (This button is available only on the Windows desktop line of operating systems.) There is also a check box to specify that this port should be captured every time the user logs on to the system. The first line in the dialog box allows you to select a port to capture or redirect, and the second line indicates the UNC path to the printer on the network.

Printer redirection in a Windows NT or Windows 2000 system can be accomplished only through the net use command. The net use command can also be employed instead of the Capture Printer Port dialog box on Windows desktop operating systems. The syntax is net use LPTx *computername**printername*. The *printername* must be the share name assigned when the printer was shared, and the appropriate LPT number replaces the x in LPTx.

Just as some applications require a mapped drive to operate properly, some applications cannot print unless a local printer port is specified. Figure 7-15 shows the same network shown in Figure 7-9, except that the workstation named Gt-166 uses printer redirection to specify that print jobs to LPT1 should be sent to the \\GLT_WIN95\HP-Laserjet share.

7

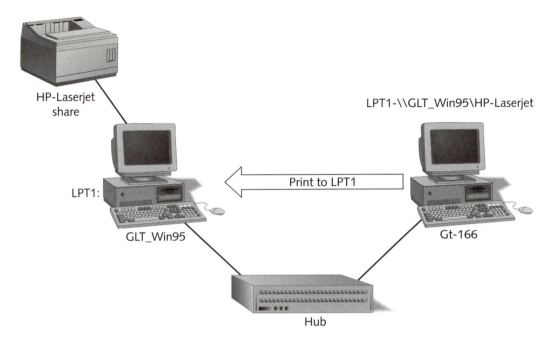

LPT1-\\GLT_Win95\HP-Laserjet

HP-Laserjet
share

LPT1:

Print to LPT1

GLT_Win95

Gt-166

Hub

Figure 7-15   Printer redirection

A problem can arise with printer redirection when the printer ports specified in an application are **hard-coded**. This means that the user does not have an option to select the printer to which to send a print job. When the user prints, the job always goes to LPT1, LPT2, or whatever the default is. The problem occurs when a user has a printer attached to his or her workstation that is not suitable for handling the print job. For example, the print job may require an impact printer because it uses multipart forms, but the user may have an inkjet printer attached to the workstation. What can you do? You can ask the application developer to rewrite the software to allow a printer port to be chosen before sending the print job. That way, the user could have LPT2 redirected to the computer that has the impact printer attached. Then, when the user wishes to print the job requiring the impact printer, the application allows the printer port to be changed to LPT2. Unfortunately, this is not always possible. The application developer may be unknown, unwilling, or just too expensive.

Now what? Well, there is a solution that doesn't cost anything other than a few moments of your time. Remember the net use command and batch files? This solution requires two batch files. The first batch file redirects the local LPT1 port to the impact printer, and the second batch file deletes the redirection. When the user is ready to run the application that requires the impact printer, he or she double-clicks the shortcut that redirects LPT1 to that printer. When the job is finished, the user double-clicks the shortcut that deletes the redirection allowing the use of the inkjet printer. Hands-on Project 7-6 walks you through the creation of these batch files.

Of course, the problems discussed earlier regarding DOS and older applications are not specific to peer-to-peer networks. However, using a client/server environment can solve many of the problems and limitations that have been discussed regarding peer-to-peer networks. A client/server network has the stability of dedicated servers and clients, which reduces some of the performance and reliability problems inherent in peer-to-peer networks.

WINDOWS CLIENT/SERVER NETWORKS

Most of the components used in a Windows server operating system are identical to those used in the desktop and workstation versions of the operating system. The File and Print Sharing Service in Windows 2000 Server and Windows XP is the same software as that in the Professional versions of the product. The Server Service in Windows NT Server is the same service that is used in Windows NT Workstation. Because the installation and configuration of these services are the same, this section focuses on what is *different*.

 The Windows 2000 and Windows XP networking components are significantly different than those found in earlier versions of Windows. The networking performance in Windows 2000 and Windows XP has been dramatically improved over earlier versions through the inclusion of many enhancements. However, the use of these components remains largely unchanged from the user's perspective.

The Domain System and Active Directory

Windows NT Server and Windows 2000 Server client/server networks are based on a security structure called a **domain**. Whereas peer-to-peer Windows operating systems use a decentralized security scheme in which each user manages the security of the resources shared on his or her workstation, the domain model centralizes security on one or more servers called domain controllers. This approach allows user accounts and permissions to be managed from a single location rather than requiring accounts to be created and passwords set on each individual computer that shares resources. Active Directory is a database and service that supports a hierarchical collection of domains and permits network resources to be organized into folders called Organizational Units (OU). The details of Active Directory occupy several volumes and it is mentioned here only for reference.

Problems Logging On to a Domain and Working Within a Domain

One of the first things that becomes apparent when you move from a peer-to-peer Windows network to a client/server Windows network is that you must log on to a domain to gain access to network resources. This process alone is responsible for a significant number of support calls in the average network.

To get acquainted with these problems, we will tackle an environment that uses Windows desktop operating systems as clients. Then, we will look at some problems related to the workstation versions of Windows.

Windows Desktop Operating Systems as Clients

A Windows 9x or Windows ME client system that will be logging into a Windows NT or Windows 2000 domain must first have the necessary networking components installed. NIC drivers and a common protocol are essential, of course, and you must also have Client for Microsoft Networks installed. That should do it, right? Well, sort of. Let's look at what happens when these components are installed and your Windows 98 computer starts.

The first thing you do is log on to the computer. All is OK so far. Figure 7-16 shows a Network Neighborhood browse window of the domain called Tomsho. If you double-click the domain controller W2k-srv1 in hopes of getting access to the shared resources on the domain, you will receive this message. There is no option of entering a user name and password—only a password. The only way you can log on to that domain controller is if you log into Windows 98 with a user name that is an administrator on the domain. Clearly, you do not want to give administrator accounts to all your users.

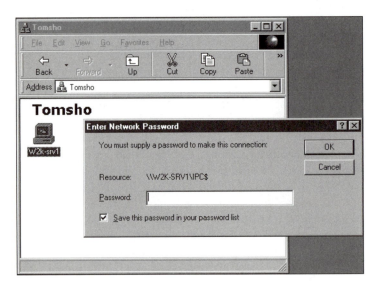

Figure 7-16 Enter Network Password dialog box

To solve this problem, you need to make one simple change in the Network Control Panel. If you select the properties for Client for Microsoft Networks, you will see an option to have the Windows 98 computer log on to a domain when it starts up. Figure 7-17 shows this dialog box. In the logon screen that greets you when you restart Windows 98, you will be allowed to specify the domain you wish to log on to. By default, it is the domain that you specify in the Client Properties dialog box.

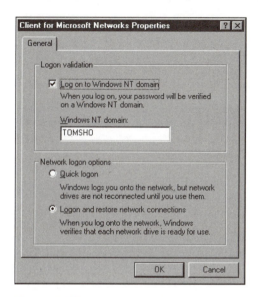

Figure 7-17   Logon validation

Computers that have Windows NT Workstation, Windows 2000 Professional, or Windows XP Professional must be configured to be a member of a domain in a domain environment. Part of the process involved with validating the logon involves ensuring that a particular workstation, not just the user, is allowed to log on to the domain. In Windows 2000 and XP Professional, you can specify that a workstation is a member of a domain or part of a workgroup through the System Properties Control Panel; you use the Network Control Panel in Windows NT Workstation for the same purpose.

If a workstation is not registered as a member of a domain with the domain controllers for that particular domain, users will not be able to log on to the domain from that workstation. This is an important point for organizations that upgrade their computers but that keep the same names for those machines. The workstation registration with the domain is based not just on the name of the computer, but on the **Security ID (SID)** as well. The SID is a unique 96-bit number that identifies domain objects such as users and workstations. If a workstation is a member of a domain, and a new computer subsequently replaces that workstation and keeps the same name, the old computer account in the domain must be deleted and a new account created for the new workstation. If you simply rename the computer, an administrator name and password for the domain are required to rename the computer account in the domain.

Figure 7-18 shows the error message that is displayed if a computer that does not have a valid account attempts to log on to a domain.

Figure 7-18 Invalid computer account error

To resolve computer account problems, you need to use the Active Directory Users and Computers Management Console for Windows 2000 Server or the User Manager for Domains utility on Windows NT Server.

Figure 7-19 shows the Windows 2000 Server Management Console. This tool allows you to create, delete, disable, and enable computer accounts. You can also reset a computer account, which you might do if a computer is replaced with a new machine but you want to assign the same name to the new computer. This option allows the new computer to rejoin the domain using the same name. Note that computer accounts are necessary only when you use one of the workstation operating system versions. Windows 9*x* and ME do not require computer accounts to log on to a domain.

 Note that when a Windows NT Workstation or Windows 2000 Professional computer joins a domain, the administrator for that domain has complete administrative rights over the computer.

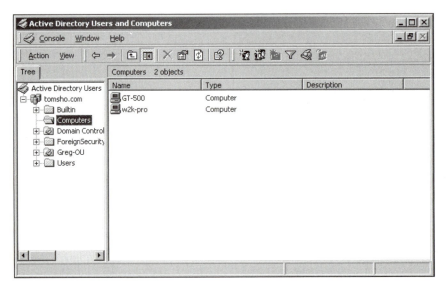

Figure 7-19 Active Directory computer accounts

Some other possible culprits to consider when logon failure occurs include an inability of the workstation to find a domain controller, user account expiration, user logon time or station restrictions, and the always-popular "forgot my password." We will examine the reasons why a domain controller might not be found later in this chapter. The user account expiration and logon time/station restrictions can all be specified by editing the user account. Figure 7-20 shows the user account Properties dialog box.

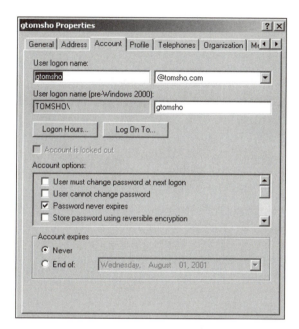

Figure 7-20   User account properties

The notification that a user cannot log on to the server usually comes in the form of a phone call. It is the administrator's job to ask the appropriate questions to determine the reason for the failed logon. Ask the user to read any error messages that may have been displayed. If a user cannot log on to a domain, verify whether the user can log on to the local computer. Do not assume that the user is entering an incorrect password, even though that reason accounts for the majority of logon failures. Walk the user through the process again, being sure that any messages displayed are reported to you. Based on the error messages received, you should be able to determine the cause of the logon failure.

Figure 7-21 shows the error message received when the user enters an incorrect password. One common password error occurs when a user leaves the Caps Lock key on—Windows server operating systems use case-sensitive passwords.

Figure 7-21   Incorrect password error

If you are running Windows NT Workstation and no domain controller is found when you try to log on to the domain, an error message will be displayed indicating that no domain controller was found. Windows 2000 Professional does not always inform you when a domain controller is not found. Instead, it uses **cached credentials** in the event that a domain controller cannot be contacted during a logon attempt. Cached credentials is a local storage of recent logon information that includes the domain name, user name, and password. If a user attempts to log on to the network but cannot locate a domain controller, the local workstation will allow the logon using the cached information. Unfortunately, the operating system does not indicate this choice to the user until the user attempts to access a domain resource.

Figure 7-22 shows the error message received when a workstation has logged onto the network with cached credentials and then tries to access a domain resource. Fortunately, you can change this default if you wish, but it involves editing the Registry. To find the details on how to make this change, visit Microsoft's support Web site and search on the keywords "cached domain logon."

Figure 7-22   Error accessing a domain resource with cached credentials

If you choose to allow cached logons without the error message, there is a definitive method to determine whether the user is indeed logged on to the domain controller or whether cached credentials are being used. If you open a command prompt from the workstation that has logged on and then type the set command, you will see a list of environment variables. Near the top of the list is the variable LOGONSERVER. If its value is set to the name of the workstation, cached credentials are being used. Otherwise, the value will be the name of the logged-on domain controller.

Once a user has logged onto a domain, problems are rare. However, problems involving access permissions to resources can occur. We discuss them next.

Shared Filed Errors

The Windows File and Print Sharing Service employs a function called **Opportunistic Locking** that can cause much grief on Windows NT and Windows 2000 systems. Opportunistic Locking is intended to increase file access performance when a single computer accesses a file using file locking. File locking and unlocking is a time-consuming procedure, and Opportunistic Locking essentially bypasses these controls if only a single user is accessing the file. The more time-consuming file locking and unlocking procedure is used only if multiple users open the same file. However, this mechanism does not always work properly and can result in data corruption, particularly in a shared database environment.

A significant number of technical notes from various corporations specify how this feature can adversely affect their applications. For this reason, Microsoft has a technical note on its support site describing how to disable this feature. Some symptoms of Opportunistic Locking problems include client stations locking up when multiple users attempt to access the same file, data corruption, or file access errors. If this feature is disabled, however, network file access performance may be decreased. Because the feature can be disabled on either the client or the server, it is recommended that you disable the feature on only those clients that are experiencing problems. For more information on this issue, visit Microsoft's support Web site.

LOCATING WINDOWS RESOURCES AND NAME RESOLUTION

Before a shared network resource can be accessed, it must be found. Once found, the computer name must be resolved to an address. Windows operating systems use a variety of methods to locate network resources and resolve names to addresses. The particular method used depends on the network protocols in use and the installed services. As we saw in Chapter 6, these methods include NetBIOS broadcasts, WINS server lookups, and DNS.

A Windows network that does not have a server depends on NetBIOS or static WINS lookups using the **LMHOSTS file** to resolve computer names to addresses. The LMHOSTS file is a plain text file that resides on the client computer and contains a table of computer names and IP address pairs.

This section of the chapter examines how resources are viewed and located on a Windows network and how names are resolved to addresses using the most common network protocols.

The Windows Browser Service

Most often, the available computers in a Windows network are displayed to users using Network Neighborhood or, as Windows 2000 and XP now refer to it, My Network Places. The list of computers shown in Network Neighborhood is called the **browse list** and the list is built using the **browser service**. The Windows browser service is available on all versions of the Windows operating system. The default status of the browser service is enabled and normally should be left that way. The browse list is maintained by broadcast NetBIOS messages, which means that special consideration must be given to any network that has more than one subnet.

 A network using Windows 2000 Server or Windows XP Server that has Active Directory installed can use Active Directory calls to locate resources. The clients must also be Windows 2000 or Windows XP clients to take advantage of Active Directory, so these server operating systems provide the browser service for backward compatibility.

Browser Roles

In a Windows network, a PC can take on one of several browser roles: nonbrowser, potential browser, backup browser, master browser, and domain master browser. Master browser and backup browser are the only two roles that actively participate in the browser process. Master browsers maintain a list of all computers that provide server services on the subnet on which the browser resides. There is one master browser per subnet; in a domain system, there is one domain master browser for the entire domain. If you are running a workgroup network, there is a maximum of one master browser per workgroup or one per subnet in the case of a workgroup that spans subnets.

Backup browsers maintain a copy of the browse list, which is copied from the master browser. A backup browser responds to client requests to display a browse list. There is at least one backup browser per subnet and one additional backup browser for every 32 computers on the subnet, with a maximum of three backup browsers.

 So how is it decided which computers become master browsers, which become backup browsers, and which are neither? It is a rather complex procedure that involves elections and a pecking order that is described in detail on Microsoft's support site. You can find the appropriate information by searching for Windows 2000 articles and using the keywords "browse list." Alternatively, you can look for Article #Q188001.

Our discussion assumes that a master browser and at least one backup browser exist on the network. For simplicity, I will use the name Network Neighborhood, with the understanding that Windows 2000 and Windows XP computers use My Network Places.

When the User Views a Browse List

When a user clicks the Network Neighborhood icon to view a browse list, a series of events occur:

1. The client broadcasts a request for a list of backup browsers. This request is called a Backup List Request and the request is formatted as a NetBIOS datagram.

2. The master browser responds with a list of backup browsers.

3. The client establishes a connection with one of the backup browsers in the list.

4. The client sends a network server enumerate command to the backup browser, which is a request for all available network servers.

5. The backup browser responds with the list of servers.

Figure 7-23 shows a trace of the sequence, albeit with some of the packets from the connection establishment omitted. Packet 2, which is highlighted, shows the master browser named W2K-SRV1 responding with a list of two backup browsers: W2K-SRV1 and JT-W2K-PRO. As you can see, the master browser in this case is also a backup browser. The client, named GT-500, then establishes a session with JT-W2K-PRO and asks for a list of servers. The last packet contains both an acknowledgment to the network server enumerate command and a list of the resources available on the network.

Figure 7-23   Browse list request and response

Master browsers and backup browsers that become unsynchronized can cause problems in the browse process. Servers and browsers that frequently leave the network can cause problems as well. In addition, if a laptop enters the network for only a few minutes, it can become the master browser or a backup browser, particularly in a workgroup environment. Because server resources announce their presence only when they first come online and every 12 minutes thereafter, when the master browser changes, it may take several minutes before a new master browser receives the list of servers and copies it to the backup browsers. The same is true if the backup browser goes offline.

To avoid problems with browsers, you can disable the browser service on those computers that should never become master or backup browsers. In Windows 95 and Windows 98, you can disable the browser service through the properties page of the File and Print Sharing Service. The Browse Master property has three possible values: Automatic, Enabled, and Disabled. To ensure that the computer will never be a master browser, select Disabled. Figure 7-24 shows these options.

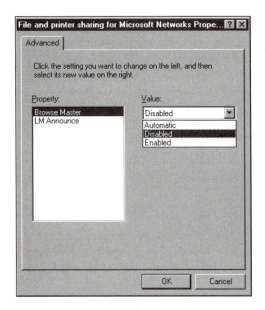

Figure 7-24 File and printer sharing

The Automatic setting—the default setting—makes the computer go through the normal process of selecting the master browser. The Enabled setting causes the computer to always try to be the master browser and should not be used unless all other computers have the Browse Master property disabled. The Disabled setting causes the computer to not participate as a master browser or backup browser.

In a peer-to-peer network in which computers frequently come online and go offline, it is desirable to make one computer always be the master browser by enabling the Browse Master property on it and disabling the Browse Master property on all other computers. Alternatively, you can set the property to Automatic for two or three computers that are always running and disable the property on the remaining computers.

The browse list may not have every computer in the network listed for several reasons:

- The File and Print Sharing Service is not enabled for every computer. The service must be installed and bound to a common protocol before the computer will be listed in Network Neighborhood.

- The computer belongs to a different workgroup or the workgroup name is misspelled. Only computers that belong to the same workgroup or domain are listed in the initial browse list. Other workgroups and domains can be found by selecting Entire Network.

- The TCP/IP protocol is being used, and NetBIOS over TCP/IP has been disabled.

- The computers are on different subnets, and you are not running a WINS server.

The first two problems listed are fairly obvious and easy to fix. The third problem should normally not be a problem unless someone has changed the default setting of NetBIOS over TCP/IP being enabled. This setting can be found in the advanced TCP/IP settings in the WINS tab.

Figure 7-25 shows the dialog box that allows you to change this setting. By default, NetBIOS is enabled over TCP/IP; Windows 2000 computers, however, can disable NetBIOS over TCP/IP, which allows for a more efficient TCP/IP network. If you choose this option, you must use it on all Windows 2000 computers and no earlier versions of Windows can run on the network.

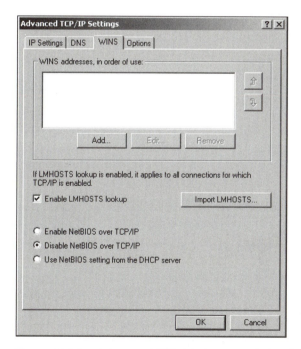

Figure 7-25   Advanced TCP/IP Settings dialog box

Sometimes you may be in a hurry and do not want to wait for the browse list to become synchronized, or you may not know which workgroup or domain contains the computer you need to access. You can still access a computer without the computer being on the network browse list. Simply go to the Start menu, select Run, and type in the UNC path to the computer, such as \\server1. If the computer can be contacted, that command will open an Explorer browse window listing all of the shared resources for that computer.

Using the WINS Service

The Windows Internet Naming Service (WINS) is a TCP/IP service that works much like DNS except that it is specific to Windows networks. You must have a Windows Server operating system to run WINS.

A WINS server eliminates the broadcasts that computers use to announce their presence to the network. To configure a computer to use WINS, select the WINS tab of the TCP/IP properties and enter a WINS server address. Because each computer has the IP address of the WINS server, name registration and browse list queries are sent as unicast packets directly to the WINS server rather than as broadcast packets. This approach allows name registration and browser list queries to travel across subnet boundaries. If you have multiple subnets in your network, you should have at least one WINS server to resolve computer names to addresses.

The alternative is to have a static LMHOSTS file on each client station. The LMHOSTS file is a simple text file that consists of computer names and their corresponding IP addresses. A sample LMHOSTS file called LMHOSTS.SAM can be found in the WINDOWS directory of Windows 9x systems and in the WINNT\SYSTEM32\DRIVERS\ETC directory on Windows NT, Windows 2000, and Windows XP computers.

The disadvantage of the LMHOSTS file is that networks using DHCP will never be able to keep up with the inevitable changes in IP addresses. Of course, you could assign static IP addresses to all computers that act as servers to resolve that problem. However, because the LMHOSTS file must reside on each computer that uses it, it would be difficult to maintain the files on a large network with many servers and clients.

NETWORKING WITH NOVELL NETWARE

Networks that use Novell NetWare as their primary operating system are, sadly, growing smaller in number. NetWare networks are usually fairly stable once they are up and running, but they are not without their occasional problems. The first thing you have to get right in a NetWare environment is the appropriate client for the version of NetWare that is running. The Microsoft Client for NetWare Networks that comes with Windows 9x and Windows ME was designed to work with NetWare versions prior to NetWare 4.

NetWare 4 was the first version of NetWare that utilized Novell Directory Services (NDS). NDS, like Active Directory, is a hierarchical database of network resources. To log on and access network resources in an NDS environment, you must have an NDS-aware client.

You have two client choices in a Windows 9*x* environment: Microsoft Client for NetWare Networks and Novell Client. We discuss each in turn.

Microsoft Client for NetWare Networks

The advantage of the Microsoft Service for NetWare Directory Services is that it comes with the Windows installation CD, meaning that you do not have to hunt down the Novell client. You can install this service by opening the Network Control Panel and adding a service.

The disadvantage of using the Microsoft client is that you cannot take full advantage of the NDS features. There is also a compatibility problem when viewing NetWare resources from a DOS prompt. The free space on NetWare volumes larger than 2 GB is incorrectly reported to some DOS applications. In addition, this client does not allow you to run many of the NetWare applications that require NDS access, such as the NetWare Administrator. For access to NetWare servers running NetWare 3.*x* and lower or for basic NDS functionality on NetWare 4 servers, the Microsoft client is fine.

Novell Client

Due to the limitations of the Microsoft NetWare NDS service, I strongly recommend installing the Novell Client only in NetWare 4 and later environments. The latest client can be downloaded from Novell's support site at *http://support.novell.com*. Once downloaded, you can configure the client to log into the NDS tree.

The NetWare client has configuration options for selecting the default NDS tree and the default user context for logging in. The NDS context specifies the location in the NDS tree in which the user can be found. If no default context is specified, the user must specify the entire NDS path that leads to his or her user account when logging in.

Figure 7-26 shows the Novell Client for Windows 2000 Properties page for the Windows 2000 NetWare Client.

7

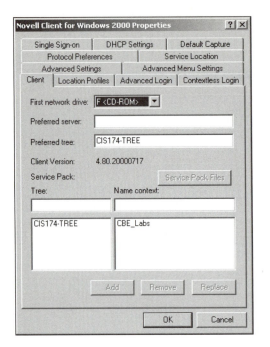

Figure 7-26 Novell Client for Windows 2000 Properties page

NetWare clients have a variety of other configuration options, a few of which will be mentioned here because of their possible effects on network performance. Note that the default IPX packet size is 576 bytes. Furthermore, the NetWare Core Protocol (NCP), which serves as the Transport through Application Layer protocol, requires an acknowledgment for every NCP packet sent.

Two client configuration options can significantly increase performance by changing these limitations. Figure 7-27 shows the advanced client settings. The two settings in which we are interested are **Burst Mode** and **Large Internet Packets (LIP)**. Burst Mode is actually a different packet format than the standard NCP packet format. It must be negotiated between the client and server before packets can be transferred using this mode.

Burst Mode allows file transfers and other large data transfers to be read in a series of large chunks, each of which is several times the size of the network MTU. In this way, several large packets can be transferred at one time without any intervening acknowledgments. If a packet is lost, the receiving computer requests that the missing packet be re-sent. The LIP option allows packet sizes to be larger than the default size of 576 bytes. It will discover and use the largest packet size supported between the client and server based on the MTU of the network.

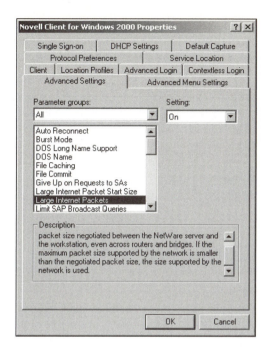

Figure 7-27   NetWare Client Advanced Settings

The default for both of these options in "on." Burst Mode must also be enabled at the server (which it is by default in NetWare 3.2 and later). Occasionally, Burst Mode will cause problems with NetWare clients, particularly if the network is operating over a slow WAN link.

Some NICs do not support Burst Mode correctly. For example, I ran into a problem on an Ethernet LAN in which the client workstation hung every time I tried to copy certain files from the server. It turned out that these files were corrupt. Rather than report an error, however, the workstation simply froze. I disabled Burst Mode on the client. The next time I tried to copy the files, I received a read error. At least then I knew that the files were corrupt and unreadable. With Burst Mode enabled, I could not identify the problem.

CHAPTER SUMMARY

❐ A network operating system (NOS) facilitates the sharing of network resources and runs and manages network applications. One network can have access to multiple NOSs. Having multiple systems allows the network administrator to choose the best NOS for the required applications.

❐ Peer-to-peer networking is a viable, inexpensive, and fairly simple way to share resources in a small business environment. Small businesses that need only the ability to share some files, a few printers, and perhaps a database application will find Windows' built-in networking capabilities to be a quick and easy solution. Peer-to-peer networking is also frequently combined with client/server networking.

❑ Most of the components used to make a Windows server operating system act as a server are identical to those used in the desktop and workstation versions of the Windows operating system. The File and Print Sharing Service in Windows 2000 Server and Windows XP is the same software as that found in the Professional versions of the product. The Server Service in Windows NT Server is the same service as that used in Windows NT Workstation.

❑ A Windows network that does not have a server depends on NetBIOS or static WINS lookups using the LMHOSTS file to resolve computer names to addresses. The LMHOSTS file is a plain text file that resides on the client computer and contains a table of computer names and IP address pairs.

❑ NetWare networks are usually fairly stable once they are up and running, but they are not without their occasional problems.

KEY TERMS

browse list — The list of computers shown in Network Neighborhood.

browser service — The Windows service that is responsible for building the browse list.

Burst Mode — An IPX packet format that allows data transfers in bursts of several packets before an acknowledgment must be sent.

cached credentials — A local storage of recent logon information that includes the domain name, user name, and password.

domain — A model that centralizes security on one or more servers called domain controllers.

hard-coded — Hard-coded software precludes a user from changing a default selection.

Large Internet Packets (LIP) — An IPX packet option that allows packets to be sized according to the MTU of the network.

LMHOSTS file — A plain text file that resides on the client computer and contains a table of computer names and IP address pairs.

mapping a drive — An action by a user that creates a drive letter designation such as F: that refers to a network share.

network bindings — The logical connections between network components.

network operating system (NOS) — Software that facilitates the sharing of network resources and that runs and manages network applications.

Opportunistic Locking — A file sharing method employed by Windows operating systems that is intended to increase performance by bypassing the time-consuming procedure of locking and unlocking files when a single user accesses the file.

printer redirection — Occurs when a print job sent to a local port is re-routed to a network printer.

Security ID (SID) — A unique 96-bit number that identifies domain objects such as users and workstations.

Universal Naming Convention (UNC) path — A path that can be used to access most types of network resources, including Windows shares and NetWare volumes.

REVIEW QUESTIONS

1. A network operating system (NOS) facilitates the sharing of network _____.

2. In a Windows environment, locating a resource may involve the use of Network Neighborhood. True or False?

3. Peer-to-peer networking is frequently combined with _____ networking when small groups of people need to share a printer but do not want the expense of buying a networked printer.

4. With file sharing, you can share an entire drive or individual folders. True or False?

5. What is the most important fact to keep in mind when sharing folders?

6. _____ means to create a drive letter designation such as F: that refers to a network share.

   a. Mapping a drive

   b. Sharing a file

   c. Sharing a resource

   d. Opening a mapped server

7. Most client/server networks designate just one or two computers to be the primary servers for peer sharing. True or False?

8. A(n) _____ path can be used to access most types of network resources, including Windows shares and NetWare volumes.

   a. NRI

   b. GLT

   c. UNC

   d. SHARE

9. A batch file is an executable file. True or False?

10. You can use the subst command to list virtual drives. True or False?

11. What are the logical connections between network components?

12. Entries can be removed from the Network Control Panel, except when the current computer is a server. True or False?

13. There is no limit to the number of connections that may be made to a Windows $9x$ file that is being shared. True or False?

14. The Windows workstation line of operating systems includes Windows NT 4.0, Windows 2000 Professional, and Windows XP _____.

15. By default, what is the name with which a Windows fixed disk is shared?

16. What is the share name of \WINNT?

17. If both sharing and NTFS permissions are used on a resource, the most _____ set of permissions apply to network users.

    a. permissive

    b. broad

    c. restrictive

    d. closed

18. NTFS permissions affect access both locally and over the network. True or False?

19. When a folder is shared, its default permissions allow Everyone _____.

    a. Full Control

    b. All Right

    c. No Access

    d. Restricted Format Access

20. Like the desktop operating systems, the workstation Windows versions place a clear limit on the number of simultaneous connections. True or False?

21. Printer redirection in a Windows NT or Windows 2000 system can be accomplished only through the _____ command.

    a. capture

    b. net use

    c. redirect share

    d. UNC forward

22. What database and service allows a hierarchical collection of domains and permits network resources to be organized into Organizational Units?

23. The _____ is a unique 96-bit number that identifies domain objects such as users and workstations.

    a. WKN

    b. PRN

    c. SID

    d. POST

24. Windows 9x and ME require computer accounts to log on to a domain. True or False?

25. A Windows network that does not have a server depends on NetBIOS or static WINS lookups using what to resolve computer names to addresses?

HANDS-ON PROJECTS

Project 7-1 Install the File and Print Sharing Service on Windows 98

This project assumes that the workstation has Client for Microsoft Networks installed but not the File and Print Sharing Service.

1. From the Windows 98 desktop, right-click **Network Neighborhood**, and then click **Properties**.

2. Click the **File and Print Sharing** button.

3. Check the **I want to be able to give others access to my files** check box and then click **OK**.

4. Click **OK** on the Network Control Panel. (You may need the Windows 98 CD-ROM at this point. Insert the Windows 98 CD-ROM if so prompted.)

5. Click **Yes** when you are asked if you would like to restart your computer. Be sure to remove the Windows 98 CD-ROM before your computer restarts.

6. When your computer reboots, right-click **Network Neighborhood**, and then click **Properties**. Verify that File and printer sharing for Microsoft networks is added to the Network Control Panel.

Project 7-2 Create and Share a Folder

In this project, you will learn to share a folder.

1. Open Windows Explorer.

2. Select the **C:** drive in the left pane, click **File** on the menu bar, point to **New**, and then click **Folder**.

3. Right-click the **New Folder** you created and then click **Sharing**.

4. Click the **Share as** option button, and type **Shared** as the share name.

5. Click **OK**, and then close Windows Explorer.

6. To verify that the folder is shared, double-click **Network Neighborhood**.

7. Double-click your computer name in the Network Neighborhood browse list. You should see a folder named Shared.

8. Close Network Neighborhood.

Project 7-3 Create a Mapped Drive Using the net use Command

This project requires students to use the Windows 98 computer from Project 7-2 and to work in pairs. Each student must know the name of his or her partner's computer and the partner's computer must be accessible on the network.

1. Click **Start**, click **Run**, type **command**, and then click **OK**.

2. At the DOS prompt, type **net use /?**, and then press **Enter** to see the help screen for the net use command.

3. You will now map a drive to the share created by your partner in Project 7-2. Type **net use m: *computer*\shared** at the DOS prompt, where *computer* is the name of your partner's computer. You should see a response that says "The command was completed successfully."

4. Close the DOS box by typing **exit**.

5. Open My Computer and verify that the M: drive is listed.

6. Double-click the **M:** drive to open the shared folder on your partner's computer.

7. Close all windows.

Project 7-4 Disable a Binding

This project uses Windows 98. It requires a computer that has TCP/IP, a dial-up adapter, and the File and Print Sharing Service for Microsoft networks installed. You will learn how to disable the binding, but you will not accept the changes that you make.

1. Right-click **Network Neighborhood**, and then click **Properties**.

2. Double-click **TCP/IP -> Dial-Up Adapter**. If a TCP/IP Properties Information dialog box opens, click **OK** to continue.

3. Select the **Bindings** tab.

4. Uncheck the **File and printer sharing for Microsoft networks** check box.

5. Click **OK**.

6. Click **Cancel** so that the changes are not recorded.

Project 7-5 Create a Batch File

This project requires a computer running Windows 98. The instructor should have a machine set up that has a shared printer. The instructor will tell the students the names of the computer and the shared printer.

1. Click **Start**, click **Run**, type **notepad**, and then click **OK**.

2. In Notepad, type **net use lpt1: *computer*\printer**, where *computer* is the computer name specified by your instructor and *printer* is the name of the shared printer.

3. Save the file by selecting **File** from the menu bar and clicking **Save As**.

4. Select **Desktop** in the Save in: drop-down box. In the Save as type: drop-down list, select **All Files**. In the File name: dialog box, type **redirect.bat**. Click **Save**.

5. Click **File** on the menu bar, select **New**, and then type **net use lpt1: /delete**. This command will delete any printer redirection for LPT1.

6. Save the file by clicking **File** on the menu bar and clicking **Save As**.

7. Select **Desktop** in the Save in: drop-down list. In the Save as type: drop-down list, select **All Files**. In the File name: text box, type **unredirect.bat** and click **Save**.

8. Close Notepad.

9. You now have two batch files, one that redirects your LPT1: printer port to the shared printer on your instructor's computer and another that deletes the redirection. Ask your instructor if you can test the batch files. If so, your instructor will give you instructions on how to test them.

Project 7-6 Reorder Bindings in Windows 2000 Professional

This project requires a computer running Windows 2000 Professional that has the TCP/IP and NetBEUI protocols installed.

1. On the Windows 2000 Professional desktop, right-click **My Network Places**, and then click **Properties**.

2. Click **Advanced** on the menu bar, and then click **Advanced Settings**.

3. Click the **Adapters and Bindings** tab.

4. In the Connections list box, click **Local Area Connection**.

5. In the Bindings for Local Area Connection list box, select **Client for Microsoft Networks**.

6. Select **NetBEUI Protocol** under Client for Microsoft Networks.

7. To move NetBEUI higher in the bindings order, click the **up arrow** on the right side of the dialog box. To move NetBEUI lower in the bindings order, click the **down arrow** to reverse the action.

8. Click **Cancel**.

9. Close the dialog box.

CASE PROJECTS

Case 7-1 Troubleshoot Network Connections on Peer-to-Peer Networks

This project requires a working network of peer-to-peer computers running either Windows 95, Windows 98, Windows NT Workstation, or Windows 2000 Professional or any combination of those operating systems. One or more computers will be designated as servers, and one or more computers will be designated as clients. Students may work individually or in groups.

Your instructor will introduce problems into your peer-to-peer network and you will be asked to find and solve the problem. The problem may be related to any one or more of the following: client software, server software, bindings, protocols, or the physical layer. You will leave the room, and the instructor will create problems either on your client workstation, the server workstation, or both. When you return, you will attempt to solve the problem until the network connection works again.

Case 7-2 Research a Opportunistic Locking Problem

Use the Internet to find a description of the Opportunistic Locking problem. You may use Microsoft's Web site but find at least one other source. Write a short description of the problems that can occur with Opportunistic Locking and explain the method used to disable this feature.

Case 7-3 Sails and Snails Printer Sharing

A small workgroup of five computers in Sails and Snails Industries wants to use the Windows 98 File and Print Sharing Service to share a new printer. Computer 1 will have the new printer attached to its LPT1 port. Describe the procedure required to make this printer accessible to all five computers from Windows applications.

Case 7-4 Sails and Snails Printer Problem

The workgroup of five computers described in Case 7-3 has been printing happily to the shared printer you set up. However, the users recently started working with a DOS-based database program. Only computer 1 can print to the printer from this DOS program. It has been determined that the DOS database program can print to LPT1 only because it does not understand UNC paths. Describe the solution to this problem.

Case 7-5 Slow Display of the My Network Places Browse List

Seven Windows 2000 Professional computers were just purchased for a small company to use in a workgroup network. The computers were shipped with NICs, and the operating system was already installed. When the PCs were hooked up to the network, they worked correctly but the browse list in My Network Places takes as long as 10 or more seconds to display. Describe your investigation into the problem, and list several possible causes of and solutions for this problem.

CHAPTER
8

NETWORK SECURITY

After reading this chapter and completing the exercises, you will be able to:

- ◆ Appreciate the many aspects and importance of network security
- ◆ Secure physical access to your network
- ◆ Understand and implement the methods available to secure and audit Windows NT and Windows 2000 servers
- ◆ Understand and implement the methods available to secure and audit Novell NetWare servers
- ◆ Identify security risks with internetworking devices
- ◆ Understand the basic principles of firewall operation and know how a firewall can help secure your network
- ◆ Understand the tools used by the hacker

Most LAN administrators would rather go in for that proverbial root canal than think about network security. Network security can be tedious because you have to think of all the ways your data could be compromised, and it can be frustrating because you have to simultaneously let the good guys in while keeping the bad guys out. Unpleasant as it sometimes can be, the design of a sound security policy and the effort required to implement that policy throughout all parts of your network will pay off in a big way. The payoff comes in the form of fewer headaches from fixing problems caused by security breaches—and fewer sleepless nights from worrying about who is accessing your data.

This chapter discusses the elements required of a sound security policy and describes many of the tools available to implement such a policy. First, we examine the various definitions of security and see what security can do for you. Next, we discuss the physical security of your network plus security in Windows and NetWare environments. Then, we present the methods and tools available to implement and verify security on internetworking equipment. Finally, we examine some of the tools that may be used to infiltrate or compromise the integrity of your network.

WHAT IS NETWORK SECURITY AND WHAT CAN IT DO FOR YOU?

Network security can mean different things to different people. To network users, security is something they have to tolerate and takes the form of logon names and passwords that they have to change too frequently. Users might also think of security as the assurance that if their hard drive burns up, the network administrator will be more than happy to restore their data from last night's backup.

Of course, network security perceptions can become very job-specific. For instance, to a pharmaceutical engineer, security might mean that the formula for the latest drug he or she has concocted is safe from the competition's prying eyes. To a network engineer, security might mean that the network cannot be brought to its knees by a 13-year-old kid trying out the latest denial-of-service attack software downloaded from the Internet. The corporate lawyer may think of network security as a means to safeguard against illegal activities such as software pirating or the distribution of copyrighted materials. The marketing team for an e-commerce site may consider network security to be a promotional tool with which to convince customers that their online purchases are safe.

To the chief information officer, network security means more than job-specific tasks. He or she knows that the goal of network security is to protect the organization, its users, customers, and business partners from any threat to the integrity of the information that resides on or passes through the network, and from the consequences of misuse of network resources.

Ideally, network security should be as unobtrusive as possible, allowing network users to concentrate on the tasks they wish to accomplish, rather than having to concentrate on how to get to the data they need to perform those tasks. The achievement of that goal not only lets people sleep better at night, but also permits an organization to go about its business confidently and efficiently. In today's security conscious world, a company that can demonstrate that its information systems are secure is more likely to attract customers, partners, and investors.

The lofty goal of good, unobtrusive security encompasses many dimensions, so where do you start? With a security policy that reflects the attitude of your business.

What Is a Security Policy?

A **security policy** is a document that describes the rules governing access to the company's information resources, the enforcement of those rules, and the steps taken in the event the rules are breached. The document should describe not only who might have access to which resources, but also the permissible use of those resources once accessed. In addition, it should follow these guidelines:

- A security policy should be easy to understand for the ordinary user and reasonably easy to comply with. In other words, if you make it too difficult to understand or follow, users will resist adhering to the policy. An example of a policy that is difficult to follow is one that requires users to change their passwords once every week.

- A security policy should be enforceable. A rule created that cannot be reasonably enforced will almost always be broken. For example, you should not prohibit the use of the Internet during certain hours of the day unless you have a method of monitoring or restricting such use.

- A security policy should state clearly the objective of each policy in place so that the purpose of the policy is clear. For example, a policy that states "Misuse of the network is forbidden" does not define misuse, making such a policy useless because of its lack of specificity.

 Refer to RFC 2196 at *www.networksorcery.com/enp/rfc/rfc2196.txt* for more information about security policies.

The Role of a Security Policy

A security policy has one giant role: to state the rules governing the use of network resources and to define the responsibilities of employees in adhering to and enforcing those rules. Of course, as with every major role, multiple subroles play a part:

- A security policy must inform your network users, staff, and management of their responsibility to protect network resources, the rules of conduct as they pertain to the use of those resources, and the consequences of failing to abide by those rules.

- A security policy must provide a blueprint for security implementation and a method to audit the status of your network security. This blueprint provides a framework for implementing security, which can be referenced to ensure that your security implementation does not stray far from your security goals.

- A security policy can guide the network administrator through certain aspects of network design and implementation. For example, if the security policy requires that all data be encrypted when it is stored on the server, then it limits the choice of network operating system to those that support that functionality, or it may require third-party software to accomplish this task.

- Another role of the security policy is to gain consensus between all key areas of the organization that will be affected by the policy. Company officers must understand how the security policy protects the interests of the organization so that they can be confident in assuring customers and investors that the organization is trustworthy.

- The security policy overtly identifies equipment or staff that needs to be kept or that must be obtained. This identification is key because it does no good to create a security policy that you cannot implement due to lack of equipment or staff.

- A written security policy forces all IT administrators responsible for network resource management to be involved and in agreement. A person who has an active part in creating or approving a policy is much more likely to uphold that policy.

- The security policy educates the organization's legal staff in case legal action needs to be taken in the event of an incident such as copyright infringement or willful destruction of data.

Elements of a Security Policy

Now that you know what a security policy is and what role it plays in an organization, you need to know some of the elements of a security policy. One of the most important aspects of a security policy is that it covers all forms of network resource access and usage. The policy must specify to whom it applies, what the scope of coverage is, how security is enforced, and who is responsible for its enforcement. You can use the following checklist to meet each of these requirements (some organizations will not need all elements):

- Definition of the policy's scope and responsibility: Describes the areas the policy covers and who is responsible for those areas.

- Software and network equipment features guidelines: Describe the required security features of purchased hardware and software and should include methods used to physically secure equipment.

- Privacy policy: Describes what staff, customers, and business partners may expect regarding the monitoring and reporting of network use.

- Acceptable use policy: Explains the manner and for what purposes network resources may be used.

- Authentication policy: Describes how users identify themselves to gain access to network resources. Logon names, password conventions, and authentication methods should be described.

- Internet use policy: Explains what constitutes proper or improper use of Internet resources, including access times and duration of access.

- Incident report policy: Details how, when, and to whom policy violation incidents should be reported as well as the procedures used to deal with such violations.

- Access policy: Specifies how and when users may access the network resources. Policies should exist for both on-site access and remote access when applicable.

- Auditing policy: Explains the manner in which security compliance or violations can be verified and the thresholds above which remedies must be made.

- System maintenance policy: Describes who may have access to network systems for the purpose of maintenance and troubleshooting. It should cover how outside help should be handled.

- Materials disposal: Describes the acceptable methods for the disposal of materials that contain sensitive data or equipment that contains sources for compromising security.

- Data protection: Details the policies for backup procedures, virus protection, and disaster recovery.

After a security policy is in place, it should not remain a static document. New technologies, changes in business practices, and the results of internal security audits may require modifications to the policy. As I said before, the policy that you put in place should reflect the current and future needs of your business.

Types of Security Policies

Before starting to design a network security policy, you need to be aware that there is a tradeoff between a highly restrictive network and the cost and difficulty required to support such a network. Security is expensive. If you work at the Department of Justice, then price should be no object in determining the extent of your security measures. However, if you are a small manufacturer of common household items, you may want to go a little easier on the security measures.

To help you decide where on the security continuum your company should reside, the next three sections consider different security levels.

Highly Restrictive Security Policies

Highly restrictive security policies will usually include features such as data encryption, complex password requirements, detailed auditing and monitoring of computer and network access, intricate authentication methods, highly restrictive usage policies on such services as e-mail and Internet access, and strict policies on the use and disposal of information media. The high expense of implementing such restrictive policies comes in the form of high design and configuration costs of software and hardware, the staff needed to implement, support, and manage the security, and lost productivity due to the higher learning curve and additional procedures that users must endure. However, if you need the security, the costs of security breaches are much more expensive than the cost of security implementation.

Moderately Restrictive Security Policies

Moderately restrictive security policies probably meet the security requirements for most companies. These policies have passwords for each user but are not required to be overly complex. Auditing is geared toward detecting unauthorized logon attempts, misuse of network resources, and hacker activity. Most network operating systems probably contain satisfactory authentication, monitoring, and auditing features to implement the required policies. The network infrastructure can be secured with off-the-shelf hardware and software such as firewalls or access control lists. The costs of moderate security policies are primarily in the areas of initial configuration and support. This type of policy is used in the typical business setting in which each user has his or her own personal files that require moderate security and in which users in some departments are responsible for files that may require additional security measures, such as payroll or personnel files.

Open Security Policies

A company that engages in an open network security policy may have simple or no passwords, unrestricted access to resources, and probably no security monitoring and auditing. This type of security policy might make sense for a small company whose primary goal for its network is to make access to resources easier. The company may not want to spend additional funds for the employee training often required with more restrictive security policies.

In this situation, Internet access should probably not be possible via the company LAN because it invites too many possibilities for outside mischief or inside abuse. If Internet access is available company-wide, a more restrictive policy is probably warranted. In an open security environment, sensitive data, if it exists, might be kept on individual workstations that are backed up regularly and are physically inaccessible to other employees.

No matter which type of security policy your company employs, some common elements should be present. Virus protection for servers and desktop stations is a must for every computing environment, and there should be policies aimed at preventing viruses from being downloaded or spread. Backup procedures for all data that cannot be easily reproduced should be in place, and a disaster recovery procedure must be devised. Remember—security is aimed not only at preventing improper use or access to network resources, but also at safeguarding the company's information, which today is often more valuable than its physical assets.

SECURING PHYSICAL ACCESS TO YOUR NETWORK

The first mantra of security is this: If there is physical access to the equipment, there is no security. This idea applies not only to servers and workstations, but also to internetwork devices and even network media. No matter how strong your logon name and password schemes are, if a user has physical access, it does not take much effort to gain access to data.

If a network server is left physically accessible, there are numerous ways to break into that server. If it is a Windows 2000 server and the administrator is logged on, the server is an open book. Even if a logon is required on the server, someone can attempt to log on using his or her own user name; if that logon is allowed, the user can potentially access the entire server. If someone is really determined, the server could be restarted and booted to a floppy disk, thereby bypassing Windows 2000 security.

 Don't forget that if a person is truly desperate, the hard drives or even the entire server could be taken and later cracked.

What do you do to prevent a physical assault on your network? Here are some steps you can take:

- When planning your network, ensure that there are rooms available to house your servers and equipment. These rooms should have locks to prevent unauthorized access and should be suitable for the equipment being housed. Sufficient power receptacles, cooling, and an environment clear of EMI sources are some of the features required. In addition, rooms should not be accessible through false ceilings.

- If a suitable room is not available, locking cabinets can be purchased to house servers and equipment in public areas. You must be certain that these cabinets have suitable ventilation for the devices so housed. Both free-standing and wall-mounted cabinets are available. Wall-mounted cabinets are particularly useful for housing hubs and patch panels.

- Wiring from workstations to wiring cabinets should be inaccessible to eavesdropping equipment. Wiring that is not concealed in floors or ceilings should be concealed in raceways or other channeling devices to discourage access.

- Your plan should include procedures for recovery from natural disasters such as fire or flood.

Securing Servers

Securing servers is sometimes operating system-dependent. For instance, a NetWare server does not have a convenient user interface like Windows does, but the NetWare console still provides methods to infiltrate the server. If a floppy drive is present and not disabled, a troublemaker could run a readily available hacker tool that permits the administrator account password to be changed. In fact, I have used such a program on a server when the person who installed the server forgot the administrator password. It worked like a charm—I was in the server in a matter of seconds. Isn't that scary?

Of course, there are tips that apply to all types of servers. For instance, securing any server from physical access should be high priority in your security plan. This goal can be accomplished in a number of ways, and sometimes a combination of methods is required, depending on your environment. Many servers are stashed away in a lockable wiring closet along with the hub or switch to which the server is connected. This setup is fine as long as the environment is suitable for the server and as long as the same people who have authority to access the wiring and hubs have authority to access the servers as well.

Servers often require more tightly controlled environmental conditions than do patch panels, hubs, and switches. Servers can generate a substantial amount of heat and therefore need adequate cooling. I have had two operating system crashes that were the result of servers being locked away in inadequately ventilated cabinets or wiring closets. In one case, the disks were overheating and errors were introduced onto the media. The operating system was unable to boot until the server was removed to a cooler environment. Some files were permanently damaged, but the drives were salvageable and the servers worked correctly thereafter as long as the rooms were kept cool and ventilated.

In at least two other instances, I walked into wiring closets that housed hubs, routers, and servers that had temperatures into the 90s. I insisted that the equipment be moved or, alternatively, that cooling units be dedicated to the wiring closets; the latter was implemented. In those environments, the servers did not fail, but I had at least one flaky hub and a flaky router that were caused by the high temperatures.

In addition to adequate cooling, your server rooms should be equipped with power that is preferably on a circuit separate from other electrical lines. The power outlets should be sufficient to eliminate the need for extension cords. Because you will be putting the servers on uninterruptible power supplies (UPSs) (won't you?), you need to verify the power requirements for your UPSs. Some UPSs require special outlet connectors and high current, such as the NEMA L5-30P, which is a twist-lock–type plug rated for 30 amps. There is nothing more frustrating than getting your brand new UPS and preparing to plug in your brand new server, only to find that the power outlets are incompatible with the UPS requirements. Yes, that is the voice of experience talking.

In some cases, you cannot avoid placing your servers in an area in which people who must have access to that area are not authorized to access the servers. For example, different people may maintain the internetworking equipment than maintain the servers, but you may not have facilities to house the different equipment in different areas. A few things can be done to increase your security beyond that offered through passwords. Many servers come with locking cabinets to prevent access to the inside of the case. Some also have lockable covers that protect the floppy drive and power buttons from unauthorized access. You can also place the keyboard and monitor in a different area than the actual server by using long-distance cable extenders. Lastly, you can place the server in a free-standing locking cabinet.

If you are forced to place the servers in a public access area, locking cabinets are a must. Even if there is no malicious intent, someone is sure to kick the server, spill coffee on it, unplug it, or impose any number of undesirable afflictions on the server. You can purchase **rack-mountable** servers, which means that the servers are designed to bolt to a standard 19-inch equipment rack like that used for patch panels and servers. To conserve space, you can purchase a free-standing cabinet that has a built-in 19-inch rack, allowing you to store several servers. Be sure that the cabinet you purchase is well ventilated or permits you to add fans for ventilation. These cabinets typically start at about $1000. Like everything else, security comes with a price.

Securing Internetwork Devices

Routers and switches contain critical configuration information. A user with physical access to these devices needs only a laptop and a few widely-published keystrokes to get into the router or switch and change the passwords and view or change the configuration of these devices. In addition, a person who has access to a hub or switch port can attach a laptop that has a protocol analyzer installed. From that point, it is simply a matter of waiting for the right data to be captured to gain access to critical information.

Obviously, internetworking devices such as hubs, switches, and routers should be given as much attention in terms of physical security as servers. These devices provide potential network infiltrators with access to the network and the opportunity to wreak havoc on the network. Configuration changes made to routers, switches, and even hubs can have disastrous consequences. In addition, access to routers can provide network topology information that you may not want everyone to know. The more that a troublemaker knows about the network configuration, the more tools he or she has to break into the network or otherwise cause problems on it.

 Not all people who try to gain unauthorized access to network resources seek to steal or view information. Some people may just want to bring the network down for spite or for fun. Access to the network equipment provides an opportunity to cause such mischief.

A room with a lock is the best place for internetworking devices but a wall-mounted enclosure with a lock is the next best thing. Such cabinets are usually heavy-duty units with doors that swing out and built-in 19-inch racks. These wall-mounted cabinets are pricey, so budget between $300 and $1000 for them, depending on the features and size required. Some racks come with a built-in fan or have a mounting hole for a fan. The racks also come with channels for your wiring to enter conveniently.

WINDOWS SERVER SECURITY

A network operating system designed as a server usually incorporates security measures in a variety of categories. Windows server operating systems are no exception. The security features built into the Windows NT, Windows 2000, and Windows XP server operating systems include user account and logon security, file system and computer security, security auditing, protection of the network from viruses, and security using patches. We discuss each in turn.

User Account and Logon Security

User account security in Windows server operating systems allows administrators to specify a number of options and restrictions regarding how and when users can log on to the Windows network. There are options related to password requirements, logon hours, logon location, and remote logon.

Password Requirements

Windows passwords can be required to be a minimum number of characters. For moderately restrictive networks, a minimum password length is recommended, and a minimum length of five characters is typical. Networks that require a more restrictive policy may want to increase this number. Windows NT permits a maximum length of 14 characters, but Windows 2000 and XP allow up to 128-character passwords. A network with an open security policy can set the minimum length to zero, which allows a blank password. The administrator account, however, should never have a blank password.

In a moderate to highly restrictive network, it is desirable to require passwords to mix alphabetic, numeric, and symbol characters to make them more difficult to guess. Windows 2000 and XP have an option to force passwords to meet complexity requirements, such as having at least one number, one uppercase letter, and one lowercase letter. Other password options include requiring users to change their passwords periodically, from as frequently as every day to once every 999 days. My advice is that you use this option but do not make users change their passwords too frequently. If a user has to change a password too frequently, he or she will forget it and, after calling desktop support a few times to have the password reset, the user will start writing the password down somewhere. Users have been known to keep their passwords on a piece of paper inside their desks and even taped to the outside of their desks! Clearly, this practice defeats the purpose of having passwords to begin with. Sixty to 90 days between password changes is usually sufficient; you can make the interim period longer if your policy is more toward the open side. To prevent users from rotating the same two passwords every time they need to change it, Windows has an option that remembers as many as 24 passwords before allowing a user to use a previously used password.

When a user fails to enter the correct password, a policy can be set to lock the user account, preventing that account from logging in. This **account lockout** option can be enabled or disabled. If it is enabled, the administrator can specify how many times an incorrect password may be entered before the account is locked. Once locked, the administrator can require a manual unlocking of the account or the account can be set to unlock in a specified number of minutes. This option is useful for preventing someone from trying to log on as another user by guessing the password. Of course, it also gives you a reason to speak to some of your users from time to time when they call you to unlock their accounts on the Monday after a long weekend!

Logon Hours

You can restrict individual users to the times and the days they are permitted to log on to the system. Each user account is associated with a grid of logon times and days, which defaults to allowing users the right to log on any time and any day. A common use for this feature is to prevent users from being logged on during the hours that backups or other standard maintenance procedures occur—usually in the wee hours of the morning.

Logon Location

A user may occasionally log on to the network from a computer that is not his or her regular workstation. This practice may be okay in your environment, but extending it to users who have access to sensitive data can be dangerous. If a user logs on at a workstation that is in a coworker's office and then walks away from that machine, the coworker now has access to the sensitive data. To prevent this problem, users can be restricted to logging on from particular workstations. Figure 8-1 shows the user account settings for logon location and logon hours.

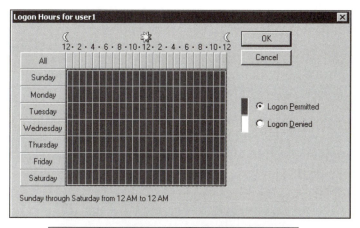

Figure 8-1   Logon restrictions

Remote Logon

If your organization permits remote access to the network through a dial-up connection or other means, you can permit or deny users the ability to log on remotely. Unless a user has a need to log on remotely, it is best to deny this capability. Remote access can be expensive to support, and there are usually a limited number of incoming lines for this purpose. Remote access should, however, be granted to your mobile sales force, telecommuters, and others who absolutely require it.

File System Security

Once a user has successfully logged on, the next level of security is the **file system security**. A network operating system with file system security permits the administrator to assign file and folder permissions to users or groups of users.

Windows Server operating systems provide two options for file security: **sharing security** and **NTFS security**. Sharing security is applied to folders that are shared over the network. The permissions on sharing can be applied only to folders. The files within the shared folder take on the same permissions that the parent folder has. Sharing security does not affect access to files or folders if a user is logged on locally; it restricts only users accessing the files across the network. It is the only security option available if you use the FAT or FAT32 disk format on your Windows server.

NTFS security is considerably more sophisticated than sharing security. It allows an administrator to assign permissions to individual files as well as to folders; thus you can assign one level of permission to a folder but a different level of permission to the individual files within the folder, if desired. Additionally, NTFS permissions apply not only to access over the network, but also to local access to files.

You must use the NTFS disk format to utilize NTFS security. The NTFS file system is proprietary to Windows NT, Windows 2000, and Windows XP, so other operating systems cannot read files stored on an NTFS-formatted disk. If security is a crucial concern, you should use the NTFS file system so that a person cannot boot to a DOS floppy disk and access the files stored on your Windows server. If compatibility is the chief concern—for example, if you want to be able to boot to other operating systems and still have access to your files—you should use the FAT or FAT32 file format.

In moderately restrictive and highly restrictive networks, permissions to files should be assigned using the most restrictive permission that still allows users to run their applications and get their jobs done. For example, users should be assigned only the read permission to directories that contain just program files, thereby preventing users from accidentally deleting or modifying a program. Users who do not need to access a folder should not be given any permission to that folder. Be aware that Windows server operating systems, unlike other NOSs such as NetWare and UNIX, default the permissions on folders and files to Full Control to Everyone. One of the first things an administrator should do after creating a folder on an NTFS drive or sharing a folder is to remove the Full Control permission to Everyone and assign access to only those users or groups of users who really need access.

Rights

Rights specify which actions a user may take on a computer. For example, a user may have the right to shut down the server, or a user may be prevented from logging on locally to the server. Rights affect only the things a user can do on a particular computer; permissions, by contrast, affect which resources (such as files, folders, and printers) a user can access on the computer. There are more than 30 rights that can be assigned to users or groups of users on a Windows 2000 or XP server and just slightly fewer on an NT server.

Default rights are assigned to various system groups when the operating system is installed. For example, Windows 2000 server permits only Administrators, Server Operators, and a few other system groups to log on locally, but all users are permitted to log on over the network.

It is a good idea to become familiar with the various rights that can be assigned and to know who has those rights so that you can fine-tune your security. However, do not do what one student of mine did. This student wanted to secure local logon to the server, so she removed all of the default groups from that right, leaving no one with the right to log on to the server locally. Now that's going a little overboard. Figure 8-2 shows the list of rights available on a Windows 2000 computer.

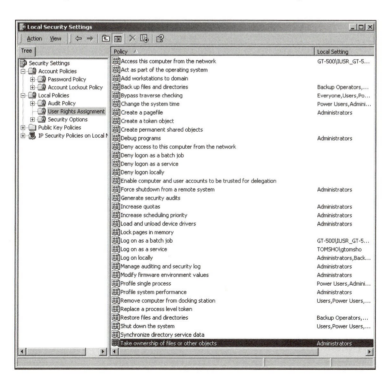

Figure 8-2   Windows 2000 rights

Security Auditing

If you are going to have security policies, you need a method to audit your security so that you can determine whether the policies are being followed or where they may be weak. Windows server operating systems provide auditing services that can be used to track many aspects of server use. When some administrators learn about the auditing features on their server, they are tempted to audit everything all the time. Note that an auditing service, like any other computer service, uses computer resources. If your server is busy auditing every little event that occurs, the server won't have any time to actually serve.

Figure 8-3 shows the types of security events that Windows 2000 can audit. These events are similar on Windows NT. You can audit both successful events and unsuccessful events. For instance, you can audit only unsuccessful logon attempts to monitor who is trying—unsuccessfully—to log on. Repeated attempts to log on as the administrator may indicate an attempt to gain unauthorized access to the network.

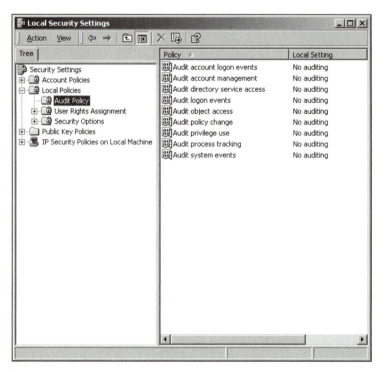

Figure 8-3   Windows 2000 security audit events

Other events that can be audited include access to files and printers. Be careful with auditing too many of this type of event, as each file access creates several entries in the security log. To audit these events, you must first turn on object access auditing and select success, failure, or both. Then, you must select the objects whose access you want to audit, what type of access to audit, and which users should be audited when accessing the objects. For example, you can select a folder to audit and then audit access by all users or just one user or a group of users.

Figure 8-4 shows the dialog box to turn on auditing for a folder in Windows 2000. File access auditing is available only if the disk is formatted in NTFS. Hands-on Projects 8-1 and 8-2 at the end of this chapter walk you through the process of enabling various auditing procedures.

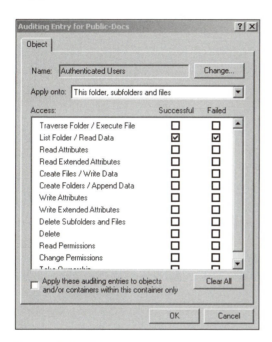

Figure 8-4   Object access auditing

You use the Event Viewer utility to view the security audit logs. Event Viewer allows you to review several logs related to system information, including security, system events, and application events. The security logs should be checked regularly on systems that have auditing enabled.

As I mentioned, you must be careful when choosing how many events and objects to audit. Figure 8-5 shows the Windows 2000 Security Log. The highlighted entry is the log entry for a failed logon attempt. The 12 entries above that entry are the success audits generated for opening of a folder only one time. Twelve entries for simply opening a folder! The auditing enabled on that folder is the List Folder/Read Data audit. As you can see, auditing creates considerable disk access and uses considerable processor time.

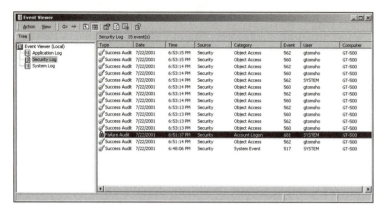

Figure 8-5   Windows 2000 Security Log

One recommendation for using auditing in a moderately secure to highly secure environment is to enable object access auditing only on very sensitive files or folders. Auditing can be turned on after security is initially set up to monitor for any problems. Thereafter, it can be turned on periodically or when problems with security are suspected. You can also elect to enable only access failures. Enabling access failures permits you to view whether users are attempting to gain unauthorized access to files. If an employee is engaging in suspicious activity, auditing can be enabled to watch for only that employee's attempts to access sensitive files.

Additional auditing functions include changes in account information, changes in network or security policies, and access to directory services. Depending on your environment, it may be wise to audit some of these events so that you have an audit trail of changes that have occurred in your security framework. The security logs can be checked and archived each day, if necessary, to prevent them from becoming unwieldy.

Securing the Network from Viruses

In today's Internet-connected networks, virus attacks are a constant threat. Users download programs that contain viruses, bring floppy disks in from home that contain viruses, and open e-mail attachments that contain viruses. The first thing you should do to help prevent the spread of viruses on your network is to require every desktop and server to have virus-scanning software active. Ideally, you should use a virus scanner that is resident in memory and scans every program file or document accessed. Documents should be scanned if the document type may contain macros, and servers should run virus-scanning software that scans every file read or written to and from the server drives.

Preventing viruses from infecting program or document files on servers is critical. I once had a virus infect several hundred computers in just a few hours because an executable file on a server became infected. When users logged on, the first thing that happened was the execution of a logon script that ran a menu program. The menu program was the infected file, so every computer that was set to run that program became infected. After the tedious task of cleaning each computer of the virus was completed, two changes were made: The menu program was flagged as read-only, and all servers were equipped with virus-scanning software. If the read-only attribute is set on a file, a virus cannot attach itself to the file. This action prevents the spread of the virus.

 Note that I am referring to the read-only file attribute, not the read-only access permission. Permissions apply to users or groups of users, but attributes apply to a particular file regardless of the access permissions.

E-mail viruses are the rage these days. Of course, the e-mail attachments are the real problem. The sad thing is that these viruses are so easy to avoid if users would only think a second before opening every e-mail that is sent to them. Your computer does not become infected with a virus simply because you read the body of an e-mail message. You must open the attachment that comes with the e-mail message. Thus, if you receive an e-mail that has an attachment and you are not expecting the file, do not open it. If the sender is someone you know, that does not mean it is safe. Such viruses usually spread from user to user by using a user's Address Book to find new victims. Call the person who sent the e-mail and ask about the attachment. If the person did not realize he or she sent you this e-mail, it is probably a virus. Simply delete the e-mail message to remove the virus.

 New virus types are developed all the time and new operating system security holes are constantly being created and discovered. Because of the nature of some of the newer versions of Microsoft's Internet Explorer Web browser and Outlook mail program, certain types of viruses can be transmitted without the receiver opening the e-mail attachments. In fact, these viruses can be transmitted simply by visiting an infected Web page. For more information on this and other virus information, see *www.sans.org/newlook/alerts/virus.htm*.

The hoax virus is one of the worst kinds of viruses. Someone sends an e-mail proclaiming that Microsoft, the U.S. government, or some other well-known organization has just discovered a new virus that will format your hard drive, erase your BIOS, or perform some other nefarious deed. Usually, you are warned that the virus appears in an e-mail message. The e-mail goes on to say that you should immediately send this message to everyone you know to inform them of this terrible virus. The flood of e-mail that inevitably occurs *is* the virus. This type of hoax clogs e-mail servers, decreases productivity, and generally wastes time. If you are really concerned that the virus warning you received is real, check the Web site of the organization that the e-mail references or check the Web site of some of the well-known antivirus software companies. If the supposed virus is not mentioned at these sites, stop this type of virus in its tracks and delete the e-mail without forwarding it to hundreds of your friends and acquaintances.

Virus protection is expensive, but the loss of data and productivity that can occur when a network becomes infected by a virus is much more costly. Keep your virus-scanning software updated! The temptation is to set it and forget it—but last year's antivirus software does not protect you from this year's viruses. Most antiviral packages can be updated over the Internet with little trouble, provided you have a paid subscription.

 For the latest on Internet security issues, particularly those dealing with Internet viruses, go to the definitive resource for Internet security: *www.cert.org.*

Maintaining Security with Patches

The first thing you should do after installing your server operating system is to install the latest security patches. Operating system releases are a work in progress. Usually within weeks after a version has been released, patches are available to fix bugs, resolve compatibility issues, and close security holes.

Windows operating systems are notorious for containing security holes. Microsoft publishes **service packs**, which are a compilation of bug fixes, upgrades, and security fixes. The service packs can be downloaded from Microsoft's Web site after they are released. Between the release of service packs, there are usually a number of other downloads that can be installed to fix problems or resolve security issues. If your network is security-conscious, you should check Microsoft's Web site regularly for security patches. The Windows Update feature, which can be found on the Start menu of your computer, can automate this process for you to some extent.

NOVELL NETWARE SECURITY

Many of the features and concerns for security that exist in a Microsoft server environment exist in a NetWare environment as well. There are some key differences, however, and it is on the differences that we will focus. For instance, the NetWare operating system differs from Windows operating systems in that it is a true client/server operating system. In other words, the server cannot be used to run user applications, and you don't have the concept of local access to files or network access to files. All access to files in a NetWare environment is done via the network, except in rare cases.

NetWare operating systems have provided a high level of security for a number of years. The NetWare operating system has been rated for class C2 security since NetWare 4.11 became available in 1997. C2 security is a rating established by National Computer Security Center and is required of operating systems used in many government offices.

 Windows 2000 is the first Microsoft operating system to achieve a C2 security rating.

The NetWare operating system provides security in four areas: logon security, NDS security, file system security, and system console security. The following sections discuss each of these areas.

NetWare Account and Logon Security

NetWare's account security has much in common with the account security available in Microsoft operating systems. There are options for minimum-length passwords, password expiration, and account lockout.

Account lockout in a NetWare environment can be found under the category of Intruder Detection in the Netware Administrator. When Intruder Detection is enabled, an entry in a log file is generated—as well as a notification on the NetWare console—when a user has failed to log on after attempting to do so the specified number of times. Other options found in a NetWare environment include restrictions on logon times and logon location, just as you found in the Windows server environment.

One restriction that prevents users from logging on at another computer and then walking away is a limit on **concurrent connections**. Concurrent connections occur when a user is logged into the network from more than one station at the same time. Users can be limited in terms of the number of times they are logged on to the server, forcing the user to log off from one location before logging on from another. This feature is especially useful if you have an IT staff member with administrative privileges who sometimes needs to log on to other users' computers. This person can get distracted and forget about the logon. Fortunately, if he or she tries to log on somewhere else, the logon will be rejected, prompting recollection of the earlier logon.

NDS Security

Novell Directory Services (NDS) is a service and a database that contains NetWare network security and resource information. NDS is managed through the NetWare Administrator, which is run from a workstation.

NDS facilitates the design of network security so that it mirrors your company's organization. When users log on to a NetWare network, they actually log on to NDS rather than to a particular server. Access to resources such as servers and printers is then controlled through NDS security. Users and administrators can be assigned rights called trustee rights to some or all of the NDS database. This approach makes control of the network simple and straightforward.

Figure 8-6 shows the NetWare Administrator's view of the NDS database. This structure makes it convenient to assign IT personnel as administrators to part of the network resources, thereby delegating administrative authority. Windows 2000 Server and Windows XP Server provide a similar capability with Microsoft's Active Directory.

8

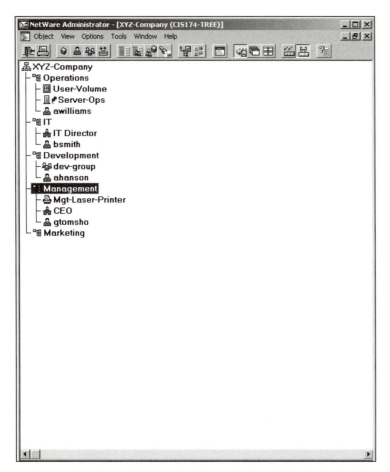

Figure 8-6   Novell's NDS

NetWare File System Security

The file system security on a NetWare server provides most of the features available in a Windows environment. A notable difference is that NetWare has a proprietary disk format and cannot use the industry-standard FAT or FAT32 file systems. You must be able to log on to the NetWare server from a workstation to gain access to the file system; this restriction applies to administrators as well as to other users. Thus, even if an administrator leaves the file server cabinet unlocked, a passerby will not be able to conveniently view the contents of the server disks. This is unlike Windows server operating systems; anyone who has physical access to a server that has someone logged on can easily view the data on the disks.

There are some rudimentary tools you can load from the NetWare console to gain access to files locally, but this endeavor would take time and require considerable knowledge of NetWare. Hopefully your server will not be unattended for that long!

NetWare Console Security

The NetWare console is the control panel for the NetWare server. It is used to configure NetWare server components, start the server, shut down the server, and perform maintenance operations. It is a plain, character-based, command-line interface, much like the command interpreter in DOS or the shell in UNIX. Figure 8-7 shows the NetWare console and the help screen that lists the available commands.

```
Z:\rconsole.exe                                                    _ □ ×
MAGAZINE INSERTED          MAGAZINE NOT INSERTED      MAGAZINE NOT REMOVED
MAGAZINE REMOVED           MEDIA INSERTED             MEDIA NOT INSERTED
MEDIA NOT REMOVED          MEDIA REMOVED              MEMORY
MEMORY MAP                 MIRROR STATUS              MODULES
MOUNT                      NAME                       NATIVE2ASCII
NCP STATS                  NCP ADDRESSES              NCP TRACE
NCP DUMP                   OFF                        PAUSE
PROTECT                    PROTECTION                 PROTOCOL
PROTOCOL REGISTER          PSM                        PUER
REGISTER MEMORY            REM                        REMIRROR PARTITION
REMOVE STORAGE ADAPTER     RESET ROUTER               RESET ENVIRONMENT
RESET SERVER               RESTART SERVER             RMIC
RMIREGISTRY                SCAN ALL                   SCAN FOR NEW DEVICES
SEARCH                     SECURE CONSOLE             SEND
SERIALVER                  SET                        SET TIME
SET TIME ZONE              SETENV                     SPEED
SPOOL                      START PROCESSORS           STOP PROCESSORS
SWAP                       TIME                       TRACK OFF
TRACK ON                   UNBIND                     UNLOAD
VERSION                    VMDISMOUNT                 VMMOUNT
VMVOLUMES                  VOLUME

Type HELP [command] to display specific command help
CONSTELLATION:                                                      O
CONSTELLATION:
```

Figure 8-7   NetWare console

As I mentioned, the NetWare console is not meant to provide access to files or to perform everyday management functions. After NetWare is installed and running, the NetWare console can be largely forgotten. Most of the day-to-day management of your NetWare network is done using NetWare Administrator. Note, however, that there are some aspects of the console that affect security.

Security Issues Surrounding the Console

NetWare servers are started from a DOS partition. This DOS partition, along with DOS floppy disks, is accessible to the NetWare console. An administrator may keep some debugging tools on the DOS partition so that they are available if the NetWare partitions become inaccessible, but therein lies the problem. Remember earlier in the chapter when we mentioned that physically securing the NetWare server was important? It's important not so much because users can easily get to the files, but rather because there are tools available that will allow someone to load a program from a floppy disk so as to subvert security. One of these programs allows the administrator password to be changed.

The only way that an unauthorized user can load such a program is if the program is carried in on a floppy disk or if the program resides on a NetWare server volume.

You can prevent access to the floppy disk or any DOS device by using the remove dos command. To prevent someone from loading a program from an unauthorized location on a NetWare volume, you can go one step better by using the secure console command. The secure console command performs the function that remove dos does, but adds some additional security by preventing certain configuration commands. Finally, before you walk away from your NetWare server, you can lock the console so that an administrator password is required to gain any access to the console—an approach much like a password-protected screen saver.

Enabling C2 Security

NetWare is capable of achieving the government's C2 security rating, but that rating is not met by default. To enable this level of security, you must type the secure.ncf command at the NetWare console. When you do so, various security-related configuration commands are executed. The secure.ncf command is a **NetWare Command File (NCF)**, which acts much like a batch file for NetWare. Some of the tasks performed by secure.ncf include disabling unencrypted passwords, enabling the automatic repair of damaged volumes, and enabling several NetWare Core Protocol commands that improve security at the packet level.

NetWare Security and System Logs

Like Windows server operating systems, NetWare has a built-in capability to audit activity that takes place on the server. Auditing is enabled, configured, and managed through a character-based program called Auditcon.exe. Auditcon supports auditing of NDS changes, logon and logout events, and file system activity.

Figure 8-8 shows the Auditcon configuration screen at the top and the audit report screen on the bottom. This report has logged users being added and renamed, and it shows passwords being changed. By default, no auditing occurs until you enable the particular events you wish to audit. Auditing can be enabled on just particular sections of the NDS structure. Figure 8-8 shows the configuration and report screen for the NDS database section called Operations.

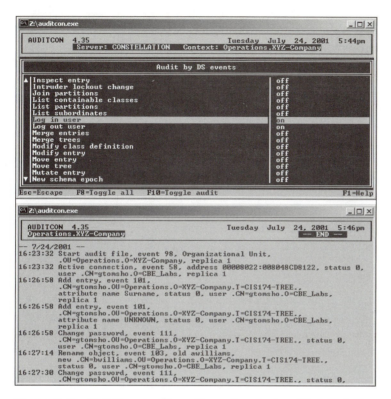

Figure 8-8   NetWare audit configuration and audit report screens

Certain events on a NetWare server are always logged. For example, it is possible to access the NetWare console remotely from a workstation. When someone accesses the console screen remotely, an entry is placed in the system log and a message is displayed on the console screen. (The system log, which is named SYS$LOG.ERR, can contain other events as well, including the NDS database opening or closing, network services starting or stopping, and system errors.)

Figure 8-9 gives you a look at the SYS$LOG.ERR file, which is opened in Notepad. The highlighted entries indicate a remote console connection and disconnection. The connection log lists the address of the workstation that made the connection. In one company, this log file came in very handy when investigating a disgruntled employee who had the remote console password and decided to create some problems on the NetWare server. Because the company knew the MAC address of the employee's workstation and the time and date when the event occurred, it was able to catch the employee red-handed. His rights were promptly revoked and all administrative passwords were changed.

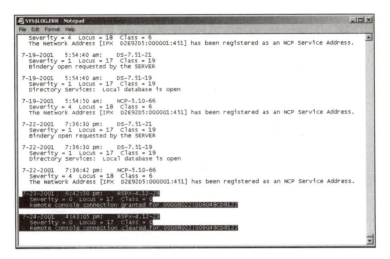

Figure 8-9   NetWare SYS$LOG.ERR file

For information on Linux security-related issues, go to *www.linuxsecurity.com*. For information on UNIX security-related issues, try *www.acm.uiuc.edu/ workshops/security/* or *www.deter.com/unix/*, which contains links to some great white papers.

INTERNETWORK DEVICE SECURITY

You may think that the security measures mentioned so far are enough to keep your hubs, switches, and routers physically secured. However, all of these devices can be configured remotely via software, so it is critical to maintain good security practices with your internetworking equipment just as you do with your servers. In this section of the chapter, you'll learn that hubs and switches must be secured to prevent unauthorized configuration of these devices. In addition, you'll learn that routers are important because they are often the window between your network and outside networks.

Securing Hubs and Switches

When we talk about securing hubs, we are not talking about securing the $19.95 variety of hub, but rather a software-configurable, $700 type of hub, as discussed in Chapter 3. These hubs can be remotely configured through SNMP software, allowing ports to be partitioned, the hub to be segmented, and remote monitoring to be configured.

The danger is not so much that users can access sensitive data if they can remotely configure your hubs; rather, it's the fact that they can create problems for your network. Some managed hubs require a password to gain access to the management capabilities; others rely on the SNMP protocol to maintain security.

SNMP functions are classified into two categories: read and write. A password is associated with the read function, and a different password is associated with the write function. By default, these passwords are "public" and "private," respectively. The read password can be safely left at its default, but you will want to change the write password to some other value. You can then set the corresponding passwords in your network management program to gain access to the hub.

Switches can be quite a bit more complex than hubs. Besides SNMP, some switches have an operating system built into the switch, much as routers do. Switches can contain VLAN settings, switching mode configurations, port security settings, and port monitoring settings, among other features. Changes to any of these settings could seriously affect the operation of your network. Some switches are accessible from a convenient HTTP interface, which, if left unsecured, provides an easy way for someone to change settings.

What harm can someone do if they have access to these switch settings? A person can change VLAN settings, for example, by making a port become a member of a different VLAN. As a result, those users who are connected to that port will lose connectivity to the network because their workstation IP address will not match the new VLAN settings. In addition, a user could change his or her workstation's VLAN to gain access to an otherwise restricted area of the network.

For security reasons, some ports can be set to accept connections from workstations only with particular MAC addresses. In a highly secure network, each switch port could be configured to accept the MAC address of only one particular workstation. For example, this setup could prevent someone from hooking up a laptop with protocol analyzer software installed for the purposes of capturing sensitive data. A user who gains access to the switch configuration would have the opportunity to change this setting so that a different computer could be hooked up to the port with unauthorized software installed. Fortunately, secure ports can be set to disable the port if an unauthorized address is detected.

The port monitoring function that was discussed in Chapter 4 allows one port to monitor traffic from one or more of the other switch ports. This handy feature allows you to analyze and monitor data in a switched network. However, if someone sets the port monitor to the port linked to his or her workstation, that person could then see and capture all data on that switch. The port monitoring function also slows the performance of the switch and should be used only for short periods of time.

As you see, there are numerous reasons to keep your switches secure. Most switches that have some of the advanced features mentioned here have console passwords to prevent unauthorized access. A switch may also have a timeout specified, after which the switch disconnects from an idle console connection. This timeout safeguards against an administrator who leaves an unattended console connection.

 There is no standard regarding how switches should implement security, and the particular commands to set security vary from switch to switch, even within products from the same manufacturer.

Figure 8-10 shows a console connection with a Cisco Catalyst 1900 switch. The screen shows the console security settings available on that switch.

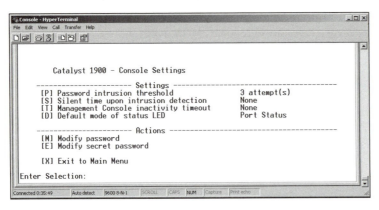

Figure 8-10   Switch console security settings

Securing Routers

Router security is a network specialty all its own. Volumes can and have been written about router security, but that level of detail is beyond the scope of this book. Instead, this section discusses some of things you can do to secure your routers from unauthorized access and takes a brief look at the use of routers to implement network security in the form of access control lists. We will also examine accounting functions that are available on some routers. The discussion in this section is based on the features available on many Cisco routers; routers from other manufacturers have similar features.

Router Logon Security

The first thing you want to do to secure your routers is to assign passwords to the various logon methods. Most routers have several methods by which the configuration and monitoring functions may be accessed: direct console connection, remote dial-up, virtual terminal, and HTTP access. It is possible to assign different passwords to each of these methods so that you can control who can access the routers through the various methods.

Direct console connections require a serial port connection with a dumb terminal or a computer that is running a terminal emulation program such as Windows HyperTerminal. Administrators use this method to access and configure routers initially. There is a password only when the router is configured, and the console password is among the first that should be set. The remote dial-up connection is usually a serial port on the router (called the AUX port on Cisco routers) that can be connected to a modem, permitting a console connection remotely. Even though the AUX port is designed for a modem connection, it should be assigned a password even if you do not connect a modem because it can be used to access the router with a direct cable connection, just like the console port.

Virtual terminal (VTY) ports are so named because they allow a terminal-like connection through a network Telnet connection. There is no physical terminal port as there is with the console and AUX ports. These ports are accessible only after the router is configured with an IP address and connected to the network. Although passwords are highly recommended for these ports, Cisco's default security is to disallow Telnet connections on these ports unless a password is set. Therefore, if you forget to set a password on the virtual terminal ports, all Telnet connections will be refused.

Cisco routers have two security modes: user mode and privileged mode. User mode permits router monitoring commands but no commands that can change the operation of the router. Privileged mode permits full configuration of the router, and access to this mode should be restricted by another password. This password usually is encrypted in the configuration file; thus someone who comes in will see the configuration file but not the privileged-mode password. User-mode passwords are normally stored in the configuration file as **clear text**—that is, text that is not encrypted. For additional security, you can turn on password encryption that will apply to all passwords entered into the configuration file.

Although it may be typical to simply assign passwords to the various methods of accessing the routers, it is also possible to assign combination user names and passwords, giving each user a different level of permission. This method for securing access to the router is preferable to simply using passwords if you have several IT staff members who must access the routers from time to time. This way, you can give employees differing levels of access.

Cisco routers permit 16 levels of access to be defined. Commands that can be executed in privileged mode can be assigned to different access levels. For example, you may want a staff member to be able to access the router privileged mode but not to enter configuration mode. Additional user name and password options permit you to store the actual user and password database list on a security server.

Cisco routers support the industry standard **Terminal Access Controller Access Control System (TACACS)** protocol, which provides authentication, authorization, and accounting security services (AAA). Other security standards that Cisco routers support include **Remote Address Dial–In User Service (RADIUS)**, which provides similar services as TACACS, and **Kerberos**, an authentication method based on encryption keys and tickets that avoids sending actual passwords across the network. For more information on these and other security methods, try Cisco's Web site at *www.cisco.com/warp/public/44/solutions/network/security.shtml*.

Because router security is of vital importance to a network's overall security, the options for securing the router from unauthorized access are numerous. For an excellent description of the options available on Cisco routers, go to the company's Web page at *www.cisco.com*, and search on the string "passwords and privileges commands." The resulting page will list all available commands and options for setting passwords and access privileges.

8

Turn Off Unused Services

Hackers can exploit any network services that are left unsecured. For example, if there is no need to use the HTTP protocol that is available to access some routers and switches, this service should be turned off. Another service that is frequently available on a router that may give valuable information to a hacker is the finger service. It can reveal to a finger client the logon names of users who are currently connected to a system. This service gives hackers information about the users in a system, the addresses from which they are connected, and the lines to which they are connected.

Figure 8-11 shows the output of the finger command used on a Cisco router. By default, Cisco routers have the finger service enabled. This service, along with services such as the UDP and TCP echo service, can and should be disabled.

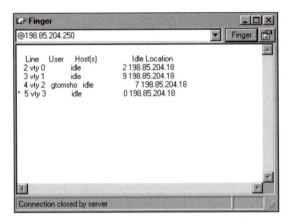

Figure 8-11   Fingering a Cisco router

One method to verify which services are active on a router (or any TCP/IP device) is to use a **port scanner**. This utility allows you to specify an IP address and a range of TCP or UDP ports to be scanned. For TCP services, the port scanner sends a TCP SYN packet for the port it is scanning. If a TCP service with the specified port is active on the device, the device will return a SYN ACK packet. If the service is not active, the device will respond with a TCP reset packet. For UDP services, the port scanner sends a UDP packet to the device with the port specified. If the service is active, there will frequently be no response and a data timeout will occur. This timeout occurs because the scanner is interested only in knowing whether the port is active.

Recall that UDP is an unreliable transport protocol and does not return acknowledgments. If the UDP service is not active, the device will send an ICMP message with the code "destination port unreachable."

Figure 8-12 shows the port scanner utility available with Wildpacket's iNetTools package. In the figure, the port scanner is scanning a Cisco router for both TCP and UDP ports. It finds the Telnet service available for TCP and UDP, the bootp service, the finger service, and the HTTP service. This type of utility is frequently used to find vulnerabilities in all types of IP devices.

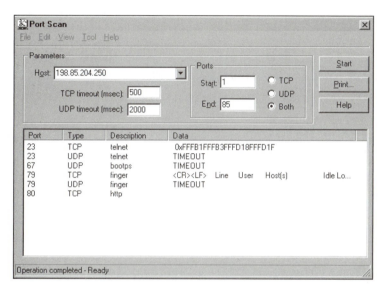

Figure 8-12   Port scanner

Router Access Control Lists

When most people think of implementing security with routers, **access control lists (ACLs)** are usually what come to mind. ACLs are rules that are applied to router interfaces and that determine what traffic should be allowed in or out of that interface. By default, routers allow all traffic in and out of their interfaces, so ACLs are designed to restrict that free flow of traffic.

> It is not my intention to go into detail about the fine art of writing ACLs; I only want to discuss some of the common uses of ACLs. For an excellent reference for ACLs (frequently referred to as simply access lists), check out *www.cisco.com/univercd/cc/td/doc/product/lan/cat6000/sw_5_4/msfc/ acc_list.htm.*

Access lists are used to keep people outside your network from accessing particular resources or services inside the network or to keep users in your network from accessing resources they should not have access to outside the network. Another common use for access lists is to protect your network from the Internet and the people out there who may want to view, steal, or destroy your data. Sometimes, would-be networking gurus simply want to bring your network down for the fun of it or just to prove that they can.

Protecting your network from those with malicious intent on the Internet is usually left to specialty devices—firewalls. Sometimes, however, routers are used as firewalls or in conjunction with firewalls. If your access list is to serve as a firewall from the Internet or as a front-line defense working with a firewall, it should be designed to allow only what is necessary into the network and deny everything else. Fortunately, an access list's default operation is to deny everything.

The rules in an access list are applied by the router to traffic that comes through a particular interface. These rules are executed sequentially—that is, starting with the first rule in the list. Once a packet matches a rule, access list processing stops. Therefore, when making your list, you need to place your most specific rules at the top of the list and allow only what is necessary.

As an example of allowing only what is necessary, assume that you have a Web server that will be accessed from the Internet. You should create a rule that allows only TCP traffic on port 80 that is addressed to the specific address of the Web server rather than allowing in all traffic that is addressed to the Web server.

The following pseudocode access list allows Web traffic to a server and FTP traffic to a different server. It also allows Telnet traffic from one particular network to one of your servers. This access list denies everything else.

1. Permit TCP port 80 from anywhere to 199.19.44.11.

2. Permit TCP port 21 from anywhere to 199.19.44.14.

3. Permit TCP port 23 from network 156.11.14.0 255.255.255.0 to 199.19.44.100.

What's missing? This access list appears to permit the required traffic but it doesn't deny everything else as required. Remember that access lists, by default, deny everything. Thus, after line 3, there is an implied "deny everything else statement" at line 4. This is not always what you intend. My suggestion is that you go ahead and add a final statement to your access list that explicitly denies everything else so that you don't forget about it. This implicit rule about access lists fooled me recently. The access list was supposed to deny access from just one particular subnet and allow everything else, so I wrote the following access list (in pseudocode):

1. Deny all IP traffic from network 144.19.22.0 255.255.0.0 to everywhere.

When the network configuration was tested, it took a couple of minutes to remember that there is an implied "deny everything" at the end of the list, so nothing was going through. I added another line to the access list:

1. Deny all IP traffic from network 144.19.22.0 255.255.0.0 to everywhere.

2. Permit everything.

Much better!

Did you know that network administrators frequently block the traffic that is created by the Ping utility, which uses ICMP? This blocking is done because an outsider could conceivably flood the network with constant pings to network resources (another form of a denial of service attack). Before you set up your access list or firewall to block all ICMP traffic, however, it is important to consider the other uses for ICMP. ICMP is used not only for determining whether a network resource is available, but also for identifying devices to send other types of status messages.

As an example of a legitimate use of ICMP, recall that Windows uses a technique to determine the smallest MTU between the source and destination device so as to optimize TCP segment sizes. Windows does so by setting the Do Not Fragment bit in the IP header of all packet transmissions. If a device receives a segment that is too large for the MTU of a link to which the packet must be sent, the device normally fragments the packet. If the Do Not Fragment bit is set, the device sends an ICMP message back to the sender indicating that fragmentation is required. If Windows receives such an ICMP message, it adjusts the segment size downward and sends the segment again. This goes on until Windows does not receive an ICMP message back. If your access list blocks all ICMP messages, this mechanism will not work and you may not be able to reach certain destinations. So, while the rule that you should allow only necessary traffic holds, be sure that you deny only what you intend to deny.

Access lists can also be set to deny particular types of ICMP messages. To deny the traffic created by the Ping and Trace utilities, set your access list to deny ICMP Echo Request messages. Because the Ping and Trace utilities are good troubleshooting tools, it is also a good idea to permit ICMP Echo Requests to leave your network and ICMP Echo Reply messages to come into your network. You should block only the ICMP Echo Requests originating outside your network.

Using access lists on routers to protect your network from Internet-based intruders is possible, but the configuration tasks can be numerous and complicated, so it is often better to leave that job to dedicated firewalls. Router access lists can, however, be put to good use to better secure your network from inside threats. Large networks with many subnets may have some resources that are open to everyone in the organization and some resources that should be accessed only by those personnel in a particular subnet or with a particular IP address. This specification gives your sensitive resources an extra layer of security beyond password security. If the network traffic cannot even get to the server, then there is no way to log on to that server, even if someone discovers a user name and password. Furthermore, this approach adds an extra layer of security to those resources in the event that someone on the outside has gotten past the firewall security.

Access lists on internal routers can also deny bandwidth-robbing applications from being used on your network. For example, it may be difficult to keep users from installing chat, instant messaging, or peer-to-peer applications on their workstations, but you can at least deny those applications from using your expensive and scarce WAN bandwidth. You need only find out which TCP ports are used by the unauthorized applications and deny packets of that type from crossing the routers.

8

Router Accounting

It is one thing to have your access lists and other security measures in place; it is another thing to know how often the security measures are being put to good use. Router accounting can give you a better picture of exactly what is being attempted on your routers and your network.

Accounting on Cisco routers is available as a built-in function that logs IP traffic by source and destination address, including the number of packets and total bytes sent. You can also log access list violations, enabling you to detect whether a large number of unsuccessful access attempts are coming from particular addresses. This type of accounting is enabled on each interface that you wish to log.

In addition, you can use more advanced accounting functions available with the Cisco AAA system. This type of accounting requires a TACACS or RADIUS server. AAA accounting can provide detailed reports regarding the bandwidth used by particular subnets for billing purposes. It also permits logging of all activity that occurs on the router, including commands entered and services used. This type of accounting can provide a detailed audit trail of configuration and access activity performed on your router. For more information, see the AAA documentation on Cisco's Web site.

Firewalls

A firewall is a network device that is designed to filter network traffic according to a set of rules. The purpose of a firewall is to protect your network from malicious or otherwise undesirable data from getting inside your network and to limit which users inside your network may access outside data. It sounds like something you can do with router access lists, but firewalls have advanced capabilities in these areas.

This section, reviews the following information: Application layer filtering of packets, security provided through encryption and decryption methods, filtering packets based on session information, network address translation, and the types of firewalls commonly available.

Application Layer Filtering

The ability to filter traffic at the Application layer is a feature needed primarily because of threat posed by the undesirable content and potentially harmful applications available on the Internet. While routers inspect packets based on the Network and Transport layer packet headers, firewalls can inspect the actual data portion of the packet to see what type of data that packet is carrying.

For those corporate networks that wish to prohibit access to adult-content sites or other undesirable-content sites, a firewall can help with that effort. A firewall can determine that a packet is carrying HTTP data by inspecting the source port number of the packet. What if the Web site uses a nonstandard HTTP port? Fortunately, a firewall can examine the actual data in the packet and determine that HTTP data is present, regardless of the port number used. In addition, while the data is being inspected, the firewall can inspect the URL to determine the address of the Web site. A database can be accessed to determine whether the URL is acceptable under the corporate Internet access policy and then accept or reject the packet.

Another source of problems is Internet applications that can be harmful or disruptive to your network or employees. A firewall can be configured to filter out Java or other application types that are not known to be safe. This way, these applications are stopped at the firewall, while still allowing some potentially useful applications to be loaded.

Encryption/Decryption

Many networks employ encryption techniques to safeguard their data as it travels across the Internet and even within the corporate network. A firewall can be made an integral part of the encryption/decryption process. If the firewall is included in the encryption/decryption process, then it can still perform some of the other duties required of it, such as Application layer filtering. If it is not included in the process, then the firewall would not be able to inspect the packet data.

Cisco firewalls can use encryption just for authenticating access to resources or for performing authentication in conjunction with data encryption. If only authentication encryption is used, once a session is established and the client has been authenticated, the transfer of data is not encrypted. For more secure applications, both the authentication process and the actual transfer of data can be encrypted.

Session-Oriented Packet Filtering

Access lists look only at source and destination addresses and at source and destination ports to determine whether a packet should be permitted or denied. Sometimes, only one or two of those fields are inspected. Hackers sometimes break into networks by taking over a communication session that is in progress or, in some cases, packets are sent for the sole purpose of making network resources unavailable to valid users of the resource.

To counteract this threat, firewalls can inspect packet headers beyond the fields that are specified in access lists. TCP packets can be inspected for reasonable values in the TCP source and destination port even if an access list is designed to inspect only the destination port. This ability prevents a hacker from interjecting TCP packets in the middle of an established session, because the source port of the hacker's packets will be different from the valid sender's source port.

The TCP Flags field also can be inspected, along with sequence and acknowledgment numbers. This inspection guarantees that arriving packets are part of the same session. One common way for hackers to cause problems on the network is to send TCP SYN packets with an invalid source address. When a server responds with the SYN ACK packet, there will never be a corresponding ACK to finish the three-way handshake. This problem leaves the server with open sessions that are not being used for valid purposes.

If enough of these packets are sent to a server, the server will not be able to respond to valid requests. This is called a denial-of-service attack. The sole purpose of this type of attack is to deny valid users from accessing the resource.

Because UDP is not connection-oriented, the same risks are not present for UDP packets. Nevertheless, firewalls can still inspect UDP packets to determine whether the packets belong to the same communication session as previously seen packets. This task is accomplished by inspecting the source and destination IP addresses, the IP protocol field, and the source and destination port information.

Network Address Translation

Network Address Translation (NAT) is an integral part of what a firewall does. NAT is generally used to change the source IP address of packets originating inside a company's network as the packets pass through the firewall. It hides the actual IP addresses assigned to workstations and servers inside a corporate LAN. This strategy not only provides additional security for the corporate network, but also helps solve the IP address shortage. A company can assign all devices inside the corporate network IP addresses from any of the three private ranges of addresses. Then, as a packet passes through the company firewall, the private address is translated into a public IP address. When an Internet host responds to the packet, the firewall translates the public address back to the correct private address.

The added security offered by NAT is obvious. An Internet user cannot try to access a workstation inside the corporate LAN if the computer inside the LAN is using a private IP address, because private IP addresses are not permitted to travel on the Internet. You would have to guess the public address being used by a particular workstation to access that workstation.

How can NAT help solve the IP address shortage? Rather than translating one public address for every private address used on the LAN, a variation on NAT called **port address translation (PAT)** can be used. PAT can use IP addresses along with port numbers in the address translation. The firewall simply keeps a table of IP address/port number pairs that correspond to the private IP addresses in the LAN. Because the port number field in the TCP and UDP header is 16 bits, conceivably a single public IP address could be used to support a maximum of 65,536 private IP address translations. The practical limit is about 4000 PAT translations per IP address.

For an extensive treatment of NAT and its configuration, see *www.cisco.com/warp/public/556/index.shtml*.

Types of Firewalls

Firewalls are available as stand-alone equipment, like a router, or as a software system you install on a computer. Software-based firewalls tend to have simpler user interfaces for configuration because the software can utilize the resources of the host operating system. Note, however, that some software-based firewalls can be installed on a PC without an operating system. In this case, the firewall is usually configured remotely from a second workstation. Software-based firewalls that run on an existing operating system such as NetWare, UNIX, or Windows depend on the reliability of the host operating system. If the operating system crashes, so does the firewall.

Stand-alone firewalls are frequently faster because the hardware was designed specifically for the purpose of firewall functions. Plus, the initial setup is often easier, and the firewall can be more reliable because there is no host operating system with which to integrate.

There can be advantages to both types of firewalls, and no one choice fits every organization. For example, if your network is based on Novell NetWare servers, Novell's BorderManager software-based firewall may be a good choice because it integrates well with NDS and can be managed using the NetWare Administrator utility. If your network uses primarily Cisco equipment such as routers and switches, Cisco's PIX stand-alone firewall may fit your needs. The advantage is that you limit the number of companies that must be called for support when a problem arises. Note that not all firewalls are created equal, and a firewall solution that fits one organization's needs may not fit another organization's needs. You must carefully evaluate the expectations you have for your firewall and then research the available products before making a purchasing decision.

Personal firewalls are also becoming popular. They are installed on an individual workstation and are intended to protect only that workstation from outside intrusion. This issue has arisen in some corporate LANs, although most often this type of firewall is installed on home computers that are connected to the Internet. Fast Internet connections that are always connected, such as cable modem and DSL, have created the need for such personal firewalls.

For information on firewalls and links to a variety of firewall vendors and firewall information sites, visit *www.firewall.com*.

HACKER TOOLS TO STOP A HACKER

If you want to design a good, solid, network security infrastructure, hire a hacker. After all, a good hacker knows how to get into your network.

There are two kinds of hackers: those who try to compromise network or operating system security for sport or out of curiosity, and those who attempt to break into systems or crack software codes for personal gain or to cause harm. The latter are sometimes referred to as crackers. Both types of hackers are adept at using a variety of tools to discover your network resources, gain access to those resources, and possibly disable or hinder your network and network services.

The term "hacker" has several connotations. In the computer field, "hacker" commonly describes a person who uses novel or unconventional methods in software development. Another connotation for "hacker" is someone who is a sloppy or poorly trained software developer. The same term is now frequently used to describe someone who tries to break into computer systems or software. The last definition is used in this book. No offense is intended to those hackers who are one of the other types and who may wear the label proudly.

We begin the discussion by looking at how your network resources are discovered.

Discovering Network Resources

Before a hacker can gain access or cause problems with your network, he or she must get information about the network configuration and available resources. Some of the tools they use are tools we have already discussed: ping, trace, finger, and nslookup. These commands can help you find out which devices are available, identify name information for those devices, and possibly learn user information.

Other hacker-friendly utilities include ping scanners and port scanners. A **ping scanner** is an automated method for pinging a range of IP addresses. A port scanner determines which TCP or UDP ports are available on a particular device. In addition, **Whois** is a handy utility for discovering information about an Internet domain. You can find out the name and address of the domain name owner, contact information for the domain, and the DNS servers that manage the domain.

Figure 8-13 shows the results of a Whois query on the domain course.com.

Protocol analyzers are also useful for resource discovery because they allow you to capture packets and determine which protocols and services are running. They require access to the network media and are therefore effective tools only if the hacker is an internal user in the organization.

To protect your network from some of these utilities, you can take a variety of actions. The finger utility can be rendered useless if you turn off the finger service on all devices that support it. If you are not sure if a device supports finger, use finger on the device and see if you get a response.

Your access lists and firewalls, including personal firewalls, can block pings. You should port scan the devices in your network and turn off port services that are nonessential. To protect your network from internal users of protocol analyzers, you should secure your hubs and switches. The use of switches rather than hubs provides some protection because protocol analyzers capture packets that the NIC sees and a switch forwards only broadcasts and packets addressed to the particular host. To further prevent the use of analyzers, you can use NICs that do not support the promiscuous mode setting that analyzers require.

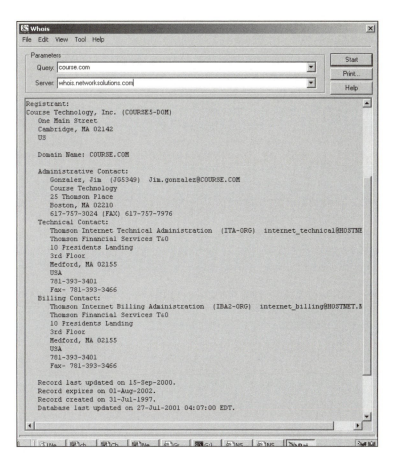

Figure 8-13   Whois results

Gaining Access to Network Resources

After a hacker has discovered the resources available on the network, the next step may be to gain access to those resources for the purposes of viewing, stealing, or destroying data. One of the first resources to open is one in which no password is set. Believe it or not, this situation happens more than you think. In my own hacker exploits (purely for educational purposes, of course), I have found numerous routers and switches that have been available through the Internet and that have had no passwords set. Your remedy to these types of exploits? Check your devices that support Telnet, FTP, e-mail, and Web services. Verify that passwords are set on resources that should remain secure and disable any services that are not required.

Often, the hacker runs into a resource that requires a user name and password. Finger can be used in some cases to discover user names. UNIX, NetWare, and Windows servers have default administrator names that are often unchanged—a fact that can be easily exploited by a hacker with a password hacking tool. Some of these utilities, such as l0phtcrack (a Windows NT password-cracking utility), use a systematic method of guessing passwords either from a dictionary of words or from an algorithm that uses all combinations of your choice of letters, numbers, and symbols. This type of cracking utility can be extremely CPU-intensive. If your passwords are strong, they are frequently impractical to use because it might take days or even weeks to guess very complex passwords. It is recommended that you use one of these password-cracking utilities on your own system to see if your passwords are sufficiently complex. A Web site that provides a very complete list of security tools and hacking tools, including password crackers, is *www.securiteam.com/tools/archive.html*.

Operating systems may have vulnerabilities that hackers can exploit to allow access without a password. Bugs in communication programs can permit hackers to gain access through methods that the operating system designers never envisioned. A well-known method of gaining access to some UNIX systems was through Web page forms. A hacker could construct input to a form that, when posted to the server, would cause the server to process the commands the hacker typed into the form.

Any Web pages developed for your servers that contain programs written with Java, JavaScript, CGI scripts, and ASP should be carefully screened before publishing. In addition, be sure to apply operating system security patches as soon as they are posted. Security holes in operating systems are usually announced and fixed quickly by the vendor. However, because the security flaw is announced, every hacker knows about it and will be trying it out—possibly on your systems.

Disabling Network Resources

A **denial of service (DoS)** attack is a hacker's attempt to tie up your network bandwidth or network services so that it renders those resources useless to legitimate users. Some may execute a DoS attack for fun; others may do it to satisfy a grudge. Three of the more common types of DoS attacks focus on tying up a server or network device: packet storms, half-open SYN attacks, and ping floods. There are readily available programs that can create these attacks for anyone willing to download the programs.

Packet storms typically use the UDP protocol because it is not connection oriented. One packet storm program called Pepsi5 sends a stream of UDP packets that have spoofed host addresses, causing the host to be unavailable to respond to other packets. A **spoofed address** is a source address that is inserted into a packet that is not the actual address of the sending station.

 An attack that exploits an operating system bug is a UDP bomb. A UDP bomb sends packets with an incorrect length field, which causes some systems to crash or freeze.

Half-open SYN attacks use the three-way handshake in TCP to tie up a server with TCP sessions that are invalid, thereby preventing real sessions from being created. The attacker sends a series of SYN packets with a valid port number, causing the server to respond with the SYN-ACK packet. The original SYN packet contains a spoofed source address, resulting in the server waiting for the final ACK in the three-way handshake until the server times out. If enough of these SYN packets are sent, the server will use all available connections and will be unable to service legitimate attempts to make a connection. Commonly available programs that create this type of attack include synk4.c and netpune.c.

A ping flood is exactly what it sounds like. A program sends a large number of ping packets, which are ICMP echo requests, to a host. They cause the host to reply, tying up CPU cycles and bandwidth. A variation is the smurf attack, in which echo requests are sent to a broadcast address. All of the requests contain the spoofed source address of the host that is to be smurfed. When the computers respond to the broadcast echo request, they send echo replies to the single host whose address is spoofed in the request packets. That host is then flooded with echo reply packets.

There is no end to the methods available to wreak havoc in a network. It is a good idea to become familiar with the tools that may be used against your network. If you know what the tools are, you can prepare defenses against such attacks. You can also use these tools to test the integrity of your network security. Firewalls, access lists, and strong operating system security are some of the ways to prevent these attacks or reduce their effects. Regardless of your tools, you should always start by devising a sound security policy that maps out your overall network security plan and contains provisions for auditing and revising the policy as your needs and technology change.

CHAPTER SUMMARY

◻ To the chief information officer, network security means more than job-specific tasks. He or she knows that the goal of network security is to protect the organization, its users, its customers, and its business partners from any threat to the integrity of the information that resides on or passes through the network, and from the consequences of misuse of network resources.

◻ The first mantra of security is this: If there is physical access to the equipment, there is no security. This concept applies not only to servers and workstations, but also to internetwork devices and even network media. No matter how strong your logon name and password schemes are, if a user has physical access, it does not take much effort gain access to data.

◻ The security features built into the Windows NT, Windows 2000, and Windows XP server operating systems include user account and logon security, file system and computer security, security auditing, protection of the network from viruses, and security using patches.

◻ The NetWare operating system differs from Windows operating systems in that it is a true client/server operating system. In other words, the server cannot be used to run user applications and you don't have the concept of local access to files or network access to files. All access to files in a NetWare environment is done via the network, except in rare cases.

❐ Hubs and switches must be secured to prevent unauthorized configuration of these devices. In addition, routers are important because they are often the window between your network and outside networks.

❐ There are two kinds of hackers: those who try to compromise network or operating system security for sport or out of curiosity, and those who attempt to break into systems or crack software codes for personal gain or to cause harm.

KEY TERMS

access control lists (ACLs) — Rules that are applied to router interfaces that determine what traffic should be allowed in or out of that interface.

account lockout — A policy that can be set to lock a user account after a set number of incorrect password attempts.

clear text — Text that is not encrypted; usually refers to passwords.

concurrent connections — Two or more simultaneous logons to a NetWare server by the same user from different workstations.

denial of service (DoS) — A hacker's attempt to tie up network bandwidth or network services so that it renders those resources useless to legitimate users.

file system security — A feature of a network operating system in which the administrator can assign file and folder permissions to users or groups of users.

Kerberos — An authentication method based on encryption keys and tickets, which avoids sending actual passwords across the network.

NetWare Command File (NCF) — A text file that contains one or more NetWare commands that can be executed with a single command, much like a DOS batch file.

Novell Directory Services (NDS) — A service and a database that contains all NetWare network security and resource information.

NTFS security — Access permissions that can be applied to a file or folder on an NTFS-formatted partition and that apply to both local access and network access.

ping scanner — An automated method for pinging a range of IP addresses.

port address translation (PAT) — A type of network address translation that uses a single address to represent multiple inside hosts by using unique port numbers for each host.

port scanner — A utility that determines which TCP or UDP ports are available on a particular device.

rack-mountable — Describes a network device or server that is designed to bolt to a standard 19-inch equipment rack.

Remote Address Dial-In User Service (RADIUS) — A security protocol that provides authentication services.

security policy — A document that describes the rules governing access to a company's information resources, ways that those rules are enforced, and steps taken in the event the rules are breached.

service packs — A compilation of bug fixes, upgrades, and security fixes for an operating system.

sharing security — Access permissions that are applied to a Windows share and that apply only to network access to the files contained in the share.

spoofed address — A source address that is inserted into a packet but is not the actual address of the sending station.

Terminal Access Controller Access Control System (TACACS) — A security protocol that provides authentication, authorization, and accounting security services (AAA).

virtual terminal (VTY) ports — Ports that allow a terminal-like connection via a network Telnet connection.

Whois — A utility for discovering information about an Internet domain.

8

REVIEW QUESTIONS

1. Network security should be as unobtrusive as possible. True or False?

2. A _____ is a document that describes the rules governing access to a company's information resources.

    a. permission list

    b. resource list

    c. security policy

    d. rule constraint

3. After a security policy is in place, it should remain a static document. True or False?

4. A company that engages in a(n) _____ network security policy may have simple or no passwords at all.

5. If there is physical access to the equipment, there is no security. True or False?

6. In Windows 2000, the server can be booted to a floppy disk. True or False?

7. Wiring that is not concealed in floors or ceilings should be concealed in _____ or other channeling devices to discourage access.

8. Servers rarely require more tightly controlled environmental conditions than do patch panels, hubs, and switches. True or False?

9. Windows passwords can be required to be a minimum number of characters. True or False?

10. To prevent users from rotating the same two passwords every time they need to change it, Windows has an option that remembers a maximum of _____ passwords before allowing a user to use a previously used password.

    a. 24

    b. 12

    c. 99

    d. 1

11. If security is a chief concern, you should use the _____ file system so that a person cannot boot to a DOS floppy disk and access the files stored on your Windows server.

12. _____ are a compilation of bug fixes, upgrades, and security fixes.

    a. Operating systems

    b. Patches

    c. Security holes

    d. Service packs

13. Account lockout in a NetWare environment can be found under the category of _____ in NetWare Administrator.

14. Concurrent connections occur when a user is logged into the network from only one station at a time. True or False?

15. Users and administrators can be assigned trustee rights to some or all of the NDS database. True or False?

16. NetWare servers are started from a(n) _____ partition.

17. A NetWare Command File (NCF) replaces the batch file in NetWare version 4. True or False?

18. SNMP functions are divided into two categories: read and write. True or False?

19. Direct console connections require a serial port connection with a dumb terminal or a computer that is running a terminal emulation program such as Windows _____.

20. Virtual terminal (VTY) ports allow a terminal-like connection through a network _____ connection.

21. You can encrypt clear text after the fact. True or False?

22. Cisco routers can have a maximum of _____ levels of access.

    a. 6

    b. 16

    c. 26

    d. 4

23. For TCP services, the port scanner sends a(n) _____ packet for the port it is scanning.

24. UDP is an unreliable transport protocol. True or False?

25. ACLs are _____ that are applied to router interfaces and that determine what traffic should be allowed in or out of that interface.

HANDS-ON PROJECTS

Project 8-1 Windows 2000 Logon Auditing

This project requires a Windows 2000 Professional computer that is not part of a domain. You also can use a Windows 2000 domain controller.

 To turn on Account Logon auditing for the domain controller, open the Domain Controller Security Policy Management Console in Administrative Tools on a domain controller. Then follow the steps starting from Step 2.

1. Click **Start**, point to **Programs**, click **Administrative Tools**, and click **Local Security Policy**.

2. Double-click the **Security Settings** icon until you see a folder called Local Policies.

3. Double-click the **Local Policies** folder, and then click the **Audit Policy** folder.

4. In the right pane of the Management Console, double-click **Audit account logon events**.

5. Under Local policy setting, check the **Success** and **Failure** check boxes, and then click **OK**.

6. Close the Local Security Policy Management Console.

7. To test the new audit policy, log off Windows 2000 Professional and then log back on.

8. Click **Start**, point to **Programs**, click **Administrative Tools**, and then click **Event Viewer**.

9. Click **Security Log**.

10. View the events created in the security log by double-clicking each event. How many events were created by your logon?

11. Clear the security log by right-clicking the **Security Log** icon in Event Viewer and selecting **Clear all Events**. When prompted regarding whether you wish to save the security log, click **No**.

12. Close Event Viewer.

13. Log off your computer and attempt to log on again with an incorrect password. Log on with the correct password and check the security log as before.

14. What new events were created?

15. Close Event Viewer.

16. Open the Local Security Policy Management Console and go to the Audit account logon events policy by following Steps 1–4.

17. Uncheck the **Success** and **Failure** check boxes, and close the Local Security Policy Management Console.

Project 8-2 Windows 2000 Object Access Auditing

This project requires a Windows 2000 Professional computer that is not part of a domain. Alternatively, you can use a Windows 2000 domain controller. At least one partition that is formatted for NTFS is required.

To turn on Account Logon auditing for the domain controller, open the Domain Controller Security Policy Management Console in Administrative Tools on a domain controller. Then follow the steps starting from Step 2.

1. Click **Start**, point to **Programs**, click **Administrative Tools**, and click **Local Security Policy**.

2. Double-click the **Security Settings** icon until you see a folder called Local Policies.

3. Double-click the **Local Policies** folder, and then click the **Audit Policy** folder.

4. In the right pane of the Management Console, double-click **Audit object access**.

5. Under Local policy setting, check the **Success** and **Failure** check boxes, and then click **OK**.

6. Close the Local Security Policy Management Console. The next step is to select an object whose access you wish to audit.

7. Open Windows Explorer and select a drive that is formatted for NTFS. Your instructor will tell you which drive to select.

8. Create a new folder under the root of the drive, and name it **secure-data**.

9. Right-click the **secure-data** folder, and then select **Properties**.

10. Click the **Security** tab, and then click the **Advanced** button.

11. Click the **Auditing** tab, and then click the **Add** button.

12. In the Select User, Computer, or Group dialog box, select **Authenticated Users** and click **OK**.

13. Under the Successful column, check the **List Folder/Read Data** check box. Click **OK**.

14. Click **OK** two more times until you have exited the folder properties.

15. To test the new audit policy, double-click the **secure-data** folder.

16. Open Event Viewer.

17. Click **Security Log**.

18. How many events did opening the secure-data folder create?

19. Clear the security log by right-clicking the **Security Log** icon in Event Viewer and selecting **Clear all Events**. When prompted regarding whether you wish to save the security log, click **No**.

20. Close Event Viewer.

21. Why should you use object access auditing with care? What can happen if you try to audit too many events? Write a short description of a circumstance in which you would want to audit successful object access and unsuccessful object access.

22. Open the Local Security Policy Management Console and go to the Audit object access policy by following Steps 1–4.

23. Uncheck the **Success** and **Failure** check boxes, and close the Local Security Policy Management Console.

Project 8-3 Update Windows with the Latest Security Patches

This project requires a Windows 2000 Professional computer that has access to the Internet.

1. Click the Start menu and then click **Windows Update**.

2. Confirm that the Internet Explorer Web browser brings you to the page *http://windowsupdate.microsoft.com/*.

3. Click the **Product Updates** link located near the top of the page. If a Security Warning dialog box appears, indicate that you will trust content from Microsoft.

4. Click the **+** sign next to the title Show Individual Updates, which is underneath the Critical Updates Package check box.

5. Scroll down and see how many updates are related to security.

6. To download the selected updates, click the **Download** button near the top of the screen.

7. To see which updates are currently installed on your computer, click the **Show Installed Updates** button. The updates already installed on your computer will have Already Installed next to the update description. Critical updates that have not been installed will be checked. It is highly recommended that you install these updates, as most of them are security-related.

8. Close Internet Explorer.

Project 8-4 Using a Port Scanner

This project requires the use of Wildpacket's iNetTools package. It can be run on Windows 2000 Professional or Windows 9*x*, but better results will come from running the project on Windows 2000 Professional.

1. Click **Start**, point to **Programs**, and then click **WildPackets iNetTools**.

2. Click **Tool**, and then click **Port Scan**.

3. You will scan your own computer. In the Host: box, type the local loopback address of **127.0.0.1**.

4. In the Start: box under Ports, type **1**. In the End: box under Ports, type **500**.

5. Click the **Both** option button to select the TCP and UDP transport protocols.

6. In the TCP Timeout and UDP Timeout boxes, type **100** and **200**, respectively.

7. Click **Start**.

8. Which ports did the port scanner find that were active on your computer?

9. If there is a Windows 2000 server available, change the Host: entry to the name or IP address of the server and run the port scanner again. Were any more ports discovered with Windows 2000 Server?

10. Close all open windows.

Project 8-5 Using Name Scan

This project requires the use of Wildpacket's iNetTools package. It can be run on Windows 2000 Professional or Windows 9x. For best results, the computer running the program should have access to the Internet.

1. Click **Start**, point to **Programs**, and then click **WildPackets iNetTools**.

2. Click **Tools**, and then click **Name Scan**.

3. In the Starting Address: box, type **207.46.196.100**. In the Ending Address: box, type **207.46.196.120**.

4. Click **Start**.

5. Which names were found?

6. Write a brief description of how this tool might be helpful to a hacker. Is there any way to prevent this program from finding host names?

Project 8-6 Using a Password Checker/Cracker

This project requires two computers on the same network, where one of the machines is a Windows 95 or Windows 98 computer with the File and Print Sharing Service installed. (You need the IP address of a Windows 9x computer on the network that has sharing enabled and a password applied to at least one share.) The other computer should be running Windows 2000. Access to the Internet and the ability to download files and unzip files are also required. All steps are completed on a Windows 2000 Professional computer.

1. Open Internet Explorer, type **http://www.securiteam.com/tools/archive.html** in the Address: box, and then press **Enter**.

2. Select **Edit** from the Internet Explorer menu bar, and then click **Find (on This Page...)**.

3. In the Find what: box, type **Share password checker**, and then click **Find Next**.

4. Click the **Share Password Checker** link.

5. Under the section of the page that says Links, click the **http://www.securityfriday.com/spc_001.html** link.

6. Read the Agreement to Download SPC, and then click the **Agreement to All button** on the bottom of the page. (If you do not agree with the terms, do not continue!)

7. Select **OK** when the dialog box asks whether you want to save the file to disk.

8. Select the **Save** button in the Save As dialog box. Note where the file is being saved.

9. When the download is complete, select **Open**. (This step requires an unzip program such as Winzip. If the workstations are not equipped with Winzip or a similar unzip program, the instructor should provide each student with the necessary files.)

10. Extract the files to your desktop using the unzip program.

11. Close the unzip program and Internet Explorer.

12. Double-click the **SPC.exe** icon on your desktop.

13. Click the **Agree** button.

14. In the Target IP Address: box, type the IP address of a Windows 9*x* computer on the network that has sharing enabled and a password applied to at least one share.

15. Click **Start**. A message telling you whether the Share Password patch has been applied to the computer will appear. Click **OK**.

16. Review the list of shares that appears. If a password is applied to a share, you will see asterisks (*) instead of the password; otherwise, you will see No Password.

17. If the patch has not been applied, click the **Show** button. The passwords that showed asterisks now show the actual password.

18. Close all windows.

CASE PROJECTS

Case 8-1 Scan for Security and Virus Risks on Your Computer

Sails and Snails Industries has asked you to check its computers for security holes and virus infection. The company currently has no virus scanners available. You have heard that Symantec Corporation has an online security and virus checker that can be used over the Internet. As all of Sails and Snails' computers have an Internet connection, you feel that this option is an ideal way to complete this task. You do not know the exact Web address of the online security and virus scanner and you want to look professional when you arrive, so you decide to check this service out for yourself first. Go to Symantec's Web site at *www.symantec.com*, locate the free online security and virus checker, and run these tools on your own computer. Report the procedure you used and the results to your instructor.

You may have to search for the security and virus checker. At the Symantec home page, click the Search button and then search for the key phrase "security check." You will be able to find the utilities in one of the returned search results.

Case 8-2 Research a Variety of Virus Types

You have been asked to write a summary of the various types of computer viruses. Include in your summary descriptions such as "worm", "Trojan horse", and "macro virus." Describe how these viruses infect a computer, what kind of damage they can do, and how they spread. To start, you can refer to *www.symantec.com/securitycheck/maliciouscode.html*.

Case 8-3 Campus Security

This project can be done in groups. Each group's goal is to perform a security audit of the campus or school network. Do visual inspections of network equipment to ensure that it is secure. Use some of the tools mentioned in this chapter to discover potential security weaknesses, and interview the campus IT staff to determine the level of security currently in place on network equipment, servers, and workstations. List any weaknesses discovered and construct a report that suggests how these weaknesses might be eliminated.

CHAPTER

9

NETWORK DOCUMENTATION

> **After reading this chapter and completing the exercises, you will be able to:**
>
> ♦ Understand the importance of accurate and complete documentation
>
> ♦ Determine what should be documented in your network
>
> ♦ Create an overview description of your network
>
> ♦ Document network cable plant and equipment rooms
>
> ♦ Document internetworking devices
>
> ♦ Document servers
>
> ♦ Understand the importance of documenting MAC and IP addresses
>
> ♦ Document moves, additions, and changes

Ask the typical network administrator about network documentation, and he or she will likely expound on the importance of documentation. Ask the network administrator if you can take a look at the documentation for the network, and he or she will probably shuffle a bit, look at the floor, and mumble something about being overworked. Few tasks in the life of an administrator receive more lip service than network documentation. Why? Because it takes time, it is rarely recognized as an accomplishment outside the IT department, and it is easy to put off until tomorrow because lack of documentation rarely keeps employees from getting their jobs done—at least not directly.

This chapter discusses why network documentation is so important and why and how this task actually saves you time in the long run. It also examines some of the tools available to make documentation less of a drudgery and more of a tolerable task. (We stop short of actually classifying these tasks as fun, because even the kindest of you will know that's an exaggeration.)

NETWORK DOCUMENTATION: WHAT CAN IT DO FOR YOU?

Some network administrators actually believe that failing to document the network means job security. It makes sense when you think of it from a narrow point of view. If your servers, cable plant, and internetworking devices are a mystery to everyone except you, it follows that you are indispensable. However, I am sorry to say that even you cannot keep the details of 1000 cable terminations, 10 server configurations, and dozens of network devices straight in your head.

If you think you can keep it all in your head, what happens when the boss comes to you all excited about the latest security vulnerability found in one of the operating systems you use? What happens if the boss asks whether your servers are vulnerable? If you are an administrator with all of your documentation ducks in a row, you will click the mouse three times, punch a few keys, and respond confidently about the status of the servers, thereby gaining much admiration and trust from the boss.

Of course, if you are an administrator who believes your job is more secure without documentation, you won't have this information at your fingertips. Instead, you will respond with a confidence-draining "I don't know." Sure, you can find the information by wandering down to the server closet and doing a little investigating, but the boss is right there watching. Can you guess the next question that the boss will ask?

If the preceding scenario doesn't scare you, try this one on for size: The boss tells you that 10 new offices on the third floor are to be occupied by the end of the month. He asks how much that will cost in new switches, patch panels, and cable runs. If you are a well-prepared administrator, you will pull up a database or spreadsheet with the information for the wiring closet on the third floor and promptly tell the boss how many ports are currently available on existing switches and patch panels. Perhaps the answer is that no additional equipment is required or that a new switch is needed, but your ability to respond nearly instantly will not go unnoticed.

Of course, if you are a documentation slacker, you will tell the boss that you need to go to the third floor closet and count the available ports and that you will get back to him tomorrow afternoon. You will need the extra time because you are busy trying to locate which workstation has been sending a large number of broadcasts on the network. Of course, if you had kept proper documentation on the workstation MAC addresses, that problem would have been solved yesterday.

The following is a list of just some of the many reasons network documentation is good for you and your network:

- It provides a reference for determining the hardware and software required for network additions.

- It makes equipment and workstation moves, adds, and changes easier. (The phrase "moves, adds, and changes" is sometimes shortened in the industry to "MAC," but this book won't use MAC in this context.)

- Documentation provides needed information for troubleshooting.
- It offers justification for additional staff or equipment.
- It helps determine compliance with standards.
- Documentation supplies proof that your installations meet manufacturer hardware or software requirements.
- It reduces training requirements.
- It facilitates security management.
- It allows for better compliance with software licensing agreements.

In a network, a change is some procedure that requires modifications at the workstation, such as a change of address, a NIC replacement, a software change, or a complete change in the workstation. Moves, adds, and changes in your network are greatly facilitated by accurate documentation. When a workstation is moved, the person doing the moving must know which hub or switch port is currently being used so that the port may be disconnected. After the workstation is at the new location, the mover must know which patch panel port to use and which hub or switch port is appropriate for the workstation. Without proper documentation, cables must be traced, questions must be answered, and time will be wasted. Documentation of the current configuration will make most of the changes proceed more smoothly, and documentation of the change results will facilitate future dealings with the workstation.

Additions made to your network can be accomplished more quickly and with fewer chances for error if documentation is up-to-date. As noted, documentation of hub and switch port usage, wiring diagrams, and the like can make estimation of costs and scheduling significantly more precise and less time-consuming.

The following sections discuss areas in your network that documentation can affect and outline the advantages you can realize from having proper and complete documentation. They include a discussion of how documentation can affect network troubleshooting, IT staffing and training, standards compliance issues, technical support, and network security.

Documentation and Troubleshooting

One of the first steps in troubleshooting is gathering information. If a user is experiencing connectivity problems, your network documentation can provide a wealth of information almost instantly. Physical and logical addressing, connectivity to devices, and even data about the cabling may be useful pieces of information when trying to solve a problem. In a recent job of mine, accurate documentation of workstation MAC addresses helped me quickly find which workstation caused an IP address conflict. In contrast, repeated IP address conflicts at another company went unresolved for weeks because the network lacked the proper documentation.

Staff Burnout

Is the network running you and your staff ragged? Documentation of the type and frequency of support calls can provide the necessary justification for additions to staff or, at the very least, additional tools to make support more efficient. You can also use statistics on network response time and bandwidth load as justification for upgrading servers or adding a new switch.

Speaking of staff—the first thing you should hand a new network technician is his or her very own copy of the network documentation manual. Tell the new employee to read it and learn it. You now have a trained technician! Well, maybe not quite, but it is a really good start. Imagine not having to tell Joe Newtech where Mary User's workstation is located and where it is connected when Mary calls with a connectivity problem. Joe can simply look it up in the documentation and start solving the problem. Now that's an efficient and professional IT staff!

Compliance Issues

Compliance with standards is a necessity in today's standards-based networks, both for ensuring correct network operation and for reducing the possibility of installation or configuration errors. Here is an example: I worked on an Ethernet network that had Category 5 cable installed throughout. While observing a technician punch down an RJ45 jack, I noticed that he punched down the green wires in the orange slots and the orange wires in the green slots. When I pointed this out to him, he explained that this was the only way to get the cabling to work, but that he did not know why he had to swap the orange and green wires. After a little investigation, I discovered that the patch panels were wired according to the 568-A wiring standard and the jacks were wired according to 568-B! The technician didn't know that two wiring standards existed. Had a network manual been available that explained which standard was in use at the patch panel (and had the technician been required to read it), the jacks would have been correct.

Interacting with Technical Support

If you call technical support for help in solving a network device problem, one of the first things that the manufacturer of that device will check is whether your equipment, power supply, and cabling meet all applicable standards. For example, if you cannot tell the manufacturer of a 100 Mbps switch that your cable installation passed the appropriate cable tests, and possibly even provide the test results, it might just tell you to call back after you have confirmed that your cabling is not the problem. If a new database server installed on the network is not working, be prepared to tell the database vendor details about the server hardware, operating system version, and patch installations. If you cannot provide this information without walking over to the server and inspecting it, the database vendor will tell you to call back, which means another hour wait on hold in the support queue.

Documentation and Security

Physical and software security of devices, operating systems with the latest security patches, and up-to-date virus protection are some of the issues involved with maintaining security. Documentation of these items helps you adhere to your security policies, and it provides confirmation of your resistance to current threats or warns you of your vulnerability to these threats.

Recently, a worm virus called **Code Red** was unleashed on the Internet; it affected certain Microsoft IIS Web servers. A patch was available for free download, so I downloaded the patch for the server in my home network (which was infected—I even have a packet trace of its attempt to spread). I tried to install the patch but was informed that the patch required Windows 2000 service pack 2, which was not installed. You know, up to that moment, I did not even know if *any* service pack was installed. This lack of information was not a big deal for my one-server home network. However, if I were in charge of 10, 50, or 200 servers, I better be able to quickly determine which servers require the security patch and, among those servers, which require the service pack 2 installation first. If I had this information at hand, I could easily deploy technicians with strict instructions regarding which installations should be applied to which servers.

When the software auditors come calling, believe me, you will be glad that your documentation is in order. You really don't want to start walking from workstation to workstation to determine which computers have software XYZ installed. Also, the auditors are not likely to trust your memory. What they will trust is a nicely printed report of your workstations and servers, in serial number order, listing all of the applications installed on each machine. Your organization and efficiency will astound the auditors, prompting them to put a gold star by your company's name, indicating that no audits are required for the next 10 years! They will probably even take you out to lunch, given that they won't be following you around from workstation to workstation for the next two days.

As you can see, a lot can be gained from good network documentation. The hardest part is determining what to document, and then establishing procedures and garnering appropriate tools to make the documentation easier.

WHAT SHOULD BE DOCUMENTED?

"What should be documented?" is the first question that should be answered before you start your documentation project or define your documentation policies. The answer to the question is not always straightforward. Networks of different size and complexity, and with differing security and usage policies, will likely have different documentation needs. To aid you in this determination, this section discusses the elements of your network that you will most likely want to document. Although it is not an exhaustive list and some environments may have additional requirements, we'll cover enough to make you comfortable.

Description of the Network

The description of your network should be the section of your documentation manual that anybody could pick up, read, and have a basic understanding of how your network works and what it includes. This section should include information about the network topology, the network architectures in use, the operating systems installed, and the number of devices and users served. It should also provide contact information for the individuals who are responsible for various aspects of the network. In addition, you might want to include information on key vendors and related contact information. This section is meant to be read as an overview, with the fine details being described later, so keep tables and graphs to a minimum.

The Cable Plant

The documentation of your cable plant is among the most critical of your documentation tasks. This section describes the physical layout of your network cabling, the terminations used, and the conventions for labeling your cable and connectivity equipment. It also includes the results of tests completed on the cable plant. This section of your documentation will probably become worn from frequent use. Whenever there are moves, adds, or changes, this document is likely to be consulted and possibly modified.

The cable plant is also one area of your documentation that must be kept current. In fact, incorrect documentation in this area is actually worse than none at all. Imagine moving a user workstation and unplugging the now-unused patch cable from the hub, only to find that you unplugged a critical server because the documentation was outdated. If you do this a few times, neither you nor anyone else will trust the documentation, and you will go back to tracing cables every time a change must be made. In this case, you might as well discard the documentation.

Equipment Rooms

Your **equipment rooms** house your internetworking devices and your servers, and they are the junction points for your work area and backbone cabling. An equipment room is also sometimes referred to as a telecommunications closet, a computer room, or an intermediate or main distribution facility. Such rooms are often dedicated to network cabling and equipment but can also be shared with telephone equipment.

The selection of the features and locations of the equipment rooms is very important to maintaining an efficient and reliable network infrastructure. In addition, the proper documentation of the items contained in each room and their location is crucial to the performance of fast and effective changes or troubleshooting.

Internetworking Devices

The efficiency of network changes and troubleshooting is greatly enhanced by the proper documentation of your internetworking devices. You need to know which devices are connected to other devices, the capabilities and limitations of each device, network management features available on each device, port usage, and physical and logical addresses. Model numbers and both hardware and software revision numbers might also be important when troubleshooting or considering upgrades.

When you are finished, you should be able to point to a switch, describe its capabilities, state which software version it is running, list the physical and logical addresses assigned to the switch, determine to which other internetworking devices it is connected, and mention the critical resources attached to it. If these properties are not readily available, your documentation work is not finished.

Servers

All computers that provide shared resources or network services require detailed documentation. These machines include file and print servers, Web servers, DNS and DHCP servers, and any other resource or service on which the company depends. Hardware configuration, operating system and application version numbers, NIC information, and system serial and model numbers are just some of the items that should be available at a moment's notice.

Remember that a server is not a stagnant piece of equipment, so you cannot simply install it and forget it. The interaction with internetworking devices, workstation client software, and new applications requires server hardware and software that is compatible and up-to-date. Very often, the installation of a new device or application will require a particular operating system version or service pack, so you need to know how your server is configured before proceeding with the installation of a hardware or software upgrade.

Workstations

Documentation on workstations is often the most difficult to maintain because there are usually a lot of them and because users, rather than the LAN administrator, are in control of them. Don't let that challenge dissuade you from keeping accurate workstation documentation.

Workstations, and the people who use them, are likely to be the source of the majority of support and troubleshooting events. Knowledge of a workstation's hardware and software configuration, along with both physical and logical addresses, can save you considerable time and effort when resolving a problem. Furthermore, your network policies should limit how much users can change their workstations without the knowledge of the administrator.

If you enforce appropriate rules, your records won't become hopelessly out-of-date. Maintaining accurate records on 20 or 30 workstations can be a significant task, but maintaining records on thousands of stations may appear too daunting a task to even attempt. Fortunately, there are many applications available to help automate the process so that much of the documentation can be gathered remotely and on a periodic basis. Some of these applications will be discussed later in this chapter.

Moves, Adds, and Changes

When changes are made in your network, it is not sufficient to simply replace the old documentation with the new documentation. For example, if a NIC is changed in a workstation, the MAC address changes, and the manufacturer and model number of the NIC may change as well. You may think that it is sufficient to change only the pertinent records in your workstation database. Although changing the workstation database is a requirement, complete documentation will include a log entry noting what was changed, when, by whom, and why.

 All changes that can affect the operation of the network or devices on the network should be logged. This practice provides an accurate audit trail that can be referenced for troubleshooting or security purposes.

Now that you know what should be documented, how do you accomplish this formidable task? You start by looking at the big picture of your network.

DESCRIBING YOUR NETWORK: THE BIG PICTURE

If you hire a new network technician or bring in a consultant to do some work on your network, that person needs to know how your network works to be effective. The description of your network should include the following elements:

- A network diagram
- The topologies and network architectures in use
- Protocols and logical addressing schemes
- The operating systems in use
- Directory services
- Cabling standards
- Conventional practices
- Equipment manufacturers
- Vendor contact information
- IT department contact information

This list is merely a guide and is probably the minimum amount of information that you want to include in your network description. We discuss each element in turn in the following sections. Note that your network may have features that require additional items not found on this list.

Physical Network Diagram

The **physical diagram** of your network depicts the type and location of major inter-networking devices, major servers, and approximate populations of workstations in various locations. The diagram should also include network architecture, addressing, and the types of media in use. Figure 9-1 shows an example of a physical network diagram.

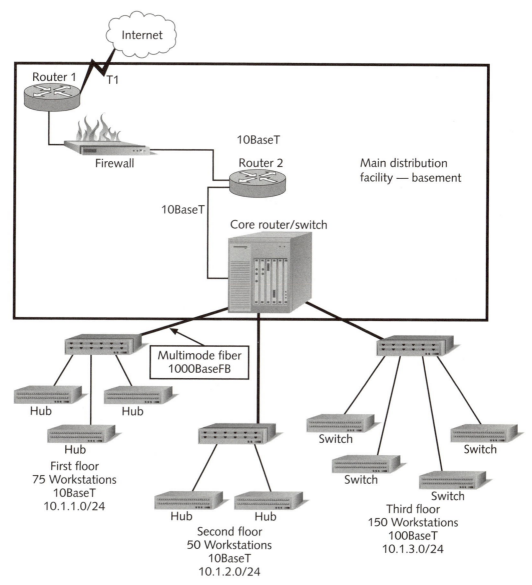

9

Figure 9-1   Physical network diagram

There is no one right way to create a network diagram, and you will run across many different styles created with many different tools. A favorite tool for many network administrators is Microsoft's Visio. There are two versions of Visio available: Visio Standard and Visio Professional. Visio Professional is required to create basic network diagrams. For extremely detailed network drawings, Visio Enterprise Network Tools is an add-on product that can perform network discovery, provide reports, and provide access to an extensive library of network equipment shapes.

 Visio is a general-purpose diagramming tool that can come in handy for creating other types of diagrams, such as flowcharts, organizational charts, and project schedules. More information on Visio can be found at Microsoft's Web site at *www.microsoft.com/office/visio/*.

Another diagramming tool, NetViz, is designed specifically for creating network diagrams. Information on this product is available at *www.netviz.com*. Other tools include Cisco's ConfigMaker, which allows you to create diagrams involving Cisco equipment. ConfigMaker is available as a free download at *www.cisco.com/warp/public/cc/pd/nemnsw/cm/index.shtml*.

Topologies and Architectures

A written discussion of the network topologies and network architectures in use in your network should accompany the network diagram. This discussion should identify areas of the network that use Ethernet, Token Ring, FDDI, or other network architectures, explain why the architecture was selected, and indicate the speed at which the network architecture is being utilized. WAN architectures such as Frame Relay or ISDN should be included as well. The most common physical topology in use today is a star or extended star topology, as depicted in Figure 9-1.

Protocols and Logical Addressing

All protocols in use on the network and the network addresses used for each protocol should be clearly specified. If more than one protocol is in use, the resources available with each protocol should be listed. This type of documentation can be written in descriptive prose or, if there is extensive information to convey, a table may be appropriate. Table 9-1 shows an example of such a table.

Table 9-1 provides a quick reference of the protocol usage throughout this network. At a glance, the reader can see what protocols are used, where they are used, and which resources use the various protocols.

Table 9-1   Network protocols and addresses

Protocol	Network Number	Location	Notes
TCP/IP	10.1.1.0/24 10.1.2.0/24 10.1.3.0/24	First floor Second floor Third floor	Internet access and Windows 2000 servers
IPX/SPX	802201 802202 802203	First floor Second floor Third floor	NetWare servers with an 802.2 frame type
AppleTalk	2-9	First floor	MAC servers for the Marketing and Advertising departments

Operating Systems in Use

The content of this part of your network description is straightforward. Which operating systems are you using and for what purposes are you using them? You should start with the server operating systems, explaining how each operating system is being used and how many users are being served. You then should list the desktop operating systems in use and indicate where they are being used. This information may be expressed in tabular form or paragraph form depending on how much information must be conveyed. If you have only one server operating system and one desktop operating system, a short paragraph is probably sufficient. Tables 9-2 and 9-3 are examples of tables describing operating system usage.

Table 9-2   Server operating systems

Server Operating System	Number of Clients	Usage
Windows 2000 Server	300	SQL server, intranet server, DNS and DHCP servers
Novell NetWare 5.0	250	File and Print Services and NDS
UNIX	N/A	Public Web server and FTP server

Table 9-3   Desktop operating systems

Desktop Operating System	Number of Desktops	Usage
Windows 95	50	Office applications, NetWare Client32, and Windows Client
Windows 98	200	Office applications, NetWare Client32, Windows Client, and SQL client
Windows 2000 Professional	50	AutoCad, Windows Client, and Engineering department only

You may want to explain the rationale behind choosing a particular operating system for the function that it provides. This explanation provides a reference as to why your environment is configured as it is. It gives the reader of your documentation a sense that some thought and planning went into your network configuration. With it, you have something to refer to when you are asked years later why certain decisions were made.

Directory Services

Directory service is the term used for the database and network service that stores and provides access to all of your network resources and security information. The two most common examples are Novell's Directory Service (NDS) and Microsoft's Active Directory. This aspect of your network may or may not require its own section in your network documentation. If you are using a single service such as NDS to manage NetWare, Windows, and UNIX resources, then perhaps this section is required so that it is clear to the reader that a single directory service is used to manage all of your resources. Also, if your network is very large, with many departments and organizational units being defined within your directory service, it may be wise to include some information on how your resources are organized within the directory. In this case, a diagram showing the most critical resources is a good idea.

Figure 9-2 is a diagram of an NDS directory service. Similar diagrams of Active Directory can be drawn with Microsoft's Visio. Visio can even import all of the necessary information from a live network, even if that network is the one on which you are running Visio.

Depending on how extensive your resource directory is, you may want to include a description of which servers participate in the directory service management and who has administrative control over the various branches of the directory tree.

Cabling Standards

This section of your network description tells the reader what type of cabling is being used and in which areas of the network, how the cable is terminated, and what are the predominant standards in use. A sample write-up might look like the following:

> Belden Category 5 enhanced plenum-rated cable is used for connections to all workstations from the patch panel to the jack. All jacks and patch panels are Hubble Category 5E with 568-A termination. All workstation patch cables are six feet in length and are factory made with boots. Fiber-optic cabling is Corning cable multimode fiber using MT-RJ terminations.

Putting this type of information in writing not only provides the reader of your documentation with important information, but also encourages you to stick with the chosen standards. If your standards change, you should note the reason for the change and include in your documentation the areas of the network that use the new standard. Manufacturer names need not always be mentioned, but when possible, it is desirable to stay with just a few manufacturers. Mentioning the manufacturer names will encourage you or future administrators to do so.

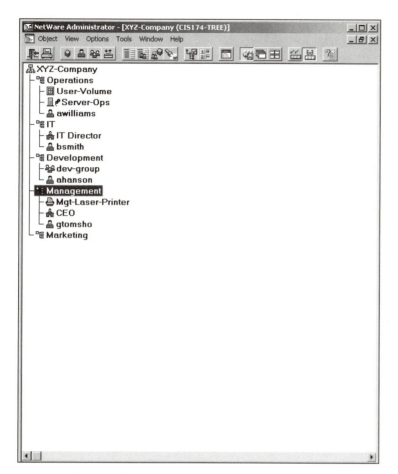

Figure 9-2   NDS directory service

Conventions Used in the Network

A **convention** is a common practice or way of doing things that makes procedures easier to follow and remember. For example, you may decide by convention that patch cables used to connect server NICs from the patch panel to the hub will always be red and that workstation patch cables will always be white. This consistency makes it easy to look at a hub or switch and know which ports your servers are on. You may also want to always use a particular port number on your hubs and switches for uplink connections and designate particular port numbers to be used only for particular types of devices such as servers or printers.

Other conventions might include using port 1 on a patch panel for connections from an **intermediate distribution facility (IDF)** to the **main distribution facility (MDF)**. An IDF is a wiring closet that serves as the connection point for work area connections. An MDF is a wiring closet in which one or more IDFs tie into the network backbone.

Backbone, or vertical, cabling is best installed using a different color than that for horizontal cabling.

Other conventions may include naming conventions and labeling conventions. You may want to explain how you name your servers and internetworking devices in the network description so that the reader understands these names when they are encountered in later parts of the documentation or when the technician sees devices and labels in the actual network. The idea of using conventions is to minimize errors during configuration and troubleshooting, to reduce the learning curve for new employees or consultants, and to maximize understanding of how the network is configured.

Equipment and Software Manufacturers

This section of your network description should list the names of all manufacturers used throughout your network; the devices used from these manufacturers; contact names including sales, customer service, and support contacts; and phone and e-mail addresses. You should also include each manufacturer's support and sales Web site addresses, along with any special procedures used to contact the manufacturer. If you have account numbers related to sales or support, passwords, Web site logins, and so forth, list them as well. If you are on vacation on a day when one of your switches blows up, anyone should be able to look in this section of your documentation and know who to call and what procedures to use in getting support.

This part of your documentation can save you lots of time when you need to talk to someone about a device you purchased three years ago. Often, finding who to call can take more time than the support call itself. Keep this information up-to-date. When you get a letter or e-mail from a manufacturer telling you that its contact information or support procedures have changed, be sure to update your documentation, because incorrect documentation is as bad or worse than none at all.

Vendor Contact Information

You will most likely purchase smaller items, such as cabling, patch panels, jacks, and so forth, from a vendor. Vendors are the companies from which you buy equipment, parts, or software, if you do not buy directly from the manufacturer. If you buy exclusively from vendors, you should still keep information on the manufacturer. Manufacturers often provide support or change distributors.

The information on vendors should be similar to the information that you keep on manufacturers. In some cases, because several vendors may supply the same products, you might want to include notes as to why certain products were purchased from a particular vendor. For example, if both Vendor A and Vendor B sell the Category 5 cable you use, and Vendor A is 5 percent cheaper, but you use Vendor B because Vendor A is frequently late in shipping, you should note this fact in your documentation. This practice avoids the problem of your manager asking why you are using a more expensive vendor for the product.

IT Department Contacts

Each staff member and consultant to your IT department should be listed, along with contact information, perhaps a short biography, and areas of expertise and responsibility. This information permits an outsider or a newcomer to quickly determine whom to contact for information about any aspect of your network.

DOCUMENTING THE CABLE PLANT

The **cable plant** includes all cables and termination points such as jacks and patch panels. It makes up the bulk of your Physical layer—minus, of course, Physical layer devices such as hubs and transceivers.

Cable plant documentation is probably the most useful and most hated part of any overall documentation. It is useful because once cables are run, tucked away in ceilings, and terminated, it may be quite difficult to find a particular cable that is causing problems unless it is labeled. Plus, when moves and changes are required, you need to know which cables are safe to disconnect and which are not.

 If you can document only one thing, the cable plant should be that one thing.

Cable plant documentation is hated because it is tedious. Cable installation is largely a physical job. When you are standing at the top of a ladder with your head inside a hot ceiling, it's difficult to think about labeling each end of the cable and then labeling the jack and patch panel. You just want to get it done and move on to less distasteful tasks, but believe me, the extra care and time you take during installation will save you many headaches afterward.

The following sections discuss the details of cable plant documentation. You will learn about documenting cable terminations, creating a cut sheet, and describing cable runs, patch panels, and jacks. We also discuss the documentation of cable tests as well as known problems in a cable plant.

Description of Cable Types and Terminations

Your cable plant documentation should begin by describing what types of cables are used in your network, for what purpose, and what kinds of terminations are used. This information expands on what was written in the network description section of your documentation. You should list each area of the network that uses a different cable and termination type, plus any exceptions to the norm. For example, part of this section may look like the following:

- Horizontal cabling:
    - Category 5E, white, Belden, plenum-rated
    - EIA/TIA 568-A termination
    - Verified to have a maximum 0.5-inch untwist at termination point
    - Tested with Agilent WireScope 155 to Cat-5E standard
- Patch panels:
    - Hubble Cat-5E 568-A (floor 1 and 2 IDF and MDF)
    - Siemon Cat-5E 568-A (floor 3 IDF)
    - Punched down with Paladin 110 punchdown tool

The main idea is to give the reader of the documentation information on what materials were used and to what standard the materials were installed.

The Cut Sheet

A **cut sheet** is a document, usually in tabular form, that lists each cable run. The information on the cut sheet should specify the connection made by the cable, the length of the run, the ID of the cable, the patch panel port used, the type of cable, and the status of the cable (that is, whether it is currently in use). You should also include the test status of the run, including whether it has been tested and, if so, any notable results. The cut sheet is proof that your network infrastructure is documented and tested and that you know where everything goes. Table 9-4 is an example of a cut sheet.

Table 9-4 Cut sheet for Intermediate Distribution Facility—Floor 2

Connection	Cable ID	Patch Panel/Port	Length (feet)	Test Status	Use Status	Cable Type
IDF2 to Room 202	202–001	PP1–IDF2/23	73	OK	Used	Cat-5E
IDF2 to Room 202	202–002	PP1–IDF2/17	78	OK	Used	Cat-5e
IDF2 to Room 202	202–003	PP1–IDF2/12	70	OK	Unused	Cat-5e
IDF2 to Room 203	203–001	PP1–IDF2/29	121	OK	Used	Cat-5e
IDF2 to Room 203	203–002	PP1–IDF2/11	133	OK	Used	Cat-5e
IDF2 to Room 210	210–001	PP1–IDF2/38	101	Failed NEXT	Unused	Cat-5e
IDF2 to MDF	IDF2 MDF–01	FP1–IDF2/01	211	OK	Used	MM-Fiber

The cut sheet lets you see at a glance the points connected by every cable and the cable's status. It is one of the key documents in your documentation, so the cut sheet should be kept accurate and up to date at all times. The use status is important because it permits you to quickly see whether any unused cables in an area might be used to add workstations or be used as spares in the event that a cable fails.

Labeling Cable Runs

All cable runs should be labeled on both ends of the cable, a few inches above the termination point. Cable runs are usually labeled after the cable has been terminated and tested because if a termination must be redone, you will need to strip more cable jacket, which might remove the label. If you are on a tight budget, a permanent marker will do. Alternatively, you can use preprinted wire markers, which are self-adhesive numbers.

While these methods work okay in a pinch, I recommend a professional cable labeler if you have a lot of labeling to do. These hand-held labelers print on vinyl labels specifically designed to adhere to cabling. They also can be used to label jacks and patch panels. Examples are the Kroy K2500 and the Brady IDPRO.

Cables should be labeled so that their approximate destinations are clear. It is not sufficient to simply slap a number on the cable if you have cables going from a wiring closet to several different rooms. You want the label to indicate which room the cable is going to so that locating the other end is easier. Of course, the label you put on the cable should match the cable ID on your cut sheet. If you are using a cable tester that allows you to identify, store, and later print your test results, you can identify the test result using the same ID used for the cable label.

Labeling Patch Panels and Jacks

Patch panels should be labeled so that a name or number in your documentation can identify them. Jacks, or rather jack faceplates, should be labeled to specify to which ports on which patch panels they are connected.

For patch panels, decide on a naming convention and then use your label maker to apply a label to each patch panel in the network. For example, if you have an IDF on the second floor, you might label the patch panels in that IDF as PP1-IDF2, PP2-IDF2, and so forth. Patch panels in the IDF on the third floor would be labeled PP1-IDF3, and so on. The important thing is to convey information with your naming scheme and then be consistent throughout your network.

Jacks can be labeled only after you have named the patch panels. A typical label for a jack on the second floor whose cable goes to the fourth port on patch panel 1 in IDF2 might be PP1-IDF2/04. Using such a scheme makes it easy to connect, disconnect, and move a workstation that is plugged into that particular jack. You know exactly which port on which patch panel to use. This information then is transferred to the cut sheet in the Patch Panel/Port column. The cut sheet can be posted in the IDF so that a technician can determine where each port on each patch panel is connected.

Cable Test Results

Installing, testing, and labeling cable runs can be hard, hot, and tedious work. When you test a cable, you want to hear only the familiar tone that the cable tester emits when the cable has passed all tests. You can then label the cable and move on to the next one.

Of course, there is one more step in the testing process, even when you hear what you want to hear from the cable tester—assign a label and store the test result for each cable tested, which can be printed later. Take advantage of this feature of your cable tester. It provides solid proof that the cables were tested, it lists to what standard they were tested, and it indicates that they passed.

After the test, simply punch in the cable ID and store the results. You can attach the tester to a PC via a serial port to extract the results and import them into a spreadsheet or similar document. This document can be added to your documentation manual. If you do not use a tester that has this capability, document your test results the old-fashioned way—write down the cable ID, the time and date the test was performed, the equipment used, and the tester's name.

Most testers show you the length of the cable during the test, and this information should be noted so that it can be transferred to the cut sheet. If your tester does not report the length of the cable, you can determine the length by subtracting the foot markers on each end of the cable.

Known Problems or Concerns with the Cable Plant

This section of your cable plant documentation, if included, simply states any anomalies that occurred during testing or installation and any concerns regarding your cable plant that might be useful to know later. For example, if an inordinate number of failed cable tests (more than 1 percent) occurred, this fact should be noted so that you can investigate why there were so many failures. Perhaps the cabling is substandard, or perhaps you didn't realize you were running a number of cables near a large EMI source. It's also possible that you ran out of the standard cable halfway through installation and had to use a different brand on a dozen cable runs. While this inconsistency may not present a problem, it should be noted so that future inspectors of your cable plant understand why the change was made. Almost anything that came up during the installation, testing, or documentation of your cable plant that was of concern or out of the ordinary should be noted just in case that concern becomes an issue later.

 The cable plant is probably the most difficult and most important part of your documentation effort. If you survive its documentation, the rest should be a breeze.

DOCUMENTING EQUIPMENT ROOMS

Equipment rooms should be described in detail, including the room location, room dimensions, type of doorway, type of ceiling and walls, cooling and heating, and the lighting used, among other details. A standard defined in TIA/EIA-569 governs how your equipment rooms should be configured. A nice reference to this standard and others can be found at *www.siemon.com/standards/*. If you wish to purchase a copy of the standard, go to *www.tiaonline.org*.

For an outstanding example of a drawing of an equipment room with the relevant features labeled, go to *www.siemon.com/standards/ansi_tia_eia.asp#CLOSET*. If you have the ability to make such drawings, great! If not, a written description will suffice.

Description of Cable Runs and Areas Served

Along with the physical parameters of your equipment rooms, the cables housed in each room and the areas of your facility each room serves should be documented. For example, you might state the following:

> Entering the room through conduit 4 in the northeast corner is a bundle of 50 Category 5E cables serving rooms 202 and 203. Conduit 1 in the southwest corner contains a 12-strand multimode fiber cable running to the MDF. Four fiber strands are in use.

This detailed information provides the reader with the knowledge necessary to make additions and changes confidently and easily. When building renovations are under way, this information may prevent unfortunate cable breaks or other accidents.

Location and Description of Devices in Each Room

This part of your equipment room documentation will be the most frequently referred-to document by you and your staff. When changes or additions need to be made anywhere in your network, you want a quick reference indicating what devices are in each equipment room and their capacities. For example, if you plan to add three workstations to room 103, you must determine whether the existing patch panels and hubs or switches have sufficient available ports to accommodate the additions. This information lends itself to table or spreadsheet form, as in Table 9-5.

Table 9-5   IDF2 equipment list

Device Type	Device Name	Location#	Ports/# Free
Category 5E patch panel	PP1-IDF2	Rack 1	48/3
	PP2-IDF2	Rack 1	48/0
	PP3-IDF2	Rack 2	24/4
Synoptics 2814 hub	MH1-IDF2	Rack 1	16/0
Synoptics 2803 hub	H2-IDF2	Rack 1	16/0
	H3-IDF2	Rack 2	16/3

Power Considerations in Equipment Rooms

You might think that electricity can be taken for granted, but many network devices require a considerable amount of power, and some have special electrical outlet requirements. Your equipment rooms should be carefully examined for the type and number of available power outlets. Once your existing equipment is satisfactorily installed, the power budget should be documented. Your power budget should include how much total power (measured in watts or volt-amps) is available to the room, how much is currently in use, and how much is available. This way, you will know if your equipment room is able to handle additional devices.

In primary equipment rooms that house your major servers and large switches, consider the number of power circuits that are available. Major equipment often comes with redundant power supplies, each of which should be plugged into a different power circuit. This way, in the event of a loss of power on one circuit, the equipment can continue to run.

Most equipment rooms use an uninterruptible power supply (UPS) to supply power to the network devices. Your documentation should specify the type and number of each UPS in each equipment room, the number of outlets available, and the power budget for each UPS. The larger UPS models require considerable current and have special outlet requirements. For example, the APC Smart-UPS 2200 requires a NEMA 5-20P power outlet, which differs significantly from a standard 15-amp outlet. Check your outlet requirements carefully.

Diagrams of Racks and Installed Equipment

For the most complete documentation of your equipment rooms, consider making drawings of your racks with the installed devices shown and labeled. Ideally, these drawings will show the physical location in the equipment room, or you can simply describe the location.

Figure 9-3 shows an equipment rack with devices installed and labeled. Providing such detailed drawings is an excellent way for the readers of your documentation to gain a virtual tour of your network without having to visit each equipment room.

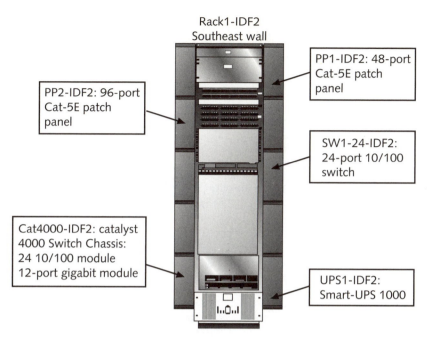

PP2-IDF2: 96-port Cat-5E patch panel

Rack1-IDF2 Southeast wall

PP1-IDF2: 48-port Cat-5E patch panel

SW1-24-IDF2: 24-port 10/100 switch

Cat4000-IDF2: catalyst 4000 Switch Chassis: 24 10/100 module 12-port gigabit module

UPS1-IDF2: Smart-UPS 1000

Figure 9-3   Equipment rack with installed devices

You can include more detail on these drawings if you feel it necessary, but at the minimum they should contain the information included in Figure 9-3. You may want to add the manufacturer and part number of each device and possibly even the serial number. Be careful about including information such as logical addresses and port usage. These pieces of information can change, and you don't want this information included in too many places or documentation maintenance becomes difficult.

Known Problems or Concerns with Equipment Rooms

In this section, you should include information such as rooms that do not meet your specifications for cooling, power, or lighting. You should also include any steps planned or recommended to address the concern. This discussion documents your recognition of a problem or concern and indicates that you have set into motion the necessary steps to resolve the problem.

As an example of a known problem, you might have an equipment room that is inadequately cooled. If you have mentioned that concern to management with no results, there should be no surprise if the boss comes to work one day, only to find that the core switch has overheated and the network is down. Your concern has been documented, and while it is still your job to get things up and running, at least the powers that be had been warned, and you will hopefully get to keep your job.

DOCUMENTING INTERNETWORKING DEVICES

Internetworking device documentation plays a key role in network troubleshooting and support. This documentation should include the manufacturer and model of each device, physical and logical addresses, port usage information, device locations, areas served, connections to other devices, and firmware version, where applicable. This information can be put into a spreadsheet or database. Databases can be useful for searching and creating reports. Because of the differences in the documentation requirements for each device, you may want to create a separate table for each device type.

 It is a matter of preference whether this part of your documentation appears as a separate section or is included in the equipment room documentation. I prefer to have a single document showing the internetworking devices in the network.

Table 9-6 is an example of what a spreadsheet table might look like for hubs and switches.

Table 9-6   Hubs and switches spreadsheet

Device Type/Label	Model/ Serial #	Location	Location Served	Interconnection/ Port Number	IP Address	MAC Address	Ports/Free	Firmware
Managed Hub MH1-IDF1	Synoptics 2814 324234657	IDF1	Room 202	H2-IDF1/BP, SW1-MDF/P1	192.168.1.240	00000cab3546	16/0	Rev1
Hub H2-IDF1	Synoptics 2803 324234658	IDF1	Room 202	MH1-IDF1/BP, H3-IDF1/BP	N/A	00000cab3305	16/0	N/A
Hub H3-IDF1	Synoptics 2803 32434659	IDF1	Room 202	H2-IDF1/BP	N/A	00000cab3254	16/10	N/A
Switch SW1-MDF	Cat4000 8443901224	MDF	Campus	MH1-IDF1/P1, SW1-24-IDF2/P2	192.168.2.245	00000cab8744	48/10	Rev4.4

Some columns in Table 9-6 may need further explanation. The fifth column refers to other internetworking devices to which the device in that row is connected. For example, the first device, hub MH1-IDF1, has a connection to hub H2-IDF1 through port BP ("BP" stands for backplane). Thus this hub is stackable and has a special backplane connector to stack other hubs. MH1-IDF1 has another connection to a switch labeled SW1-MDF, which goes through the hub's port 1. Your documentation should provide a key to any abbreviations and other terms that may not be obvious to the reader.

In a large network, this table could be quite large. Having the information in a spreadsheet or database allows sorting by column header and searching so that information is easily accessed. For example, you may want to sort the information by location so that you have a quick reference to all of the internetworking devices in a particular equipment room. Alternatively, you could sort by model number if you need to determine how many of a particular model device your network has. Depending on the type of devices and the feature set, your table may have different columns than those shown in Table 9-6.

In addition to the spreadsheet or database of devices, this section should include a description of each model device that is installed in your network. The description provides the reader with information about important features available with each device type, such as port speed, duplex modes supported, SNMP capabilities, and so forth.

Advanced features on devices are difficult to document with a table, so a narrative description is needed. These advanced features might include chassis-based switches, VLANs on switches, and configuration files for switches and routers. For those devices, it is wise to create a small section for each device and document those features. For example, to further document the switch labeled Cat4000-IDF2 in Figure 9-3, you might create the following section in your documentation:

Cat4000-IDF2
Device model: Cisco Catalyst 4000
Number of slots: 3
Installed modules:
- Slot 1: Supervisory Module/ 29489-8a
- Slot 2: Catalyst 4000 E/FE/GE Module/ 29489-1a
- Slot 3: Catalyst 4000 10/100 Auto Module/ 29489-3a
Configuration:
- Three VLANs configured.
  - VLAN01: Ports 1–12 Slot2–192.168.1.0
  - VLAN02: Ports 13–24 Slot2–192.168.2.0
  - VLAN03: Ports 1–24 Slot3–192.168.3.0
- Configuration file:
  Here, you would insert the configuration file from the switch but exclude any passwords.

The preceding section is incomplete, but it is intended to give you an idea of what information should be included. Each device type will likely require differing amounts of information. Include as much information as is necessary to completely describe how the device functions in your network. For routers, you would create a similar section, being sure to include the configuration file from the router, but no password information.

Now that you've got your network infrastructure documented, it is time to turn your attention to the computers in your network. We will start with the servers.

DOCUMENTING SERVERS

Accurate and up-to-date server documentation is crucial to maintaining a reliable and secure network. This information not only helps you find needed information in a hurry, but can drastically reduce the learning curve for new employees who are assigned to manage the servers.

There are several categories of information that you should cover in your server documentation. You should start with a general description of the server.

Server Description

This section of your server documentation should provide a general description of the server's purpose in your network. It should include two or three sentences describing the primary service that the server provides and noting to whom it provides that service. For example, you might describe a server that is named MKT-SRV1 in the following manner:

MKT-SRV1:

A Windows 2000 server providing Marketing department document sharing and print services along with Internet Information Server Web services for the marketing intranet. This server serves approximately 30 employees located in the main office on the third floor. This server is configured as a member server in the XYZ-Corp domain.

Include any additional information that may be useful, but do not be too specific here as the details will appear later. Remember that several types of people are likely to read your documentation manual, so it is best to start with more general information. That way, less technical people can get the information they want without having to wade through pages of technical data.

Server Hardware Configuration and Operating System

The server hardware configuration should start with the manufacturer, model number, and serial number of the server. The operating system information should list the version number and any updates or patches that are installed. If you have several servers, a table of information can be created so that all of your servers are documented uniformly. Table 9-7 is an example of a server hardware and operating system configuration table.

Table 9-7 is merely an example; you may have to experiment to find a format that fits your environment well. The important thing is to include the most pertinent information about the hardware configuration of your server so that upgrades and repairs can be made hassle-free. You should not have to open up the server to determine the type of memory installed and the number of free memory slots. Nor should you have to restart the server to determine the BIOS version. Details that are not likely to be referenced frequently can be accessed through hyperlinks if your documentation is electronic. In the preceding example, for instance, you might construct a hyperlink from the model description to a detailed specification sheet for that server.

Table 9-7   Server hardware configuration

Server: MKT-SRV1				
Model: <u>**Dell PowerEdge 500SC**</u> Serial# DCS-50049443 Location: IDF1 Operating System: Windows 2000 Server – Patches: SP2, IE5.5 SP1, Code Red Virus Cleaner				
CPU **#/Speed**	**RAM** **Amount/Type/Free Slots**	**Bus Slots** **Type/Free**	**Drives** **Type/Size**	**NIC/MAC/IP**
Pentium III 1/1 GHz	512 MB/ECC SDRAM/ 2 DIMM	PCI-32/1 PCI-64/2	EIDE/30 GB HD EIDE/CD-ROM SCSI-2/8 GB DAT	Intel 10/100 04AB33126900 192.168.1.33
I/O Ports **Type/Number**	**Additional Information**		**Drive Bays** **Size/Free**	**Modem**
USB/2 Serial/2 Parallel/1	Phoenix Bios Version 4.4 250W ATX Power Supply Tower Chassis PS/2 Keyboard and Mouse		5.25 inches/2 3.5 inches/2	3Com-56 K

The MAC address and the IP address should be listed along with the NIC. This puts all of the critical information about this server in one handy location. You do not want to overload the table with too much information, as it then becomes difficult to follow. Additional information about your servers can be discussed in other sections of your documentation.

Available Services

The services that are available on your server should be listed along with their purpose. This information also lends itself well to tabular form. Some of the services you might see here include File and Print Services. You also can include shared folder names and printer names, Web services, FTP services, DNS, DHCP, Active Directory, backup, Telnet, database, e-mail, and terminal services. A host of other services may be possible depending on your operating system.

One reason to include all of this information is so that you understand the ramifications if this server were to go down. Another reason to list the critical services is so that you can configure your security appropriately. You need to know what services are available to properly allow or restrict access to each server.

Resource Configuration and Limitations

This section should describe how your hard drives are configured and what your limits are regarding hard drives and memory. For example, you should specify how your drives are partitioned and formatted along with the size of each partition. You should specify the amount of free space available after installation and the least amount of free space allowed before upgrading the drive. You should also indicate whether any drives are configured for

9

redundancy, such as mirroring or RAID-5. This section should include the maximum number of drives that the server can support.

Memory configuration should include the total amount of memory and the amount of free memory, (and virtual memory) available when the server is running. You should determine a minimum amount of free memory permitted before a mandatory memory upgrade. You should also specify the maximum amount of memory supported by each server.

Another resource parameter you may want to include is the maximum number of users that a server is designed to support or, as in the case of a Web server, the maximum number of transactions per minute that the server is designed to handle. This information can help you determine when you need to upgrade or make some design changes in your network.

Administrative Contacts

The administrative contacts section of your server documentation should list the people who should be called for various support issues. You may have different personnel assigned to creating users, setting security permissions, making changes to services, and performing software or hardware upgrades. The responsible staff members should be listed along with their contact information.

Server Documentation Tools

Collecting all of the information you may want about your servers can be a time-consuming task. Fortunately, there are some tools available to help automate the task. Some tools to help document a Windows 2000 and Windows NT machine are available with those operating systems. For extensive hardware and software information, the winmsd.exe program can be run to create a text file report that contains the information available from the System Information shortcut in the System Tools folder. Hands-on Project 9-4 goes through the process of creating this report.

The System Information utility can be run in GUI mode to provide browsable information about a particular computer. Figure 9-4 shows the System Information utility. This utility can be run on any Windows machine, starting with Windows 98. You can print this information or save a text file copy of it to disk using the toolbar icons.

UltraAdmin is a third-party utility that has an easy-to-use interface. This computer management tool allows you to manage and view information on all computers in a Windows NT or Windows 2000 domain.

Figure 9-5 shows UltraAdmin. UltraAdmin can be used to gather information about your servers remotely but it is also a handy and easy general-purpose administration tool for Windows NT or Windows 2000.

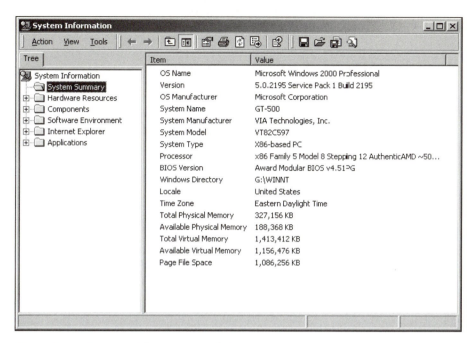

Figure 9-4   System Information utility

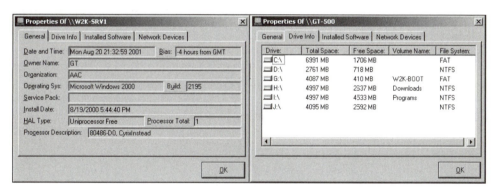

Figure 9-5   UltraAdmin utility

For detailed disk usage information, a simple, but effective utility is Directory Report by AWB Software. It scans one or more drives and creates a report showing the amount of drive space used by each directory. This utility has a host of options, including filtering, finding duplicate files, and displaying cluster sizes. Both Directory Report and UltraAdmin, along with many other Windows NT and Windows 2000 utilities, can be downloaded from *http://home.ntware.com*. A screen shot of Directory Report's output is shown in Figure 9-6.

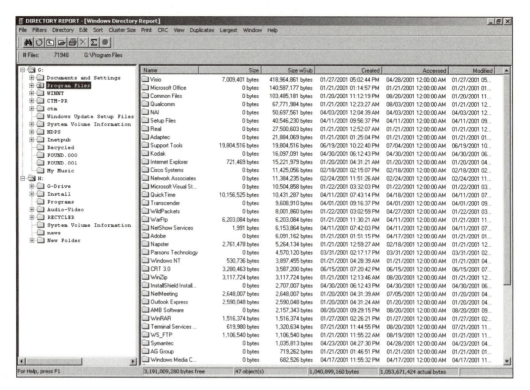

Figure 9-6   Directory Report utility

There are several major commercial products available to help you manage and document your servers. Intel's LanDesk Management Suite is available for Windows NT and later and Novell NetWare. BindView produces bv-Control and bc-Admin for both Windows and NetWare environments. These products are comprehensive management and documentation tools. BindView's tools can be located at *www.bindview.com*, and information on Intel's LanDesk can be found at *http://developer.intel.com/network/ products/landesk/landesk_mgmtsuite_v6.htm*.

Documenting Workstations

The documentation that you keep on workstations should be similar to that which you keep for servers. You should include hardware configuration, addresses, and available services, if applicable. Additional documentation on each workstation should include a list of the installed applications, primary users of the workstation, and policies and restrictions applied to it. Many of the same tools used to automate collecting server information can be used to collect workstation information. For example, UltraAdmin can provide a list of installed applications on any workstation quickly and easily. Figure 9-7 is a screen shot of the installed applications screen from UltraAdmin.

Intel's LanDesk has a host of workstation configuration and management tools and allows you to collect complete information remotely from the LanDesk management station. For large networks with hundreds or thousands of nodes, a tool such as LanDesk, with its remote control, remote software distribution, and software metering functions, can be a huge time saver.

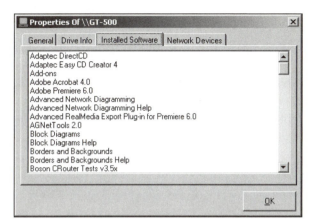

Figure 9-7   UltraAdmin's installed applications screen

DOCUMENTING MAC AND IP ADDRESSES

Even if you skimp on every other aspect of your documentation, you absolutely must have a list of your MAC and IP addresses. I recommend maintaining a searchable database of every MAC address and IP address for every node in your network. This database should include all servers, workstations, managed hubs, switches, and routers. It need not be complicated; the only information required is the MAC address, IP address, device name, and device location. If you assign all of your IP addresses using DHCP, you can skip the IP address.

For me, a MAC and IP address database has come in handy countless times in the process of troubleshooting various problems. For example, users may, if allowed, change the IP addresses of their workstations. If a user changes the address to one that is already in use, a message will appear on the other station indicating that a duplicate IP address was detected. The MAC address of the station with the duplicate IP address will be listed in the message. To find the offending machine, simply pull up your database, enter the MAC address from the message, and then locate that machine.

Such a database may also be useful in situations in which a network monitoring session turns up an extraordinary number of error packets from one MAC address. You can locate the machine quickly in the database and discover a bad NIC.

This database can have many other uses as well. In a NetWare environment, certain events, such as remote console sessions, are logged with the MAC address of the connecting station. This information, along with the database, allowed me to catch an intruder who had discovered the password to the NetWare console.

DOCUMENTING MOVES, ADDS, AND CHANGES

You must always be able to determine what has changed in your network (in case the change causes a problem in the network) and to keep track of users and devices. No work you do on your network is complete until you have documented it.

There should be two sections in this part of your documentation. The first section should specify in detail the procedures for moves, adds, and changes, and the second section should provide a detailed log of actions taken.

Documenting Procedures

Any changes that are made to the network require a detailed procedure so that changes are made consistently and then documented. If a user moves his or her workstation to a different location, the procedure document for a workstation move must specify a list of actions required when making the move. The procedure may look like Table 9-8.

Table 9-8   Workstation move procedure

Action Taken at Old Location	Action Taken at New Location
Remove the patch cable from the hub/patch panel	Install the patch cable in a new patch panel/hub
Update the cut sheet	Update the cut sheet
Update the hub documentation to reflect a new free port	Update the hub documentation to reflect one less free port
Update the MAC address database to show the workstation's new location and enter information related to the move into the workstation log	

Procedures for every type of common change in your network should be documented and rigorously followed. Otherwise, your documentation will become hopelessly out-of-date and all of that hard work will be wasted. You should have similar procedures for server and workstation changes such as new application installations, hardware or software upgrades, address changes, and so forth. This part of your documentation might easily be made into its own booklet that you can hand to all new technicians who come to work for you.

Logging of Moves, Adds, and Changes

Logging of changes in your network will probably be placed in one or more journals rather than being a part of your documentation manual. I maintain a journal for each server, one for each equipment room, and a workstation journal for each area of the network. It need not be fancy; a simple notebook with columns for the time and date, the technician's name, the change made, and the reason for the change should be sufficient. This kind of log provides a running history of work done on the network. This way, when something goes horribly wrong with your network, you can try to determine whether recent modifications may have played a role in the problem.

CHAPTER SUMMARY

The following is a list of some of the reasons network documentation is good for you and your network:

- It provides a reference for determining the hardware and software required for network additions.

- It makes equipment and workstation moves and changes easier.

- It provides needed information for troubleshooting.

- It offers justification for additional staff or equipment.

- It helps determine compliance with standards.

- It supplies proof that your installations meet manufacturer hardware or software requirements.

- It reduces training requirements.

- It eases security management.

- It allows for better compliance with software licensing agreements.

9

❐ You should include, at a minimum, a description of your network, the cable plant, equipment rooms, internetworking devices, servers, and workstations. In addition, whenever information regarding these devices changes, you should document those changes.

❐ If you hire a new network technician or bring in a consultant to do some work on your network, this person needs to know how your network works to be effective. You should have a complete description of your network available for their use.

❐ Cable plant documentation is useful because once cables are run, tucked away in ceilings, and terminated, it is quite difficult to find a particular cable that is causing problems unless it is labeled. Plus, when moves and changes are required, you need to know which cables are safe to disconnect and which are not.

❐ Equipment rooms should be described in detail, including the room location, room dimensions, type of doorway, type of ceiling and walls, cooling and heating, and the lighting used, among other details. A standard defined in TIA/EIA-569 governs how your equipment rooms should be configured.

❐ Internetworking device documentation plays a key role in network troubleshooting and support. This documentation should include the manufacturer and model of each device, physical and logical addresses, port usage information, device locations, areas served, connections to other devices, and firmware version, where applicable.

❐ Accurate and up-to-date server documentation is crucial to maintaining a reliable and secure network. This information not only helps you find needed information in a hurry, but also can drastically reduce the learning curve for new employees who are assigned to manage the servers.

❐ You should maintain a searchable database of every MAC address and IP address for every node in your network. This database should include all servers, workstations, managed hubs, switches, and routers. It need not be complicated: The only information required is the MAC address, IP address, device name, and device location. If you assign all of your IP addresses using DHCP, you can skip the IP address.

❐ You should document all moves, adds, and changes. There should be two sections in this part of your documentation. The first section should specify in detail the procedures for moves, adds, and changes, and the second section should provide a detailed log of actions taken.

Key Terms

cable plant — All cables and termination points, such as jacks and patch panels, within your network.

Code Red — A worm virus that affected certain IIS Web servers.

convention — A common practice or way of doing things that makes procedures easier to follow and remember.

cut sheet — A document that lists the details of each cable run in the network.

directory service — The database and network service that stores and provides access to all of your network resources and security information.

equipment rooms — Rooms that house your internetworking devices and your servers and that are the junction points for your work area and backbone cabling.

intermediate distribution facility (IDF) — A wiring closet that serves as the connection point for work area connections.

main distribution facility (MDF) — The wiring closet in which one or more IDFs tie into the network backbone.

physical diagram — Drawing that depicts the type and location of major internetworking devices, major servers, and approximate populations of workstations in various locations.

Review Questions

1. Moves, adds, and changes in your network are greatly facilitated by accurate
   _____.

2. A worm virus called _____ affects certain Microsoft IIS Web servers.

3. A network description should contain detailed information. True or False?

4. A(n) _____ houses your internetworking devices and your servers.

   a. junction point

   b. equipment room

   c. service junction

   d. telephone bank

5. A server is a stagnant piece of equipment, so you can simply install it and forget it. True or False?

6. Users are often in control of workstations. True or False?

7. What type of information should be included in the description of a network?

8. The _____ of your network depicts the type and location of major internetworking devices, major servers, and approximate populations of workstations in various locations.

9. A written discussion of the network topologies and network _____ in use in your network should accompany the network diagram.

10. What term is used for the database and network service that stores and provides access to all of your network resources and security information?

    a. Active Directory

    b. network documentation

    c. directory service

    d. critical diagram

11. A(n) _____ is a common practice or way of doing things that makes procedures easier to follow and remember.

12. An MDF is a wiring closet. True or False?

13. The _____ includes all cables and termination points such as jacks and patch panels.

14. What document lists each cable run in a network?

15. All cable runs should be labeled on both ends of the cable, a few inches below the termination point. True or False?

16. Jacks can be labeled only after you have named the _____.

17. Most cable testers show the length of the cable during the test. True or False?

18. Major equipment often comes with redundant power supplies, each of which should be plugged into a different power circuit. True or False?

19. The server hardware configuration should start with the manufacturer, model number, and _____ of the server.

20. Memory _____ should include the total amount of memory and the amount of free memory, (and virtual memory) available when the server is running.

21. You can have different personnel assigned to creating users, setting security permissions, making changes to services, and performing software or hardware upgrades. True or False?

9

22. The _____ utility is a computer management tool that allows you to manage and view information on all computers in a Windows NT or Windows 2000 domain.

    a. Ultra Admin

    b. System NT

    c. MDF config

    d. cut sheet

23. Intel's LanDesk Management Suite is used with Windows NT and later and Novell NetWare. True or False?

24. Ultra Admin cannot provide a list of installed applications on any workstation. True or False?

25. In a NetWare environment, certain events, such as remote console sessions, are logged with the _____ of the connecting station.

HANDS-ON PROJECTS

Project 9-1 Download ConfigMaker

In this project, you will download a program called Cisco ConfigMaker. This exercise requires a workstation that has access to the Internet. You will download this 9.5 MB file using Internet Explorer.

1. Open Internet Explorer and enter the address **http://www.cisco.com/warp/public/cc/pd/nemnsw/cm/index.shtml**.

2. Click the **Click here to download Cisco ConfigMaker Software** link.

3. You will be greeted with a form that you must fill out. Fill out the fields marked with an asterisk (*); they are the required fields.

4. Click the **Submit Form** button at the bottom of the page.

5. Click the **Click here to continue** link at the bottom of the confirmation page.

6. Click the file name in the Select a File to Download text box.

7. You are greeted with the license agreement. Click **Yes** if you agree. If you do not agree, click **No** and do not finish this project.

8. Click the file name to begin the download.

9. Click the **Save this program to disk** option button and then click **OK**.

10. Note the file name and location where Internet Explorer will save the file and click **Save**.

11. When the download is complete, click **Close**.

12. Close Internet Explorer.

Project 9-2 Install ConfigMaker and Run the ConfigMaker Tutorial

In this project, you will install the file that you downloaded in Hands-on Project 9-1.

1. Find the file that you downloaded in the previous project using Windows Explorer.
2. Double-click the file name to start the installation.
3. Click **Next** and then click **Yes** to accept the software license agreement.
4. Click **Next** to accept the default install location or browse to reach a different directory.
5. Uncheck the **Readme** check box and click **Finish**. ConfigMaker is now installed.
6. To run ConfigMaker, click **Start**, point to **Programs**, and then click **ConfigMaker**.
7. Click **Yes** when ConfigMaker asks if you would like to view the tutorial.
8. Follow the tutorial instructions until you have finished the tutorial.
9. Exit all programs and close all windows.

Project 9-3 Download and Install UltraAdmin

9

In this project, you will download a program called UltraAdmin. This exercise requires a workstation that has access to the Internet. You will use Internet Explorer to download this 5 MB file.

1. Open Internet Explorer and go to **http://home.ntware.com**.
2. Type **ultra admin** in the Search WinNT/2000Archives: text box, and then click the **Search!** button.
3. Find the search result that says "Administration 5" and click that link.
4. Scroll down the page until you see UltraAdmin. Click the **Download Now!** button.
5. Click the **Save this file to disk** option button and then click **OK**.
6. Note the file name and location where Internet Explorer will save the file, and then click **Save**.
7. When the download is complete, click **Close**.
8. Close Internet Explorer.
9. Find the file that you just downloaded in Windows Explorer.
10. Double-click the file name to start the installation.
11. Click **Yes**.
12. Follow the instructions in the setup program.
13. Restart your computer when prompted to do so.
14. To run UltraAdmin, click **Start**, point to **Programs** point to **UltraAdmin**, and then click **UltraAdmin**.

15. When prompted, enter the domain or workgroup for which your computer is configured, and then click **OK**.

16. To find out information about any of the computers in your network, select the computer in the list and click the **Computer Info** button.

17. Examine UltraAdmin by clicking several of the buttons on the toolbar.

18. Exit all programs and close all windows.

Project 9-4 Use WinMSD to Create a Report About Your Computers

This project requires Windows 2000 Professional or Windows 2000 Server on your computer.

1. Click **Start**, click **Run**, type **cmd**, and then press **Enter**.

2. Type **winmsd /?**. You will see a help screen.

3. Examine the options available for this command and then click **OK**.

4. From the command prompt, type **winmsd /report C:\mypcinfo.txt** (you may substitute C:\ with a different drive and path if desired).

5. Wait until the report is finished. It may take several seconds to complete or even more than a minute.

6. Exit the command prompt by typing **exit**. (You can close the command prompt even if the report isn't finished.)

7. Using Windows Explorer, locate the file you created. When the file size is greater than 0 bytes, the report is finished. Double-click the file and examine it in Notepad. (You can limit the amount of information in this report by using some of the other options in WinMSD.)

8. Exit all programs and close all windows.

Project 9-5 Use WinMSD

This project requires Windows 2000 Professional or Windows 2000 Server on your computer. You will use WinMSD to create a report for another computer on your network.

1. Click **Start**, click **Run**, type **cmd**, and then press **Enter**.

2. At the command prompt, type **winmsd /computer** *computername* **/report C:***computername***-info.txt** (where *computername* is the name of another Windows 2000 computer on your network). (You may substitute C:\ with a different drive and path if desired.)

3. Wait while the report finishes. It may take several minutes.

4. Exit the command prompt by typing **exit**. (You can close the command prompt even if the report isn't finished.)

5. Using Windows Explorer, locate the file you created. When the file size is greater than 0 bytes, the report is finished. Double-click the file and examine it in Notepad.

6. Write a short note to your instructor explaining how the /computer option used with WinMSD in this project could save you time in documenting the computers in your network.

7. Exit all programs and close all windows.

CASE PROJECTS

Case 9-1 Create a Diagram of Your Network

Using ConfigMaker (directions for downloading it are in Hands-on Project 9-1), create a network diagram of your school or classroom network. (*Hint:* Under the View menu, select Options, and then select the Advanced tab. Uncheck the five check boxes you see there.)

Case 9-2 Create a Cut Sheet for Your Classroom Network

Create a cut sheet for your classroom network. If possible, use a tester to determine the length of each cable run; otherwise, use the feet marks on the cable to calculate the length.

Case 9-3 Create an Equipment List for Your Campus Network Equipment Rooms

Using the sample equipment list in Table 9-5, create an equipment list for your campus equipment rooms. If this documentation does not already exist, you can provide a service to your IT department by helping gather this important information.

Case 9-4 Create a Database of MAC and IP Addresses

Create a database of the MAC addresses and IP addresses in your campus or classroom network. This database should be searchable by device name, MAC address, or IP address. If your devices are not labeled, create a naming scheme and label the devices first.

Case 9-5 Investigate Tools

Go to *http://home.ntware.com* and browse the available tools listed on that site. Write down the names of the tools that you think would be useful in maintaining your network documentation. If permitted, download one of the tools and demonstrate it to the class.

Case 9-6 Research Documentation and Management Tools

Research the Intel LanDesk Management Suite and the BindView development tools for NetWare. These tools can be found at *developer.intel.com/network/products/landesk/landesk_mgmtsuite_v6.htm* and *www.bindview.com,* respectively. Compare and contrast the features available in both tools for documenting and managing a NetWare network.

9

CHAPTER

10

TOOLS FOR NETWORK TROUBLESHOOTING AND SUPPORT

After reading this chapter and completing the exercises, you will be able to:

♦ Discuss a variety of tools for testing and troubleshooting a network

♦ Discuss procedures involved with monitoring and baselining a network

♦ Describe and select from a variety of network monitoring tools

All of the knowledge in the world about cabling standards, frame formats, and packet headers can be useless if you cannot get the information you require from your network. A good network administrator needs technical knowledge, but he or she also needs tools to collect the information from the network.

In this chapter, we look first at the network testing and troubleshooting tools that you can use to get your network in top shape. Then, we concentrate on strategies for monitoring your network. Afterward, we look at the network monitoring tools that you can use to maintain the network in optimal condition.

TOOLS FOR TESTING AND TROUBLESHOOTING YOUR NETWORK

An untested network is a long, sleepless weekend waiting to happen. You may be the cable-installation guru of the universe, heeding every rule ever written about cable bend radius and cable termination, but no amount of knowledge and care on your part is going to make up for a bad batch of cable, a fault in the patch panel manufacturing, a bad NIC driver, or a bad hub port. The worst part is that the network may even work with some of these faults, but with errors and retransmissions that can seriously rob your network of the performance your users crave.

Back in Chapter 3, we discussed the Physical layer and its importance to the health of your network. We begin this chapter with a closer look at what tests are required to ensure a healthy cable installation and some of the tools available to perform those tests.

Testing Cable

Your first goal is to understand what should be tested in a cable installation. This understanding will help you see why a $10 tester that consists of some LEDs and a 9-volt battery will not do the job. As discussed in Chapter 3, different cable standards require different levels of testing. For example, the tests required to certify Category 5 cable include wiremap, near-end crosstalk (NEXT), length, and attenuation as specified by TSB67 from TIA/EIA. A newer standard, TSB95, specifies additional tests required for Category 5E and Category 6 cable. These tests include the equal-level far-end crosstalk (ELFEXT) test and the return loss test. We discuss each in turn.

Wiremap

The **wiremap** test checks for continuity of each wire from each pin on the connector on one end of the cable to the corresponding pin on the other end of the cable. In addition, the wiremap checks for common wiring pair faults such as reversed pairs, transposed pairs, and split pairs.

The most difficult of these faults to detect is the split pair. Split pairs were discussed in Chapter 3. This type of fault cannot be detected by simple continuity checks, but rather requires the tester to use information gained from the NEXT test. The wiremap test is usually the only test that can be performed by the simple LED cable checkers, and those tests cannot detect split pairs. Although the wiremap test is extremely important and detects some of the more common wiring faults, it cannot guarantee the reliability or performance of your cable installation.

Near-End Crosstalk (NEXT)

Crosstalk occurs when the signal transmission on one pair of wires leaks onto a nearby pair. Near-end crosstalk is the ratio in volts between the test signal injected into one pair of wires and the crosstalk signal detected on another pair when both pairs are measured from the same end of the link. The NEXT value is expressed in decibels (dB), and the higher the value the better. The reason we want a high NEXT value is because we are calculating the *ratio* between the injected signal and the crosstalk signal. We want the injected signal to be at a much higher level than the signal created by crosstalk.

NEXT is measured from every pair to every other pair. Thus, in the four-pair wiring scheme found in UTP cabling, 12 different NEXT tests will be conducted. Furthermore, NEXT tests must be done from both ends of the cable because NEXT checks the effects of crosstalk only on the end of the cable from which the test signal is generated. Some cable testers have the ability to perform NEXT tests at both ends of the cable at the same time; this failure is a worthwhile option if you have a lot of cable to test.

Cable Length

As you well know from the lengthy discussion in Chapter 3, cable length is critical in a network installation. The usual result of cable that exceeds the maximum length requirement is increased attenuation, or an increase in possibility for late collisions, particularly at higher transfer rates.

Cable length is measured using **time domain reflectometry (TDR)**. TDR is the measurement, in nanoseconds, of the time it takes a signal to travel the length of a wire and return, or reflect, back on that same wire. In a properly installed cable, the signal will reflect after it finds the end of the wire, giving you the total length of the cable run.

Installation faults can also cause the signal to reflect. These problems include cables of differing impedance used in the same cable run, crushed or pinched cable (possibly caused by overly tight wire wraps or staples), and kinks caused by extreme bends in the cable. The TDR function can help you find faults of these types in addition to cable runs that exceed the maximum length.

Electrical signals do not travel through all types of wire at the same rate. The rate at which the signals travel is referred to as the **nominal velocity of propagation (NVP)**. Even within the same cable type from the same manufacturer, this value can vary by several percent from manufacturing lot to manufacturing lot. If extreme accuracy in your length measurements is critical, you may need to calibrate your test equipment using a known length of wire from the lot of cable you are running. For typical installations, it is sufficient to merely select the cable type (Category 5, Category 5E, and so on); the NVP used will be typical for the type selected.

Attenuation

Recall that attenuation is the decrease in signal strength as the signal travels the length of the wire. Attenuation becomes greater with longer links and higher transmission speeds. Unlike NEXT, attenuation need be measured from only one direction. Attenuation is expressed as a loss of energy measured in decibels. The higher the value, the poorer the quality of the signal.

10

Attenuation must be measured at the highest frequency rated for the cable type. Both Category 5 and Category 5E cables require a testing frequency of 100 MHz. The proposed Category 6 cable requires attenuation to be tested up to 250 MHz. The highest allowable attenuation for Category 5 and Category 5E cable at 100 MHz is 22 dB; it is 32 dB for Category 6 cable tested at 250 MHz.

Another factor that affects attenuation is temperature. The previously mentioned values are specified for an operating temperature of 20°C and will increase slightly as the temperature increases. Cabling installed in metal conduit may see the attenuation increase a couple of percentage points as well.

You must have the four testing parameters to certify Category 5 cabling. Category 5E and Category 6 require additional tests. The additional tests required of Category 5E cabling can also be performed on cable specified as Category 5 cabling to certify it to carry 1 GB Ethernet. It is believed that most Category 5 cabling installations, having passed the Category 5 tests, will be able to carry 1 GB Ethernet.

ELFEXT

Far-end crosstalk (FEXT), as the name implies, measures the crosstalk ratio at the opposite end of the link from where the test signal is being applied. **Equal-level far-end crosstalk (ELFEXT)** is the ratio of the FEXT and the attenuation measured in the wire pair being tested. It provides an **attenuation to crosstalk ratio (ACR)** on the far end of the cable, which is critical when two or more wire pairs carry data in the same direction as does 1 GB Ethernet. This value is not critical for 10BaseT and 100BaseT Ethernet, because only one wire pair carries data in one direction at a time in those schemes.

Return Loss

Return loss is a value resulting from impedance mismatches along an entire cable link segment. Any differences in impedance within the cable run or connecting equipment such as jacks and patch panels along the link causes reflections that result in loss of signal. Return loss is measured in decibels and varies significantly with frequency, which is why it is a particularly important testing parameter for 1 GB Ethernet.

Impedance mismatches are most common at connectors, but variations in impedance can be introduced along a length of wire during manufacturing as well. The amount of impedance mismatch found within the cable is usually small because manufacturers must have procedures in place to monitor for irregularities. Nevertheless, this important testing parameter is required for Category 5E and Category 6 cabling.

 For a more thorough treatment of these cable testing parameters and more, an excellent Web resource is *www.cablemeter.com*.

Now that you have some idea of what is expected of your cable tester, we can examine some cable test equipment and discuss various features available with several of the leading testers now on the market.

Cable Testers

In this section, we examine cable testers from the three dominant cable test equipment manufacturers in the industry: Fluke Networks, Microtest, and Agilent Technologies. Each of these manufacturers carries cable testers of varying features and capabilities, and it is up to you (and your budget) to decide which tester has the right features to meet the requirements of your network now and in the future. The last thing you want to do is purchase a cable tester that will have to be replaced next year because of your lack of forethought.

There are no doubt other cable testing products available, and I cover only the low-end, mid-range, and high-end testers from each of the three dominant cable test manufacturers. This discussion is designed to give an overview of the variety of products available, not to endorse any particular product.

The low-end basic testers discussed range in price from around $300 to $600. The mid-range products range in price from nearly $2500 to more than $5000. In addition, the higher-end products range in price from almost $5000 to more than $6000. Additional accessories, such as fiber modules, can cause the price of these cable testers to top $10,000. As you can see, a certified cable plant comes at a price, but the security of a certified cable plant, along with the troubleshooting time that can be saved and the solid documentation these tools provide, is well worth the cost.

10

Fluke Networks

For basic testing of correct wiremap and length, Fluke Networks (*www.flukenetworks.com*) offers a low-cost solution in the Fluke 620 LAN CableMeter. This tester is convenient to check for correct termination if you do not have time to do a complete performance test. It is available as a single-ended tester, meaning that you do not need a second unit at the other end of the cable to detect basic wiring faults such as opens, shorts, and split pairs. An optional cable identifier, which is used at the other end of the cable, is also available; it eases cable identification and can check for reversed and transposed pairs.

This tester will not certify your cable plant to EIA/TIA standards but rather is a low-cost basic checker that can be used when certification is not necessary or when performance and certification tests will be done at a later time. You can find out more about the Fluke 620 LAN CableMeter by going to *www.flukenetworks.com/us/Cabling/default.htm*.

For a Category 5 certified installation, Fluke offers the DSP-100 Digital CableMeter. This cable analyzer certifies your cable to EIA/TIA TSB67 standards by performing a battery of tests including the NEXT test on both ends of the cable, saving you the trouble of performing tests from both ends. In addition, this tester will store more than 1000 test results, permitting you to download these results to be included in your cable plant documentation. In addition to UTP cabling, the DSP-100 can test STP and coaxial cable. With an optional fiber test kit, the DSP-100 can test for power loss, breaks, and poor connections in fiber-optic cable assemblies.

Fluke's high-end tester, the DSP-4000, provides cable certification up to Category 6; it conforms with the TIA/EIA-568B draft specification for cable testing. The DSP-4000 offers a modular approach to cable testing by using adapters to match the type of cable being tested. Thus, even though the Category 6 standard was not complete as of fall 2001, the DSP-4000 offers link adapters for products sold by the majority of Category 6 jack, plug, and patch panel manufacturers.

After the Category 6 standard is completed, Fluke will offer a Category 6 link adapter to match standardized equipment. In addition to providing higher-performance testing, the DSP-4000 offers test management software that collects, organizes, and provides searchable cable test results. This modular product also offers fiber-optic test adapters providing single-mode, multimode, and gigabit Ethernet over multimode fiber-optic testing.

Microtest

Microtest (*www.microtest.com*) offers a range of cable testing products similar to Fluke Networks' line. The basic cable test unit from Microtest is the Microscanner, which performs tests similar to those performed by the Fluke 620 CableMeter, including cable length and wiremap tests. The Microscanner includes a wiremap adapter, which must be used on the other end of the cable to perform wiremap tests.

Like the Fluke 620, the Microscanner is not intended to certify your cable installation; rather, this tool is designed to quickly detect common installation faults so that they can be corrected on the spot. A cable analyzer should then be used to certify the installation.

For Category 5 certified cabling installations, Microtest offers the PentaScanner+ and PentaScanner350. Both models test cable to see whether it meets or exceeds the TIA/EIA TSB67 standard. The PentaScanner350 comes with a two-way signal injector that allows NEXT testing from both ends of the cable simultaneously, whereas the PentaScanner+ requires that the test be done twice, once at each end of the cable. Both PentaScanner models can store a maximum of 500 saved test results for download to a PC for documentation.

Microtest's flagship cable scanner is the OmniScanner II, which is able to certify cable through Category 6 and even claims to test cable to the proposed Category 7 cable standard. The OmniScanner II uses link adapters to match manufacturers' Category 6 equipment, similar to the Fluke DSP-4000. This tester includes cable test management software with graphical displays, allowing you to present your results professionally. As many as 10,000 test results can be stored using flash memory, so your results are safe even if the unit's battery dies.

Because the OmniScanner uses a modular approach to cable testing, single-mode and multimode fiber-optic testing can be accomplished with the optional OmniFiber adapter. For more information on the OmniScanner II and the rest of the Microtest cable testing products, see *www.microtest.com/ntmhome.jhtml.* As an added bonus, Microtest has a downloadable document at *www.microtest.com/omniscanner/Cpr_Prem_Req.jhtml* that can be used for specifying cabling acceptance requirements. This document can be included in a bid for performing cable installation and testing.

Agilent Technologies

Agilent manufactures two cable testers, foregoing an entry-level basic tester. The Wirescope 155 tests cable to Category 5E standards, meeting all TSB67 requirements for that category. In addition, like some of the other products discussed previously, the Wirescope 155 can store test results for later uploading and analysis on a PC. Optional fiber modules, called Fiber SmartProbes, are available to test single-mode and multimode fiber. The Wirescope 155 is designed to perform the tests necessary to certify cable ready for gigabit Ethernet, and it can perform most of the tests required for Category 6 cabling, up to 160 MHz. (The proposed Category 6 standard requires testing to 250 MHz.)

The Wirescope 350 certifies cable to the Category 6 standard and beyond with a testing frequency range up to 350 MHz. It sports a user-friendly color touch screen for easy navigation and on-screen color graphics. The large display screen makes viewing of cable faults clear and easy to understand. Test results can be stored on removable flash cards, allowing for the storage of as many as 59,000 cable tests with the optional 192 MB flash card. Like the Wirescope 155, the Wirescope 350 supports the Fiber SmartProbes for easy and accurate fiber-optic testing. An abundance of information on Agilent's Wirescope products is available at *http://wirescope.comms.agilent.com/products/.*

Cable testing is first and foremost used as a method to ensure that your network infrastructure works after initial installation, but it can also help solve problems that occur after the network is installed. Some of the advanced cable testers discussed here have troubleshooting features that detect data errors on a working network. To perform a detailed examination of data packets and frames, however, a protocol analyzer is the tool of choice.

Protocol Analyzers

A protocol analyzer's primary purpose is to capture and decode frames as they travel your network. Your Physical layer installation may be certified and working perfectly, but applications, protocol stacks, internetworking devices, and device drivers can cause network problems that a cable tester alone cannot diagnose. In addition, while some protocol analyzers can detect data errors such as CRC errors, fragments, and jabbers, their strength lies in decoding frames so as to allow people to easily see Data Link, Network, and Transport layer headers as well as the data contained in each frame. In this section, we examine protocol analyzers from three different companies: Wildpackets, Fluke Networks, and Sniffer Technologies.

This look at three common protocol analyzers will give you an idea of the features and capabilities of this category of products. It is not intended to provide an in-depth or exhaustive look at the features of each product. Please refer to the Web site addresses listed for detailed examination of each.

The prices for these products range from nearly $1000 to more than $20,000—again, the capabilities of these products come at a price. Without such a tool, the solution to a problem may elude you for days, weeks, or longer, whereas the detailed information these products can provide may help you find a solution in minutes.

It is worth mentioning that there are less expensive products whose features may not be as extensive, but which may do what you need. An example of such a product is CommView from TamoSoft. This product (which lists for less than $125) captures and decodes packets with few frills but may be just the tool you need in the absence of a more expensive package. A free evaluation can be downloaded from *www.tamos.com*. If you want to try an absolutely free product, try PackAnalyzer from *www.cs.umd.edu/~cpopescu/NetAnalyzer/*. Although this product does not have many of the advanced features of some of the commercial products, such as expert diagnosis or plug-in modules, it provides basic packet capture and decode functions.

Wildpackets' EtherPeek

By now, you should be reasonably familiar with packet capturing, filter creation, and decoding with EtherPeek. EtherPeek does a fine job at all of these tasks and makes filter creation particularly easy. Some of the other capabilities of this product come in the form of plug-ins that perform specific filtering tasks on captured or monitored data. **Plug-ins** are special filters that collect statistics or watch for particular types of packet, such as Internet attacks or viruses. For instance, a virus called Code Red that was going around the Internet at the time of this writing can be detected by a downloadable plug-in from Wildpackets' Web site.

Plug-ins, such as InternetAttack, can detect a variety of attack types, including well-known ones such as Land, WinNuke, and Teardrop. Figure 10-1 shows the InternetAttack screen and the EtherPeek plug-ins configuration screen. In addition to the plug-ins shipped with EtherPeek, plug-ins can be easily developed with the included software developer kit.

Another nice feature of EtherPeek is the Summary Statistics screen, which shows a detailed summary of packets captured or total packets seen while EtherPeek has been running. The summary includes general utilization statistics as well as statistics specific to the packets filtered by the plug-ins. The general statistics that this screen shows include total packets, total broadcasts, and percentage utilization. Error, packet size, and protocol statistics can also be viewed. Figure 10-2 shows statistics for currently active plug-ins.

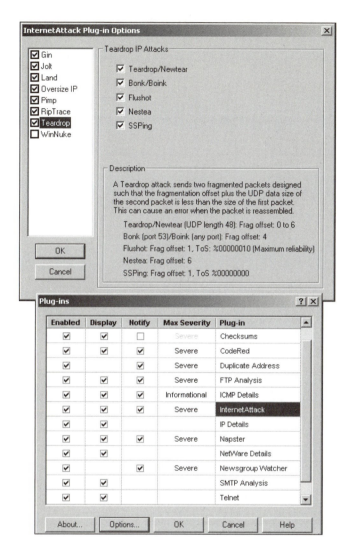

Figure 10-1   EtherPeek screens

As you can see, this protocol analyzer can do more than capture and decode packets. It can provide important statistics on those packets, which may aid you in network problem solving. For more information on EtherPeek, see Wildpackets' Web site at *www.wildpackets.com*.

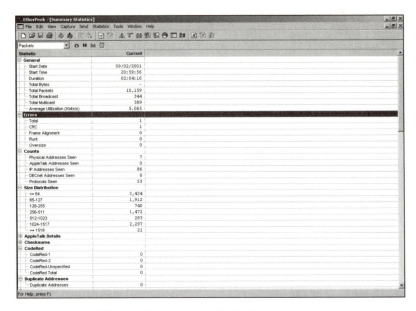

Figure 10-2   EtherPeek Summary Statistics

Fluke Networks' Protocol Inspector

The Protocol Inspector from Fluke Networks uses a three-paned display as its packet capture interface, in contrast to EtherPeek's single-pane display. The three-paned display shows the list of captured frames at the top, a layer-by-layer display of the selected frame in the middle, and raw data on the bottom. The display is color-coded by protocol, allowing you to scan the list of frames and easily pick out packets of a particular type, such as HTTP or FTP. Figure 10-3 shows a Fluke packet capture display.

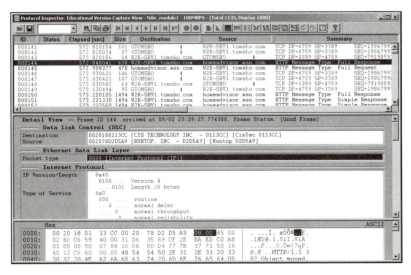

Figure 10-3   Fluke packet capture

Creating and applying filters is somewhat less straightforward with the Protocol Inspector than with EtherPeek's simple point-and-click interface, which offers several ready-made filters from which to choose. However, Fluke's filter creation capability is nonetheless powerful and there is little you cannot do with it. The filter creation interface uses a visual state machine, allowing you to combine filter criteria in complex ways. This option can be a powerful feature but you'll probably want to make additional filters, so that you can choose common protocols to filter on with a single click. Figure 10-4 shows the filter creation interface, and Figure 10-5 shows the Quick Filter dialog box in which you can build filters.

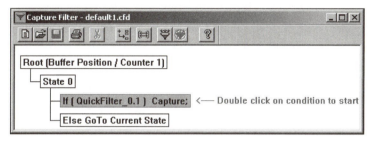

Figure 10-4   Fluke filter creation

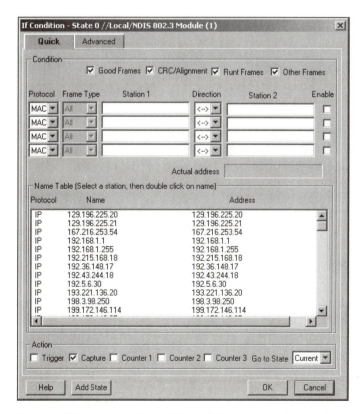

Figure 10-5   Fluke Quick Filter dialog box

Protocol Inspector is chock full of buttons for bringing up graphs displaying statistics such as top sending and receiving stations, protocol distribution, and application conversations, among others. This ability can be handy when you want to get the big picture on your network as it is currently operating. Figure 10-6 shows several of these displays.

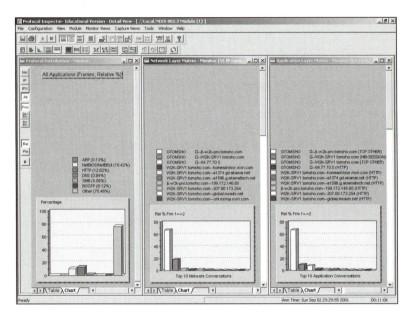

Figure 10-6   Fluke graphical displays

Protocol Inspector even has a display for showing switch VLAN statistics by examining Cisco's ISL protocol packets. If you need to monitor network segments other than the one on which Protocol Inspector is installed, Fluke offers a software remote-control option as well as hardware-based distributed inspector modules for use in switched environments. Additional software options include an expert analysis module that scans your packet captures, detects problems, and suggests solutions. Voice over IP analysis can also be purchased as an option.

 More information on Protocol Inspector and its optional accessories can be found at *www.flukenetworks.com*.

Sniffer Technologies' Sniffer Pro

The Sniffer line of products from Sniffer Technologies (a business unit of Network Associates) has long been the standard for protocol analysis. Sniffer decodes almost any protocol you will encounter and also decodes database transactions from Oracle and the Sybase/Microsoft SQL servers.

Sniffer's configurable three-pane display permits the network administrator to see as much or as little information in the packet summary pane as he or she wishes—from Data Link layer information to Application layer information. What really makes Sniffer stand out is its real-time expert diagnosis system. This product watches for a variety of symptoms as packets are captured and flags potential problems as they occur. Many of the symptoms Sniffer searches out are based on configurable thresholds, which the administrator has the ability to modify.

Figure 10-7 shows the Expert summary display, and Figure 10-8 shows the Expert detail on a flagged symptom. Notice that each symptom listed in Figure 10-8 has a question mark button associated with it. Clicking this button brings up the Expert explanation shown on the right, which includes an explanation of the symptom and a list of possible causes. Note that many of the symptoms flagged are only possible problems; and in some cases, it is the administrator's responsibility to determine whether the symptom represents a real problem or a normal situation for the network. That explains why thresholds can be set on many parameters so that Sniffer can be configured to report only symptoms of parameters that cross the threshold. Examples of configurable thresholds include TCP acknowledgment times, low throughput, and server response times.

10

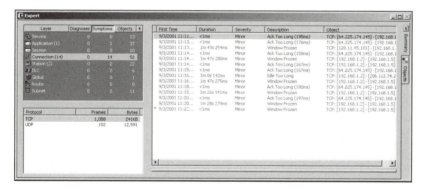

Figure 10-7   Sniffer Expert summary display

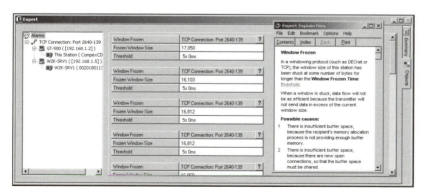

Figure 10-8   Sniffer Expert detail display

Like the other protocol analyzers discussed here, Sniffer can display a variety of graphs and statistics to provide an overall picture of the operation of your network. It also has the ability to work with switches that support port mirroring and RMON, which allows a single Sniffer station to monitor several switch ports and display information gathered by the RMON software built into the switch. A short discussion of RMON appears later in this chapter. For more information on the complete line of Sniffer products, see *www.sniffer.com*.

Sometimes you do not need to look at packet headers and traffic flow and simply need to determine whether a device is responding. For this simple task, you have tools available on your PC right now, or you can get some inexpensive products that simplify the monitoring of the status of several devices.

Basic Connectivity Tools

For basic connectivity verification, there is the old standby, the Ping utility. In addition, if the Ping utility fails on a device on a different network, you can use the Trace Route utility. The problem with Ping is that it is a command-line utility and you have to enter the ping command to get results; the same applies to the Trace Route utility.

If all that you need to do is monitor a device's up/down status on a regular basis, there are a variety of inexpensive products available. An interesting one that offers an evaluation download is Alchemy Network Monitor, from Dek Software. You specify the servers or devices you wish to monitor by supplying the name or address of the server and the service you wish to use to contact the server. What makes this option interesting is that you are not limited to using ICMP messages (used by the Ping utility) to determine the status of a server. This flexibility is ideal because some Internet devices may block ICMP echo requests. If you are more interested in whether a particular service, such as HTTP or FTP, is available, rather than just in whether the server can respond to a ping, you should use Alchemy Network Monitor as well.

Figure 10-9 shows the server display for Alchemy Network Monitor. Simple ICMP messages are being used on the first four devices in the list, whereas the fifth device is checking on the HTTP service and the last device is using TCP on port 110 to check on the POP3 mail service. The ability to specify a TCP port is useful because you can monitor a specific service operating on a server.

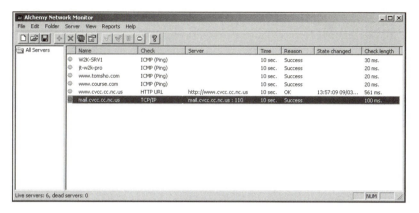

Figure 10-9   Alchemy Network Monitor

You can also specify how many attempts Alchemy Network Monitor should make to contact the server before deciding that it is down and who should be notified if the server goes down and when it comes back up. These configuration options are shown in Figure 10-10. More information and a free evaluation can be found at *www.deksoftware.com*.

10

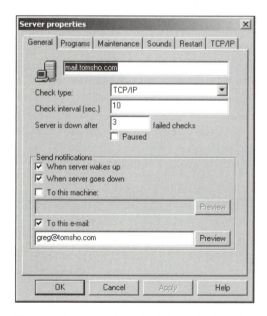

Figure 10-10   Alchemy Server properties dialog box

VisualPulse, from Visualware, is another resource status program that provides additional information besides simply whether the server is up or down. VisualPulse provides information on response time or latency of the server and dropped packet statistics as well as up/down status. It also has a convenient Web interface so that the information can be viewed with any Web browser. VisualPulse relies on ICMP echo request messages, meaning that you cannot verify specific services; if the server is behind a firewall that blocks ICMP, the server will always appear down. Figure 10-11 shows the latency display interface.

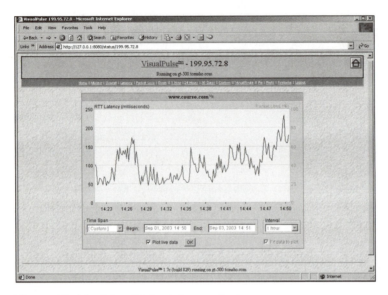

Figure 10-11   VisualPulse latency display

An add-on utility available separately or packaged with VisualPulse is VisualRoute. VisualRoute does Trace Route one better by providing a graphical look at the route taken from the VisualRoute server to a specified host. Figure 10-12 shows this utility tracking the route from the VisualRoute server run by Visualware in Dulles, Virginia, to www.microsoft.com. For more information on VisualPulse and other Visualware products, go to *www.visualware.com*.

An abundance of utilities that provide similar capabilities to the programs discussed here can be found on the Internet for free or evaluation downloading. Some of the Web sites to try include *www.tucows.com* and *http://home.ntware.com*.

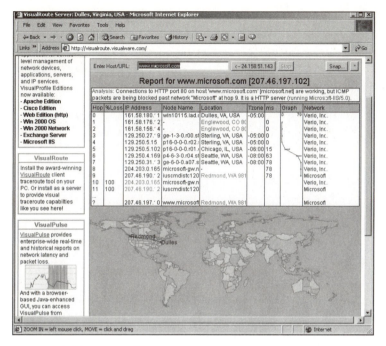

Figure 10-12 VisualRoute

MONITORING YOUR NETWORK

Monitoring your network means collecting information about the operational and performance parameters of your network devices and media. You monitor your network to locate problems, determine trends, and maintain security. You can use this information to solve problems and, ideally, to prevent problems from occurring in the first place by detecting trends or security holes that may later become a problem. In this section, we discuss what should be monitored and how to use this information to create a baseline against which you can compare future monitoring sessions.

 Network monitoring and measuring network performance are not exact sciences. They take time and experience to master. In addition, approaches may differ depending on your environment and equipment. This section serves as merely an introduction to the subject.

Creating a Baseline

A baseline is a measure of a network's current performance. The raw data in a baseline is not sufficient to tell you how your network is performing; rather, you must analyze the information collected and compare your results against the perceived operation of the network. Ideally, a baseline is taken when the operation of the network is considered good—by user standards. Remember, as a network administrator, your job exists to ensure timely and secure access to your company's network resources. When creating your baseline and determining results, the results must be put into the context of how the network users perceive the usability of the network.

Creating your baseline requires the following steps:

1. Determine what type of information should be gathered.

2. Decide which devices can best reflect the information you require.

3. Determine the baseline intervals and duration.

4. Gather the necessary tools to collect the required information.

We discuss each in turn.

What Should Be Baselined?

What information do you want to collect? You need to choose information that best reflects the requirements of your users in their use of the network. Do not go overboard with data collection. Collecting too much information will merely confuse and overwhelm you when it comes time to analyze the data.

If database server response and Internet access times are among the most critical factors to your users, then that is perhaps where you should start. Baselining is not a static undertaking. You can start small and expand the reach of your baseline as time goes by and you become more practiced.

To start, you may want to do some experimentation to determine which parameters in your network best reflect your final goal. For example, which factors in your network most affect database server response time? You may think that CPU utilization on the server and network congestion affect it most. You can test this theory by cranking up CPU utilization with a test program and creating traffic on some network links (preferably when normal network usage is low) while accessing the database.

After testing, you may find that available server RAM has more effects than CPU utilization does. If that is the case, you can adjust the parameters you will measure in your baseline. The point is that you should attempt to measure those factors that will most likely affect the performance issues with which you are concerned.

The following are some common performance-related categories and subcategories for which you may want to gather data:

- Utilization
  - Server and router CPU
  - Switch and hub links
  - Router links

- Response time
  - File and print servers
  - Database servers
  - Web and e-mail servers
- Resource availability
  - All servers
  - Gateways (such as links to the Internet and other networks)

Pick Your Baseline Points

Now that you have decided what to measure, you should decide where to measure it. Select the servers, network links, and device ports that are most critical to showing the information you need. Here is where your good documentation practices come in handy. Which devices are serving the most critical users, and through which links will the majority of the traffic in which you are interested (database and Internet accesses, for example) travel? If your documentation is wrong, you may end up monitoring ports that have little to do with the scenario you are trying to baseline. Pick your points carefully and monitor only a limited number of devices and device ports at first so that your picture is clear and easy to understand. More information can be added in future baselines, if necessary.

Determine Your Baseline Schedule

Your baseline schedule will, in part, be determined by how your organization operates. You want to get a picture of how your network operates throughout a day, throughout a week, and perhaps throughout a month. Your baseline, therefore, should be scheduled to collect information for at least one week and probably for at least four weeks. If your network is not used 24 hours per day, you may not need to monitor it during nonoperational hours; if there is no activity on weekends, you need not include weekends either. Remember, however, that if you have remote access capabilities or your network houses publicly accessible resources such as Web or FTP servers, people may access the network at odd times, day or night.

Try to avoid baselining the network during unusual usage periods, regardless of whether "unusual" means unusually high or unusually low. If you have periods throughout the year or within a month that are unusual compared to other periods, a separate baseline is warranted for those times. If you are a retailer or toy manufacturer, for example, you don't want statistics gathered during the Christmas shopping period to be used as a baseline to compare against the month of July!

Once you decide on the duration for the baseline, you need to determine an interval between baselines. Whether it is every other month, quarterly, or some other interval, you need to stick to it so that you can accurately predict trends by comparing one baseline to another.

You will be collecting a considerable amount of data, so you need to ensure that your storage capacity is set to handle that amount of information. Do not use a floppy disk to store data collected for a month, for example.

Gather the Tools Needed for the Baseline

Once you know what to baseline and when you are going to baseline it, you need the appropriate tools that allow you to gather the information required. This requirement probably means network monitoring tools and server performance monitors.

In a switched and routed network, you will need monitoring tools that can collect information across switch and router segments, or you will need a way to consolidate information that has been collected in a distributed fashion. Thus you probably need switches, hubs, and routers that support remote monitoring protocols such as RMON and that can be remotely managed via SNMP. If you do not have this capability in a large network, the job will be much more difficult.

You'll want to collect the data for the duration and times you require, so the ability to schedule monitoring sessions is desirable. We have discussed some network monitoring tools that are available with protocol analyzers. Some of those packages may do the job for you. We will look at additional monitoring software and hardware options later in this chapter.

Analyze the Baseline

You have collected the data; now it is time to use that information. It will take some time and experience, but you will learn what the data collected means to you and to your network users. The analysis of the baseline is your interpretation of the data that you have collected and its effects on your network. Unfortunately, there is no magic formula that works in every situation. Because each network is different, you cannot look up in a reference book what each number you see means to your network. That is something that comes with experience, consistent application of your baseline, and careful attention to your users. Your baseline will be helpful to you in several key areas:

- Determining utilization of resources
- Predicting trends
- Defining thresholds
- Justifying network upgrade plans

We discuss each in turn.

Determine Utilization of Resources

Just as the utilization of our nation's roads and interstates has varying levels of use, your network links and servers will vary in their usage—sometimes dramatically. You can use this information to pinpoint pathways that are used to capacity or in excess of capacity and to find pathways that are underutilized. In some cases, you may be able to adjust your routing tables or switch port usage to ease the burden on one link by offloading traffic to another, less heavily used link.

If a server appears underutilized, you can install additional services on it while disabling the corresponding services on an overburdened server. Even if you cannot make adjustments to improve matters immediately, at least you will have a better picture of how your network is operating, allowing you to plan for future changes in design or configuration.

The data you examine can tell you not only what is being used and to what capacity, but also who is monopolizing the resource or at least which applications or protocols are predominantly used. For example, if switch port 5 on SW1-IDF2 shows extreme amounts of FTP traffic at 4 P.M. every day, you may find that Jim in engineering is taking advantage of the fast Internet connection to download demos of his favorite games and utilities every day.

Predict Trends

Your network may be in fine shape this month. If you take regular baselines, however, you may see trends in utilization or error rates that indicate pending problems. Perhaps Internet usage is increasing by 10 percent per month, or error rates on a particular segment have been climbing steadily. Or perhaps a trend shows up that is not performance-related in of itself, such as use of particular TCP port numbers. This type of information can tell you whether use of applications such as ICQ or Napster is on the rise. Any gradual change in traffic or usage patterns can be significant in the long run, and regular baselines can reveal these patterns.

Define Thresholds

After you have an idea of what is normal or typical for your network, you can use this information to define thresholds for various data points. This step permits you to do daily monitoring with assigned thresholds on such parameters as bandwidth utilization, CPU utilization, broadcast rates, transaction rates, and error rates, among others. If the threshold value is exceeded, you can set the monitoring software to create a log entry or, in the event of a critical threshold, page or e-mail someone. The baseline is used to determine what is normal over a period of time, so when usage becomes abnormal compared to the baseline, you probably want to know about it.

Justify Network Upgrade Plans

Remember that your network exists to provide a certain level of service to its users. Using the baseline data, you can determine at what performance level the network must operate to provide the desired level of service. When it becomes apparent that the service level will fall below user expectations, you can plan for and implement a network upgrade before the level of service becomes a problem. Your baseline data can help you show that an upgrade is needed to maintain proper service—just the kind of data the boss needs to justify the expenditure.

10

Now that you know some of the reasons for network monitoring and a little about what to monitor in your network, and why, we turn our attention to some of the tools available to monitor and baseline your network.

TOOLS FOR MONITORING YOUR NETWORK

There is no single tool that you can buy that can perform all of your network monitoring tasks. You will likely need and use a collection of tools, just as you do for troubleshooting and testing your network. This section introduces several commonly used and widely available software and hardware packages that do one or more of the tasks you require. We will start by looking at some software-based tools that are comparatively inexpensive but that may be just what the doctor ordered to get your network under control.

Software Network Monitors

We will start by examining a couple of tools with which you may already be familiar and which do not cost anything beyond the cost of the operating system on which they are installed. We will then look at some simple-to-use and comparatively inexpensive tools that go beyond what the freebies can do. Last, I will mention and provide references for a few industrial-strength products whose detailed examination is, unfortunately, beyond the scope of this book.

Windows Performance Monitor

Windows Performance Monitor is not really a network monitoring tool but rather a tool for gathering performance data on your servers, which are an integral part of your network performance picture. Performance Monitor is part of the standard installation of Windows NT Workstation and Server, Windows 2000 Professional and Server, and Windows XP.

Performance Monitor lets you view server or workstation performance in real time, or you can log the results and examine the data later. The former option is useful for responding to user calls complaining about slow server response time. The latter option is what you use for baselining your server or for determining what your server is up to when you are not watching it.

Figure 10-13 shows Performance Monitor graphing CPU utilization, page faults, and NIC utilization. Windows maintains counters on a variety of system objects such as memory, page-file access, disk drive access, and CPU access. The key to using Performance Monitor is to select the best counters to log that will show the performance statistics in which you are interested. If you are not certain what a particular counter does, you can click the Explain button in the Select Counter dialog box to see an explanation.

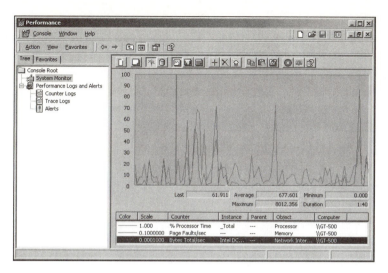

Figure 10-13   Windows 2000 Performance Monitor

Windows 2000 supplies a sample set of counters in the Counter Logs folder that provide a quick system overview. These counters monitor CPU utilization, memory pages accessed, and disk drive queue length. A nice feature of Performance Monitor is that you can collect counter information remotely, which permits you to use one station as the data collector for all of the Windows NT/2000/XP computers you wish to monitor. Hands-on Project 10-5 walks you through the process of using the counter log to collect performance data over a period of time for later examination.

IPSwitch's Whatsup Gold

Whatsup Gold, from IPSwitch, has a variety of features useful for monitoring your network. It can create a map of your network by discovering devices using a variety of methods, including ICMP, SNMP, a hosts file, and Network Neighborhood entries. This product saves you from having to manually enter each of the devices on your network. Additionally, Whatsup Gold can create several maps, each representing a separate subnet, and link these maps together so that you can see the big picture from one main map and drill down to your subnets to view detailed information.

Polling is used to determine the status of devices. You can also scan each device for services and have those services monitored in addition to monitoring simple connectivity. Polling for up/down status can be done with either ICMP or TCP/IP. Color-coded icons are used to indicate the status of devices.

While Whatsup Gold polls devices for status, it maintains performance data, which is logged and can be used later to create graphs and reports. These reports can be selected using a date range, which makes it ideal for helping with your baseline figures. An event log is also maintained that keeps information on events such as devices or services that go down or come up.

Figure 10-14 shows a simple network map created with Whatsup Gold. More information about Whatsup Gold can be found at *www.ipswitch.com/Products/WhatsUp/index.html*.

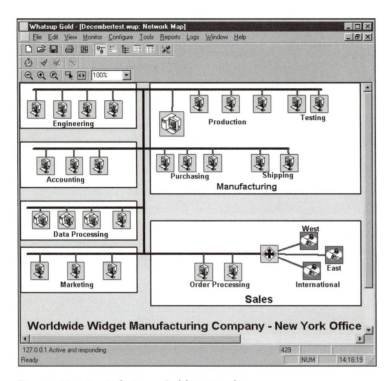

Figure 10-14   Whatsup Gold network map

Fluke Networks' Network Inspector

Network Inspector, from Fluke Networks, has many features similar to Whatsup Gold, albeit with a very different user interface. Network Inspector presents a Windows Explorer-style two-pane interface, with device and network categories appearing in the left pane and the contents of those categories shown in the right pane. This setup makes navigating to the information that you require fairly easy and familiar.

Network Inspector's trending reports are excellent and professional. This product uses RMON to get statistical information from routers and switches; by comparison, Whatsup Gold, uses only round-trip transfer times of ICMP messages.

Network maps are created automatically through an interface with Visio, provided that Visio is installed on your workstation. An example of one of Network Inspector's trending reports on a Cisco 2900 switch is shown in Figure 10-15. This type of report, which provides time-stamps on data points, is a great tool for creating baseline data for your switch and router interfaces. Reports that list IP devices and their offered services, as well as IPX devices, and reports that graph the top error, broadcast, and utilization rates are also available.

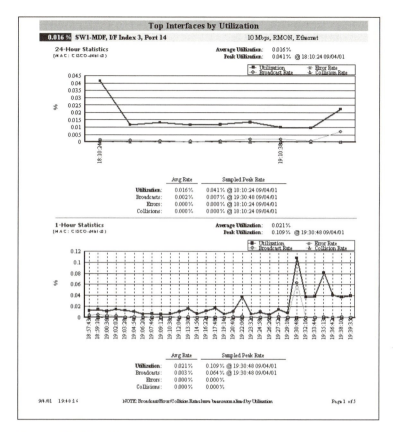

Figure 10-15   Network Inspector trending report

Fluke Networks offers other network monitoring tools, including the Fluke LANMeter, which is a hardware-based monitor. Network Inspector has an interface to collect data from the LANMeter and then graph and trend that data. Overall, Network Inspector is a very capable product that would make an excellent addition to your network toolbox.

High-End Monitoring and Management Tools

The tools we have discussed so far for monitoring your network can be had at a reasonable price (starting at $800) and are quite capable tools for small to medium-sized environments. Beyond that, there is a breed of products that are intended for large and complex networks and that perform both network monitoring and network management tasks.

Some of these products are hardware manufacturer-specific and do their best work when the majority of devices being monitored and managed are manufactured by one company. Examples of such products include Nortel's Optivity Campus and Cisco's CiscoWorks2000. These products allow you to configure, monitor, and upgrade your network devices from a single management console using RMON and SNMP. A third product, HP OpenView, has long been a standard in network monitoring and management. There is a complete line of HP OpenView products that can help you with the complete management and performance monitoring of your network.

These high-end products cost well into the thousands of dollars. Of course, if your network infrastructure costs into the hundreds of thousands of dollars (or more), these products may be the tools you need to get your network under control. More information on HP OpenView can be found at *www.managementsoftware.hp.com*. Information on Nortel's Optivity is at *www.nortelnetworks.com/products/01/unifiedmanagement/index.html*. For more information on CiscoWorks2000, point your browser to *www.cisco.com/warp/public/cc/pd/wr2k/*.

Hardware Network Monitors

At times, you may need to bring the monitor to the network. In such a case, a handheld hardware monitor can be just the right tool. A hardware network monitor is typically lightweight and portable so that you can pick it up and take it to the network segment you need to monitor.

Most of the products in this category perform similar functions, and their goal is generally to monitor the network, report any problems found, and attempt to make a diagnosis of their cause. Some of the tasks performed by these devices include displaying top senders and receivers, detecting duplicate IP addresses, displaying error and collision statistics, showing overall utilization statistics, and listing IP and IPX devices. Some of them can perform cable tests and test hub ports and NIC cards as well. Devices in this category include the Fluke Networks' LANMeter, Microtest's Compas, and Acterna's LANChecker 100.

Among these three devices, the LANChecker 100 is the most portable and least expensive, but also carries the fewest features. The LANMeter is the largest, most expensive, and most capable of these three devices. These products range in price from around $2500 to more than $10,000. A portable network monitor is indispensable for those situations where a software-based product is inconvenient or unavailable.

Remote Monitoring

Remote Monitoring (RMON) is a specification that describes how network monitoring software and networking devices exchange network monitoring data. RMON gives network administrators the ability to install RMON-compatible console software on a workstation in the network and collect data from any device that contains an **RMON probe**.

RMON probes are software or firmware modules that can be embedded in devices such as routers and switches, or that can be installed on workstations on remote network segments. They collect network statistics on the ports associated with the device and present that data to a network management station using RMON and SNMP packets. All of the devices in a network that can be managed are described in a **management information base (MIB)**. A MIB is a database of objects that contains network device information and describes the statistics that may be collected for a particular device. It resides on the network management station, allowing the management software to interpret the information that it collects from the RMON probes.

In addition to collecting network statistics, RMON filters can be set to collect certain types of data, and thresholds can be configured to generate alarms when network parameters cross administrator-defined limits. RMON has many other capabilities as well and should be a standard part of any sizable network.

Several of the software and hardware products discussed in this chapter rely on RMON probes being present in the devices that are being monitored. Note that RMON probes can be installed as dedicated, external probes on network segments, thereby relieving the internetworking devices from the added burden of collecting network statistics. For optimal performance, many manufacturers recommend the use of external probes rather than full-time use of the RMON probes embedded in the internetworking devices.

The leader in dedicated RMON probes is NetScout, whose products can be reviewed at *www.netscout.com*. RMON is a standard-based protocol, and RMON over Ethernet networks is defined in RFC-1757. A newer standard, RMON II, is defined in RFC-2021. A good overview of RMON can be found at *http://support.baynetworks.com/library/tpubs/html/router/soft1101/114070B/N_24.HTM*.

10

How Do I Know Which Products to Use?

When your network is in trouble, how do you know to which product type you should turn? That decision will largely depend on the symptoms displayed by the network. It all goes back to your troubleshooting flowchart. You need to define the problem and the scope of the problem before you start troubleshooting. In general, localized problems such as poor performance or lack of connectivity by a particular application or workstation are more likely to require the use of a protocol analyzer. These products gather real-time network data, not just statistics, and can help you resolve problems related to protocol, NIC driver, and upper-layer implementations. Poor network performance on one network segment may best be resolved by a hand-held network monitor that can quickly provide a picture of the traffic and error patterns on a single segment. Network performance issues that encompass many segments or your entire network typically require examination of baseline data that has been collected by RMON probes distributed throughout the network. Suspected Physical layer problems are best resolved with cable performance analyzers.

Many times you will need to use a combination of products to resolve problems and improve performance in a large network environment. Experience and careful attention to details, as well as diligent documentation and careful monitoring of your network, will help you determine which type of product is best for a given situation.

CHAPTER SUMMARY

❑ Different cable standards require different levels of testing. For example, the tests required by Category 5 cable include wiremap, near-end crosstalk (NEXT), length, and attenuation as specified by TSB67 from TIA/EIA. A newer standard, TSB95, specifies additional tests required for Category 5E and Category 6 cable. These tests include the equal-level far-end crosstalk (ELFEXT) test and the return loss test.

❑ Fluke Networks, Microtest, and Agilent Technologies all offer cable testers with varying features and capabilities. It is up to you (and your budget) to decide which tester has the right features to meet the requirements of your network now and in the future.

❑ A protocol analyzer's primary purpose is to capture and decode frames as they travel your network. Your Physical layer installation may be certified and working perfectly, but applications, protocol stacks, internetworking devices, and device drivers can cause network problems that a cable tester alone cannot diagnose. In addition, while some protocol analyzers can detect data errors such as CRC errors, fragments, and jabbers, their strength is in decoding frames to allow people to easily see Data Link, Network, and Transport layer headers as well as the data contained in each frame.

❑ You monitor your network to locate problems, determine trends, and maintain security. You can use this information to solve problems, and, ideally, to prevent problems from occurring in the first place by detecting trends or security holes that may later become a problem.

❑ There is no single tool that can perform all of your network monitoring tasks. You will likely need and use a collection of tools, just as you do for troubleshooting and testing your network. Tools include software network monitors, hardware network monitors, and RMON.

KEY TERMS

attenuation to crosstalk ratio (ACR) — The ratio of the attenuation of a signal to the crosstalk level at the far end of the cable being measured.

equal-level far-end crosstalk (ELFEXT) — The ratio of the far-end crosstalk to the attenuation in the wire pair being tested.

far-end crosstalk (FEXT) — The crosstalk ratio at the opposite end of the link from which the test signal is being applied.

management information base (MIB) — A database of objects that contains network device information and describes the statistics that may be collected for a particular device.

nominal velocity of propagation (NVP) — The rate at which the signals travel across the media.

plug-ins — Special filters used in protocol analyzers that collect statistics or watch for particular types of packets such as Internet attacks or viruses.

polling — Checking the status of a device by querying it to determine its up or down state.

Remote Monitoring (RMON) — A specification that describes how network monitoring software and networking devices exchange network monitoring data.

return loss — A loss of signal value resulting from impedance mismatches along an entire cable link segment.

RMON probes — Software or firmware modules that can be embedded in devices such as routers and switches or that can be installed on workstations on remote network segments for the purpose of gathering network statistics.

time domain reflectometry (TDR) — The measurement, in nanoseconds, of the time it takes a signal to travel the length of a wire and return, or reflect, back on that same wire.

wiremap — The arrangement and continuity of wires in a UTP cable. A wiremap test checks for continuity of each wire from each pin on the connector on one end of the cable to the corresponding pin on the other end of the cable.

REVIEW QUESTIONS

1. Different cable standards require different levels of testing. True or False?

2. The _____ test checks for continuity of each wire from each pin on the connector on one end of the cable to the corresponding pin on the other end of the cable.

3. The NEXT value is expressed in _____.

   a. megahertz

   b. decibels

   c. megabytes

   d. megabits per second

4. NEXT tests can be done only from the origination end of a cable. True or False?

5. Cable length is measured using _____.

6. The rate at which the signals travel is referred to as the _____.

   a. MRI

   b. MHz

   c. NVP

   d. Category 5 rate

7. Attenuation must be measured at the highest _____ rated for the cable type.

8. Temperature affects attenuation. True or False?

9. Far-end crosstalk (FEXT) measures the crosstalk _____ at the opposite end of the link from where the test signal is being applied.

    a. ratio

    b. link

    c. or RJ outlet

    d. certification level

10. _____ is a value resulting from impedance mismatches along an entire cable link segment.

11. Return loss is measured in decibels. True or False?

12. A wiremap adapter is used during the performance of wiremap tests. True or False?

13. A protocol analyzer's primary purpose is to capture and decode _____ as they travel your network.

14. _____ are special filters that collect statistics or watch for particular types of packets such as Internet attacks or viruses.

    a. Plug-ins

    b. EtherPeeks

    c. Data code segments

    d. Diagnosis modules

15. A packet is the best measure of a network's current performance. True or False?

16. What steps should you take to create a baseline?

17. You should avoid baselining a network during unusual usage periods. True or False?

18. In which operational areas are baselines useful?

19. A baseline is used to determine what is normal over a period of time. True or False?

20. Polling is used to determine the status of _____.

21. RMON probes are software or firmware _____ that can be embedded in devices such as routers and switches.

22. A MIB resides on the network management _____.

23. Some Internet devices may block ICMP echo pings. True or False?

24. By definition, baselining is not a static undertaking. True or False?

25. List and describe some common performance-related categories and subcategories for which you might want to gather data.

HANDS-ON PROJECTS

Project 10-1 Review the Options in an EtherPeek Plug-In

In this project, you will review some of the options available with an EtherPeek plug-in.

1. Click **Start**, point to **Programs**, and then click **Wildpackets' EtherPeek**.
2. Click **Tools** on the menu bar, and then click **Plug-ins**.
3. In the Plug-in column, select **Internet Attack** and then click **Options**.
4. Review each Internet attack monitored by EtherPeek by selecting the name of the attack in the left side of the screen. Read the details of how each attack works.
5. Notice that some of the attacks have configurable options. Write down the options available for the Jolt and Pimp attacks and explain what they mean.
6. Click **Cancel** twice, and then close EtherPeek.

Project 10-2 Review EtherPeek Summary Statistics

In this project, you will explore the value of the statistics offered by EtherPeek.

1. Click **Start**, point to **Programs**, and then click **Wildpackets' EtherPeek**.
2. Click **Statistics** on the menu bar, and then click **Summary**.
3. Watch the statistics update for four or five minutes.
4. What is the average utilization reported?
5. Scroll down until you see the section called Size Distribution.
6. What type of packet do you see most in this section?
7. Scroll down until you see the IP Analysis section.
8. Which type of IP packet is seen most on your network?
9. Close the Summary Statistics screen, and then close EtherPeek.

Project 10-3 Create a Statistics Report with EtherPeek

In this project, you will learn about creating a statistics report with EtherPeek.

1. Start EtherPeek.
2. Click **Statistics** on the menu bar, and then click **Statistics Output**.
3. Click the **Save statistics report every...** check box.
4. Change the number of seconds to **120**.
5. Write down the location of the Reports folder. You will need it later.
6. Click **OK**.
7. Select **Yes** at the next prompt. Three statistics windows will open.
8. Wait about two minutes and then open Windows Explorer.
9. Browse to the location of the Reports folder you wrote down in Step 5.
10. Double-click the Reports folder.

11. Double-click **Stats.htm** to open it in your Web browser.

12. Examine the Node Statistics report.

13. Click each of the Statistics reports listed on the left side of the screen and review it.

14. Close your browser.

15. Return to the EtherPeek window and click **Statistics** on the menu bar, and then click **Statistics Output**.

16. Uncheck the **Save statistics report every...** check box, and then click **OK**.

17. Close EtherPeek.

Project 10-4 Graph Real-Time Statistics with Windows 2000 Performance Monitor

This project requires Windows 2000 or Windows XP. Windows NT may be used, but there will be some differences in the steps required.

1. Click **Start**, point to **Programs**, point to **Administrative Tools**, and then click **Performance**.

2. In the left pane, select **System Monitor**.

3. In the right pane, click the button with the **+** sign.

4. In the Add Counters dialog box, select **Processor** in the Performance object drop-down list.

5. Select **Processor Time** in the Select counters from list drop-down list.

6. Click **Add**.

7. In the Performance object drop-down list, select **Memory**.

8. Select **Pages/sec** in the Select counters from list drop-down list.

9. Click **Add**.

10. Click **Close**.

11. Examine the chart for several minutes. Open Windows Explorer or your Web browser to create CPU and memory accesses that cause the values to change.

12. Close Performance Monitor.

Project 10-5 Save Performance Monitor to a Log

In this project, you will learn about saving information to a log.

1. Click **Start**, point to **Programs**, point to **Administrative Tools**, and then click **Performance**.

2. In the left pane, expand **Performance Logs and Alerts**.

3. Right-click **Counter Logs**, and then click **New Log Settings**.

4. Type **New Log** as the name, and then click **OK**.

5. Click **Add**.

6. In the Select Counters dialog box, select **Processor** in the Performance object drop-down list.

7. Select **Processor Time** in the Select counters from list drop-down list.

8. Click **Add**.

9. In the Performance object drop-down list, select **Memory**.

10. Select **Pages/sec** in the Select counters from list drop-down list.

11. Click **Add**.

12. In the Performance object drop-down list, select **PhysicalDisk**.

13. Select **Avg. Disk Queue Length** in the Select counters from list drop-down list.

14. Click **Explain** and read the explanation for that counter.

15. Click **Add**.

16. Click **Close**.

17. Click the **Log Files** tab.

18. Under Log file name, note the location where the log file will be stored and the log file's name. You may change the name and location if you wish.

19. Click the **Schedule** tab. If you are presented with a dialog box asking if you would like to create the folder that was specified for the log folder, click **Yes**.

20. Under Start log, click the **At** option button.

21. Under Stop log, click the **After** option button, and then set the time to **5** minutes.

22. Click **OK**.

23. Click **Counter Logs** under Performance Logs and Alerts until New Log appears in the right pane. If New Log appears in red, right-click **New Log**, and then click **Start**. New Log should turn green.

24. After five minutes, note that New Log will turn red, indicating that it has stopped. Close Performance Monitor when New Log has turned red.

Project 10-6 Examine Logged Performance Data

In this project, you will examine performance data.

1. Click **Start**, point to **Programs**, point to **Administrative Tools**, and then click **Performance**.

2. In the left pane, select **System Monitor**.

3. In the right pane, click the **View Log File Data** button.

4. Browse to the location of your log file and select the **log file** listed there.

5. Click **Open**.

6. Click **Add**.

7. In the Select Counters dialog box, select **Processor** in the Performance object drop-down list.

10

8. Select **Processor Time** in the Select counters from list drop-down list.

9. Click **Add**.

10. In the Performance object drop-down list, select **Memory**.

11. Select **Pages/sec** in the Select counters from list drop-down list.

12. Click **Add**.

13. In the Performance object drop-down list, select **PhysicalDisk**.

14. Select **Avg. Disk Queue Length** in the Select counters from list drop-down list.

15. Click **Add**.

16. Click **Close**.

17. Examine the graph of your saved counter data.

18. Close Performance Monitor.

CASE PROJECTS

Case 10-1 Baseline Your Network

Over the course of one week, you are to baseline your network. Use whichever tools are available to you that you think will be helpful. Before you begin, write a description of the methods and tools you will use to baseline the network. Discuss the statistics that you plan to gather and note on which devices you will gather statistics. Also, discuss the time periods in which you intend to gather statistics.

Case 10-2 Resolve a Network Response Problem

Sails and Snails Industries reports that network response time has deteriorated over the past two weeks. The company has called you to resolve this problem. Discuss how you might approach this case. Include in your discussion the questions you will ask and the steps you will take to resolve the problem. Finally, mention some of the tools you might use to collect information.

Case 10-3 RMON Research

Prepare a paper on the capabilities of RMON. Include a description of the differences between RMON and RMON II. Also, discuss why you would want to use RMON and the requirements for working with this standard.

Case 10-4 UTP Cable Standards

UTP cable standards continue to evolve. By the time you read this book, changes will have likely occurred in the current standards for cable use in LANs. Write a short paper discussing the current status of the Category 5E, Category 6, and Category 7 cabling standards.

Glossary

Abstract Syntax Notation Number One (ASN.1) — A formal Presentation layer protocol.

access control lists (ACLs) — Rules that are applied to router interfaces that determine what traffic should be allowed in or out of that interface.

account lockout — A policy that can be set to lock a user account after a set number of incorrect password attempts.

Address (A) record — A DNS resource record that consists of a host name/IP address pair.

agent — A program that runs on a computer or networking device and that gathers information on behalf of a program running on a console or management station.

Application layer — Layer 7 of the OSI model, which provides networking services to user applications.

application programming interface (API) — An operating system subroutine that an application developer can call from a program to request an operating system service.

ARP cache — A storage area, usually in RAM, where MAC address-to-IP address mappings are kept.

attachment unit interface (AUI) — A 15-pin interface that allows you to connect a transceiver that supports the media type of your choice.

attenuation — The loss of signal strength as a signal travels the length of the media.

attenuation to crosstalk ratio (ACR) — The ratio of the attenuation of a signal to the crosstalk level at the far end of the cable being measured.

Automatic IP Addressing (APIPA) — A range of IP addresses that is automatically assigned to a host when no DHCP server is available.

autonegotiation — An approach used for two devices to decide whether the connection should be established as half duplex or full duplex; specified in the IEEE 802.3u standard.

AutoSense — A method by which a device automatically detects the speed of the device to which it is connected—for example, 10 Mbps or 100 Mbps.

backoff — A delay period that occurs after an Ethernet collision, during which a station does not transmit data.

bandwidth — The amount of data that a medium is capable of carrying, measured in bits per second.

baseline — A periodic measurement of a variety of network statistics intended to provide an administrator with a reference for judging current network performance.

bit-time — The amount of time it takes a bit to travel about 20 meters in copper, or 0.1 μs (100 ns).

blocking mode — A mode in which a switch port will not forward frames to avoid a bridging loop.

bridge — A Data Link-layer device that is used to segment a network into multiple collision domains. It filters and forwards data based on MAC addresses.

bridging loop — A condition that occurs when switches are connected in such a way that it is possible for frames to be forwarded from switch to switch in an infinite loop.

broadcast — A frame sent and intended to be processed by all stations; in Ethernet, it is a physical address of all binary 1s or hexadecimal Fs.

broadcast domain — A group of computers and devices that reside on the same network.

broadcast storm — A network condition in which several hundred broadcasts per second are generated.

browse list — The list of computers shown in Network Neighborhood.

browser service — The Windows service that is responsible for building the browse list.

Burst Mode — An IPX packet format that allows data transfers in bursts of several packets before an acknowledgment must be sent.

byte stream protocol — A protocol, such as TCP, that sends and acknowledges data based on the number of bytes sent rather than the number of packets sent.

cable plant — All cables and termination points, such as jacks and patch panels, within your network.

cable segment — A section of cable bounded by a switch, bridge, or router port; also referred to as a collision domain.

cached credentials — A local storage of recent logon information that includes the domain name, user name, and password.

caching DNS server — A DNS server that does not contain any DNS zone information but that passes DNS requests along to primary or secondary DNS servers while caching the responses.

cancellation — The effect that occurs when wires carrying a differential signal are twisted tightly together, resulting in the cancellation of each other's electrical field.

Carrier Sense Multiple Access with Collision Detection (CSMA/CD) — The method used by Ethernet to control access to media.

clear text — An unencrypted method of transferring data; usually refers to passwords.

cleaver — A sharp ceramic or diamond-edged cutting tool used to prepare fiber-optic cables for termination.

client — In general, a computer that has the capability to access shared resources on a network. It also is the software required to make a stand-alone workstation operate in a network environment.

Client for Microsoft Networks — The client software required to communicate from one Windows computer to another.

client software — The software installed on a workstation that allows the workstation to access shared resources on another computer.

client/server model — A network of designated server and client computers with centralized administration.

coaxial cable — A cable type that consists of a single conductor inside a layer of insulating material, surrounded by a metal shield and plastic outer jacket.

Code Red — A worm virus that affected certain IIS Web servers.

collision domain — The area in which an Ethernet collision is propagated; it is bounded by a switch or router interface.

concurrent connections — Two or more simultaneous logons to a NetWare server by the same user from different workstations.

connection-oriented protocols — Protocols that use flow control, acknowledgments, and other methods to ensure the reliable delivery of data.

connectionless communications — A form of communication in which there is no confirmation to the sender as to whether the data arrived at the destination.

content addressable memory (CAM) — Memory that contains the switching table, which itself contains source addresses and port numbers.

convention — A common practice or way of doing things that makes procedures easier to follow and remember.

crossover cable — A cable that has been wired purposely with transposed pairs.

crosstalk — The leaking of signals from one wire onto another wire.

cut sheet — A document that lists the details of each cable run in the network.

cut-through switching — A method of switching in which a frame is forwarded to the destination as soon as the destination address is determined.

Cyclic Redundancy Check (CRC) — A calculation performed on the data in a frame that results in a 32-bit value that is used for checking the integrity of transmitted data.

daisy-chain — The connection of two or more devices with what amounts to a continuous line of cable without connecting to a central device.

Data Link layer — The layer at which network packets are formatted into frames to be sent to their destination address along the physical medium.

decode — A process used by protocol analyzers that allows the display of network packets in a user-friendly format.

default gateway — The address of the device, usually a router, to which all packets should be sent if the destination IP address of the packet is not on the same network as the source.

delay — The amount of time that the devices on a network must wait before sending data that is ready to go.

denial of service (DoS) — A hacker's attempt to tie up network bandwidth or network services so that it renders those resources useless to legitimate users.

Denial of Service (DOS) attack — A problem that occurs when real clients are being denied service because the server is overwhelmed waiting for fake three-way handshakes to complete.

Desktop Management Interface (DMI) — A standard framework for managing and tracking components in a PC or server.

Destination Service Access Point (DSAP) — The first byte of an 802.2 LLC header; used to inform the receiver what type of information is contained in the frame.

device driver — The software interface between an operating system and computer hardware.

differential signal — Two wires are used to send the same signal using different polarities.

directory service — The database and network service that stores and provides access to all of your network resources and security information.

DNS zone — The top- and second-level domains in an internet.

domain — A model that centralizes security on one or more servers called domain controllers.

Domain Name Service (DNS) — A TCP/IP service that resolves host computer and domain names to IP addresses.

dotted decimal notation — The uses of decimal numbers, separated by periods, to express a value.

driver — Software that serves as an interface between an operating system and a hardware device.

Dynamic Host Configuration Protocol (DHCP) — A TCP/IP standard that allows a workstation to request from a DHCP server its TCP/IP configuration settings rather than having a network administrator configure the settings manually.

electromagnetic field — The energy field that surrounds a conductor carrying electrical signals.

electromagnetic interference (EMI) — Interference of data traveling on copper wires caused by such things as motors, electrical cables, and fluorescent lights.

encoding — The method used to represent a 0 or 1 bit on the physical media.

Equal-level far-end crosstalk (ELFEXT) — The ratio of the far-end crosstalk to the attenuation in the wire pair being tested.

equipment rooms — Rooms that house your internetworking devices and your servers and that are the junction points for your work area and backbone cabling.

Ethernet — A 10-Mbps, broadcast-based network architecture that dominates in the LAN arena.

far-end crosstalk (FEXT) — The crosstalk ratio at the opposite end of the link from which the test signal is being applied.

fiber optic — A networking medium, usually made of glass, that uses light signals to transmit data.

File and Print Sharing for Microsoft Networks — The Windows Server software component that permits a Windows computer to share resources.

file system security — A feature of a network operating system in which the administrator can assign file and folder permissions to users or groups of users.

flooding — A situation that occurs when a switch does not know the port for a destination address, and the switch forwards the frame out all ports.

fragment — A runt frame with a bad CRC; it usually results from a collision that is not detected.

fragment-free switching — A switching method in which a switch will discard the frame if the length is not at least 64 bytes.

frame — The final packaging, or encapsulation, of data before it is broken into individual bits to be delivered to the Physical layer by the Data Link layer.

frame check sequence (FCS) — The 32-bit value that results from the CRC calculation performed on each frame and that is used to validate the frame.

Frequently Asked Questions (FAQ) — A document that contains common questions and the responses to those questions regarding the support or installation of a manufacturer's product.

full-duplex — Allows a device to send and receive data simultaneously.

Fully Qualified Domain Name (FQDN) — The name of a resource that includes the host name followed by the domain name, including the top-level domain, separated by a period.

Get Nearest Server (GNS) query — A broadcast packet sent by a NetWare client looking for a NetWare server to respond to a login attempt.

giant frame — A frame that is larger than the allowed maximum of 1518 bytes, but that does have a valid CRC.

half-duplex — Allows a device to send or receive data, but not simultaneously.

hard-coded — Software that precludes the user from selecting a printer.

hub — A multiport repeater.

Hypertext Markup Language (HTML) — The syntax used to create Web page documents that include special formatting and multimedia content.

impedance — The amount of resistance to the flow of electricity exhibited by a media, measured in ohms.

Individual/Group (I/G) — The first byte of a MAC address; it is used to determine whether the frame is addressed to an individual station or multiple stations.

interframe gap — The amount of time between the end of one frame on the medium and the beginning of the next frame.

intermediate distribution facility (IDF) — A wiring closet that serves as the connection point for work area connections.

International Standards Organization (ISO) — An international organization composed of national standards bodies from more than 75 countries.

Internet Assigned Numbers Authority (IANA) — An organization that maintains a variety of numbering schemes used on the Internet.

internetwork — Two or more networks that communicate with each other using hubs, bridges, routers, or gateways.

Internetwork Packet Exchange/Sequenced Packet Exchange (IPX/SPX) — A protocol suite used primarily at the Network and Transport layers of the OSI model.

internetworking device — A piece of equipment such as a hub, switch, or router that allows your network to grow beyond the confines of its media specifications.

jabber — A frame that exceeds the maximum frame size and that does not have a valid CRC.

jack — The point in the work area where media are terminated to allow connection to a workstation.

Kerberos — An authentication method based on encryption keys and tickets, which avoids sending actual passwords across the network.

knowledgebase — A database maintained by an organization that contains technical support information.

Large Internet Packets (LIP) — An IPX packet option that allows packets to be sized according to the MTU of the network.

late collision — A collision that occurs after the first 64 bytes of a frame have been transmitted.

least significant bit (LSB) — The rightmost bit in a byte.

light-emitting diodes (LED) — A low-energy light source used in multimode fiber-optic cabling transmitters.

link segment — A segment in which there is a maximum of two medium attachment units connected together by a full-duplex medium.

LMHOSTS file — A plain text file that resides on the client computer and contains a table of computer names and IP address pairs.

Local Area Network (LAN) — A local grouping of computers and devices configured to communicate through network media. It may be a stand-alone network or part of a larger internetwork.

logical address — The address assigned to a device that provides both network and host information and operates at the Network layer.

MAC address — The physical address of an Ethernet station consisting of 48 bits and expressed in hexadecimal digits.

main distribution facility (MDF) — The wiring closet in which one or more IDFs tie into the network backbone.

management information base (MIB) — A database of objects that contains network device information and describes the statistics that may be collected for a particular device.

mapping a drive — An action by a user that creates a drive letter designation such as F: that refers to a network share.

Maximum Segment Size (MSS) — The maximum number of bytes that can be received by a client in a single TCP segment.

Maximum Transmission Unit (MTU) — The largest datagram size accepted by the media or Network layer protocol.

media converter — Converts signals to a type that can be used by a specified medium.

media-dependent interface (MDI) — The IEEE standard for the interface to unshielded twisted-pair cable.

medium attachment unit (MAU) — A device such as a transceiver that connects to an AUI. The MAU then allows the medium to attach to the network.

minimum bend radius — The amount of cable that must be used to circumvent a 90° angle.

misaligned frame — A frame that contains extra bits at the end of the frame that do not form a complete octet.

mixing segment — A cable segment in which there can be more than two MDIs attached to the segment, as you have with a coaxial 10Base2 segment.

multiplatform network — A network environment that includes more than one operating system, computer type, or network architecture.

Name Server (NS) record — A DNS resource record that specifies the name of a server that is authoritative for a domain.

NetBIOS API — An API that allows programs designed for NetBIOS to access network resources.

NetBIOS Enhanced User Interface (NetBEUI) — A simple, efficient protocol designed for Windows LAN environments.

NetBIOS Frame Protocol (NBF) — The NetBIOS API used by NetBEUI applications.

NetBIOS over IP (NetBT) — One of the NetBIOS APIs that permits NetBIOS applications to run over the IP protocol.

NetBIOS over IPX (NBIPX) — One of the NetBIOS APIs that permits NetBIOS applications to run over the IPX protocol.

NetWare Command File (NCF) — A text file that contains one or more NetWare commands that can be executed with a single command, much like a DOS batch file.

NetWare Core Protocol (NCP) — An Application layer protocol that is part of the IPX/SPX protocol suite and that provides some Transport layer services.

NetWare Link State Protocol (NLSP) — Novell's proprietary link-state routing protocol.

network architecture — Networking technologies such as Ethernet and Token Ring that describe logical and physical topology as well as the media access method.

network bindings — The logical connections between network components.

network interface card (NIC) — The interface card between a workstation and the network media.

Network layer — Layer 3 of the OSI model, which defines logical addressing and is responsible for best-path selection in a routed internetwork.

network operating system (NOS) — Software that facilitates the sharing of network resources and that runs and manages network applications.

network redirector — An Application layer client component that determines whether a requested resource is local to the requesting application or a network resource.

networking media — The pathway by which networking signals travel, much as roads represent the pathways by which automobiles travel.

networking model — The manner in which data and devices are shared.

nominal velocity of propagation (NVP) — The rate at which the signals travel across the media.

Novell Directory Services (NDS) — A service and a database that contains all NetWare network security and resource information.

NTFS security — Access permissions that can be applied to a file or folder on an NTFS-formatted partition and that apply to both local access and network access.

octet — A grouping of 8 bits that represent a byte.

Opportunistic Locking — A file sharing method employed by Windows operating systems that is intended to increase performance by bypassing the time-consuming procedure of locking and unlocking files when a single user accesses the file.

Organizationally Unique Identifier (OUI) — The first 24 bits of a MAC address; used to identify the manufacturer of the NIC.

OSI model — A framework for describing the travel and transformation of data as it is sent from its source to its destination on an internetwork. The OSI model consists of seven layers.

packet burst mode — A mode of transferring IPX data in which acknowledgments are not required for each packet.

pad — Extra characters added to a frame or packet as required to meet the minimum frame size.

passive transfer mode — An FTP mode of operation that requires the FTP client to establish the data transfer session with the server using a random port number.

patch panel — A centralized connecting point, usually located in a wiring closet, for terminating media coming from the work area.

path delay value (PDV) — The time it takes for a bit to travel through all cable segments and through all repeaters to the farthest destination.

peer-to-peer model — A network of computers that has both clients and servers and where administration is distributed.

physical diagram — Drawing that depicts the type and location of major internetworking devices, major servers, and approximate populations of workstations in various locations.

Physical layer — Layer 1 of the OSI model, which consists primarily of things you can get your hands on and which describes the physical signals that make up network data, such as electrical or light pulses.

Ping (Packet InterNet Groper) — A troubleshooting utility used to determine if a device with a particular IP address is available on the network.

ping scanner — An automated method for pinging a range of IP addresses.

Ping utility — A utility that helps determine whether a workstation has end-to-end connectivity with a particular destination and that identifies the amount of time it took the destination to respond.

plug-ins — Special filters used in protocol analyzers that collect statistics or watch for particular types of packets such as Internet attacks or viruses.

polling — Checking the status of a device by querying it to determine its up or down state.

port address translation (PAT) — A type of network address translation that uses a single address to represent multiple inside hosts by using unique port numbers for each host.

port partitioning — Disconnecting a port from the rest of the hub such that no data is repeated out that port and no data that goes into the partitioned port is repeated to any other port.

port scanner — A utility that determines which TCP or UDP ports are available on a particular device.

port segmentation — A process that allows an administrator to create two or more groups of ports on a hub or hub stack that operate in separate collision domains.

preamble — A string of alternating ones and zeroes, which the receiver detects and prepares for the incoming frame.

Presentation layer — Layer 6 of the OSI model, which translates data types when necessary between communicating machines.

printer redirection — Occurs when a print job is sent to a local port.

promiscuous mode — A mode of operation supported by many NICs that allows a network monitor program or protocol analyzer to view and process all network traffic on the cable segment.

protocol analyzer — A program or device that captures data packets and displays each packet in a user-friendly format for analysis by the user.

PTR record — A DNS entry that make reverse lookups possible.

quality of service (QoS) — A factor that determines the reliability of data transfers and the performance level of those transfers.

rack-mountable — Describes a network device or server that is designed to bolt to a standard 19-inch equipment rack.

radio frequency interference (RFI) — Interference to data signals caused by radio broadcast sources such as radio transmitters, microwaves, and X-rays.

recursive lookup — A DNS lookup that starts with the top-level domain server and returns the address of another DNS server, which is then queried, and so forth.

redirector — Software installed on a workstation that allows the workstation to access resources on a particular network operating system; also called a requestor, network shell, or client.

registered ports — TCP and UDP ports in the range 1024 to 49,151 that may be used by private applications within an intranet or extranet.

Remote Address Dial-In User Service (RADIUS) — A security protocol that provides authentication services.

Remote Monitoring (RMON) — A specification that describes how network monitoring software and networking devices exchange network monitoring data.

repeater — An internetworking device used to extend the length of a cable segment by conditioning and amplifying incoming signals and repeating them out all other ports.

Request for Comments (RFCs) — An open forum for creating documents that describe networking processes or procedures.

resource records — Information about DNS resource types maintained by a DNS server.

return loss — A loss of signal value resulting from impedance mismatches along an entire cable link segment.

reverse DNS lookup — A DNS query that returns an FQDN.

RJ45 — Registered jack type 45 is a common connector used in twisted-pair Ethernet cabling.

RMON probes — Software or firmware modules that can be embedded in devices such as routers and switches or that can be installed on workstations on remote network segments for the purpose of gathering network statistics.

round-trip collision delay — The amount of time that it takes for a sending station to send the first bit in a frame, have that bit collide with another station's attempt to send a signal, and have the first station hear the collision.

router — The device that routes packets through an internetwork.

routing table — A map of all networks known to the router. Routing tables are created by the exchange of information between routers.

runt frame — A frame that contains fewer bytes than the minimum frame size of 64 bytes.

Security ID (SID) — A unique 96-bit number that identifies domain objects such as users and workstations.

security policy — A document that describes the rules governing access to a company's information resources, ways that those rules are enforced, and steps taken in the event the rules are breached.

segment — A data portion created when the Transport layer breaks data into smaller pieces prior to hand-off to the Network layer.

Server Message Block (SMB) datagram — A protocol developed by Microsoft, IBM, and Intel that contains commands used by network redirectors to indicate what type of request or response is contained in a packet.

server services — A device or software component that provides access to shared resources to network clients.

server software — Software installed on a computer that allows other computers to access resources on that computer.

Service Advertising Protocol (SAP) — A protocol that creates a special IPX packet that is broadcast by NetWare servers to inform the network of the resources that server has available.

service packs — A compilation of bug fixes, upgrades, and security fixes for an operating system.

Session layer — Layer 5 of the OSI model, which coordinates conversations between networked applications.

sharing security — Access permissions that are applied to a Windows share and that apply only to network access to the files contained in the share.

Signal Quality Error (SQE) Test — A test that ensures that the collision detection circuitry on the transceiver is working correctly.

signal reflection — The phenomenon that occurs when electrical signals travel down a wire and meet a change in impedance such as an open, short, or end of the cable.

Simple Network Management Protocol (SNMP) — A TCP/IP standard that allows agents on network devices to collect network statistics and send the information to a network management station.

Source Service Access Point (SSAP) — Informs the destination about which application the information contained in the frame originated.

Spanning-Tree Protocol (STP) — A protocol used by switches to ensure that a bridging loop does not occur when switches are connected in a redundant fashion.

split pair — A wiring error in which the differential signals from one circuit are traveling on two different pairs of wires, negating the cancellation effect.

spoofed address — A source address that is inserted into a packet but is not the actual address of the sending station.

stackable — A hub has this characteristic when there is a method, usually through a proprietary cable, to connect hubs such that the entire stack of hubs counts as only one repeater in the 5-4-3 repeater rule.

Start of Authority (SOA) record — A DNS resource record that lists information for a DNS zone.

store-and-forward switching — A switching method in which the entire frame is buffered on the switch until the CRC can be checked.

straight connector (SC) — A connector type used with fiber-optic media.

straight tip (ST) — A connector type used with fiber-optic media.

subnet mask — Defines which part of the IP address is the network portion and which part is the host portion; used in combination with an IP address to specify the number of bits that make up the network part of the address.

subnetting — The act of dividing one large IP address space into two or more smaller address spaces.

switch — A multiport bridge.

TCP segment — The entire unit of information that includes the TCP header and data.

TCP/IP networking model — A four-layer design that combines the upper three layers of the OSI model into the Application layer and the lower two layers of the OSI model into the Network Interface layer.

TDR (Time Domain Reflectometer) — A device used to measure the length of a cable by measuring the amount of time needed for the signal to reflect back when it meets the end of the cable.

Telecommunications Industry Association/Electronics Industries Association (TIA/EIA) — A standards body governing, among other things, telecommunications wiring in buildings.

Terminal Access Controller Access Control System (TACACS) — A security protocol that provides authentication, authorization, and accounting security services (AAA).

termination — The method used to end a length of network media, either with a connector or by securing the wires in a jack or patch panel.

thickwire Ethernet — 10 Mbs Ethernet running on a thick coaxial cable; also called Thicknet and 10Base5.

Thinnet — Thinwire Ethernet.

thinwire Ethernet — 10 Mbps Ethernet running on thin coaxial cable, type RG58; also called Thinnet and 10Base2.

time domain reflectometry (TDR) — The measurement, in nanoseconds, of the time it takes a signal to travel the length of a wire and return, or reflect, back on that same wire.

Trace Route utility — A TCP/IP utility found in most operating systems that shows the path that a packet takes from source to destination. The Trace Route utility uses the same technology as the Ping utility. In Windows systems, the program name is TRACERT.EXE.

transceiver — A device that contains the transmit and receive circuitry and the appropriate connector for the media used.

translation bridges — Bridges that can translate between network architectures by changing the frame header before passing the frame on to the destination.

transparent bridging — A situation in which Ethernet frames pass through a switch unaltered.

Transport Control Protocol/Internet Protocol (TCP/IP) — A protocol suite used primarily at the Network and Transport layers of the OSI model.

Transport layer — Layer 4 of the OSI model, which is responsible for reliable transmission of data, disassembly and reassembly of large data transmissions, and the maintenance of multiple data streams between multiple applications.

transposed pair — A wiring error where one end of a cable is terminated according to the 568-A wiring standard and the other end is terminated according to the 568-B standard.

unicast — A frame that is addressed to a single MAC address with the intention that only one station will process the frame.

Universal Naming Convention (UNC) path — A path that can be used to access most types of network resources, including Windows shares and NetWare volumes.

Universal Resource Locator (URL) — The standard naming convention for Internet resources in the form *protocol://host.domain*.

Universally/Locally Administered (U/L) — Used to determine whether a MAC address is burned in or assigned locally.

unshielded twisted-pair (UTP) — An unshielded cable type that contains from two to four pairs of wires twisted together.

User Datagram Protocol (UDP) — An unreliable Transport layer protocol that is part of the TCP/IP protocol suite.

virtual circuit — A communication method in which a connection is established between the sender and receiver before data transfers begin. Once the transfer is finished, the circuit is broken.

virtual terminal (VTY) ports — Ports that allow a terminal-like connection via a network Telnet connection.

wake-on-LAN — Allows an administrator to remotely turn on the computer by sending a signal to the NIC.

Whois — A utility for discovering information about an Internet domain.

Windows Internet Naming Service (WINS) — A Windows service that resolves Windows computer names to IP addresses.

Winsock API — An API that provides TCP/IP services to applications.

wiremap — The arrangement and continuity of wires in a UTP cable. A wiremap test checks for continuity of each wire from each pin on the connector on one end of the cable to the corresponding pin on the other end of the cable.

Index